Normalizing Japan

Studies in Asian Security

A SERIES SPONSORED BY THE EAST-WEST CENTER

Muthiah Alagappa, Chief Editor
Distinguished Senior Fellow, East-West Center

The aim of the Asian Security series is to promote analysis, understanding, and explanation of the dynamics of domestic, transnational, and international security challenges in Asia. Books in the series will analyze contemporary security issues and problems to clarify debates in the scholarly and policy communities, provide new insights and perspectives, and identify new research and policy directions related to conflict management and security in Asia. Security is defined broadly to include the traditional political and military dimensions as well as the non-traditional dimensions that affect the survival and well-being of political communities. Asia, too, is defined broadly, to include Northeast, Southeast, South, and Central Asia.

Designed to encourage original and rigorous scholarship, books in the Asian Security series seek to engage scholars, educators, and practitioners. Wide-ranging in scope and method, the series welcomes an extensive array of paradigms, programs, traditions, and methodologies now employed in the social sciences.

★   ★   ★

The East-West Center is an education and research organization established by the U.S. Congress in 1960 to strengthen relations and understanding among the peoples and nations of Asia, the Pacific, and the United States. The Center contributes to a peaceful, prosperous, and just Asia Pacific community by serving as a vigorous hub for cooperative research, education, and dialogue on critical issues of common concern to the Asia Pacific region and the United States. Funding for the Center comes from the U.S. government, with additional support provided by private agencies, individuals, foundations, and corporations and the governments of the region.

Normalizing Japan

POLITICS, IDENTITY, AND THE
EVOLUTION OF SECURITY PRACTICE

Andrew L. Oros

SPONSORED BY THE EAST-WEST CENTER
Stanford University Press • Stanford, California 2008

Stanford University Press
Stanford, California

Printed in the United States of America

Library of Congress Cataloging-in-Publication Data

Oros, Andrew.
    Normalizing Japan : politics, identity, and the evolution of security practice /
Andrew L. Oros.
    p. cm. — (Studies in Asian security)
Includes bibliographical references and index.
ISBN 978-0-8047-0029-0 (cloth : alk. paper)
    1. Security, International—Japan. 2. Militarism—Japan. I. Title.
    JZ6009.J3O76   2008
    355'.033052 DC22   2007038750

This book is printed on acid-free, archival-quality paper.

Typeset at Stanford University Press in 10/13.5 Bembo

TO MY FAMILY

Contents

Tables

Preface

My first contact with Japan was in Los Angeles at the height of Japan's economic boom (later seen as "bubble"). It was an outwardly self-confident Japan I experienced, often telling America how it needed to reform its inefficient and profligate ways. As a young student anxious about my own future, I was drawn to learn more. In Japan, however, I learned and read that under this confident exterior was a nation deeply questioning what was at its essence, and what it should seek to project to others. Bookstores in the 1980s were full of lengthy pseudo-academic treatises on what it meant to be Japanese—the so-called *nihonjinron* (treatises on Japaneseness). Any student of Japanese trade policy at the time would see the effect of this self-conceived unique identity on policy. METI (then MITI) trade ministers were famous for their assertions that foreign skis had to be tested on unique Japanese snow, that Japanese stomachs digested foreign beef differently, and that "not a single grain" of foreign rice could be allowed to pollute Japanese cuisine.

Times have changed. Japan's national self-confidence was shattered by the collapse of the "bubble economy," fueling a new, yet related, literature on what place Japan had in the world if not to spread its superior economic practices. The death of the Showa emperor, Hirohito, and end of the Cold War between the United States and the Soviet Union (if not the Cold War in East Asia related to North Korea and China) further pushed Japan to reconsider its identity. As this process continues, Japan's security practices are being transformed. Japan may not ever become "normal" from the perspective of a foreigner, but the process by which it seeks to become so nevertheless can be understood.

The past sixty years of Japanese historical development have been a time of incredible social change and great economic success, and as well, a continuing battle to imagine and reimagine Japan's place in a hostile world. At the turn of the new century Japan faces not only a new domestic demographic and political composition, but a shifting and dangerous international environment as well. In this context it is seeking either to build a new security identity to ground its defense policies or to reform the security identity that contributed so much to the previous half century of peace and prosperity. This book explains the politics of this fundamentally political process in Japan and, more broadly, suggests some theoretical insights that can be applied from the Japanese case to other states grappling with security issues in the past and into the twenty-first century.

This book would not have been possible without the intellectual, logistical, and emotional support of a large number of people—to whom I owe a great debt. Research for this project has been supported by generous grants from Columbia University, the Japan Foundation Center for Global Partnership (CGP), the Japanese Ministry of Education, the Smith Richardson Foundation, Washington College, and the Weatherhead Foundation. I acknowledge in particular grants from the Japan Foundation CGP and the Washington College Christian A. Johnson Fellowship for funding of a one-year junior sabbatical leave to complete the final work on this manuscript.

I cannot personally thank all those individuals who provided support (both substantive and emotional), but several groups of people deserve particular mention, beginning with the two people who have most influenced my thinking on Japan through their careful guidance of my graduate and professional development: Gerald Curtis and Richard Samuels. I have been fortunate indeed to have benefited from such insightful and sustained support from them.

Also for patiently contributing to my formal studies at Columbia University, I would like to thank Robert Jervis, Lisa Anderson, Richard Betts, Kimberly Marten, Andrew Nathan, Jack Snyder, and Robert Uriu; and I wish to acknowledge the debt I owe to Professors Peter Nosco, Gordon Berger, and Peter Berton of the University of Southern California for encouraging me to deepen my study of Japan beyond the first steps of my early undergraduate years. These professors, together with Professors Martin Krieger and Abraham Lowenthal, have continued to serve as important mentors and sources of advice. As well, my new colleagues at Washington College—Melissa Deckman, Tahir Shad, John Taylor, and Christine Wade—have helped smooth my transition from graduate student to assistant professor and have become good friends in the process.

My research in Japan was greatly facilitated by the University of Tokyo's Faculty of Law, Institute for Oriental Culture, and Institute of Social Sciences, and in particular Professors Akihiko Tanaka and Nobuhiro Hiwatari for supervising my extended stays at their institutions. Moreover, I would like to thank the library of the International House of Japan, and in particular its librarian, Ms. Koide. I was fortunate to be able to conduct over one hundred interviews in Tokyo with a range of government officials, politicians and political staff, academics, journalists, and members of the business community. I offer my collective thanks to them all, many of whom requested anonymity. Finally in Japan, I would like to express my gratitude to my former classmates of the Osaka University of Foreign Studies, many of whom provided useful advice and friendship during my stays in Tokyo. In particular, Soo-Im Kim and Masaki Fujiwara provided me a place to stay over countless short visits to Tokyo and, even more importantly, a window on what it means to be Japanese in Japan today.

I was fortunate to be able to complete the final stages of this project in Washington, D.C., where many practitioners of Japanese security policy reside. I have benefited from the advice of far too many people to recognize individually, but I would like to offer a collective note of appreciation to members of the Washington policy and academic community for their support. A special thank-you is due to the New America Foundation for allowing me the privilege of a quiet space to write in the fall of 2001 and spring of 2002, and to the East-West Center Washington and the George Washington University Sigur Center for Asian Studies for hosting me during a junior sabbatical leave period in 2005–2006. Finally, but foremost in Washington, I wish first to thank a small group of dedicated professionals who agreed to participate in a monthly critique of my final manuscript-in-progress, which greatly improved the clarity of my thinking about the subject, and the prose itself: Muthiah Alagappa, Daniel Bob, Bill Breer, Richard Bush, Emma Chanlett-Avery, Steve Clemons, Richard Cronin, Eric Heginbotham, Kimihiro Ishikane, Shin'ichiro Ishio, Komei Isozaki, Nobukatsu Kanehara, Weston Konishi, Mindy Kotler, Ed Lincoln, Mark Manyin, Hitoshi Marui, Akihiko Maruya, Mike Mochizuki, Katsuhiko Nakao, Valerie Ploumpis, Chris Preble, Amy Searight, Bruce Stokes, Yuki Tatsumi, Elizabeth Turpen, Barbara Wanner, and Tom Watanabe. I would like to single out Muthiah Alagappa, Mike Mochizuki, and Leonard Schoppa for special insights into multiple versions of the complete manuscript. Naturally, all remaining errors of fact, interpretation, and omission are my own.

I also would like to thank my editor, Muriel Bell, for her supportive and careful shepherding of the manuscript, her assistant, Joa Suorez, and series editor, Muthiah Alagappa, for his years of guidance and advice. John Feneron and Geoffrey Burn of the Stanford University Press also deserve credit for patiently guiding a first-time author through the final stages of publication.

Most important, I thank my family for their unflinching support of my career in higher education. My parents and grandparents, and my long-time domestic partner, Steve Clemons, instilled in me the confidence to see through the long process of completing this book and provided important financial support. This book is dedicated to them.

Andrew L. Oros
Washington, D.C.

Acronyms

ABM	Anti-Ballistic Missile
AFTA	Asian Free Trade Area
APEC	Asia-Pacific Economic Cooperation
ARF	ASEAN Regional Forum
ASDF	Air Self-Defense Forces
ASEAN+3	Association of Southeast Asian Nations plus Japan, China, and South Korea
BDS	Boost Defense Segment
BMD	ballistic missile defense
BPI	Boost-Phase Intercept
CFR	Council on Foreign Relations
CIRO	Cabinet Intelligence Research Office
CISTEC	Center for Information on Strategic Trade Control
CLB	Cabinet Legislation Bureau
COCOM	Coordinating Committee on Multilateral Strategic Export Controls
CSICE	Cabinet Satellite Intelligence Center
DMZ	demilitarized zone
DOD	Department of Defense
DPC	Defense Production Committee
DPJ	Democratic Party of Japan
DSP	Democratic Socialist Party
ETCO	Export Trade Control Ordinance
FEFTL	Foreign Exchange and Foreign Trade Law
FMS	Foreign Military Sales
GATT	General Agreement on Tariffs and Trade

GDP	gross domestic product
GNP	gross national product
GPS	Global Positioning System
GSDF	Ground Self-Defense Forces
IGS	information-gathering satellites
INTELSAT	International Telecommunications Satellite Organization
JAE	Japan Aviation Electronics Industry Corporation
JAXA	Japan Aerospace Exploration Agency
JCP	Japanese Communist Party
JDA	Japan Defense Agency
JMTC	Joint Military Technology Commission
JSP	Japan Socialist Party
KMT	Komeitō
LDP	Liberal Democratic Party
LST	land-sea transport
MD	missile defense
MDAA	Mutual Defense Assistance Agreement
MELCO	Mitsubishi Electronics Company
METI	Ministry of the Economy, Trade, and Industry
MHI	Mitsubishi Heavy Industry
MITI	Ministry of International Trade and Industry
MOD	Ministry of Defense
MOF	Ministry of Finance
MOFA	Ministry of Foreign Affairs
MOU	Memorandum of Understanding
MPT	Ministry of Post and Telecommunications
MSDF	Maritime Self-Defense Forces
NAD	Navy Area Defense
NASA	National Aeronautics and Space Agency
NASDA	National Space Development Agency
NATO	North Atlantic Treaty Organization
NDPG	National Defense Program Guideline
NDPO	National Defense Program Outline
NEC	Nippon Electric Company
NKP	New Komei Party
NMD	national missile defense
NPL	nonperforming loan
NPR	National Police Reserves
NPT	Non-Proliferation Treaty
NSAC	National Space Activities Council
NSC	National Security Council
NTW	Navy Theater Wide
OECD	Organization of Economic Cooperation and Development
PLA	People's Liberation Army (China)

PSI	Proliferation Security Initiative
RA&D	Requirements Analysis and Design
RMA	revolution in military affairs
SAC	Space Activities Commission
SAGE	Study of Attitudes and Global Engagement
SAPC	Space Activities Promotion Council
SCAP	Supreme Commander of the Allied Powers
SCC	Security Consultative Committee
SDF	Self-Defense Forces
SDI	Strategic Defense Initiative
SDP	Social Democratic Party
SIPRI	Stockholm International Peace Research Institute
SMDS	Sea-Based Midcourse Defense System
STA	Science and Technology Agency
STF	Systems and Technology Forum
TDS	Terminal Defense Segment
THAAD	Theater High-Altitude Area Defense
TMD	theater missile defense
UAV	unmanned aerial vehicles
UN	United Nations
UNPCC	United Nations Peace Cooperation Corps
UNPKO	United Nations Peacekeeping Operations
USTR	United States Trade Representative

Normalizing Japan

Introduction

There is a palpable fear among many that Japan is on the verge of a major break from the past sixty years of peaceful security practice, that recent incremental changes in long-standing policy—such as the dispatch of Japan's military forces, the Self-Defense Forces (SDF), abroad for the first time, and the creation of a Ministry of Defense (MOD), to name just two—foretell even greater changes in the near future. The fear is that Japan is being "normalized" into developing military capabilities and approaches in line with its great power status.

Such fears are misplaced at best and at worst stand to inhibit solutions to the real security problems faced by Japan and the East Asian region as a whole. In the larger global context Japan faces no shortage of substantial security contingencies, including conventional and nuclear weapons proliferation, tense standoffs over the divided states of China/Taiwan and the Koreas, Islamic-related terrorist activity in a number of Southeast Asian states, and widespread concerns over the "rise" of China. Japanese security practice is evolving to respond to new threats, but it is evolving along a predictable path—one guided by the same central tenets that have shaped Japan's security practice in the past fifty years. Contestation over these tenets has been a basic fact of politics in Japan for half a century and will continue to be in the foreseeable future. This is what is "normal" in Japan.

This book seeks to explain how such normal politics have evolved to allow Japan's security practice to adapt to new challenges within a framework deemed acceptable by Japanese citizens and the complex system that determines security policy. Within the framework of such central principles—Japan's postwar "security identity"—policy evolution is possible and indeed common. The likelihood of a substantial departure from these central tenets—an identity shift—is a central question addressed in this volume, utilizing a general theory of policy change that builds on existing theory and is supported by evidence gathered through an examination of several important cases illustrating the evolution of Japan's security practice in the past half-century.

Japan is not nearly the security outlier it is often mischaracterized as being: it has one of the largest military budgets in the world,[1] and by many measures of military capability ranks among the top few states in the world (Lind 2004). Still, observers of Japanese security practice have noted a series of shifts in Japanese policy in the past decade, most dramatically the contrast between a hamstrung Diet (Japan's parliament) unable to dispatch troops for the 1991 Iraq War to SDF participation in the coalition led by the United States in the 2003 Iraq War—albeit still in a noncombat and largely humanitarian role.[2] By 2005, the SDF had been dispatched abroad to fourteen countries or areas since its first overseas deployment to Cambodia in 1992.[3] The SDF also has expanded its defense cooperation and training with the United States military in other areas, reflected in new defense "guidelines" issued in 1997 and other areas of increased cooperation in response to the global war on terrorism. At home as well, the extent of SDF activity in disaster relief and other domestic assistance is a striking contrast to the delay experienced in authorizing the SDF to help respond to a devastating earthquake in the Kobe area in 1995. Beyond the issue of deployment, SDF capabilities also have risen in the past decade, including the controversial areas of surveillance satellites and missile defense detailed in this volume.

Yet a number of Japan's security policies continue to depart from expected standards. The much-referenced dispatch of the SDF abroad has taken place only in conjunction with other international forces, and only in a very limited manner—at their peak, troop rotations to Iraq of about 1,100 members at a time (200 ASDF, 600 GSDF, 330 MSDF) of a total force of over 240,000 at home.[4] Japan refrains from pursuing most offensive military capabilities, including nuclear weapons, which it has the technological and economic capability to produce. Despite possessing one of the world's most advanced manufacturing bases, which produces the majority of weapons for Japan's own SDF, Japanese firms export no weapons abroad: in part due to this absence of arms exports, only one Japanese defense manufacturer ranks in the top twenty defense producers worldwide, despite Japanese industrial firms generally being among the largest and most competitive in the world.[5] Further, despite adhering zealously to a "defensive defense" military posture, Japan's stated policy regarding the use of outer space has precluded—until very recently—the use of military surveillance satellites to balance its lack of offensive weapons capability, and even today Japan's intelligence capabilities are quite limited and activities highly constrained. By contrast, the consensus among security specialists is that states pursuing a defensive military posture require greater intelligence resources. More broadly, many intellectuals and opinion leaders in Japan continue to encourage a role for Japan that differs from that of a typical "great power" or "normal nation" (as this term generally has come to be understood). In particular, the idea of Japan as a "civilian power" or "middle power" continues to attract significant attention.[6]

The appropriate level of Japan's future militarily related global engagement first and foremost will be determined by Japanese seeking to make sense of their state and their view of Japan's appropriate position and role within the evolving international environment. The question is not what is "normal" in the abstract, but what is considered normal by Japan, and by Japanese. Thus, although the substance of this book focuses on Japan's evolving security practices, at its core this study attempts to reveal and to benchmark Japan's self-perceived security identity: how it is envisioned, how it has been institutionalized and reproduced over time, and how this factor continues to affect the politics and practice of external defense in Japan today. This is not a question of a security "strategy"—in the sense of an approach to the world developed by political elites—but a resilient identity that is politically negotiated and comprises a widely accepted set of principles on the acceptable scope of state practices in the realm of national security. It is within the framework of these core principles that specific policy practices are developed and will be developed in the years to come. As such, both specific policies and the broader principles upon which they are based must be examined to consider Japan's security future.

A Shifting Wind in Japan Today?

If we compare national power to a strong wind, national identity is the weather vane that tells us which direction this wind is blowing. (Nau 2002, p. 6)

Which direction will the wind blow in Japan in the early twenty-first century? Will the nascent nationalism apparent for the past several decades suddenly burst more into the open, capitalizing on Japan's incremental rearmament, perhaps reversing a deepening military alliance with the United States, perhaps sparking a further arms race—or even open military hostilities—in East Asia? Or will the power of pacifism, or at least "antimilitarism"—long a powerful constraining force in Japan's security policies—persuade a new generation of supporters to continue to thwart the efforts of those seeking the reemergence of Japan as an independent, fully armed great power in East Asia, a so-called normal nation? The popular press is full of articles warning of rising Japanese nationalism, militarism, or "realism." Japanese political leaders' visits to the controversial Yasukuni Shrine—which enshrines the souls of fourteen Class A war criminals and along with its accompanying museum openly celebrates Japan's militarist rise in the 1930s and 1940s—in particular have fueled articles in the press about a future, more muscular and robust Japan.

The answer to these questions will be determined in part by the international security environment in East Asia and the world in the coming decades—either conventional warfare or nuclear conflagration on the Korean peninsula, or interstate warfare in the Taiwan straits certainly would affect Japan's conduct profoundly; the outbreak of the "Long War" on global terrorism already has led to a shift in Japanese policy. The decisions of individuals and groups of political actors inside Japan and pressure exerted by the United States and others on Japan will also form the basis for which direction the wind will blow in Japan's future. Already a charismatic, popular leader—Prime Minister Junichiro Koizumi—has taken Japan quickly down a path of increased military activities surprisingly quickly in the early twenty-first century. His successor, Shinzo Abe, sought to lead Japan further down this path—though he encountered significant resistance that led, in part, to his abrupt resignation in September 2007. American pressure for Japan to "normalize" its security practices has been powerful—captured in former Deputy Secretary of State Richard Armitage's counsel to the Japanese to "show to the flag" after the September 11 attacks on the United States—notwithstanding past U.S. efforts to "contain" Japan. To some degree these efforts have been quite successful.[7]

To understand the way in which Japanese security practice is evolving, however, it is not sufficient to look at changes in the past few years; one must instead consider how Japan has responded to previous changes in its international environment. Contestation over the content, and later the contours, of Japan's security identity has been an enduring facet of postwar Japan, experiencing ebbs and flows in line with substantial changes in Japan's domestic and international environment—despite continuity in the core principles upon which the identity is based.

A security identity is not a static phenomenon, however, but rather a set of principles that must be reinforced and conveyed through human action. The gradual and contentious formation of Japan's postwar security identity is central to Japan's understanding of its present and future. It is not just a matter of "history"—in terms of a scholarly reexamination of Japan's past.[8] The contemporary debates in Asia over history drive major political and diplomatic contests in Asia in the early twenty-first century. This volume therefore focuses on both aspects of Japan's security identity—the content of the identity as well as contestation over this identity over time. The origins of what would become the three central tenets of Japan's postwar security identity—no traditional armed forces, no use of force by Japan except in self-defense, no Japanese participation in foreign wars—and examples of each are the subject of Chapter 2 of this volume. Also in Chapter 2, the critically important question of why these three tenets and not others is addressed. Despite a greatly changed international and domestic political environment in the twenty-first century, these tenets continue to fundamentally shape Japan's security practices today. They are therefore worthy of sustained reconsideration vis-à-vis previous characterizations of Japan's postwar security practice.

Security policy making in Japan is a deeply political process. Throughout the postwar period, Japanese political activists have spanned the full gamut from principled pacifists who believe that Japan should possess no armed forces at all (as opposed to being one of the largest military spenders in the world, after the United States and perhaps China, Britain, or France[9]) to those who argue for Japan once again to play the role of an independent military power, including the possession of nuclear weapons.[10] Between these extremes lie the majority of Japanese voters and political leaders, often espousing foreign policy positions that are driven less by worldview than by attempts to further their political or material interests. In the immediate postwar period (1945–60), Japanese politicians, party supporters, and the general public devoted significant time debating security questions, which played a formative role in the ideological shape of the newly forming democratic party politics.[11]

Since roughly 1960, Japan's security policy making has been filtered through a set of guiding principles which were negotiated in the preceding fifteen years and which greatly limited the scope of Japan's postwar security practices. These principles specify the degree to which Japan's reconstituted armed forces can become involved in domestic and international politics and are embodied in the new postwar security identity of "domestic antimilitarism."

Domestic antimilitarism is not a "pacifist" security identity in that it explicitly incorporates some role for a postwar military. The idea of a "pacifist" Japan, one that is disappearing as Japan faces new security threats, is in fact a double fiction. First, as carefully and correctly argued by Thomas Berger (1998), while believers in pacifist principles helped to shape Japan's security identity of domestic antimilitarism, this group alone never determined foreign policy outcomes in postwar Japan. Second, believers in pacifist—or antimilitarist—principles to ground Japanese security practice are not disappearing in Japan today, though they also are not the dominant intellectual force. Neither is this identity entirely "antimilitarist," in that it is openly accepting of military activity on the part of other states, including Japan's military ally and supporter, the United States.[12] Rather, the security identity is one of *domestic* antimilitarism—focusing on limits to the reemergence of militarist elements at home, yet still accepting as legitimate a defensive role for a military at home.

Policy practitioners who help formulate Japanese security policy as well as handlers of the U.S.-Japan security relationship are confronted daily with the effect of security identity on Japan's security policy-making process. In the world of scholarship, however, there is a wide gap between those who studiously endeavor to explain how such an identity is "constructed" and maintained, and those who seek to explain Japan's position in the international system as well as the strategic choices it faces based on shifting international power dynamics driven by such factors as divergent economic growth rates, technological progress in military hardware, and exogenous factors such as the recent U.S.-proclaimed outbreak of "the long war on global terrorism," to name but a few. This study brings these two approaches and concerns together, offering a unified study of Japan's view of its appropriate security role as well as the forces that help determine this view and resulting policy.

The early postwar origins of what would become Japan's security identity, and how this identity is institutionalized into the political process, has been a subject of intensive scholarship.[13] Three important questions remain largely unaddressed, however: First, how can we explain change, or lack of change, in security practice despite a stable security identity—change evident in Japan today? Second, what has been the effect of continued opposition to the long-standing security identity in terms of identity reproduction and actual security practice? Finally, the predictive question of the likely longevity of Japan's domestic antimilitarist security identity remains an important question: What makes this identity so resilient? Answers to these questions form the core of this volume.

While some argue that Japan today is on the verge of developing a new security identity manifesting a true "normalization" of Japanese security practice, this study suggests that it is more likely that Japan's existing security identity will continue to exert a predictable and measurable influence on Japan's security behavior for many more years to come. Indeed, for most Japanese the past fifty years of security practice is "normal," and they are not keen to depart dramatically from policies which have successfully kept a single Japanese soldier from dying in combat for over sixty years and have seen Japan literally rise from the ashes to the second-largest economy in the world today.

The Argument in Brief

The argument of this book has two fundamental pieces. The first examines the political process filtered through a postwar security identity that shapes Japanese security behavior and decision making, incorporating domestic political actors and international environmental variables to explicate change in security practices over time. It is not only in the post–Cold War period that significant changes in Japanese security practice took place—despite a stable security identity. Such change demands attention. In contrast to previous scholarship, this study employs case-based analysis to explore the nature of policy change over time. By examining a few areas of security practice in greater detail, an explanation for policy shift despite a fairly stable security identity is formulated.

The second piece of the argument may appear counterintuitive on the surface: that despite apparent new security policy innovation in Japan in recent years, constraints on security policy imposed by this security identity remain largely unchanged from the Cold War era. While it would appear that much-hyped new security practices Japan has adopted must be a result of dramatic new thinking about security, in actuality what better explains the evolution of security practice—what some perceive as a rising "militarism" or, more neutrally, a rise in "realist" thinking in the post–Cold War period—is the changed international strategic environment and changes in the relative power of different domestic political actors (such as the major political parties and other domestic interest groups), filtered through the long-standing security identity of domestic antimilitarism. While systematic polling indicates some shift in public and elite attitudes toward security issues (a topic addressed in Chapter 7 of this volume), change in the area of security identity does not constitute the primary explanation for new security practices in Japan in recent years. Thus, in addition to investigating Japan's security identity of domestic antimilitarism, it is important to examine the constellation of domestic political forces, and pressure put upon them by changes in Japan's international environment, to explain the evolution of Japanese security practice today. A framework for understanding such change is set out in Chapter 1 of this volume.

Here Robert Lieberman's (2002) observations about political change are instructive. He writes, "where friction among multiple political orders is more prevalent, the likelihood of significant, extraordinary political change (as opposed to normal variation) will increase" (p. 703). Japan today is a society where much such "friction" is apparent—leading many to question the future course of Japanese security decisions. While it can be a challenge empirically to identify and measure "friction among orders," this task is aided by careful extant scholarship about numerous aspects of Japanese security policy in the postwar period, much of which focuses on political contestation. Chapter 2 of this volume utilizes a large body of scholarship to illustrate the politics surrounding the creation and maintenance of the security identity of domestic antimilitarism. Subsequent chapters consider this "friction" more explicitly in relation to specific security practices that chafe against the hegemonic security identity of domestic antimilitarism: arms exports, the military use of outer space, missile defense, and other recent developments such as deployment of the SDF abroad and practices related to a closer military alliance with the United States.

Although it would be convenient to tell a simple causal story of the decline of pacifist ideas and the party that supported such ideas in postwar Japan along with the concomitant rise of realist thinking and new political actors to support it (a story often seen in mass media accounts), such a story is deeply misleading. Moreover, such an account is too superficial to be useful both in hypothesizing about Japan's future security direction and in explaining the nature of security policy innovation that already has taken place in recent years.

The changes that have occurred in contemporary Japan are not simply the values of key "independent variables" such as public opinion about the use of force abroad or over constitutional revision, or elite opinion about the same, resulting in a change in a "dependent variable" of security policy. Rather, the relationships have changed among the factors and processes by which a set of underlying conditions generates a set of policy outcomes.[14] Thus, this study is not designed around individual, testable "variables" but rather examines varying configurations of actors, institutions, and beliefs; it seeks to examine and explain friction and overlap among ideational and institutional elements. Careful attention to the evolving relationships among actors, institutions, and identities is necessary to explain the important political change that is taking place in Japan today in the area of security policy.

The much-discussed debate over constitutional revision in postwar Japan is illustrative of this point. It is often noted that support for revision now regularly reaches a majority of those polled, even supermajorities among elected officials (Kliman 2006, p. 46). The association of constitutional revision with "militarists" and those of the political right, however, has changed in the post–Cold War period. Today, those seeking the maintenance of Japan's postwar security identity of domestic antimilitarism also may support constitutional revision—in order to codify principles of the existing security identity for future generations. Support for constitutional revision no longer signifies support for identity shift, an attempt to change the famous Article Nine "no war clause" of the "peace constitution." Measurement of this "variable," therefore, has no meaning divorced from analysis of this changed context.

This book was written with three groups of readers in mind. First are those who follow Japanese security policy closely and are concerned with key determinants of the policy-making process, the content of specific policies, and the likely future direction of Japan's security policy. Such readers will find new insights from a reconsideration of past Japanese security practice as well as new empirical detail about several important cases of Japan's security policy past and present based on both archival and interview research conducted in Tokyo and Washington, D.C.

A second group of targeted readers are those interested in the active debate among international security specialists on the role of normative constraints and ideational factors on policy formulation, and how together with material factors policy outcomes are determined. This study seeks to build on important work published on the security policies of a number of advanced industrial democracies as well as other "great powers" in the international system, work discussed in the following sections of this introduction and in further detail in Chapter 1. In short, this volume seeks to move beyond important earlier studies which demonstrated both that security norms shaped the nature of Japanese security practice and, in separate work, how Japanese security practice has been constrained by several domestic and international factors, by setting out a framework for understanding the politically negotiated basis for Japan's security norms, and further how ideationally based security identity shapes and is shaped by political interaction.

A third group of targeted readers are general readers of foreign policy decision making. Although this study is designed around the question of security identity and its role in security practice, it also seeks to explain how security policies are actually formulated, including in particular the role of domestic politics and a changing international environment in this process. These policy case studies are illustrative of general policy-making practice, not just in Japan but in most advanced industrial democracies.

Defining Security Identity

In order to utilize such a potentially vague concept as identity in political analysis, it is important to be clear about basic issues of definition, measurement, and competing explanations. Indeed, Rawi Abdelal et al. (2005) argue that without such clarity, as well as a convergence of terminology and more rigorous methods, identity-based explanations for political outcomes will lose favor. Thus, such issues must be addressed directly at the outset of this study.

A security identity is a set of collectively held principles that have attracted broad political support regarding the appropriate role of state action in the security arena and are institutionalized into the policy-making process. Once (or if) such an identity becomes hegemonic in the polity, it serves as a structure in which all future policy decisions must operate, providing an overarching framework recognized both by top decision makers and by major societal actors under which a state shapes its security practices. A security identity, by definition, enjoys broad

legitimacy at the level of the general public—it is not merely a creation by political elites—but should not be conflated with amorphous "public opinion." Rather,
attention to the political bargain of Japan's postwar security identity allows one to
understand that what is often mistaken for "public opinion" is in fact the result of
a political negotiation among major domestic actors who traded off contending
foreign policy preferences.[15] Likewise, a security identity is neither an ideology
nor a set of beliefs about legitimate state action held by individuals;[16] though, of
course, *some* individuals within the state may share such beliefs, and indeed many
may do so.

Central to determining the role of a security identity in policy outcomes is
the *content* of the collective identity as well as the *level of contestation* over this content.[17] The *content* of Japan's security identity of domestic antimilitarism can be
summarized in three central tenets—no traditional armed forces, no use of force
by Japan except in self-defense, no Japanese participation in foreign wars—that
reflect both unwritten and institutionalized barriers to action beyond these limits.
The *contestation* element of Japan's security identity similarly is both explicit (self-
referential) and implicit (hidden from public discourse). It involves society-wide
discourse on "Japaneseness" (the so-called *nihonjinron*) as well as covert practices
of intimidation and political activism—both sides of which must be measured and
examined to understand how security identity affects security practice.

Simply arguing that multiple political actors had to cooperate to codify a particular security identity which then affected subsequent security practice in itself
is not an ideational argument. If the identity, even a compromise one, reflects the
interests of the politically powerful—even those powerful only in a coalition—the
"identity" in question is merely the result of material political factors. The argument of this study begins with such material considerations but then demonstrates
how these material factors are influenced directly by the security identity, which
generates a new political vocabulary, provides a focal point for public opinion, and
enables cooperation among diverse political actors who would not have acted
together absent the identity; moreover, the security identity indirectly influences
policy outcomes through institutionalization into the policy-making process.[18]

Thus, the conception of security identity developed here differs from previous work employing the terms *norms, ideas, ideology, political culture,* and *strategic
culture*—although this study draws on the insights of much of this previous work.
Among the many identity-based terms recently employed in political research,
ideology comes closest to the term *security identity* which is employed in this volume. To the extent that an ideology, as Richard Samuels (1994) writes, constitutes
"the ways in which history and political structure conspire to constrain the strategic choices of nations" (p. x), *ideology* is quite similar to *security identity* as employed
here. However, more often writers have conceptualized an ideology as more like

an "idea" or a "belief," both of which are individually held and affect the prefer-ence structures of individual political actors.[19] For the purposes of this study, *secu-rity identity* is not comparable to *ideology* in this sense—the three central tenets of the security identity of domestic antimilitarism are not argued to be universally shared beliefs among postwar Japanese. If they were, the role of political contesta-tion over security practice would be greatly diminished, and substantial change in security practice would be difficult to reconcile with a stable security identity.

Ideas overlap with a security identity conceptually, however, where they estab-lish a type of worldview or framework for understanding a state's position or role in the international system—as discussed by Henry Nau (2002) and Jeffrey Legro (2005). Ideas—and, in this study, a security identity—can provide a *focal point* for strategic situations with multiple equilibriums, such as the way in which decision makers sought to enact a common market among members of the European Eco-nomic Community (Garrett and Weingast 1993). Similarly, a state's security iden-tity provides a sense of coherence to foreign policy decision making by making certain policy options more desirable than others would be absent the overarch-ing identity.[20]

Some argue further that ideas provide a "road map" for policy decisions by informing one's *causal or principled beliefs* about a given situation—such as how an adversary is likely to respond to a reduction in the number of troops deployed on a border or how the economy will respond to increased government spend-ing (Goldstein and Keohane 1993, p. 12). Recent scholarship demonstrating this point for the Japanese case makes an important contribution to understanding the nature of recent policy change in Japan (e.g., Midford 2006, Vosse 2006). This is *not* a role ascribed to security identity in this study, however—though clearly many Japanese hold causal beliefs about the ineffectiveness of military power to attain state goals, which reinforce the postwar security identity of domestic antimili-tarism. The security identity of domestic antimilitarism does set boundaries for appropriate action in the foreign policy arena, but this does not rise to the level of a uniformly held causal or principled belief.

Also similar to the role of ideas, a security identity can act both to change the terms of political debate and discussion, as well as to affect political outcomes through its institutionalization into the political process. In addition, a hegemonic security identity influences "organizational design," affecting the policy-making process in another important, though distinct, manner. What Judith Goldstein and Robert Keohane (1993) write about the role of ideas, which they define as beliefs held by *individuals*, can be extended for the purposes of this discussion to an over-arching security identity:

> Regardless of how a particular set of beliefs comes to influence politics, use of those
> ideas over time implies changes in existing rules and norms. Ideas have a lasting influ-

ence on politics through their incorporation into terms of political debate, but the impact of some set of ideas may be mediated by the operation of institutions in which the ideas are embedded. Once ideas have influenced organizational design, their influence will be reflected in the incentives of those in the organization and those whose interests are served by it. In general, when institutions intervene, the impact of ideas may be prolonged for decades or even generations. *In this sense, ideas can have an impact even when no one genuinely believes in them as principled or causal statements.* (Goldstein and Keohane 1993, p. 20, emphasis added)

The final sentence of the above quotation deserves underscoring: as with Goldstein and Keohane's view of ideas, a security identity can influence security practice even if an individual political actor does not believe in the underlying principles of the identity, because the security identity has been institutionalized into the policy-making process.[21]

Also related conceptually, Berger's (1998) view of the power of "culture" in Japanese security practice is far broader than is ascribed here to Japan's postwar security identity. In contrast to Berger, security identity here does not provide the "goals and norms" for individual political actors, but rather it sets such goals for the state as a whole, and in doing so sets boundaries for the appropriate political action of individual political actors.[22] Crossing these boundaries requires substantial political capital and subjects those who attempt such to substantial political costs, similar to the costs of violating a "norm" as Peter Katzenstein conceptualizes them.

Katzenstein (1996b) defines *norms* as "social facts" which "inform how political actors define what they want to accomplish" (p. ix). By contrast, the security identity of domestic antimilitarism is concerned not with *what* political actors seek to accomplish but rather with *how* they will attempt to accomplish their goals given the overarching framework (and content) of the security identity of domestic antimilitarism. For example, given a corporate interest to export weapons, the security identity of domestic antimilitarism can shape the strategy a corporate actor employs to achieve this goal, or at an extreme, lead to the abandonment of this goal as too costly or unattainable; it does not, however, alter such a firm's desire to export weapons but does limit its ability to achieve this aim and may increase the costs of doing so. Despite the focus of this volume on security practice, it should be stressed at the outset the important contribution the norms-based literature makes to our understanding of political outcomes. As Katzenstein (1996b) correctly argues, "to disregard norms and take the interests of actors as given is thus to short-circuit an important aspect of the politics and policy of national security" (pp. ix–x). Previous examinations of norms related to postwar Japanese security practice are central to Chapter 2 of this volume, and to the study overall.

Methods, Cases, and Evidence: Measuring
Security Identity and Policy Shift

This volume examines three important cases of postwar Japanese security practice that are critical components of previous identity-based scholarship and that also have special relevance to recent security discussions in Japan: restrictions on the export of weapons, the limitation on the use of outer space to peaceful purposes, and military cooperation with the United States in the realm of missile defense. Together with a broader examination of other important changes in Japanese security practice—such as SDF deployment abroad, the expanding military capabilities of the SDF, and the deepening alliance with the United States—the three core cases of this volume present the most often cited, crucial cases of Japan's "abnormal" security practices and therefore are most often discussed in the context of Japan's imminent "identity shift."

Careful examination of these cases demonstrates two important points. First, in none of these cases has there been a dramatic break with past practice in recent years—despite much media hype to the contrary. Only incremental change— much like what has taken place in preceding decades—has occurred to date. An unusual level of continuity is apparent over time, continuity best explained by reference to Japan's long-standing security identity. Second, neither ideational nor material explanations alone can explain the policy evolution that has taken place.

Case Selection

The cases presented in this volume can be conceptualized on three levels. First, the evidence collected and presented here is about a single case—the case of postwar Japan. Following a number of other single-country studies in research areas related to security identity (e.g., Friedberg 2000, Johnston 1995a, Kier 1997, Katzenstein 1996a, Nau 2002), the goal is to link specific observations from a single case to a larger research agenda.[23] Second, however, this volume presents findings from three temporal cases of "critical junctures" in Japanese security policy, seeking to explain and conceptualize instances of identity shift. Thus, despite a single-country analysis, methodologically the volume does not constitute a single case.[24] Finally, this volume presents findings from three detailed cases of evolving Japanese security practice, demonstrating the effect of a consistent security identity on security practice, within a changing material political environment. Examination of these three detailed cases illustrates commonalities that can be used to examine policy change more broadly.

The dearth of scholarly attention to Japan's postwar arms export and outer space policies is notable, since in many ways it is these policies that most demand explanation.[25] First, they are among the most puzzling of Japan's postwar security policies in that existing theories uniformly predict a different outcome. Second, the cases are studied infrequently in the literature despite their importance both as discrete and important issues in themselves and for their potential contribution to theory building. Third, the two policies are of particular interest in the post–Cold War period due to their influence on major new security policy decisions, such as the decision to manufacture and deploy domestically produced surveillance satellites (explained in this volume within Chapter 5) and the decision to participate with the United States in joint research on a missile defense system for East Asia (the final case study examined in Chapter 6).

Despite common reference to the arms export "ban" and the peaceful-use-of-space policy in relation to surveillance satellites and missile defense, little focused research has been conducted on the origins of these Cold War–era policies, and their continued relevance today. By contrast, a great deal of attention has been paid in recent years to the broader issue of defense production as well as to issues related to the SDF, particularly the issue of foreign deployment of the SDF as part of UN Peacekeeping Operations (UNPKO).[26] Findings from these existing studies therefore can be combined with new research from the three case studies developed in this volume to provide a broader picture of the direction of Japanese security policy in the twenty-first century, the topic of Chapter 7.

Japan's individual security policies are not formulated in isolation, however. Rather, they are closely connected by political actors seeking to balance contending political objectives and interests within the framework of Japan's postwar security identity of domestic antimilitarism. Accordingly, the outcome of one policy case is often contingent on the outcome of another. For example, as discussed in later chapters, Japan's policy decisions to support its U.S. ally in its war in Vietnam and to aggressively pursue the reversion of Okinawa to Japanese administrative control (two policies which themselves are linked) led to countervailing policies such as restrictions on nuclear weapons and arms exports, the formal declaration of a policy regarding the peaceful use of outer space, and restrictions on defense spending overall. It is impossible to fully explain one of these policies without reference to several others. This interaction among cases parallels the central thesis of Kent Calder (1988a), who argues that conservative elites "compensated" in certain policy areas when "crisis" was evoked in other areas.[27] Like Calder, this study follows an integrated approach, utilizing detailed analysis of several important cases of postwar Japanese security policy but also embedding these cases in a broader theoretical and empirical context.

Strict positivists and methodological purists will quickly shout "tautology" to this approach. It is not. The argument here is that guiding principles apparent in an early stage of institutionalization and political debate over an emergent security identity help determine the acceptability and political viability of future policy decisions. These future policies themselves do not determine the identity, though they can help delineate guideposts and do serve to reproduce the identity over time. Chapter 1 delves further into the methods by which one can employ the concept of security identity in empirically based explanations for the evolution of Japanese security practice.

Sources of Data and Measurement

Lieberman (2002) identifies three "clusters of order" to aid in a case-based analysis that takes the ideas of friction and contestation seriously: (1) *"governing institutions"* such as legislatures, executives, courts, and bureaucracies; (2) the *"organizational environment"* such as political parties, interest groups, and nongovernmental organizations; and (3) *"ideological and cultural repertoires"* that organize and legitimate political discourse (p. 703). This study similarly focuses on the role and institutionalization by the *governing institutions* of the prime minister, the Diet, and relevant bureaucracies such as the Ministry of Foreign Affairs (MOFA), the Japan Defense Agency (JDA),[28] the Ministry of International Trade and Industry (MITI, later METI), and the Cabinet Legislation Bureau (CLB). As well, it considers the policy positions of the actors within what Lieberman calls the *organizational environment*—the major political parties of the Liberal Democratic Party (LDP), the Japan Socialist Party (JSP), Kōmeitō (KMT), and the Democratic Party of Japan (DPJ), and important interest groups such as the Federation of Economic Organizations (Keidanren) and labor unions. The *ideological repertoire* is examined through evaluation of newspaper editorials, articles from the popular press, statements of major intellectual figures, and even representations in popular culture such as films, novels, and songs.[29]

At its heart, the battle over a security identity is a political process involving both public debate and private negotiations. As Legro (2005) writes, "By their very nature, foreign policy ideas will be in the public realm. They cannot be reproduced unless all have access to them" (p. 22). Public opinion polls provide one measure of the level of subscription to competing identities, but they show only part of the picture.

The role of specific actors is discussed in each case chapter below, but each case shares in common categories of evidence collected from government documents and policy statements, newspaper accounts (particularly those collected by the National Diet Library and, more recently, archived in computer databases), political party platforms, and a number of secondary sources published in English and

Japanese. In addition, supplementary case evidence for this study was collected in over two hundred interviews conducted in Tokyo and Washington, D.C., with state actors in both countries as well as representatives from political parties and associations, private corporations, the media, and academic analysts.[30]

As with Nau (2002), Lieberman focuses his analysis on the "directionality" of these clusters of order—whether they are in harmony with one another or in tension. He stresses:

> When stable patterns of politics clash, purposive political actors will often find themselves at an impasse, unable to proceed according to the "normal" patterns and processes that had hitherto governed their behavior. Political actors in such circumstances will often be induced to find new ways to define and advance their aims, whether by finding a new institutional forum that is more receptive to their ideas or by adapting ideas to take advantage of new institutional opportunities. . . . The result of these moves is not that old orders are jettisoned but that elements of them are recombined and reconfigured into a new set of political patterns that is recognizably new and yet retains some continuity with the old ones. (Lieberman 2002, p. 704)

Japan in the immediate postwar period offered one such opportunity to reconfigure a "new set of political patterns," and one taken—leading to a dramatic recrafting of Japan's security identity from military expansionism to domestic antimilitarism in the period 1945–60, the subject of Chapter 2 of this volume. A second opportunity was presented after the end of the Cold War in Europe and the death of the Showa emperor (Hirohito) in 1989, and this is the subject of Chapter 3. In this period, despite substantial institutional reform (of political party structure, electoral system, and bureaucratic governance) and widespread public debate, no new security identity emerged. Japanese are confronted with a third opportunity today. Observers at home and abroad are witnessing daily how the friction among Japan's clusters of order is playing out in practice—between bureaucrats in the MOD and MOFA seeking to implement new defense cooperation with the United States and politicians and other bureaucrats seeking to justify such cooperation using dated legislation and terminology, among political parties seeking to quell new public security concerns yet respecting past security identity boundaries and preferences, and within civil society institutions such as the left-leaning media and nongovernmental organizations. Given the degree of tension and contradictions within and among these different nodes of order, the possibility for a shift in security identity away from domestic antimilitarism is real. An examination of the potential for such a shift—and why ultimately such a shift is unlikely in the foreseeable future—is the subject of Chapter 7, but it is foreshadowed in the following section and in the theoretical framework set out in Chapter 1.

Prediction and Falsification

The argument developed in this volume—based on Japan's long-standing security identity and its effect on security practice—leads to the following hypotheses about the future evolution of Japan's security practices. First, policy initiatives that conform to existing interpretation of the security identity of domestic antimilitarism should proceed quickly and be relatively unhindered, absent other intervening factors such a bureaucratic politics, alliance politics, or personal executive leadership effectiveness. Japan's humanitarian-based initial response to the September 11 attacks on the United States is a good example of such "normal politics."

Second, and as a corollary, policy initiatives that conflict with the existing interpretation of the security identity should take more time, require extensive use of political capital, and often necessitate substantial political concessions to the initial intent of the policy in order to proceed. Here one could contrast the speed and ease with which multiple humanitarian-based responses to the September 11 attacks were enacted (all of which fell clearly within the boundaries of the security identity) to the debacle of Prime Minister Kaifu's efforts to extend the boundaries of the security identity at the time of the first Gulf War in 1990–91.

Finally, interpretation of the security identity may evolve over time to some extent, based on a changing domestic or international environment, but even such change often requires political capital. Moreover, there are clear limits beyond which the security identity cannot be extended—as is evident in the case chapters that follow.

To the extent that these hypotheses are disconfirmed, the argument can be considered falsified. If in Japan's future, policies regularly pass which conflict fundamentally with the three central tenets of domestic antimilitarism, it will be an indication either of identity shift in Japan (in which case new central tenets could be identified) or of the failure of an argument based on security identity to explain policy change in contemporary Japan. In such an event—a shift away from the security identity of domestic antimilitarism—one would see a much more accelerated change in Japanese security policy, and in ways that are unpredictable until a new security identity is crafted and negotiated, a process that likely would take several years (if not a decade or more) and thus could have significant ramifications for regional stability.

Absent the existing security identity, Japanese security policy could fluctuate unpredictably in the years to come, stymieing U.S.-Japan alliance cooperation and vexing Japan's close neighbors, perhaps leading to increased military tensions or even outright military conflict—such as over disputed territories, territorial incursions, or preemptive strikes to slow weapons development in hostile states.

TABLE I

Indicators of Possible Breaches of the Security Identity of Domestic Antimilitarism

Tenet One	Centralization of defense policy management solely within the Ministry of Defense
	Creation of a national security council to advise the prime minister that includes SDF officers
Tenet Two	Statements of threat of use of force in international discourse
	Development of explicitly offensive military capabilities
Tenet Three	Creation of offensive military plans or posture
	Commitments to the use of the SDF in active overseas conflicts
	Unilateral use of the SDF in overseas military activities

Such policy outcomes are extremely unlikely under the current security identity of domestic antimilitarism.

What would it take to produce a different security identity for Japan? Or might the existing security identity be altered to an extent that it no longer meaningfully represented the central tenets of the past security identity? The empirical research presented in this volume, together with the theoretical framework offered in Chapter 1, provides a detailed answer to these two important questions. This introduction will conclude with a few specific thresholds for measuring possible movement away from the central tenets of Japan's postwar security identity of domestic antimilitarism, as summarized in Table 1.

Successful revision of the constitution that includes a constitutional basis for SDF *military* activities overseas and poses no obstacles to Japan exercising its sovereign right of collective self-defense would signify a shift away from the security identity of domestic antimilitarism. The enactment of legislation that took advantage of these new constitutional entitlements would signify the crossing of a threshold away from this security identity toward something else. Such change is unlikely, though, divorced from growing evidence in public discourse about new underlying principles for Japan's security future, new coalitions among political and social actors, and new proposals for institutional rules and legislation in line with this "something else." As argued in Chapter 1, the presence of alternative visions to ground new general principles for state action and of political entrepreneurs to articulate these visions in socially salient ways is critical to the consolidation of a new security identity. Such alternative principles and actors to articulate them are evident in today's Japan (Samuels 2007) and must be considered carefully. In the area of constitutional revision, the creation of numerous task forces—public and private—to propose alternatives and to advocate for new grounding principles is evidence of such a vibrant ideational environment. Thus, the potential for identity shift certainly is present, but at the earliest it is several years away.[31]

Constitutional revision is not the only route to security identity shift. It may be possible to enact legislation in a number of areas that departs from the core principles of domestic antimilitarism without following this path.[32] Indeed, conservatives seeking a more "normal" Japan may choose to follow this route of nonrevision given the obstacles to enacting constitutional revision along the lines they seek. The elevation of the JDA to the MOD would appear to be an example of the crossing of such a threshold. It seems likely in the years to come that the MOD will begin to exercise new powers and authority in line with its new status that could lead to the negation of the first tenet of domestic antimilitarism, which prohibits active military involvement in policy making. Some would argue that this threshold has already been crossed, as the de facto status, functions, and institutional capabilities of the JDA were increased in the late 1990s in preparation for elevation of the agency to ministry status, and the role of the uniformed SDF members in the JDA bureaucracy increased.

Certainly the visibility of the SDF has increased markedly in recent years—from coverage in the media and appearance of uniformed SDF officers in public places to the shiny new headquarters of the MOD in Ichigaya, Tokyo. More substantively, a greater SDF presence has been visible in policy-making institutions within the JDA for several years, and equally so—though not yet *more* so—within the MOD. Still, MOFA continues to play a leading role in the management of one of Japan's principal security issues—its alliance with the United States—and the prime minister and members of the Diet have limited direct contact with the SDF or even the MOD. Discussions are under way to set up an upgraded National Security Council (NSC) in Japan to advise the prime minister, though current proposals do not include uniformed officers of the SDF (as the U.S. NSC does, in the form of the head of the Joint Chiefs of Staff), and the civilian MOD will be just one voice among many. If in Japan's future, the SDF and MOD begin to play a leading role in planning and implementing Japan's security strategy—as the individual military services and the Department of Defense (DOD) do in the United States—it should be seen as an example of the abandonment of the first tenet of domestic antimilitarism.

Similar indicators can be imagined for the resilience of the other two central tenets of Japan's security identity, as summarized in Table 1. For example, regarding the second tenet of no use of military force to resolve international disputes, public acceptance of explicit threats of the use of Japan's formidable military to achieve state objectives would indicate an abandoning of this tenet.[33] As well, development of explicitly offensive military capabilities—as opposed to capabilities that might incidentally have some offensive applications in principle—would provide further evidence of a crossing of a threshold that would signify the collapse of a core principle. Creation of new military plans or "contingencies" that included offensive action would also violate a principle central to the existing security identity. Other indicators are also imaginable for this tenet, and for others.

The third tenet of domestic antimilitarism—no Japanese participation in foreign military conflict—has already been pushed close to the limit of reasonable implementation of the principle through the deployment of the SDF to participate in counterterrorism activities in the Indian Ocean and areas in and around Iraq. Still, the activities of the SDF overseas are almost exclusively humanitarian in nature—though Maritime Self-Defense Forces (MSDF) activities in the Indian Ocean to refuel warships and Air Self-Defense Forces (ASDF) resupply activities from Kuwait get perilously close to violating this principle. Consistent with the argument of this volume, however, this policy is deeply contested politically. Moreover, at the time of publication of this volume, the future of this "special measure" is uncertain, as political opposition has become emboldened. Future such activities seem to be on hold for now as well—following the long-standing pattern of "reach, reconcile, reassure" discussed in Chapter 1—but routine participation in such activities could well signal an abandonment of this principle. Such abandonment could come both from the number and frequency of such activities or from future "mission creep." Public statements by former Prime Minister Abe and former Foreign Minister Aso clearly indicated that their government would have liked to have seen this happen. But, to date, such statements do not reflect mainstream opinion in contemporary Japan (Oros 2007b). That these officials served less than a year in office also suggests their views were not politically viable.

Is there a security identity beyond domestic antimilitarism in Japan's near future? Historically speaking, one can observe a "fifteen-year rule" in Japanese historical development.[34] The forced opening of Japan in 1853 by U.S. naval force led fifteen years later to the 1868 Meiji "restoration" of imperial authority—a dramatic reshaping of political order. The 1945 defeat in the Second World War led fifteen years later to the 1960 renewal of the U.S.-Japan security treaty and codification of the security identity of domestic antimilitarism. Will the 1991 dissolution of the Soviet Union and the collapse of the bubble economy (on the heels of the 1989 death of the Showa emperor) lead to the codification of a new security identity for Japan in a multipolar Asia in 2006 or soon after? To answer these important questions, one must look to the broader theoretical arguments for policy change developed in Chapter 1 and illustrated empirically in subsequent chapters.

Primary Alternative Explanations

It is useful to briefly consider at the outset two primary alternative explanations to the argument presented here, with more detailed discussion of alternative and complementary theories to follow in Chapter 1. One alternative explanation is that changes in material factors largely account for changes in security practice to date. Material factors in this sense would include both the domestic configuration of political power and the international environment. While on the surface this basic explanation has some traction, detailed examination of multiple cases of Japanese security practice provided in following chapters demonstrate clearly that such materially based explanations alone cannot account for more than the surface evolution of Japan's security practice over time.

A second alternative explanation concedes the past role of the security identity of domestic antimilitarism but argues that this identity has since disappeared in favor of a more realist orientation in post–Cold War, post-Taepodong, and post-9/11 Japan. This explanation as well cannot account for the substantial limits still evident on a large swath of Japanese security practice today, including SDF deployments abroad, the tortured pace of missile defense codevelopment, capability restrictions on surveillance satellites, and consecutive declines in overall defense spending in recent years. Instead, the evolution of security practice in Japan clearly is still shaped fundamentally by a security identity whose central tenets were negotiated decades ago but which continue to be reproduced, reinterpreted, and reified regularly in new security legislation and overall practice.

Such a framework for Japan's security outlook seems fairly certain for the medium term, absent a dramatic external or internal shock to Japan. Even such a shock does not necessitate a broader shift in security identity, as seen in the 1990s after a series of international and domestic security shocks failed to lead to a recrafting of the long-standing security identity of domestic antimilitarism. Still, the possibility of identity shift must be considered carefully. This, together with an explanation for general policy change within an existing security identity, is the focus of the next chapter.

1

Security Identity and the
Evolution of Security Practice
Explaining Policy Change

Explaining policy change has been a core task for policy makers and scholars alike, but a particular problem for advocates of structural theories such as those based on "culture" or "polarity" of a system. The then-dominant structural realist theories of international relations widely failed at anticipating the end of the Cold War, for example, and culturally deterministic wartime explanations for Japan's military aggression were hard-pressed to explain Japan's policy turn after defeat in the Second World War. Today, when change in states' foreign policies is broadly apparent, renewed attention to this question is necessary. Recent changes in Japanese security practices have alarmed many observers and called into question past explanations for Japanese security practice. In particular, there is widespread concern that Japan is on the verge of disengaging the "brakes" (*hadome*, in Japanese) that limited Japanese military activity in the past half century. What often is overlooked in contemporary discourse, however, are the many cases throughout the postwar period when Japanese security policy changed in response to shifting political inputs and changes in its international environment. Further consideration of such cases offers insight into the ways in which policy change in Japan today conforms to past practice and the extent to which it suggests a new direction. Before examining the specifics of policy change in Japan, however, it is useful to consider the broader question of how policy change has generally been conceptualized.

This chapter lays out, first, three factors that contribute to general policy change. It then seeks to develop how security identity can contribute to understanding this process. Next, this general discussion is brought back to the specific case of Japan, suggesting how broader theories of policy change can illuminate existing scholarship on policy change in Japan. Finally, a theory of policy change based on the conception of a security identity is offered and contrasted with other prominent and contending explanations for Japanese security practice.

Explaining Policy Change

Three factors—individually or in combination—explain policy shift and therefore must be considered in conjunction with an explanation rooted in security identity.[1] Each of these factors contributes to a general explanation for Japanese security policy evolution over time (see Table 2). First, ideas about the appropriate course of action may change, leading to policy change. For example, changing notions of race may lead to new policies regarding racial segregation. In the security realm, new ideas about the utility of particular strategies or military technologies may lead to policy change. In the most extreme cases, wholesale change in ideas about security may explain dramatic policy shift, such as when comparing the cases of prewar and postwar Japan. Chapter 2 of this volume demonstrates how such a shift occurred in early postwar Japan, while Chapter 3 shows the opposite—stability despite a changed domestic and international environment. Jeffrey Legro (2005) offers one conceptualization of why such ideas change, which is applied to the case of Japan below.

Second, the distribution of power within a political system may shift, resulting in policy change. In democracies, this most often happens with a change to the party in power, but it also may take place even under a single party's rule due to changes in support levels among different groups within a single party or coalition. In the case of Japan, the ascendancy or decline of particular factions within the long-ruling LDP can explain some degree of policy shift, as could the periods where the LDP majority was fundamentally challenged. This factor often is related to the first factor in that change in support for a particular party or group may be based on changes in ideas held by supporters: voters may vote a party or a candidate in or out based on ideas they advocate. In later chapters of this volume, policy evolution due to shifting political support is widely evident.

Third, the context or environment in which a policy is made may change, resulting in policy change. In the realm of security policy, a change in threat, threat perception, or system stability may lead to a policy response, even if there is no change in the previous two factors. This aspect of policy change forms the basis of structural realist theory and accounts for a high degree of security policy evolution in Japan in recent years due to an objectively changed level of threat as well as greater Japanese perception of this threat.

To what extent do each of these reasons for policy change explain evolving security practice in postwar Japan? Each of the three factors contributed to a dramatic change in Japanese security practice after defeat in the Second World

TABLE 2

Why Policies Change

---

1. Ideas about appropriate action change, perhaps even so far as an identity shift
2. Political power distribution or the party in power changes
3. The context or environment in which policy is made or to which it is targeted changes

---

War: (1) a thorough discrediting of military expansionist ideology; (2) a purging (for a time) of wartime politicians and bureaucratic leaders and release of political prisoners who enjoyed new political support; and (3) a new international environment that soon would be characterized by a bipolar Cold War. In the first years of the twenty-first century, it is the second and third factors that best explain the degree of change in Japanese security practices, while the first factor has served both to limit and to shape the nature of policy change. Although perception of threat clearly has increased among the Japanese public in recent years, ideas about the best way to ameliorate such threats—reliance on the United Nations and international cooperation highest among them—have not changed substantially.[2] By contrast, a changed international environment—beginning first with the collapse of the enemy state Japanese security strategy was built around, the Soviet Union—necessitated changes in Japanese security policy and practice, despite similar ideas held by most Japanese and the same political party dominating the political system. Thus, on the surface, an explanation for policy change rooted in changes in the international environment—international relations realist theory— would appear to be the best starting point for explaining the evolution of Japanese security practice. However, the cases examined in this volume illustrate clearly that reliance on this school of theory alone leads to inaccurate prediction and inadequate explanation of postwar Japanese security practice overall. Failure to consider Japan's long-standing security identity leads one to incorrect predictions regarding future policy direction and outcomes and, conversely, fails to provide an explanation for the striking stability of Japanese security policy over the past fifty years. A rigorous conceptualization and application of Japan's security identity is necessary to understand Japanese security practice and its evolution over time.

Security Identities and Security Practice: Toward a General Framework

The nature of a state's security identity is critical not only to understanding postwar Japan, but to understanding the security posture and policies of most states. A quick scan of the major transformative events of the twentieth century quickly underscores how changed domestic circumstances, and a state's perception of

these changes as institutionalized in a security identity, can have dramatic consequences for domestic security policies as well as the broader international system.
The end of the Cold War, the rise of the United States after the Second World
War, the rise of China on the international scene in recent decades, and the outlier status of Japan in the late twentieth century are all due primarily to factors
linked to each state's self-perceived security identity in the context of domestic
political change.[3]

One of the more popular theoretical literatures in the study of international
politics at the end of the last century, hegemonic stability theory, ultimately had
poor predictive power due to the lack of sufficient attention paid to such domestic factors, including specifically the nature of Japan's security identity: Japan did
not, in fact, rise to challenge the United States for global hegemony, but rather
cooperated with the United States in extending the latter's military "hegemony"
into the Asian region and beyond. As Henry Nau (2002) notes, "domestic change
is often the primary source of external power shifts" (p. 237). But such "domestic
change" must be contextualized and understood by citizens through an understandable lens: a defined, reproduced, and institutionalized security identity. The
process by which such a lens is formulated, institutionalized, and maintained over
time is inherently political. The next section develops a framework by which
these processes can be understood, setting the basis for the empirical work of the
following chapters.

While ideas about specific policies within the broader identity may evolve on
a regular basis, a change in the principles underpinning the basic direction of state
policy is much less common and thus a more significant occurrence. Change in
this area when applied to the security realm gets to the core of possible security
identity shift and therefore deserves special attention here.

Explaining Identity Shift

Security identity—or other forms of state identity, as discussed below—therefore can be used to explain the evolution of policy practice in two distinct ways.
First, in periods of "normal politics" the identity structures political action in
line with the central tenets of this identity. This process, and the way by which it
comes about, is discussed in the following sections of this chapter. Second, major
policy change can take place through the adoption of a new security identity—an
identity shift. While such shifts do not, by definition, occur frequently within
states, across states they do occur frequently enough to allow general theory to be
formulated about what factors contribute to identity shift, and to the important
corollary question of how a *new* identity can become hegemonic.

Here Legro's work on state conceptions of the international system—an ideational variable similar in many ways to a security identity as postulated in this study—is instructive. Underlying wholesale identity shift, in Legro's view, is a disjuncture between what he calls "social expectations" resulting from "collective ideas about what should be expected to occur and what is desirable" (Legro 2005, p. 32) and what actually happens in the material world. Instances of substantial disjuncture *in a negative way* can precipitate identity shift. However, he argues, importantly, that it is insufficient to consider only the "collapse" of an identity, but that equally one must consider the likelihood of "consolidation" of a new identity. As he rightly notes, "Individuals may agree that the old view has to go but may not be able to agree or coordinate on what new orthodoxy should be the guide" (p. 15). This perceptive observation may be quite important to explaining the direction of contemporary Japanese security policy.

Legro studies one case of identity shift in Japan, in the late nineteenth century, which demonstrates how the collapse of the old identity of isolationism greatly preceded any new consensus about a new identity which could be consolidated. The following chapter of this volume shows a similar phenomenon in the case of immediate postwar Japan, where it took fifteen years for a new identity to begin to be consolidated, despite the thorough collapse of the old identity. The cases of immediate post–Cold War and contemporary Japan are less clear. Some argue that Japan today is in a process of ideational collapse. Critical to this question, therefore, are the alternative identities that can be consolidated. As Legro notes, a common limitation in this search—at least initially—is that "when serious problems arise, policymakers go looking for new ideas but have to choose from the existing supply, those notions developed in the preceding period" (p. 35). As discussed in later chapters of this volume, however, this is less the case in Japan today (where political entrepreneurs have had nearly twenty years to articulate new post–Cold War visions for Japan) than in the immediate post–Cold War period.

From a theoretical perspective, therefore, this conceptualization of identity shift does make the viability of adopting and consolidating a new security identity seem more likely in Japan today than a framework based solely on collapse. Still, the critical theoretical issue facing the case of contemporary Japan is what would precipitate a "collapse" of the old identity, in order for another contending set of principles to take root. The argument of later chapters of this volume is that there is nothing approaching the level of discontinuity necessary to precipitate such a collapse in Japan today. Moreover, Legro argues that new ideas must achieve "social salience"—that is, they must be "backed by important constituencies or activist subgroups . . . that have the ability to vie for new dominant orthodoxy" (p. 35) in order for principles to be consolidated into a new identity. What is important in this approach, as well as the approach advocated in this volume, is that the presence or absence of alternative ideas, and the social salience of these ideas, becomes central to theorizing the likelihood of identity shift—apart from realpolitik international and domestic political concerns. Simply put, identity shift cannot take place without the presence of an alternative set of unifying principles and respected political actors to advocate for them. Renewed attention to this area of discourse on foreign policy visions for Japan's future is therefore an important part of the research agenda, one usefully pursued by Richard Samuels (2007).

Conceptualizing Multiple and Competing Identities over Time

At one level, as Legro conceptualizes, state identity is a lens through which citizens determine a framework for a state's appropriate response to the demands and challenges of the international environment. Multiple such lenses are imaginable—activist or passive, internationalist or isolationist, revolutionary or status quo are several general postures often considered by states.[4] Choosing just one identity is impossible for an individual (e.g., which is more important to you—your skin color or your religion?); even more so for a state. As with individuals, a state will not assume only one identity but will manage multiple, and at times possibly even conflicting, identities in the course of its choices and policy making. Rawi Abdelal et al. (2005), among others, usefully delineate measurement of identity into two parts—*content* of the identity and *contestation* over the identity, a framework employed in this volume as well. This latter category might be further expanded to consider contestation over overlapping or conflicting identities rather than over a single identity, such as a security identity, since our choices of identity in particular contexts affect our actions—both as individuals and as states.[5] In the cases considered in this volume, for example, Japan's security identity of domestic antimilitarism frequently comes into conflict with Japanese elite views of Japan as a technonationalist or trading state.

State identity is, by definition, a *collective* identity, which requires a conceptualization and tools of analysis different from those used in an examination of individual identity. States institutionalize the identities they seek to reify and project them to others in laws and other norms of behavior. What identity will be institutionalized is a fundamentally political question—one which is simply understood in some rare states, never reached in unfortunate others, and the subject of continual battles and rearticulation in the majority of cases.

A security identity is a subset of the larger question of national identity, which pervades much of the recent literature on identity factors in international politics. It is not the position of this study that a security identity arises from a shared worldview among decision makers or the general public. Rather, a security identity may become hegemonic as a result of a political solution that reflects the individual beliefs of some political actors but also accommodates the interests of powerful political and economic actors who benefit materially from the identity in the short term yet do not necessarily embrace its ideological content.[6] Moreover, the contestation element over the security identity may continue even after it has become hegemonic—a critical element of policy change discussed in subsequent chapters. Thus, a security identity cannot be defined by individual beliefs—whether present or absent—nor negated by the presence of opposition alone. The factors that lead to the adoption and codification of a security identity therefore demand special attention.

In postwar Japan, the security identity of domestic antimilitarism is not a "grand design" propagated by the politically or economically powerful, reflecting both their interests and worldview. Nor, as noted in the introduction, is it an ideology or a national culture. However, over time many actors who initially supported the emergent identity only for reasons based solely on material interest later supported the ideological component of the security identity more broadly once it was institutionalized. Herein lies an important "identity" component of the analysis offered here—it is not just a matter of logrolling, nor of institutionalization. Through the negotiation and adoption of a series of policies and precedents, an identity can be created that exerts a presence of its own.

To examine this process, it is useful to break discussion of the role of security identity on policy practice into temporal stages, as the subsequent case chapters of this volume are organized, following Kathryn Sikkink's approach to the study of the role of ideas in Latin American economic development policy. Sikkink (1991) implements a separation of the role of ideas analytically into three temporal stages—adoption, implementation, and consolidation. Ideas matter at each stage of the process, but in different ways. In a similar vein, it is useful methodologically to trace policy formulation on one issue over time—from initial debates through implementation and later consolidation and revision—to see how security identity affects the outcome. While the role of ideas and the impact of a security identity are not identical, it is useful methodologically to conceptualize their effects in a similar fashion. Such an approach also serves, methodologically, to maximize the number of observations from a smaller number of cases—an important factor in extending the theoretical breadth of a single study.

One must be careful not to take this logic too far to a point where competing elites support an appealing security identity only to propagate and legitimate their interests, but where the actual content of the identity plays no causal role. This way of thinking, as Judith Goldstein and Robert Keohane (1993) argue, closely approximates some rationalist views where identity is merely a "hook" on which to place one's predetermined policies—which are based on an actor's conception of his or her interests. In such a rationalist view, interests are given and logically prior to any beliefs held by the actors, as seen in the international relations schools of realism and liberal institutionalism.[7] Preferences are formed prior to any social interaction or historical evolution in the case of neorealism and largely fixed in the case of neoliberalism, where preferences may be adjusted at the margin during negotiations or through interactions under institutional contexts. Theories situated within this rationalist framework rely on the assumption of a utility-maximizing actor, whether the actor has political, economic, or social interests. The goal of any action is to maximize one's interests and preferences. This study argues, by contrast, that within the state some actors' conception of their interests will be fixed and lead to support of one conception of security identity over another, but that other actors' preferences are altered by the content of the adopted security identity through socialization and through institutionalization. Moreover, while some political actors may choose to support the identity for purely material reasons, others will support the identity based on its content. Kimberly Zisk Marten and Alexander Cooley (2003) apply a similar framework to allow us to better understand the politics of protest against U.S. bases in Okinawa, Japan.[8]

The Effect of Security Identity on Security Practice

Promoting the notion that interaction among political actors over identity issues is an important aspect of decision making is a contribution made by a number of recent identity-based studies of foreign policy, including those employing variables such as "norms," "ideas," and "strategic culture."[9] However, what is necessary to move forward in theory-building on the role of identity in foreign policy making is an explanation of not only how a hegemonic security identity is deployed and becomes adopted, but also how this identity then affects the process of policy making as well as actual security practice. Scholars need to understand better how, once hegemonic, a security identity can constrain the interests of powerful political and economic actors, or conversely, how a security identity can at times be violated or transcended. Finally, and more difficult to assess, one must consider the question of how security identity and interests interact to shape each other. These latter questions have been weak points in the first generation of constructivist literature applied to Japan (e.g., Berger 1998, Katzenstein 1996b), but they have begun to be addressed by a new round of scholarship which would include this study as well as that of several empirically based Japanese scholars such as Yasuhiro Izumikawa (2005) and Miyashita (2007). As is evident from the front pages of mass media publications throughout Asia, a clear understanding of the politics and events of the past century in Japan is still far from being reached and thus requires additional careful study.

Among important factors in foreign policy outcomes, public opinion is one variable that is especially subject to alteration based on the content of security identity over time. Rather than reflecting fresh views on a particular issue at a given time, public opinion is the most likely of all variables affecting security practice to reflect the ideological content of the security identity. Given that public opinion is only one variable in determining a particular outcome, however, this does not ensure a policy outcome consonant with the security identity. Indeed, the spectrum of Japanese foreign policy decisions—as in most advanced industrial democracies—is replete with instances of foreign policy decisions that ignore mass public sentiment. A recent example of this in the Japanese case would be the foreign deployment of the SDF to Iraq in 2004 to participate in the U.S.-led coalition, a policy overwhelmingly opposed by the Japanese public.[10]

The rationalist assumption of a utility-maximizing agent is challenged by the existence of networks of norms, social structures, and shared meanings that warp utilitarian preferences and open the process of interest formation to scrutiny. Contrary to the parsimony of rationalist frameworks, constructivist scholars argue that actors influence their own environment, and this environment reciprocally constrains actors' preferences and practices. There is an "intersubjective" relationship where interest and identity are linked.[11] As Jeffrey Checkel (1998) writes: "Material factors are only given meaning by the social context through which they are interpreted" (p. 2). Thus, this school pays more attention to how identities are shaped and what leads to the formation of actors' preferences and conceptions of interest.[12] Although "rationalists" and "constructivists" treat interests differently, this does not mean that they are in fundamental opposition. Rather, the questions on which they focus often are different. In the case of rationalist accounts, it is not necessarily the case that interests are seen as fixed, but rather they may be *treated* as fixed for the purpose of theoretical parsimony. In such cases, constructivist, or reflectivist, concern with the process of interest and preference formation can complement rationalist approaches to the study of international relations, a line of argument apparently congruent with Peter Katzenstein and Nobuo Okawara's (2001/02) idea of "analytical eclecticism." Indeed, even within the realist school of international relations thought, scholars are increasingly problematizing ideational aspects such as threat perception, hostile intentions, or the ideological power basis of a regime. In this sense, so-called constructivist concerns already have been integrated into some rationalist approaches. This study seeks to contribute further to such systematic consideration of the ideational-material connection in theory and practice.

Structuring Japan's Security Practice: Explaining
Continuity and Change

Identity alone does not dictate a predetermined policy outcome. Japan's security identity structures specific policy outcomes in three ways (see Table 3): through its influence on policy rhetoric, its structuring of public opinion and the coalition-building opportunities this enables, and its institutionalization into the policy-making process. In tandem with these processes, domestic and international polit-ical actors seek to influence policy outcomes to fulfill their own objectives, based on their own understanding of their interests, and through a routinized political process—a "politics of antimilitarism" in the case of postwar Japan. These politics often take the form of a pattern of "reach, reconcile, reassure," as discussed in the next section. Thus, a focus on Japan's security identity of domestic antimilitarism alone is not enough to understand security policy outcomes in Japan today or in the past. But attention to security identity does provide a useful framework for developing a full explanation for policy change.

In conjunction with shifts due to a changing political environment, policy change evident in the case chapters that follow illustrates the three roles of Japan's security identity on specific security practices. First, on the rhetorical level, the security identity allows political cooperation among political actors who would be unlikely to cooperate absent the unifying framework embodied in the security identity. To offer an example from Chapter 4, the rhetoric of domestic antimili-tarism allowed the conservative Ministry of Finance (MOF) and far left pacifists together to oppose redevelopment of an arms industry in the early postwar period despite their underlying reasoning being quite different—for the former, to con-serve limited capital and foreign exchange, and for the latter, to promote pacifist principles by eschewing weapons production. Absent such a unifying security identity, these common policy objectives would appear unrelated and may well be less effective. Second, a security identity provides a focal point for public opin-ion, which helps to explain the striking continuity in public opinion on security questions related to the hegemonic security identity of domestic antimilitarism, though not in foreign policy questions outside the scope of the security identity (such as Japan's military alliance with the United States). Third, the security iden-tity becomes institutionalized into the foreign policy–making process, creating political incentives to follow the grooves of the identity and imposing political costs for violating the identity; thus, it operates simultaneously as a constraint to some policies and as a tool enabling actors to pursue their interests. This aspect of security identity is similar to the effect Peter Katzenstein, Thomas Berger, and

TABLE 3

How Security Identity Affects Policy Outcomes

---

1. Provides a vocabulary to enable political cooperation around specific policies
2. Provides a focal point for public opinion, explaining policy continuity over time
3. Becomes institutionalized into the policy-making process, exacting costs for violators of the security identity

---

others ascribe to norms of Japan's "antimilitarist culture." Each of these effects shaped policy outcomes in the cases considered in this volume.

This model of policy making departs from realist models of international relations that conceptualize the state as a unitary actor pursuing objectively determined strategic interests. It also departs from traditional interest-based models in comparative politics by incorporating how rhetoric and identity affect how actors choose to pursue their interests within a political arena. Finally, it departs from the views of radical constructivists and critical theorists who reject the notion that identity and interests can be disaggregated. Although the approach advanced here departs from each of these theoretical schools, this study seeks to build on several important works on Japan and on literature in political science and related fields. Since identity alone cannot explain the motivations and environmental factors affecting political actors, other existing theory must also be employed to explain the nature of specific policy outcomes. For example, Jennifer Lind's (2004) "buck-passing" theory, Paul Midford's (2002) reputational theory, and Richard Samuels's (1994) theory based on "technonationalist" ideology each can help explain specific security practices, but absent a grounding in the security identity of domestic antimilitarism, each misses the mark—as discussed further in the next section.

Reach, Reconcile, Reassure: The Politics of Antimilitarism

During the Cold War period, powerful political actors in Japan at times were able to enact policies that were contrary to the security identity of domestic antimilitarism. These policies were always contentious, and those actors seeking such exceptions understood them as such, expending extra political capital to attain such objectives—such as the brief surpassing of the 1 percent of GDP ceiling on defense spending under Prime Minister Nakasone, or the passing of the first U.S.-Japan Defense Guidelines in 1978.

Moreover, typically such exceptions were balanced by countervailing policies to reinforce the established security identity in another arena. It was a policy of "reach, reconcile, reassure"—the "three Rs" of postwar Japanese security policy.[13] For example, as Japan's participation in the American war in Vietnam deepened, the three nonnuclear principles, the three principles on arms exports, and policies regarding the peaceful use of space were all declared. In the 1980s, after exceptions to the arms export restrictions were made to allow joint defense production with the United States and the 1 percent ceiling on defense spending was breeched, defense spending quickly returned to below the 1 percent threshold and the new doctrine of "comprehensive security" replaced the idea of Japan being the "unsinkable aircraft carrier" for the United States.[14] Overall, the three central tenets of domestic antimilitarism—no traditional armed forces, no use of force by Japan except in self-defense, no Japanese participation in foreign wars—set a context under which political interactions on security issues have been negotiated for half a century.

Beginning in the late 1990s, some saw the pattern of "reach, reconcile, and reassure" giving way to a new pattern of extending the limits of the central tenets of domestic antimilitarism without compensating in other areas. To critics, it was a pattern of "reach, reach, and reach." A more reflective treatment might cast it as a new "three Rs"—"reach, replace, and review." The reach remains the same, but rather than reconciling this new policy with existing practice, at times now we see a replacement of old policy; rather than reassuring the public after a new reach, today we often see a review once again of existing policy to identify areas of further reach.

The 2001 dispatch of the MSDF to the Indian Ocean to play a rear-area support role to U.S. combat operations, followed in 2004 by both the MSDF and the ASDF to play a similar role in Iraq (though not the prominent Ground Self-Defense Forces [GSDF] dispatch, which continued with the 1990s practice of offering only humanitarian and reconstruction assistance), is often cited as an example of reach, reach, and reach. To date, however, one also still could understand even such dramatic new security policies in terms of the old "3 Rs"—for example, reach to dispatch the SDF abroad, reconcile this with SDF law by greatly limiting rear-area support scope and simultaneously stressing the humanitarian mission of the GSDF in Iraq, and reassure the public by limiting the duration of the enabling legislation.

The greater reach of contemporary policy makers toward more "normal" security practices can be explained to some extent by a changed international strategic environment and domestic political configuration, but new attitudes toward security that are increasingly apparent in recent public opinion polls should also be considered in an analysis of the staying power of Japan's current security identity.[15] Indeed, the new domestic political configuration itself is in part the result of shifting public attitudes about security issues that contributed to a new domestic political environment—in Japan's democratic political system, voters choose among politicians advocating different security practices.

One of the most interesting and important questions in the area of Japanese security policy today is whether this mooring in domestic antimilitarism will continue, or whether the recent series of extensions of previous limits will continue until the limits no longer have meaning or simply disappear. Prediction deep into the future, particularly given the quickly shifting international strategic environment in East Asia, is difficult, but in the short to medium term, there are strong indications that the central tenets of domestic antimilitarism will continue to act as the central grounding principles of Japan's security policies. It is notable that in a period of great change, relatively speaking, in Japanese security practice the long-standing principles of the existing security identity simultaneously are extensively reinforced and reified for a new generation through public debate, media interpretation of opinion polling, and new legislation designed to adapt Japan's long-standing security identity to new demands from abroad, new military technologies, and a new international environment. Evidence of the continued reproduction and reification of existing principles while extending the limits is examined in greater detail in the chapters that follow. The final section of this chapter briefly sketches out major contending—and at times complementary— theories for explaining and predicting the future course of Japan's security practices.

Complementary and Contending Explanations for Japanese Security Practice

Contending explanations for changes in Japanese security policy specifically—as opposed to policy change in general, discussed at the beginning of this chapter—typically stress one of three approaches: (1) international politics and external pressure models rooted in the realist school of international relations theory, which draws on factor 3 and, internationally, factor 2 of Table 2; (2) domestic politics explanations rooted in traditional power and interest-based analysis, drawing in particular on factor 2 of Table 2; and (3) culture and norms-based arguments which draw in particular on factor 1 of Table 2. Each of these approaches offers valuable insights into actual policy-making practice in Japan today or in the past. Most individual studies focus on one of these three approaches and incorporate other factors as necessary to account for significant empirical anomalies. For example, of the prominent book-length studies touching on military security issues, Samuels (1994) focuses on technonationalist ideology; Michael Green (1995; 2001) and Daniel Kliman (2006) on domestic politics, influenced by realist international relations theory; Thomas Berger (1998), Glenn Hook (1996), Peter Katzenstein (1996b), and Susanne Klien (2002) on ideational variables, influenced by domestic and international politics; and Christopher Hughes (2004a; 2004b) on domestic politics and ideology based on the notion of "comprehensive security." One exception to this trend is the literature that has developed around so-called two-level games, which has been applied especially to U.S.-Japan trade negotiations. Among Japan scholars, the related idea of *gaiatsu* (foreign pressure) has been examined in depth, with particular attention paid to linkages between international and domestic actors (e.g., Calder 1988b, Schoppa 1997, Yasutomo 1995).

Each of these studies makes an important contribution to our understanding of Japan security practice and to the factors that lead to change or continuity. An approach based on security identity is able to draw on insights from these studies and can account for broader continuities. Legro's argument for the need to consider collectively held state ideas about the international system applies equally to this study. He writes: "By their very nature, foreign policy ideas will be in the public realm. They cannot be reproduced unless all have access to them" (Legro 2005, p. 22).

Internationally Rooted Explanations

Among international-level theories, realist theories most often are used to explain the security policies of "great powers" such as Japan. Realist theories of international relations conceptualize an anarchical international system consisting of unitary, rational states engaged in a struggle for power.[16] At the core of realist theory is the belief that state security practice derives from the distribution of material power resources (which, importantly, are conceptualized as fungible between the military, economic, and cultural realms) and from changes in this distribution of power over time.[17] Given the dramatic rise of Japan's capabilities during the Cold War period, realist theories predict Japan to play a greater military role in the world. For example, Herman Kahn (1970) argues this position in the early 1970s, Kenneth Waltz (1981) in the early 1980s, Richard Betts (1993/94) in the early 1990s, and Green (2001) and Kliman (2006) in the early twenty-first century. For realists, the end of the Cold War was widely seen as the last barrier to a fully remilitarized Japan (Betts 1993/94, Layne 1993). Rajan Menon (1997) reflects the central tenet of realist logic: "at some point Japan is likely to build a military machine that matches its economic might" (p. 1). The critical question of when exactly is "at some point" is not well specified, however.

By themselves, international politics-level explanations—of which realist theories are only one, though dominant, variety[18]—are insufficient to explain Japan's postwar security practices, and in particular the cases examined in this volume. Realist theories do succeed to some degree in accurately predicting the direction of the postwar policies studied here, but they cannot account for the important changes in the policies over time. To some extent, this can be said to be an unfair criticism particularly of neorealist approaches to international relations since their principal proponent, Waltz (1979), explicitly states that neorealism is not a theory of foreign policy.[19] Despite this disclaimer, however, numerous scholars within this tradition attempt to apply realist theory—or new iterations of it—in order to understand foreign policy outcomes.[20] Consistent with such approaches, one finds the general trend in postwar Japan toward rearmament and a greater role within the U.S.-Japan alliance as Japan's power in the international system grows. Japan's military is among the most equipped, best-funded, most highly trained forces in the world. Over the decades since their creation, they have played expanded roles which now include limited overseas deployments. In reference to the cases studied in this volume, one sees more and greater exceptions to limitations on arms exports and the policy regarding the peaceful use of outer space as Japan emerges as an economic superpower in the 1970s and as a challenger to American hegemony by the late 1980s; in the post–Cold War period, development of new military capabilities of surveillance satellites and missile defense further support realist predictions. What cannot be explained within this framework is why the restrictive policies discussed in this volume continue to this day, and why several restrictions have actually been further strengthened and institutionalized. Central tenets of realist theory would predict that these vestiges of Japan's defeat over half a century ago would long since have been discarded. Realists' standard response is that there is simply a time lag.[21] Many policy analysts buy into this argument and expect a "normalized" Japan to emerge shortly. As with such expectations in the past, however, they are bound to be disappointed, as such a shift is not forthcoming absent an unexpected shock to the system.

A second, growing response to apparent anomalies regarding Japan in realist theory is to modify realism's core assumptions, or to develop alternate lines of argument. New strands of "realist" scholarship—which relax the unitary-actor assumption, the fungibility-of-power assumption, and the implications of anarchy—have come up with plausible reasons why Japan has not developed military capabilities to the degree structural realists predict. In this sense, it is not necessarily the case that some realists cannot explain the case of Japan—but, importantly, they do so by violating (or modifying) the core assumptions of existing realist theory.[22]

A variant of the international politics-level explanation would more directly consider the role of the United States as a political actor within the Japanese security policy apparatus. Reference to the United States as an important actor in Japanese domestic politics is common in the foreign policy literature, particularly in the research area of two-level games. This literature has the benefit of systematically testing the role of *gaiatsu* (foreign pressure), but the findings are complex and mixed. The cases of limited arms exports, the peaceful use of outer space, and missile defense cooperation with the United States appear broadly consistent with the preferences of the United States, suggesting this approach as a viable alternative explanation. While the United States was able to procure defense manufactures for its war efforts in Korea and Vietnam, it did not face potentially stiff competition in international arms markets, nor in the international satellite market. The case of joint research on missile defense also clearly supports U.S. preferences—though there is a significant delay in achieving the congruence that must be explained, and the ultimate level of cooperation is far less than sought. The case of Japanese surveillance satellites poses a challenge to this theoretical approach in that the United States consistently opposed Japanese development of this technology until *after* Japan announced independently that it would develop such capabilities. In sum, however, this aspect of international-level explanation merits the further consideration extended to it within the following chapters of this volume. Without a doubt, the United States has been a sustained force for the normalizing of Japan in the image of the United States.

Domestically Rooted Explanations

In studies of Japanese foreign policy, there long has been a division between discussions of military security policy and economic policy—one that is unfortunate given the overlap between military security and economic security conceptions evident in the cases considered in this volume, a point underscored by the work of Samuels (1994), Green (1995), and Hughes (2004b). International factors, particularly the role of the United States, have often been seen as predominant in military security, but domestic factors—notably the debate over politician versus bureaucratic dominance models—have reigned in studies of foreign economic policy, with the exception of the two-level game literature popular among specialists of international political economy.[23]

It is counterintuitive to assume that security policy would respond only to objective conditions dictated by the international system. As Elizabeth Kier (1996) rightly stresses, "Military doctrine is about state survival, but military policy is also about the allocation of power *within* society" (p. 200). Given this, it is clear that domestic political factors are certain to play a role in the determination of Japan's security practice. Indeed, such factors provide the starting point of this study. Attention paid solely to the power and interests of domestic political and economic actors, however, does not provide a complete explanation at critical decision points without reference to the security identity of domestic antimilitarism (as well as important material international system-level factors). Most studies of Japanese foreign policy rooted at the domestic level acknowledge—indeed, rely on—the phenomenon conceptualized here as the security identity, using such terms as *public opinion,* political costs and benefits, or naming alternative unifying strategies such as the Yoshida or Fukuda "doctrines." When and how such factors affect policy outcomes are generally not problemized in this literature, however. One contribution of this study is to subsume many of these exogenous factors systematically in order to specify the mechanisms whereby security identity structures security practice.

In sum, these two contending explanations, at the domestic and international levels, achieve some success due to their foundation in concepts of power, interests, and coalitions among competing groups. They fail to address the nature of the domestic political institutions that arose in the postwar period to constrain these factors, however, and thus ultimately fail on their own to explain and predict the actual shape of Japanese security practices.

Ideationally Rooted Explanations

Recent years have witnessed a proliferation of scholarship employing such concepts as culture and norms.[24] Studies of Japanese foreign policy have been at the forefront of this literature. Katzenstein (1996b) writes of "normative constraints" which preclude a wide range of domestic and international security policies in postwar Japan; Berger (1998) writes of a "culture of antimilitarism" arising in postwar Japan (and Germany); Hook (1996) writes of postwar Japan's "pacifist" foreign policy, focusing in particular on the role of discourse in policy making. Even more traditional explanations for Japanese foreign policy outcomes typically resort to these types of terms (though not necessarily using constructivist vocabulary) or employ residual categories such as "public opinion" or "structural constraints" to explain why traditional interest politics models of domestic policy making or realist international relations theory often fail to accurately predict the evolution of Japanese security practice. This study builds on such explanations by examining the political context in which what others refer to as norms or culture operate to shape specific security practices over time, and, importantly, how understandings of security identity can be renegotiated to adapt to a new domestic or international political environment. Contrary to the assertions of many who have examined Japan's postwar security policy (whether or not explicitly employing a cultural or norms-based framework), there has never been a domestic consensus on Japan's appropriate role in the international system. Certainly a majority of Japanese support the postwar security identity of domestic antimilitarism, though often for different reasons, but even still there is a sizable minority that does not. The failure to reconcile this empirical reality to their theoretical models is an unfortunate oversight of the primary culturalist approaches to the study of Japanese security policy. Among the primary studies of postwar Japan in this tradition, Berger (1998) does the most to recognize this problem. However, he fails to reconcile it. This is unfortunate because the framework he sets out—which acknowledges the diversity of Japanese views on security—and much of his empirical argument is so promising.[25]

While domestic politics approaches have trouble integrating ideational factors into their analyses, however, culturalist approaches suffer from the opposite flaw—ad hoc incorporation of key domestic and international political factors. The result is significantly overdetermined outcomes and an inability to explain "dogs that did not bark"—cases where one would have expected policies to materialize to support cultural or norms-based claims but where they did not.[26] As argued in Chapter 2, in postwar Japan a number of foreign policy decisions were made that contradicted or at least seriously strained any "norm" or "culture" of antimilitarism or pacifism—such as alignment with the United States in the Cold War against the Soviet Union and China, support of the war efforts in Korea and Vietnam, and (re)creation of an arms industry and armed forces (under the name of a "Self-Defense Force"). These decisions cannot be explained from a pacifist or antimilitarist culture or norms-based perspective. Moreover, even with regard to the specific security practices examined in later chapters of this volume, a norms or culture-based explanation cannot explain the complicated and mixed nature of actual security practice.[27]

A number of authors similarly have attempted to answer the related but distinct question of how Japan's postwar security identity developed—both in Japan and elsewhere, and from a variety of disciplinary backgrounds in the social sciences and humanities.[28] Despite regular mention of identity issues in the existing literature, however, little attention has been devoted to the question of how contending views of security identity in Japan have structured specific security practices in postwar Japan.[29] By contrast, in recent literature focusing on Japan's security policy outcomes, terms such as *norms* or *identity* often operate as code words for complex political negotiations that are left unexplored.[30] This study, by contrast, advocates attention to the political nature of identity throughout the Cold War and post–Cold War periods while also considering the effect of this identity on security practice.

In sum, this study builds on previous scholarship addressing the question of how Japan's new postwar security identity arose (and how it might change) as well as how security identity is filtered through a political process to shape actual security practice. The next chapter focuses on the former—how Japan's postwar security identity of domestic antimilitarism was crafted from the ashes of Japan's defeat and remained the hegemonic security identity throughout the Cold War period.

2

Negotiating and Institutionalizing a
New Postwar Security Identity

Japan's defeat in the Second World War required a fundamental reexamination of Japan's place in the world and its resulting foreign policy. The challenge this posed was on an entirely different scale to the shocks Japanese faced in the 1970s over the oil crisis or the switch to floating exchange rates, or in the 1990s as the Cold War drew to a close, or after September 11, 2001, marked the beginning of a new era characterized by globalization and the long war against global terrorism. Post-1945, nothing less than a shift in security identity would suffice. As argued in Chapter 1, however, collapse of an identity alone is not sufficient for identity shift: a successor identity also must be articulated, adopted, implemented, and consolidated. The immediate postwar years indeed see multiple identities articulated, with the security identity of domestic antimilitarism taking shape by 1960, being implemented, consolidated, and reproduced throughout the postwar period.

Japan's security policy in the years immediately following the Second World War does not point uniformly in the direction of either a truly pacifist security identity or a return to an identity as a great power. Rather, it illustrates the contestation over the future vision of the Japanese state in the world that would continue throughout the postwar period. Political actors in immediate postwar Japan actively debated numerous possible future visions for the defeated Japanese state, from plans to reemerge as a major world power to developing a model of unarmed neutrality that other world states could follow. Ultimately, political actors crafted a compromise identity from among several options—options that may have been foreclosed once the emergent identity of domestic antimilitarism became hegemonic, but clear options at the time.

Against the wishes of those who sought a nonaligned "pacifist" Japan, Japan signed a comprehensive security treaty with the United States and re-created a fledgling army, navy, and air force under the label of a "self-defense force." By contrast, there were a number of apparent successes of the pacifist/antimilitarist political forces: no Japanese troop deployment in the Korean War, no Japanese participation in a multilateral security framework for East Asia, no full-fledged armed forces, and only an unequal "alliance" with the United States that did not require Japan to aid the United States militarily if the United States were attacked. Other commonly cited examples of Japan's "abnormal" security policy either cannot be attributed to *Japanese* decision makers (e.g., Article Nine of the postwar constitution or the prohibition on weapons production and their export) or were instituted later in the postwar period (e.g., the three nonnuclear principles or the 1 percent of GNP ceiling on defense spending). However, the maintenance of Article Nine and the lack of redevelopment[1] of a major arms industry after the Occupation ended in 1952—which later would be reinforced by a formal ban on the export of arms—are examples of apparent triumphs of the pacifist and antimilitarist proponents in the immediate postwar period. A ban on the military use of outer space would emerge later, at a time when domestic political actors again became active and vocal in their concerns about the direction of Japan's military policy—especially vis-à-vis the United States. The continuity among the seemingly haphazard nature of these disparate decisions becomes understandable when the tumultuous politics of the time are viewed through the lens of the emergent security identity of domestic antimilitarism.

Attention to the political arrangements which led to the codification of domestic antimilitarism in addition to the more traditional attention to the distribution of political power at the time is essential to understanding Japan's resulting postwar security policy. In contrast to some conceptions of culture, norms, and national identity, security identity is not treated here as monolithic but rather as hegemonic. The lack of a single, uniformly held security identity requires one to appreciate the effect of minority voices on policy outcomes—both in the immediate postwar period (when Japan's future international role was unclear) and more recently (when peace activists and outspoken rightists continue to play a disproportionately strong role in shaping Japan's foreign policy agenda).

The security identity of domestic antimilitarism began to take shape in the late 1940s, both as a consequence of the shock of defeat in the Second World War and due to direct political intervention on the part of the United States, and had become the hegemonic security identity by 1960. This chapter details how domestic antimilitarism became the hegemonic identity in postwar Japan over the fifteen years after Japan's surrender in the Second World War. In addition, drawing from the extensive primary and secondary literature available on this period, the chapter highlights the central characteristics of domestic antimilitarism that shape the policy outcomes discussed in the chapters which follow.

Competing Visions for Postwar Japan

At least five alternative visions played a role in the emergence of the political compromise of a security identity of domestic antimilitarism, demonstrating the presence of a great supply of ideas upon which political actors could draw.[2] Variations on each of these postwar visions continue to drive the politics of security policy in Japan today; their lineage therefore continues to be important and worth review. First, on the right, reconstructed prewar and wartime militarists sought to restore Japan to its rightful place as a great power militarily and economically, politically enabled by Cold War–inspired depurges by Occupation authorities. Such actors were joined by a younger generation who sought a new, active-yet-accountable armed force for Japan. The children of this camp—in some cases literally as well as figuratively[3]—are driving forces in Japan's security policy recrafting in the early twenty-first century. Second, at the center-right politically, some in both Japan and the United States envisioned a multilateral security framework for East Asia based on a "Pacific Pact," modeled on the North Atlantic Treaty Organization (NATO) in Europe.[4] Today this camp is evident in calls to forge deeper security ties with South Korea and calls for Japan to play a greater role in Asia's emerging international institutions of ASEAN+3, ARF, APEC, and AFTA.[5] Third, toward the political center, leaders in business and some in the political center sought to fashion a new role for Japan as an economic power in Asia and the world, focusing on the daunting task of rebuilding the war-torn economy.[6] Analogous figures today fret about Japan's declining economic competitiveness vis-à-vis China and continue to fuel the Japanese obsession over the development of indigenous technology. Fourth, on the left, pacifists sought to make Japan the "Switzerland of Asia" by advocating unarmed neutrality, essentially sitting out the emerging Cold War. A more activist version of this alternate identity envisioned Japan playing a leading role in the spread of pacifist beliefs worldwide, focusing in particular on conveying the message of the horrors of nuclear war based on Japan's status as the only target of a nuclear weapon to date.[7] Such actors today are in decline but still constitute a visible and active section of the Japanese political spectrum. Finally, on the far left, communists and radical socialists sought to align Japan with their party allies in communist China and the Soviet Union. Given the variety of nasty encounters Japan experienced from the Soviets in the early postwar years—particularly the horrific treatment of Japanese soldiers marooned in Soviet territory at the end of the war as well as the emerging Cold War rivalry with the United States—this final alternate vision had perhaps the least chance of being adopted widely, though it too exercised influence on the eventual compromise identity that was forged in the immediate postwar period.[8] This camp alone has few visible supporters today.

If identity is to be understood—as most rationalists claim—as a way for the powerful to justify their privileged position or to further their interests, it would suggest that the identity is adopted because it is *useful* to those in power, rather than due to any aspect derived from the identity itself. An analysis of the politics surrounding Japan's new security identity shows actors attempting exactly this—advocating for their preferred security identity, which they saw as furthering their interests, however defined. In the immediate postwar period, however, no single actor—nor coalition of like-minded actors—had the political power to institutionalize its preferred security identity. Instead, this identity was the subject of intense political negotiation over a period of fifteen years. In the end, no single actor was able to fully institutionalize its preferences into a new security identity; a compromise identity therefore was forged. This compromise was based on both material and ideational factors. Moreover, it did not exhaustively spell out all aspects of Japan's foreign policy—nor even all key aspects, such as the alliance with the United States or the subsequent "economy first" policy of Prime Minister Shigeru Yoshida.

One actor played a disproportionate role in the creation of Japan's postwar security identity: the United States. The initial moves to create a "pacifist" Japan in the postwar period came from the United States, serving its interest of preventing another devastating war in the Pacific. This goal on the part of the United States is evident first in Japan's surrender document and was later institutionalized into the postwar Japanese political structure in the so-called MacArthur Constitution of 1947 with its famous Article Nine. If U.S. interests in the region—and preferences for Japan—had not changed dramatically in the late 1940s, one might plausibly argue that the institutionalization of Japan's postwar security identity could largely be attributed to the political power of the United States over its defeated opponent. U.S. interests did change dramatically, however; moreover, domestic interests inside Japan quickly and deeply embraced pacifist or antimilitarist ideals for their own varied reasons. As the Cold War deepened in Asia, it was in the interests of the United States—which maintained formal control of Japan's foreign policy until the end of the Occupation in 1952—for Japan to remilitarize in order to support U.S. war efforts. Importantly, Japan's security identity did *not* change in line with new U.S. interests. Despite at times intense pressure from the United States, Japanese leaders—particularly the unusually effective Prime Min-

TABLE 4

Central Tenets of Japan's Postwar Security Identity of Domestic Antimilitarism

1. No traditional armed forces involved in domestic policymaking
2. No use of force by Japan to resolve international disputes, except in self-defense
3. No Japanese participation in foreign wars

ister Shigeru Yoshida[9]—managed to codify the security identity of domestic anti-militarism which maintained to a considerable degree the pacifist characteristics that the United States wished Japan to discard.

Ultimately, by 1960, the security identity of domestic antimilitarism emerged clearly as the hegemonic identity in the domestic political arena. In particular, three central tenets would emerge to define Japan's new security identity, as set out in the introduction to this volume. These principles therefore move from a few among many proposals for defining Japan's future role into the stages of adoption and implementation by the Japanese state, illustrating the temporal model Kathryn Sikkink (1991) envisions in her work. These tenets are summarized in Table 4.

The first tenet is the rejection of the establishment of a traditional armed force, one that would participate in policy planning as do the leading government ministries in Japan (particularly MOF, MITI, and MOFA in this area) or the Department of Defense (DOD) or National Security Council (NSC) in the United States. This first tenet best exemplifies the antimilitarist basis of the new postwar security identity. It goes beyond the concern with "civilian control" evident in all advanced industrial democracies by completely rejecting the rise of the sort of military-industrial complex developed in the United States in the early years of the Cold War.[10]

This first tenet of domestic antimilitarism was institutionalized in practice through the creation of the Self-Defense Agency (later the Defense Agency, or Japan Defense Agency, JDA, in English) as an "agency" (*cho*) rather than a "ministry" (*sho*), and through the practice of seconding officials from the ministries of finance (MOF), foreign affairs (MOFA), and international trade and industry (MITI) to high positions within the JDA. Numerous studies of early postwar Japanese defense policy point to this restriction as fundamentally hamstringing rational defense planning in Japan, citing controversies over practices that are routine in other states such as setting multiyear goals for defense procurement or establishing contingency battle plans for likely threats.[11] In this way, the security identity is affecting not just discrete policy outcomes but the overall policy-making process. This tenet also limited Japan's ability to collect military intelligence for defensive purposes by contributing to the establishment of a "peaceful use of outer space" policy that went beyond other states' definition of the term *peaceful* by interpreting the word as meaning *nonmilitary* rather than *nonaggressive.*

The second tenet of domestic antimilitarism is the rejection of the use of force to resolve international disputes, though importantly *not* the rejection of other states'—notably the United States'—option to do this, even on behalf of Japan. The key method of institutionalization of this tenet is Article Nine of the postwar constitution, which explicitly renounces the state's right to use force to resolve international disputes.[12] There is no question that this particular area of institutionalization was imposed externally; however, numerous scholars have demonstrated convincingly how postwar Japanese embraced this aspect of the constitution.[13] Article Nine of the Constitution alone does not encompass the full scope of this second tenet of domestic antimilitarism, however. It encapsulates the Japanese force proscription aspect of this tenet but leaves open the question of Japan's support for other states' policies toward the use of force.

There was much less consensus among Japanese on this latter aspect of the second tenet than on the former. The Japanese military alliance with the United States best exposes this tension, with roughly half of the Japanese population against the alliance and half for it in the early postwar period—and even greater numbers against it before it was revised and extended in 1960. Among opponents of the security treaty, a primary argument was disagreement with the implicit acceptance of the use of force to resolve international disputes such an alliance would entail. For this reason, the very use of the term *alliance* (*domei*) was taboo and not used by Japanese officials to describe Japan's relationship with the United States until the 1980s (and even then only sparingly), evidence of the effect of security identity on the very language of politics and political discourse.

The third tenet of domestic antimilitarism is the proscription of Japanese from participation in international conflict among third parties. This tenet is distinct from the second in that it addresses acceptable Japanese conduct regarding the use of force in situations where Japan is not threatened directly. The second tenet relates to cases where Japan itself is involved in an international dispute or threatens the use of force to achieve a foreign policy objective; the third relates to Japan's role in disputes among third parties—such as U.S. conflicts in Korea and Vietnam, and more recently Afghanistan and Iraq. This third tenet of domestic antimilitarism was institutionalized at the time of the creation of the Self-Defense Forces (SDF) through legislation prohibiting the dispatch of the SDF abroad, a proscription that was respected throughout the Cold War period. Moreover, it led to the continuation of the occupation-imposed ban on arms exports, a policy consolidated in the late 1960s and 1970s, as discussed in Chapter 4.

Of the three central tenets of domestic antimilitarism, this third tenet was opposed by domestic actors with the greatest political power—wartime defense manufacturers redefining their business scope in the new postwar domestic environment. The power of this group—together with their allies in business associations and MITI in particular—partially explains the exceptions to this third tenet evident throughout the Cold War period. Still, even proponents of such exceptions understood their achievements as exceptions to the general policy prescription of domestic antimilitarism. Thus, it is appropriate to consider this third tenet as equally central to the new security identity. Indeed, periodic violation of this tenet underscores the central argument of this study: security identity alone does not determine policy outcomes, but rather plays a central role in domestic political contestation.

Key exceptions to the third tenet of domestic antimilitarism in the Cold War period, discussed further in Chapter 4, allowed extensive Japanese exports to— and other Japanese civilian participation in—the Korean peninsula in the early 1950s and to Southeast Asia in the 1960s and 1970s. These activities were severely limited, however, and were extremely controversial at the time. Not until the post–Cold War period were there perceived exceptions to this tenet that involved Japanese state—that is, SDF—participation in international disputes, and only after the terrorist attacks on the United States on September 11, 2001, was the SDF dispatched abroad to an area of active international conflict (and even then they were explicitly prohibited from playing a combat role).[14]

Subsequent chapters will examine how this security identity led to such policy outcomes as the ban on the export of weapons and related technology and the limitation of the use of outer space to peaceful purposes only. A number of other formative policy outcomes resulting from the security identity are discussed in this chapter. Renewed challenges to the hegemonic identity were mounted at various times in the Cold War period by forces advocating alternative identities for the state, as discussed in this and later chapters of this volume. An overview of this change within the continuity of Cold War Japan concludes this chapter, foreshadowing the challenges that would arise to the hegemony of domestic antimilitarism after the Cold War drew to a close—the subject of Chapter 3.

Throughout this overview chapter explaining the rise of the security identity of domestic antimilitarism, three points are underscored. First, at no point did one view of security identity become a universal belief. Contestation continued throughout the period, though after 1960 security politics were somewhat "normalized." Second, as the security identity of domestic antimilitarism becomes hegemonic, its effect on subsequent security practices becomes apparent through the three ways described in the introduction to this volume and summarized in

Table 3: by permeating the vocabulary of political actors, becoming institutionalized into the policy process, and serving as a focal point for public opinion. Third,
although the hegemonic security identity fundamentally shaped Japan's postwar
security practices, it did not in itself dictate a set outcome. Indeed, numerous
instances of policies contrary to this identity are apparent, despite the political
costs they required. This final point is especially noteworthy in the post–Cold War
context of Japanese security practice.

Facing a New Postwar Environment at Home and Abroad

In 1945, Japan was literally in a new place, having dramatically shrunk in size
from its vast colonial empire down to the four main islands it occupies today. No
longer did Japan control "the dagger pointed at its heart," the Korean peninsula,
nor the grain fields and industrial belt of Manchuria, nor the oil fields of what is
now Indonesia. The entire Asian region and international system in general were
similarly undergoing seismic shifts in the immediate postwar period, a time which
corresponds with the outbreak of the Cold War in Europe and Asia, the "hot" war
on the Korean peninsula, and the communist revolution in mainland China. The
nature of the challenge posed to Japan by this new domestic and international
environment must be examined to fully understand the new security identity that
would arise in its midst.

A New Domestic Environment: Defeat and Occupation

Defeat in the Second World War shattered Japanese prewar militarist ideology and
discredited the political and economic institutions that had actively supported it,
laying the foundation for a new security identity based on antimilitarism. Defeat
inflicted a massive shock to Japan, enabling—both institutionally and psychologically—new ways of thinking about the nature of the state and the role of the
military within it, again opening up space for identity shift. Defeat also required
Japan to rethink its place in the world and functional role within it, in contrast to
later periods examined in this volume when a new direction was an *option* (even if
presented by some political actors as a necessity).[15]

The magnitude of Japan's defeat further contributed to this nationwide soul
searching. Although the loss of life in Japan was not on the scale of Europe or of
the countries that Japan invaded (particularly China), roughly 3 million Japanese
were killed in the war and another 5 million injured. Moreover, scores of cities
were the target of intense bombing campaigns that included the comprehensive
fire-bombings of Tokyo and the atomic bombings of Hiroshima and Nagasaki.
Due to the devastation caused by these campaigns as well as extensive maritime

disruption of Japan's shipping, Japan's economy was reduced to a small fraction of its prewar level. Added to these dislocations, roughly 6 million Japanese soldiers and civilians were repatriated to Japan's four main islands after Japan's extensive overseas possessions were stripped from it, creating further strains on limited resources at home. It is estimated that between one-quarter and one-third of Japan's total wealth was destroyed in the war, including over three-quarters of all ships, a third of all machine tools, and a quarter of all rolling stock and motor vehicles (Dower 1999, p. 45). The Ministry of Finance estimates that living standards fell to 65 percent of prewar levels in rural areas and to just over a third of prewar levels in urban areas.[16] Roughly 9 million people were left homeless by widespread bombing. In immediate postwar Japan, large-scale starvation was averted only through generous American economic assistance.

Within this context, coping with the state of economic devastation was the primary concern of the vast majority of the population in the immediate postwar period. However, the hardship inflicted by defeat in the Second World War was not only economic but social and psychological as well. The shame of unconditional surrender epitomized by the new status of the emperor as mere symbol of state rather than a living god left the great majority of Japanese disillusioned and searching for new forms of order and social and economic development. Thomas Berger (1998) notes the opening this devastation created for a new security identity to be crafted: "With their wartime leaders imprisoned and the legitimacy of their nation's old political orders severely damaged, . . . Japanese elites were compelled to reexamine the definitions of their national identity and to find new moral visions and goals to build their [nation]" (p. 25). An opening was created, as John Dower (1999) writes, "of a sort possible only among people who have seen an old world destroyed and are being forced to imagine a new one" (p. 44).

Foremost in this reimagining were views of the military and its role in society. During the early years of the postwar period, the Japanese public increasingly became aware of the scale of misrepresentation that the Imperial Army spread through wartime propaganda, creating strong sentiments against the military as an institution. Newspaper letters and columns, led by the *Asahi Shimbun*, were filled with testimonials by rank-and-file soldiers recounting atrocities committed against the peoples of Asia or upon Japanese soldiers themselves by Imperial officers. This testimony was particularly damaging to the military given that the emperor himself was publicly absolved of responsibility for the war, implicitly shifting blame on military institutions as a whole and explicitly on the senior military officers condemned at the Tokyo Tribunal war crimes proceedings.

The conduct of the Japanese military even after the fighting ceased was also criticized bitterly. In the immediate postwar period, civilian Japanese witnessed firsthand how military discipline crumbled after the surrender announcement and how soldiers scrambled to secure any useful state-owned property for personal gain. Further, many questioned privately and in print why soldiers were entitled to a pension to help them through postwar life while those who contributed to the war effort at home were often left with nothing, even nothing to eat. Dower (1999) writes: "The emperor's loyal soldiers and sailors seemed to have metamorphosed overnight into symbols of the worst sort of egoism and atomization" (p. 52). Combined with the shame of defeat in itself, these new revelations that the military could be trusted neither with winning nor even acting honorably in defeat deeply affected the political debate over the future role of the military in the postwar Japanese state. These widespread antimilitary views formed the basis for a new postwar security identity, which would not again place public trust in military institutions—what would emerge as the first tenet of a new security identity. Although half a century later Japan's new military, the Self-Defense Forces, would achieve a degree of public acceptance and even respect, this would require generations of concerted effort and an entirely new identity for military forces in Japan.

Allied forces,[17] dominated by the over four hundred thousand troops from the United States, entered Japan on September 2, 1945, with their primary objective to effect the demilitarization of Japan, and the primary means a strategy of deep democratization at all levels of Japanese society. The goals of the Allied occupation—which lasted from September 1945 until May 1952—were expressly political: to fundamentally transform Japan's political governance, its economy, and even its social structures.[18] Naturally this had a dramatic effect on Japanese domestic politics and its emergent security identity, a degree of change that many have compared to the Meiji Restoration of the previous century, which had elevated Japan to world power status in only three decades. General Douglas MacArthur and his office, the Supreme Commander of the Allied Powers (SCAP), undertook an ambitious liberal program in the first years of the occupation. By publicly repudiating Japan's first postwar cabinet, led by the emperor's cousin, Prince Naruhiko Higashikuni, MacArthur signaled that superficial reform under conservative rule would not be accepted. In addition to exerting concerted pressure on Japan's first postwar prime ministers, MacArthur ordered the immediate restoration of civil liberties to the Japanese citizenry, adding many new rights which would be codified in the new postwar constitution of 1947, termed by many even today as the MacArthur Constitution.[19] Given this dramatic new level of political participation, it is no wonder that a significant shift in Japan's security identity would result—apart from exogenous changes to Japan's international environment.

Occupation reforms were not limited to the directly political. Dissolution of the *zaibatsu* (industrial conglomerates) was seen as an important part of structural reform of the Japanese prewar and wartime military-industrial complex—though, as seen below, reform of big business would be sacrificed to other goals.[20] The simple fact of large-scale wartime destruction also played a significant role as an economic leveler of postwar Japanese society. New government legislation furthered this trend. For example, the Farmer-Owner Establishment Act of 1946 directed the purchase of over 4 million acres of land by the government to be sold cheaply to former tenant farmers as a way of weakening the political power of large landholders who formed a key component of the prewar and wartime governing coalition. As a result, tenancy dropped to less than 8 percent, creating a larger class of small landholders who would become a bulwark first of the conservative Liberal and Democratic parties, and later the Liberal Democratic Party (LDP) (LaFeber 1997, p. 265).

Although the above reforms (and many others) were extended almost immediately after the occupation began, it was still necessary to codify these rights into a new constitution that would guarantee such rights into the future. For this purpose, MacArthur and his staff began simultaneously to study how the existing Meiji Constitution of 1889 should be revised. Initially this endeavor was conducted together with State Minister Joji Matsumoto, Prime Minister Yoshida, and their staffs, but several stumbling blocks quickly emerged between officials of the two states, particularly over the role of the emperor and any future armed forces in the postwar Japanese state, but over a host of other, smaller issues as well. Despite Japan's status as an "occupied" state, Japanese politicians and bureaucrats played an important role in modifying U.S. demands for the codification of political reform in immediate postwar Japan—including the famous war-renouncing Article Nine that would play a central role in Japan's postwar state identity.[21] Ultimately a tenuous compromise was reached and the new document was made public (issued in the Emperor's name) in November 1946 and became law in May of 1947.

As much as Japan had changed domestically as a result of defeat in the war, changes in the international environment and in American policy toward Japan in particular are often cited as the primary factors which explain Japan's postwar foreign policy direction and are considered in the next section. Despite all of these effects of the United States and the international system on domestic Japanese politics, however, it was the Japanese themselves who determined their course for this new era in their history—albeit under significant constraints.[22] Taking advantage of externally imposed democratic reforms (though within the limits noted above), political actors across the ideological spectrum debated Japan's international role for the new era—the freest discussion of Japan's future achieved to that point in Japanese history. It is in this arena that the new security identity of domestic antimilitarism was debated, negotiated, and ultimately crafted.

The United States and the Postwar International Environment

Japan entered the postwar period greatly influenced by the wishes of the United States and the dictates of the new postwar international environment. Among the starkest breaks with its past international role was the ordered complete disbandment of Japan's armed forces per Directive 82 of its unconditional surrender to end the war. The introduction of the directive states: to "insure that Japan will not again become a menace to the peace and security of the world . . . the existing economic basis of Japan's military strength must be destroyed and not permitted to revive."[23] Clearly a high level of distrust of Japan's military (and Japanese in general) was communicated by the United States to ordinary Japanese. Moreover, as noted above, many Japanese embraced this distrust and blame placed on their former military institutions, forming a core component of Japan's newly emerging postwar security identity.

The hard-line sentiment of the United States advocating permanent Japanese disarmament did not last long, however, as the Cold War began to take root in East Asia. Only five years after defeat, the United States was encouraging Japanese rearmament, and some Japanese policy makers were keen to exploit this new opportunity.[24] This shift was evident more broadly in Allied Occupation policy as well. Although Japan's ultimate foreign policy direction was determined domestically, the Allied Occupation of Japan from 1945 to 1952 and the outbreak of the Cold War fundamentally shaped Japan's postwar options. Moreover, even after the United States lost its institutional control over Japan after the conclusion of the Occupation, it continued to be deeply engaged in Japanese domestic debates over Japan's future international role, playing a central role in efforts to "normalize" Japanese security practices to Cold War strategic demands.

The outbreak of the Cold War affected the nature of Japanese domestic politics in the immediate postwar period as much as the Occupation itself; importantly, it affected the nature of the Occupation as well. While the Cold War alone did not determine any specific foreign policy outcome—just as the new security identity of domestic antimilitarism did not—it vastly changed the nature of the debate in Japanese domestic politics in three ways. First, it dealt a crushing blow to any remaining backers of the wartime idea of an Asian regional bloc by making the issue of trade with China a choice between China and the United States. Second, it served to structure one of the primary political cleavages in postwar Japan between left and right over the issue of military alliance with the United States, brought to the fore by the outbreak of armed conflict on the Korean peninsula in 1950. Third, the persistence of the Cold War eventually allowed the domestic Japanese political debate to become circumscribed largely to economic issues, a policy crafted by Prime Minister Shigeru Yoshida and often called the Yoshida Doctrine.

The outbreak of the Cold War had the most visible effect on the policies of the Occupation itself, leading to what scholars have called the "reverse course," or the "second occupation." Troubled at the continuing economic dependence of Japan on the United States and with no clear signs of economic recovery, policy planners in Washington especially began to fear a society fermenting a possible socialist revolution, led by a growing and increasingly confrontational labor movement closely allied with the socialist and communist movement in Japan.[25] As discussed further in the following section, Japan's first socialist-led coalition government was formed in 1947 after the Japan Socialist Party (JSP) won the largest number of seats in that election (though not an outright majority in the multiparty politics of the time).

In response to such fears, earlier policies that had sought to punish big business and encourage decentralization were "reversed" in favor of promoting economic self-sufficiency and industrial development. As a result, earlier gains for organized labor were dealt a severe setback: MacArthur outlawed a planned general strike in February 1947 and decreed in 1948 that government employees did not enjoy the private-sector rights to bargain collectively or to strike. Suppression of the political rights of the Communist Party and supporters of the radical left and covert funding of conservative politicians followed, mirroring the growing McCarthyism of domestic politics in the United States at the time. In 1948, roughly ten thousand wartime "conspirators" were depurged, followed by the purging of over eleven thousand labor leaders across a range of industries critical to Japan's economic recovery.[26]

The outbreak of the Korean War in 1950, which indicated a further escalation of the Cold War in Asia, marks the height of change in occupation policy, and a fundamental turning point in Japan's postwar political and economic development. It also played a critical role in the development of Japan's postwar security identity, particularly vis-à-vis the politically vexing question of rearmament. Under extreme pressure from the United States to support the Free World in the "Korean Conflict," ongoing Japanese discussions regarding the reestablishment of a military (explicitly prohibited by Article Nine of the 1947 constitution) and the redevelopment of defense production (nominally prohibited by the terms of Japan's surrender and occupation) quickly became urgent and concrete. Through the United States government policy of "special procurement" (*tokujū*),[27] the United States encouraged the redevelopment of manufacturing—including defense-related—industry within the Japanese economy, as discussed in greater detail in Chapter 4. It is estimated that nearly 70 percent of Japanese exports between 1950 and 1952 were the direct result of this special procurement by the United States (Samuels 1994, p. 133).

Japan's experience with the Korean War allows one to see clearly the competing forces vying to shape Japan's postwar security identity. Contrary to the connotations of the terms *pacifism* and *antimilitarism*, many in Japan were not adverse to participating in and profiting from war efforts within certain defined parameters— namely, support of *American* war efforts. The limit set by Japan's emerging security identity of *domestic* antimilitarism was that Japanese troops would not again be deployed abroad, expressed here as the second tenet of domestic antimilitarism. Based on domestic political calculations discussed below, Prime Minister Yoshida's refusal to send Japanese troops to the Korean peninsula to fight together with the troops of the many nations that participated in the United Nations force in Korea led by the United States codified the political milieu into what would crystallize into the second tenet of the new postwar security identity. The emergence of the first tenet of a new security identity—proscription of a standard armed force—is also evident at this time, with the creation of the National Police Reserves (NPR) rather than a new "military" for the postwar Japanese state. These National Police Reserves would later become the Self-Defense Forces. Finally, another limitation of domestic antimilitarism concerned the issue of arms production in general, and arms exports in particular—the subject of Chapter 4.

Once alignment with the United States was assured as a result of Japan's support of the United States in the Korean War and the subsequent signing of the first security treaty between Japan and the United States in September 1951, the persistence of the Cold War eventually allowed the domestic Japanese political debate to become focused on rebuilding economic vitality. U.S. policy makers contributed to the success of this plan by allowing unfettered access to the U.S. market for Japanese exports and by championing Japanese entry into international trade institutions such as the General Agreement on Tariffs and Trade (GATT) and the Organization of Economic Cooperation and Development (OECD). Thus, even if the Japanese somehow independent of Cold War politics had envisioned a new security identity of domestic antimilitarism, it is unlikely to have been a successful strategy outside of the Cold War framework. This point deserves underscoring because it exposes that the foundation of Japanese postwar security identity is based on a particular international environment and domestic political configuration. A substantial change to this environment—seen in 1989 and in 2001—would lead to a need to renegotiate the basis of the security identity. Moreover, changes in the international environment apparent during the Cold War itself required political actors to adapt interpretation and provide new justifications for the compromise security identity of domestic antimilitarism.

The counterfactual to the effect of the Cold War on Japanese domestic politics is compelling: had the Cold War not arisen, Japanese politics surely would have developed in a fundamentally different way due to the importance Japan would have of necessity placed on forging peaceful diplomatic relations with its neighbors and the rest of the world. As it was, the political right in Japan was able to offer a future vision based on largely cost-free protection and economic prosperity while, by contrast, the left was hampered by its strong links to communist China and the Soviet Union. Arguably without the left's identification with communists abroad, more constituents would have been supportive of the domestic policies of the left, leading to a vastly different political outcome in postwar Japan. In particular, without the outbreak of the Cold War it is debatable whether the Liberal and Democratic parties of the right would have been able to merge into the LDP to create the so-called 1955 System that would last until after the end of the Cold War in the early 1990s. As this brief counterfactual discussion illustrates, while international constraints had a great impact on the shape of Japan's postwar security identity, ultimately it was domestic political debate, mediated through the newly emergent open party politics, that shaped Japan's postwar international role. Such interplay is considered further in the next section.

Early Party Politics Surrounding Japan's Future International Role

Japanese domestic politics in the early postwar period naturally reflected the wide diversity of opinion and extremes of the defeated Japanese. With the economy barely functioning, the public demoralized, and the role in the world for this once great power unclear, politicians faced a great challenge. Domestic political turmoil was further exacerbated by policies of the Allied Occupation such as the strong support for increased political participation of all sorts under the banner of promotion of democracy. The Communist Party and active labor unions were allowed (for a while) to express their views without limits for the first time in Japanese political history, leading to a vast array of formerly suppressed political views being aired publicly. Combined with the purges of scores of political conservatives from immediate postwar political life (though most of these purges later were reversed), Japanese political discourse bordered on the radical at times, far exceeding the range of acceptable political discourse in the United States at the time of the "red scare."

The promising political possibilities of the left in immediate postwar Japan were substantially limited by international events, however. Heightening tensions with the Soviet Union, the fall of China to the Communists in 1949, and outbreak of the Korean War led to the so-called reverse course in Allied Occupation policy: organized labor was once again curtailed, communists harassed, and covert U.S. aid to conservative political candidates was increased substantially.[28] For the first seven years after the end of the war, Japanese politics operated within the constraints imposed by Occupation authorities, notably including widespread censorship in the media and the purging and depurging of Japanese wartime political figures. Changes in Allied—namely U.S.—policy were therefore as important as changes in the domestic political environment.

In order to understand how domestic antimilitarism emerged as Japan's compromise security identity, it is necessary to consider in greater depth the turbulent party politics that were unfolding in the first years after the 1947 constitution went into effect on May 3, in particular the strength of the political left in the immediate postwar period, and how this strength was eroded by both emerging Cold War politics and the superior political tactics of the right, particularly under Prime Minister Shigeru Yoshida.

While Japan's future international direction was one of the major issues discussed in the political arena in the early postwar period, naturally it was not the only issue. Citizens' views on foreign affairs were not the only issue of differentiation used by parties to build stable support bases. Eight general elections were held in the sixteen years between Japan's surrender in 1945 and the year that the U.S.-Japan Security Treaty was renewed in 1960, the formative period for the new security identity.[29] In 1955, the conservative Liberal and Democratic parties merged into the LDP, setting up a system of conservative party rule that would last until the end of the Cold War. In the early postwar period, however, domestic politics were far more fluid.

In the first election held to uphold the new "MacArthur" Constitution on April 19, 1947, the Japan Socialist Party (JSP) emerged as the party winning the greatest number of seats. In this election the JSP won 143 seats to the Liberal's 131 and Democrat's 126. It would be the only time under the new constitution that the left would possess the electoral strength to form a cabinet to this day.[30] At the time, of course, it was not at all clear that this would be the last major electoral victory of the left. The challenge the JSP posed to the conservative Liberal and Democratic parties instigated intense competition for voters in this period, and a powerful role for the JSP, and members of the left in general, in shaping Japan's postwar security identity.

The first JSP prime minister after the election was Tetsu Katayama. In partnering with political conservatives, however, his freedom of action was severely limited. The Katayama government lasted less than a year and was replaced by another JSP coalition under the short-lived Prime Minister Hitoshi Ashida, who was forced to resign to take responsibility for the first major corruption scandal to hit postwar Japan later the same year. Ashida's government was replaced in October 1948 by a conservative coalition government created by the merged Democratic Liberal Party, which once again established Shigeru Yoshida as prime minister (who had been prime minister under the former constitution from 1946 to 1947). In the following year, 1949, the JSP was routed in the general election, with its number of seats dropping precipitously from 143 to 48. By contrast, the Democratic Liberal Party increased its number of seats from 151 to 264, an absolute majority. Not all of the losses of the JSP went right, however. The Japanese Communist Party (JCP) increased its number of seats nearly tenfold, from only 4 to 35.

In 1951, due to fierce internal disagreement within the JSP over the San Francisco Peace Treaty and the first security treaty with the United States, the party split into right and left wings. It would later remerge in October 1955 (one month before the creation of the LDP). The division of the JSP due to disagreements over Japan's foreign policy weakened the party electorally but reflected divisions within the general public over Japan's future course. For example, many opposed the signing of a security treaty with the United States, preferring Japan to remain neutral in the intensifying Cold War. In 1953, 38 percent of the Japanese public preferred neutrality over 35 percent favoring alignment with the United States (Etō and Yamamoto 1991, p. 223).

Although securing a majority of Diet seats from 1949 onward, conservatives also faced their share of electoral challenges, compounded by the shifting nature of domestic politics, international politics, and the interaction of the two under the supervision of the Allied Occupation authorities. The trump card of the right in this period was the particularly adept "political entrepreneur" Shigeru Yoshida. Gerald Curtis (1988) writes: "While the Socialists, for whatever reasons, had been incompetent at governing, Prime Minister Yoshida . . . proved himself to be a master statesman, master politician, and a master bargainer with Occupation authorities" (p. 13). This view resounds in the literature on this period both in English and Japanese.[31]

The area in which Yoshida's skills were perhaps most greatly challenged was over strenuous U.S. demands for Japanese participation in the Korean War. On this issue, Yoshida had to be both "master bargainer" with the United States and "master politician" in Japan in order for his party not to pay the electoral price for any concessions he made to the United States regarding Japanese rearmament. The creation of the National Police Reserve as the predecessor to what would become the Self-Defense Forces clearly reflected Yoshida's political acumen, satisfying for a time both U.S. demands and domestic political requirements to establish new armed forces in line with the emerging tenets of domestic antimilitarism. This decision initiated four years of political discussion and debate over the character of Japan's future armed forces.[32] Such a political compromise is not unlike the policy innovations developed by subsequent Japanese leaders seeking to adopt the core principles of Japan's security identity of domestic antimilitarism to a shifting international environment.

The 1955 System—created through the mergers of the left and right wings of the JSP on the left, and the Liberal and Democratic parties on the right—established the one-party dominance of the conservative Liberal Democratic Party (LDP) that would remain in place for the remainder of the Cold War. Although the rise of the Cold War in Asia and resulting U.S. pressure on Japan played a key role in the establishment of the 1955 System—as argued above—it did not predetermine LDP dominance. Numerous other factors were important, high among them the superior political entrepreneurship and organizational talent of the conservatives in the immediate postwar years.[33] Despite LDP one-party rule from this time until the end of the Cold War, an important check on LDP power was provided by the security identity of domestic antimilitarism, enforced by vigilant Japanese voters.[34]

Since its founding in 1955, the LDP advocated and pursued a security policy which combined a program of limited rearmament with alliance with the United States. This approach to providing for Japan's national security policy was fundamentally contested by opposition parties, most importantly the JSP.[35] The institutionalized cleavage between the LDP, as ruling party, and the (increasingly divided) progressive opposition parties over defense and alliance issues ensured an active role in the policy-making process by the LDP leadership and guaranteed that implementation of any policy related to the SDF or to the activities of the U.S. military in Japan was carefully scrutinized by opposition parties.[36]

The purpose of national rearmament was the core source of dispute, and since the JSP refused to acknowledge the constitutionality of the SDF, legislative deliberations over national military planning were fraught with conflict. Opposition party challenges of the LDP's interpretation of the Japanese constitution at every possible opportunity and its raising of the issue of civilian control were the principal mechanisms by which the JSP sought to slow the pace of rearmament, leading to further consolidation of the security identity of domestic antimilitarism over time. The LDP's secure majority in the Diet since its founding in 1955 allowed rearmament to proceed, but LDP members were sensitive to the political costs of this aspect of their national policy. As a result, much of the actual policy debates took place away from the public eye, and the rearmament process in general was handled as quietly as possible within the state.[37] Thus, it is not that there has been a consensus on security policy in postwar Japan but rather an elaborate accommodation of often-conflicting interests and policy preferences. The LDP itself typifies the accommodation of the differing conservative and liberal views on security, defense, and the U.S.-Japan alliance, albeit on a lesser scale than across the full Japanese political spectrum.

Creating New Armed Forces and a New Security Identity

Prime Minister Yoshida's creation of the National Police Reserves in 1950 generally satisfied the emerging tenets of domestic antimilitarism, though this decision was not scrutinized to the level that the SDF later would be, because Japan's security was still the responsibility of the United States under its Occupation mandate. As a fledgling organization with few resources, the NPR clearly satisfied the first tenet of domestic antimilitarism, that of not becoming a major actor in security policy formulation by itself. Also due to its limited resources and mandate under the Occupation, the NPR was not about to engage in the use of force to settle an international dispute against Japan, in line with the second tenet of domestic antimilitarism.

The NPR's status vis-à-vis the third tenet of domestic antimilitarism was more controversial, however. The NPR clearly involved Japan in the use of force in an international dispute among third parties (the United States and Korea), exactly what many Japanese feared regarding Japan's alliance with the United States. The NPR played an indirect role in the Korean War by providing technicians and mechanics, plus minesweepers and land-sea transport (LST) crews, to U.S. forces. These roles were controversial, though they did not become major political issues in the environment of Japan's first postwar economic boom generated by the war. More controversial was the redevelopment of defense-related manufacturing to support the war effort, a subject discussed in Chapter 4. The initial activities of the NPR were remembered by many Japanese, however, and invoked during discussions about the future role of the SDF since it was established. Looking ahead briefly to the late 1960s when the United States became involved in another international "conflict" in East Asia, in Vietnam, one sees that the actions accepted by the NPR in Korea were not deemed acceptable for the SDF, Japan's institutionalized, domestic antimilitarist armed forces.

The evolution of the NPR into the establishment of the Self-Defense Forces in 1954 can be seen as one of the first major instances of the emerging security identity of domestic antimilitarism shaping security practice. At the same time, this decision point served to reify and define the contours of the new security identity. Building on the issue of defense production, which had also arisen in the context

TABLE 5

Japanese Attitudes on the Re-establishment of an Armed Forces, 1950–56

Year	Yes (%)	No (%)	Other/Don't Know (%)	N
1950	54	28	18	2,641
1952	56	26	18	2,614
1954	52	30	18	2,498
1956	66	19	15	16,630

Respondents were asked: "Do you approve or oppose the idea that Japan needs military forces?"
Source: *Asahi Shimbun*, cited in Mendel (1961), p. 69.

of the Korean War, heated debate over Japan's postwar international role was pre-cipitated by the creation of the SDF. Despite widespread concerns that re-creation of armed forces would once again lead Japanese down the wrong path, the major-ity of the general public recognized the need for some type of armed forces to protect Japan from international aggression. According to surveys conducted by the left-leaning *Asahi* newspaper and summarized in Table 5, most Japanese (ranging from 52 percent to 66 percent) approved the idea that Japan needed armed forces throughout the heated period in which this issue was debated (1950–56)—a sur-prising finding if one expects to see a "pacifist" Japan in the postwar period.

As summarized in Table 5, in the year that the National Police Reserves were created, 1950, 54 percent of the public supported the re-creation of some military forces. Much of the controversy on this question therefore centered around two issues. The first was the sizable minority who did not support reestablishment of armed forces—28 percent of the public in 1950—whose views were given a large voice by the opposition JSP. The second issue surrounded the structure and character of the new armed forces: even among the majority who supported rees-tablishment, opinion ranged from support for a full-fledged prewar-style military (which would require revision of the constitution) to the bare minimum neces-sary for "self-defense." It was in this area that the emerging security identity of domestic antimilitarism structured the final policy outcome of the establishment of the SDF in 1954 through an elaborate, and enduring, political compromise.

From the beginning, the JSP positioned itself as a vehement protector of the new constitution and, according to its rhetoric, the people's rights. As such, it opposed the creation of the SDF due to their perceived incompatibility with the new constitution, whose Article Nine, the JSP pointed out at every opportu-nity, explicitly prohibits the maintenance of "war potential." The conservatives, in response, offered a more complex interpretation, but one also firmly grounded in the emerging political rhetoric of domestic antimilitarism. The unified govern-ment view (*seifu toitsu kenkai*) submitted to the Budget Committee of the House of Representatives in December 1954 states the following:

Although Japan has renounced war, it has not renounced the struggle for self-defense. What was abandoned under Article 9 was war and the use of force as means of settling international disputes. The deterring of armed attacks by other countries is in the defense of Japan, and this differs in essence from the settlement of international disputes. Accordingly, use of force for defense of national territory is not contrary to the constitutional provisions.[38]

This statement reinforces the rationale for the establishment of the SDF but also simultaneously serves to reify the central tenets of the new security identity, particularly the second tenet prohibiting the use of force by Japan to settle international disputes. This official interpretation of the constitution regarding national defense was expressed repeatedly by the ruling party—exclusively the LDP from 1955 into the post–Cold War period—after the creation of the SDF, in a number of forms other than the unified government view quoted above. These include the Defense Agency view (*boeicho kenkai*) presented to the Diet, written replies to questions posed by Diet members, remarks during parliamentary interpellations, and statements contained in the annual Defense White Paper compiled by the JDA and approved by the cabinet. Through such a mechanism, use of the language of domestic antimilitarism led to its institutionalization into Japanese postwar security practice.

The organizational structure and capacity of the SDF institutionalized the first tenet of the new security identity, that the military would not be involved as a regular actor in state policy making. This structure reflected concessions by both conservatives and supporters of the JSP, underscoring the compromise nature of the emergent postwar security identity. For example, under a separate law passed concurrently to the SDF law, the supervisory agency over the SDF, the Self-Defense Agency (later the JDA) was established as an agency within the prime minister's office, not as an independent ministry. This underscored the noncentral function envisioned for the JDA/SDF and the idea of civilian control residing in the person of the prime minister. Second, its very name, self-defense force (*jieitai*) rather than army (*guntai*), denoted its limited mission—the defense of Japan. This mission was clearly expressed in Article Three of the SDF law, underscoring the second tenet of domestic antimilitarism.

The establishment of the SDF led immediately to a drive to institutionalize a series of safeguards, or "brakes" (*hadome*)—beyond even the restrictions of the establishing law itself—that would prevent Japan's new military from exceeding its mission of defending Japan. These brakes came in the form of laws, Diet resolutions, and government declarations designed to define the scope of acceptable activities of the SDF. It is through such means that the new security identity permeates postwar security practice and is reproduced over time for future generations. The SDF law already limited the mission of the SDF to the defense of Japan itself. Soon after, the Upper House of the Diet passed a resolution that banned the dispatch of the SDF abroad, the first of many such security-related resolutions that would be declared in the postwar period to emphasize the limits imposed by the compromise security identity. This effectively codified the second and third tenets of domestic antimilitarism, keeping Japan and Japanese from participating directly in international conflicts. Later, various procurement policies were established to prevent the SDF from obtaining offensive weapons such as long-range bomb-ers or midair refueling capability for its fighter planes, reinforcing and further consolidating each tenet of domestic antimilitarism.[39] All of these restrictions were designed to ensure that the new Japanese military would not possess the ability to project force abroad, a capability necessary to violate the second and third tenets of domestic antimilitarism regarding the use of force to settle inter-national disputes. This flurry of policy making reflected the contentious nature of party politics in the period, and continuing strength of the political left, but was fundamentally structured by Japan's new emergent security identity—particularly tenets two and three—which informed the specific policy prescriptions and pro-scriptions that were institutionalized in state security policy. Looking forward, it is clear that such strict restrictions have been relaxed somewhat in the twenty-first century, but they have not been abandoned. The extensive institutionalization of the security identity of domestic antimilitarism remains a strong barrier to policy change.

One example of the extent of subscription to this new security identity is pro-vided by Japanese responses to a survey regarding a volatile international dispute of the time—the issue of fishing rights in the Sea of Japan between Korea and Japan. For a number of years in the mid-1950s Japan and South Korea were embroiled in a diplomatic dispute regarding the acceptable sea area each state's fishing ves-sels could utilize. Naturally this type of international dispute would generally not escalate into a war anywhere in the world, but the question of whether Japanese fishing vessels should be lent assistance by the new Maritime Self-Defense Force (MSDF) to protect them in asserting their rights to certain territory did arise. This issue is interesting to reexamine today in light of the post–Cold War issue of the extent to which the Japanese Coast Guard and the MSDF should be able to fire upon (primarily Chinese and North Korean) ships which illegally enter Japanese sea territory and which attempt to flee when caught, as discussed in Chapter 7.

Respondents were asked, "Should Japan use force to protect fishermen?"[40] The resounding view of the general public was that force should not be exercised in such cases, reflecting the second tenet of domestic antimilitarism embodied in the constitution and the laws and guidelines regulating the SDF. Only 8 percent of the public in 1958 thought that force should be employed in this case, though many advocated for Japan to take a more "forceful diplomatic" stand (37 percent). Only 15 percent thought Japan should negotiate "as before." The large number of respondents who answered "don't know" (also 37 percent) may be explained by the belief among many in the central tenets of domestic antimilitarism but uncertainty about how Japan could protect its interests under these constraints; alternatively, this large number may reflect the newness of this emergent security identity, one which had not yet fully congealed in the consciousness of many Japanese.

Domestic Antimilitarism and the U.S.–Japan Alliance

The security identity of domestic antimilitarism enabled Japan to enter into a security alliance with the United States, but only under certain defined parameters. Indeed it was the controversy over entering into the alliance that brought the contours of the emerging security identity of domestic antimilitarism into full relief. Within the scope of domestic antimilitarism there are a number of possible forms of alliance with the United States (or others), spanning a range of levels of coordination and responsibilities. The outbreak of the Korean War in 1950 and subsequent U.S. pressure on Japan to reconstitute armed forces and to dispatch troops to the Korean peninsula in support of the U.S. war effort led to intense discussions about the future alignment of the Japanese state in the postwar period. Contrary to a conceptualization of security identity that includes the U.S. alliance as one of its central tenets,[41] public opinion in Japan was greatly divided over the issue of alignment with the United States.[42] This stands in contrast to other decisions made in line with the new security identity, such as opinion regarding the SDF outlined above. While there was broad agreement against alignment with the communist states, which encumbered the left, there was no agreement on aligning with the United States among the general public. In 1953, after the first security treaty with the United States was in force, the SDF law was being debated, and the Korean War had ended in stalemate, more Japanese preferred neutrality (38 percent) than alignment with the "free world" (35 percent). Later, amid discussions of revising the U.S.–Japan Security Treaty (including mass political demonstrations protesting such action—the largest ever in Japanese history), Japanese preferred neutrality over continued alignment with the United States nearly two to one, 50 percent versus 26 percent respectively. A clear majority preferred neutrality despite the eventual, controversial decision by the conservative government to sign a new security treaty with the United States in 1960.

The instability of public opinion over the issue of alignment during this period demonstrates the importance of a grounding security identity such as the ultimately hegemonic domestic antimilitarism. The central tenets of domestic antimilitarism provide guideposts to political leaders regarding the acceptability of foreign policy options regarding military security, enabling continuity over time and allowing routine decision making that does not generate mass controversy. By contrast, an issue such as alignment with the United States—which lies outside of the tenets of the new security identity—evoked great swings in public opinion, where support for the alliance fluctuated nearly twenty percentage points from 37 percent at the minimum to 55 percent at its peak between 1950 and 1980 (Etō and Yamamoto 1991, p. 223). Other polls show even less support for the alliance at times, as little as one-quarter of the general public (Nishihara 1981, p. 27). Despite being a central aspect of Japanese security policy during the Cold War, Japan's alignment with the United States was not part of its core security identity.

The contrast between stability of public attitudes regarding alignment with the United States and support of the SDF is instructive. Despite heated debate over the scope of the SDF's mission at the time of its establishment, Japanese attitudes remained continuously supportive of the SDF throughout the postwar period, growing from a low (but still strong majority) of 65 percent responding "good to have it" in 1959, to a high of 86 percent in 1978, the year of the first proclaimed U.S.-Japan Guidelines for Defense Cooperation.[43] Only between 5 and 12 percent of those polled responded "better not to have it" in this period, though "don't know" responses reached as high as 24 percent in 1959, steadily declining to 9 percent in 1978. Such attitudes reflect the character of public opinion one would expect to find in support of a central tenet of a security identity. In the case of the SDF, as discussed above, the way in which the SDF was established and regulated reflected all three tenets of the security identity of domestic antimilitarism, which accounts for the stable support of the institution.

By contrast, while Japan possesses the right of collective self-defense under international law, the view of the Japanese government articulated in the mid-1950s was that it exceeds the limits of the domestic antimilitarist tenet of "self-defense" to take any military action on behalf of a foreign country, no matter how closely Japan is associated with it.[44] As a result, Japan cannot enter into an agreement to protect an alliance partner from external aggression even if the partner makes a commitment to the defense of Japan—as in the security treaty with the United States. In fact, even into the 1980s it was controversial in Japan to refer to Japan's relationship with the United States as an alliance (*domei*). It was Prime Minister Zenko Suzuki who took the step of labeling the relationship an alliance in a joint communiqué issued after he met President Ronald Reagan in May 1981. The wording was so controversial even within the Japanese government—let alone among the broader public—that it resulted in the resignation of the foreign minister (Umemoto 1985, p. 56). Due to this prohibition on the exercise of the right of collective self-defense, the Japanese government maintained that the dispatch of troops outside of Japan would fall outside the scope of self-defense until the 1990s.[45]

Policy development between Japan and the United States regarding the U.S.-Japan alliance continued to be limited by the central tenets of domestic antimilitarism throughout the Cold War period. For example, routinized military cooperation within the alliance did not begin until twenty-four years after the Mutual Defense Assistance Agreement (MDAA) was signed in 1954, demonstrating the continuing controversial nature of the alliance. The SDF was allowed to join in a bilateral security dialogue with the United States only in 1978, when the Guidelines for U.S.-Japan Defense Cooperation were negotiated to allow discussions and planning for how the two states' militaries would work together in case of a threat to Japan.[46] Although the text of the 1978 Guidelines included the possibility of military collaboration in case of a contingency in the region, no actual progress was made on agreeing in advance to potential military cooperation between the United States and Japan in cases of conflict beyond Japanese territory during the Cold War under this framework—at least publicly. This outcome is not surprising given that such cooperation would violate outright the third tenet of domestic antimilitarism and would also serve to elevate the role of the SDF in security policy making, which would violate the first tenet of the security identity as well.

Foreshadowing discussion in Chapter 7, the distinction between the security identity of domestic antimilitarism and the security alliance with the United States becomes more clear in the post–Cold War period, when many Japanese feared a U.S. withdrawal from Asia. Although, as in the Cold War period, political actors on the political right actively promoted a greater military role for Japan if this were to happen, moderate voices advocated Japan playing a greater role within the existing alliance framework. Despite this continuing debate, however, the central tenets of domestic antimilitarism remained firmly in place.

The fact that security alliance with the United States does not constitute a central tenet of domestic antimilitarism does not mean that the alliance was irrelevant to the codification of this identity in the postwar period. Without the U.S. alliance, Japan probably would not have been able to pursue its identity of domestic antimilitarism during the Cold War. Moreover, it probably would not have been able to form the domestic political coalition necessary to reach the compromise embodied in domestic antimilitarism. Even if an alternative political coalition had been forged, it would not likely have been centered around political conservatives. Dower (1979) makes this point in his analysis of Prime Minister Yoshida's political life: "the reconsolidation and recentralization of conservative authority during the Yoshida era was inseparable from the strategic settlement reached between the United States and Japan" (p. 369). Michael Green adds the important point that U.S. assistance reached out to both the moderate and right wings of the LDP in order to secure support for the alliance.[47]

What made the compromise of domestic antimilitarism possible, however, was that in addition to appealing to conservatives, political actors outside of the LDP were also brought into the compromise by adapting the language of the pacifists and institutionalizing constraints on rearmament that appeased not just doves within the conservative party but also sympathetic members of other parties and, importantly, the general public. This broader political coalition differentiates the security identity of domestic antimilitarism from the decision to enter into the security alliance with the United States, the latter of which was forced on Japan's political world through collusion between the right wing of the LDP and policy makers in the United States and later accepted only grudgingly by many Japanese.

Cold War Security Politics Under the Hegemony of Domestic Antimilitarism

It is a common misconception that the renewal of the U.S.-Japan Security Treaty in 1960—which ensured the indefinite stationing of U.S. forces in Japan and Japan's protection under the U.S. nuclear umbrella—allowed Japan to avoid serious debate about security policy from this time until the end of the Cold War. This view is perpetuated by overuse of the catchphrase Yoshida Doctrine, meant to connote consensus on the U.S.-Japan alliance and on Japan's limited military role in the postwar period. Although it is clearly the case that discussion of security issues after 1960 did not continue at the same scale as in the formative period discussed in this chapter (which, after all, had led to the largest demonstrations in Japanese history), discussion of security issues continued to be at the forefront of the 1955 System that divided Japanese politics between left and right for the remainder of the Cold War period. Discourse over security practice had been "normalized," but political disagreement did not disappear. Contestation over security policy was normal for Japan throughout this period.

A critical difference between discussion of security policy that took place in the formative period examined above and such discussions in the remainder of the Cold War period is the codification of the new security identity that had taken place: the hegemony of domestic antimilitarism. The three central tenets of domestic antimilitarism were firmly established by 1960 and institutionalized into a wide range of laws, Diet resolutions, bureaucratic regulations, and policy-making conventions. The concrete political negotiations surrounding Japan's security policy from the 1960s forward focused on the implementation of security cooperation with the United States under the framework of domestic antimilitarism, rather than the question of what international role Japan should play in the postwar period. It is in this period, after 1960, that other policies that further expanded the institutionalization of the security identity of domestic antimilitarism emerged—such as the three nonnuclear principles, the 1 percent ceiling (of GNP) on defense spending, restrictions on arms exports, and restrictions on the military use of outer space.

Only three years after Prime Minister Kishi was ousted from power in 1960, the LDP won 55 percent of the vote and 60 percent of the seats in the 1963 Lower House elections. By contrast, the JSP won only 29 percent of the vote. Similar percentages were evident in the Upper House as well, where the LDP held roughly 57 percent of the seats compared to the JSP's 26 percent.[48] Despite this evidence that the LDP had won the battle with the left over the future direction of Japan, the LDP did not have a free hand in its foreign policy decision making. Rather, structured by the security identity of domestic antimilitarism, debates over foreign policy continued throughout the Cold War period, such as the cases of arms exports and the military use of outer space examined in Chapters 4 and 5.

One example of the continuing fundamental difference of opinion regarding national security at the mass level is seen in three polls conducted by the *Mainichi Shimbun* in 1968 and 1969 (at the height of the Vietnam War and during the initial discussions of the reversion of Okinawa) which confirmed the continuing presence of three views: nearly 40 percent seeking a nonaligned Japan with a capability to defend itself militarily, roughly one-quarter endorsing the U.S.-Japan bilateral alliance, and slightly more than a quarter advocating unarmed neutrality.[49] The end of the Vietnam War and the reversion of Okinawa to Japanese administrative control in 1972, along with the consolidation of U.S. bases on the Japanese main islands, erased much of the antipathy to the bilateral security arrangement by the mid-1970s. Moreover, the economic hardship of the first oil crisis (1973–74) shifted the attention of the general public to economic concerns. Tetsuya Umemoto notes that public division over the U.S.-Japan alliance begins to lessen at this time in favor of a growing acceptance of the security treaty and the alliance with the United States. Although there is a move toward greater acceptance of the alliance in the late 1970s and 1980s, it is not the case that the cleavage disappears. Umemoto notes that between 1968 and 1983, the number of respondents who approved of the security treaty as contributing to the security of Japan increased by 15 percent from 30 percent to 45 percent, but even still less than half of the respondents saw this security arrangement as Japan's preferred security option.[50] Surveys cited in the previous section show even greater acceptance of the alliance

(55 percent in 1980), yet they also show over a quarter of the population firmly against it, and others undecided.[51]

Thus, even thirty-five years into the postwar period, Japan's security identity of domestic antimilitarism has not shifted in this area to include consensus on the alliance relationship with the United States. By contrast, surveys show dramatically growing support for the constitution—an embodiment of domestic antimilitarism given the way it was interpreted in the early formative years of the security identity. Those against constitutional revision (and thus, supporting the constitution as written) grew steadily from 42 percent in 1955 to 78 percent in 1983. Conversely, those supporting constitutional revision dropped to only 12 percent of those polled in 1983.[52]

Umemoto asserts that Japan underwent a substantial shift in public opinion in the 1970s, comparable, he argues, to the U.S. shift away from isolationism in the 1940s. Indeed, public opinion did change on some major foreign policy issues in this period, exemplified in particular by growing acceptance of the SDF and the security alliance with the United States. However, it cannot be demonstrated that Japan's security identity underwent a dramatic shift in this period. The central tenets of domestic antimilitarism remained firmly in place, signifying solid—if uneasy—political agreement on the acceptable framework for Japan's security practices. Thus, the example of changing views on the alliance serves to illustrate the difference between a focus purely on mass public opinion and the larger issue of security identity.

In the 1980s, the selection of hawkish Yasuhiro Nakasone as prime minister ensured that national security policy would remain in the headlines. Once again, however, the security identity of domestic antimilitarism set the boundaries of acceptable security practice, despite much public discussion of a possible new security identity for Japan, the rising economic hegemon.[53] Policy shifts did occur, in particular in the areas of defense cooperation with the United States, levels of defense spending, arms exports, and use of outer space—but each of these policy changes represents minor tinkering with the boundaries imposed by the security identity, not a wholesale departure, underscoring the 3 Rs of Japanese policy making: reach, reconcile, reassure. Thus, these debates and the nature of the limited policy shifts serve as examples of the resilience of the security identity rather than a transcendence of it and, moreover, underscore a central argument of this study—that policy change within a static security identity is to be expected and is explainable.

Curtis (1988) notes that by the end of the Cold War period "Japanese society . . . was remarkably free of wrenching social cleavages. Extremists of the left and the right had been pushed to the sidelines of political life" (p. 2). While it certainly is the case that the acrimony and mass demonstrations of earlier years had dissipated by this time, extremist voices from both sides of the political spectrum continued to play a role in shaping foreign policy discourse even late in the Cold War period. The hegemonic identity was not the only identity that deserved attention. In particular, the role of two sets of actors should be noted prior to a discussion of the specific cases to which Chapters 4 and 5 are devoted. On the left, the peace movement continued to mobilize support in the 1970s and 1980s, particularly for its antinuclear policies and its opposition to the continued U.S. military presence in Japan.[54] In the 1990s, as discussed in Chapter 3, this group would become particularly active regarding U.S. military presence in Okinawa.

On the right, militarists and other members of the far right (*uyoku*) continued to influence public opinion and political leaders in particular through methods of intimidation often associated with the criminal underworld. Regular visits to newspaper and commercial publishers, broadcast studios, and offices of political leaders to protest perceived slights on Japanese honor and historical memory (particularly regarding Japan's conduct in the Second World War) gave pause to those on the left and even in the center before expressing their views publicly. Although murder and assassination as a political tool greatly declined after the immediate postwar period, occasional incidents such as the shooting of the chairman of the left-leaning *Asahi* newspaper and, separately, the mayor of Nagasaki after he imputed responsibility for the war on the dying Showa emperor, Hirohito, served as a brake on public expression of views more powerful than the number of supporters of such groups would suggest.[55]

In sum, Japan's postwar security identity did not arise from a shared worldview among decision makers or the general public. Rather, the identity of domestic antimilitarism became hegemonic as a result of a political solution that reflected the individual beliefs of some political actors but also accommodated the interests of powerful political and economic actors who benefited materially from the identity in the short term and did not necessarily embrace its ideological content. Considered in the longer term, however—as seen in the cases presented in the following chapters—adoption of a particular identity results in the altering of the interests of some actors over time through socialization and through institutionalization. Interest- or power-based rationales do not provide a complete explanation, nor even a satisfactory one by themselves. Moreover, the development of the security identity precedes many policies that later are affected by it. Domestic antimilitarism provided a remarkably stable context for security policy making throughout the postwar and into the post–Cold War periods, despite a dramatically altered domestic and international political environment.

It is an apparent paradox that while a politics constrained by the security identity of domestic antimilitarism characterizes the postwar Japanese political process over security issues, domestic political actors enjoyed substantial opportunities to enact policies beyond apparent constraints[56]—building a large military, exporting weapons components, even sending Japanese troops abroad in recent years. The contradiction between appearance and reality in Japan's arms export and outer space use policies are two such cases which expose the limits of explanations based on norms or identity alone and which have important implications for Japan's post–Cold War policies, including the cases of joint ballistic missile defense (BMD) research with the United States and deployment of surveillance satellites—examples discussed later in this volume. This apparent contradiction directs attention back to the domestic determinants of foreign policy, and in particular the evolving politics of antimilitarism in Japan in recent years. Thus, before a case-based analysis can proceed, it is important to consider how the security identity of domestic antimilitarism fared in the years immediately following the end of the Cold War—the subject of Chapter 3. Once this issue is addressed, an analysis of cases that cross these periods can proceed.

3

Reaffirming Core Principles in a "Lost Decade," 1989-1998

The Japan of the 1990s displayed a number of parallels to immediate postwar Japan. While not saddled with the immense physical destruction that followed the Second World War, Japan's national self-confidence had collapsed along with its "bubble economy."[1] More abstractly, the death of the Showa emperor, Hirohito, in 1989[2] opened many troubling questions about past war responsibility that caused increased stress between Japan's more hawkish, nationalist right, which did not want the past to constrain Japan's progress toward a greater military role in the world, and the left, which feared that Japan's political system was not mature enough to prevent the kind of extremism that had led Japan to war five decades earlier. The end of the Cold War and the outbreak of the Persian Gulf War in 1991 opened political space for a renewed discussion about Japan's place in the world[3] and whether the Cold War compromise of domestic antimilitarism was appropriate for the new Heisei era.[4]

Unlike the immediate postwar period, however, a dramatic new security identity was not forged out of the sense of crisis that emerged in Japan in the early 1990s. Instead, the basic constraints of domestic antimilitarism were maintained, though at times rearticulated and adapted to a new international environment. Only a decade after the end of the Cold War and the death of Hirohito, spurred by a North Korean Taepodong test missile launch, rising concerns about China, and ultimately the September 11, 2001, attacks on the United States, an avalanche of new security policies were enacted—the subject of Chapter 7. Prior to the Taepodong launch of August 1998, however, debate over Japan's security practices yielded few dramatic departures from past practice beyond the gradual evolution seen in the Cold War period discussed in Chapter 2 and in later case chapters.

A key difference for Japan between the immediate postwar period and the post–Cold War period is that the former reflected a "crisis of security" while the latter a "crisis of expectations" (Green 1998, p. 13)—at least early in the post–Cold War period. In 1945 Japan could not continue on its former foreign policy trajectory, which had led to a humiliating unconditional surrender to the Allied powers. Not only had the former course been discredited, but Japan's future options were unclear—complicated by civil wars taking place within the borders of its close neighbors and the early stages of the emerging Cold War rivalry between the United States and the Soviet Union. By contrast, in the early 1990s Japan faced the reverse situation: the course it had been following for the previous forty years had led to great success—though the severity of the developing economic downturn had not yet been fully appreciated, nor were its broader implications understood. Thus, Michael Green (1998) rightly notes: "the debate in the early 1990s was about Japan becoming a 'normal' country, rather than about protecting Japanese interests in a hostile world," or of finding a new path for Japan of necessity (p. 13).

Beginning with the bursting of the financial bubble by the Bank of Japan,[5] the dissolution of the Soviet Union, and the creation of the U.S.-led coalition against Iraq in the Gulf War, Japan's domestic and international political environment changed markedly and rapidly in the 1990s. Japan ran through nearly ten different prime ministers in these ten years.[6] Both during the period of the first Gulf War as well as through a series of other major domestic and international crises for Japan—including the 1995 Kobe earthquake that killed more than five thousand people, the sarin gas attack on the Tokyo subway by a religious cult later that year, and the takeover of the Japanese ambassador's residence in Lima, Peru, in 1996—many Japanese citizens became discouraged by their national government's inability to take decisive action on behalf of the public. Slow decisions by ineffective prime ministers raised Japan's sense of international and domestic insecurity. Further eroding Japan's insulation from international crisis, in 1993–94 hot conflict on the Korean peninsula came to its closest point in decades as the United States engaged in a standoff with North Korea over North Korea's development of a nuclear energy reactor that was thought capable of yielding weapons-grade plutonium.[7] In this climate, the two components for identity shift—discrediting of the old identity and options for a new identity articulated by major political actors—were both apparent.

With diminishing economic resources and a greater sense of international vulnerability, numerous security analysts predicted a more active security role for Japan.[8] This prediction proved accurate to a degree, but the set of policy choices made by Japan were constrained significantly by Japan's existing security identity, an identity which proved surprisingly resilient to many. Though the boundaries of this long-codified security identity were seriously tested in this decade, the postwar compromise of domestic antimilitarism continued—and continues—to fundamentally shape political discourse on Japan's international role and resultant security practices. In addition to the role of domestic antimilitarism both in constraining policy and in shaping outcomes, a number of diverse factors affected new security policies in the 1990s, including changing threat perceptions, the role of the 1993 and 1998 North Korean missile tests, general and elite public opinion, changing political coalitions within the Diet, bureaucratic politics, changing regional security dynamics, and alliance politics with the United States.[9] Pressure for identity shift was, and is, evident in both the international and domestic political arenas.

Despite widespread discussion about—and fears of—a dramatic break from Japan's postwar security practice in the post–Cold War period, only one long-standing policy constraint of the Cold War era, the blanket prohibition of foreign deployment of the Self-Defense Forces (SDF), was abandoned in the first decade of the post–Cold War period (and only after strict new limits on SDF action were put into place). Although this decision certainly set an important new policy precedent, it should not be viewed primarily as a departure from Japan's long-standing security identity but rather as an example of the continuing effect of this security identity in the post–Cold War era in that such deployments in almost every way followed the spirit of the long-standing security identity. As such, it is an example of how policy can change in response to a new international or domestic environment within an existing security identity. Established restrictions on other aspects of security practice such as arms export restrictions, the policy regarding the peaceful use of outer space, the three nonnuclear principles, the 1 percent ceiling on defense spending, and the limited capability and mission of the SDF also were largely observed in the first decade of the post–Cold War period. New agreements with the United States to bolster Japan's military alliance with that country form a second, less dramatic but equally significant area of policy evolution that pushes the boundaries of the hegemonic security identity, a subject discussed further below and continued in Chapter 7.

That such long-standing postwar policies constraining Japan's military role remain, however, does not mean they remain fully unaltered. As with the 1980s, a number of previous policy constraints were further modified in the first post–Cold War decade. Such change is the result not of changes in Japan's security identity, however, but rather a changed configuration of political power domestically and internationally, and a new international security environment. This chapter discusses the evolution of such constraints, but more importantly notes their continued resilience despite considerable pressure for change. Chapters 4, 5, and 6 then examine in greater detail the politics of policy shift and mechanisms of identity influence with specific reference to arms export restrictions, the policy regarding the peaceful use of space, and growing cooperation with the United States on missile defense. One further point to stress at the outset of this chapter: while the evolution of security practice was not as dramatic in this period as many people expected, the extended political discussion that took place, as well as additional incremental policy shifts themselves, laid an important foundation for more dramatic change to come post-1998. In this sense, the 1990s were far from a "lost decade" in the evolution of Japanese security practice and therefore deserve fresh consideration.

Confronting a New International and Domestic Environment

Japan was buffeted by change in four areas simultaneously in the early 1990s: in its international environment, in its relations with its principal security guarantor (the United States), in its domestic confidence, and in its domestic politics—each discussed in subsections below. On the international level, the end of the Cold War is the most dramatic change in the international environment to face Japanese policy makers, but not the only one. This change affected not only the level of threat perceived by Japan, but also the strategic calculations made by the United States vis-à-vis Japan and East Asia in general. In the early 1990s there was great fear among Japanese policy makers that the United States would withdraw its military forces from Japan and East Asia to reap a post–Cold War "peace dividend." Such fears constituted one of the major sparks to renewed debates over Japan's post–Cold War international role. Aside from the end of the Cold War, other changes at the international level also affected Japanese foreign policy calculations. The corollary to the bursting of the bubble economy in Japan was the resurgence of the U.S. economy and emergence of the United States as "the world's only superpower"—not only because it defeated the Soviets in the Cold War but because its economy had recovered to once again outshine the economies of Japan and Europe. Finally, despite the floundering Japanese economy and the East Asian Financial Crisis of 1997, the continued rise of the economies of East Asian states as a whole contributed to Japan's reconceptualization of itself as an "Asian" nation with strong interests in that region.[10] The growth of the Chinese economy in particular posed a potential security threat of a rising regional hegemon.[11]

Throughout these changes, the continued privileged role of the United States as a political actor within the Japanese system was evident. It was the United

States that drove discussion of Japan's role in the Persian Gulf War more than any other actor; it was the perceived threat of the United States' withdrawal from Asia that sparked renewed debate over Japan's international role; and it was the United States that pressured Japan to take a greater lead in economic and security affairs in Asia.

Domestically, the bursting of the bubble economy and death of the Showa emperor, Hirohito, sent shockwaves throughout Japan, followed politically by the Liberal Democratic Party's (LDP's) loss of its Diet majority in 1993 in the House of Representatives (after already having lost its majority in the House of Councilors in 1989), indicating the end of the 1955 System with the 1993 accession of a non-LDP prime minister, Morihiro Hosokawa, for the first time since the creation of the LDP in 1955. The dramatic changes in Japan's domestic and international environment did not result in the extent of policy shift predicted by material power-based international- or domestic-level theory, however. Instead, despite some incremental shift in security policy outcomes, the security identity of domestic antimilitarism continues well into the post–Cold War period to structure Japan's security practices.

An Evolving Post–Cold War International Environment

The outbreak of the Persian Gulf War in 1991 demonstrated to the Japanese, and the world, that the post–Cold War international system would not be conflict-free. Moreover, the Cold War had not fully ended in East Asia, where over a million troops were still positioned along the demilitarized zone (DMZ) between North and South Korea, and where a tenuous standoff between China and Taiwan (which China maintains remains its wayward province) regularly threatens to erupt in open military hostilities. Given the continued simmering of historical resentments in Japan's close neighborhood, relief at the end of the Cold War between the West and the then-dissolved Soviet Union transitioned to fear that the United States would withdraw from the region, leaving Japan to manage security tensions in the region on its own—to put it in scholarly realist terms, Japan shifted once again from fearing "entrapment" to fearing "abandonment." This anxiety, evident both among Japanese and among Japan's neighbors (who feared a Japan that would not only rearm but shed its self-imposed constraints on military behavior), led to renewed discussions about the role of the U.S.-Japan security alliance, which over the course of this decade resulted in a deepening of the relationship rather than a withering away.

The reinforcement of the U.S.-Japan security alliance, which had begun in the Cold War period, was hastened by new open conflict with North Korea and growing fear of China's increasing power resources. For most of the 1990s, Japan's most immediate security threat had emanated from North Korea, both from its nuclear and missile development (the Nodong and Taepodong medium-range missiles) and from periodic intrusion of North Korean ships into Japanese territorial waters. The threat from Chinese missile development also lurked in the background and was thought by many, including many Chinese, to be the true motivation for Japan's defense policy responses such as joint research on missile defense with the United States and the indigenous development of surveillance satellites.[12] Without the increased Japanese perception of threat from North Korea, however, Japanese policy makers would not likely have been able to move forward with ambitious plans to develop surveillance satellites or to engage in joint research with the United States on theater missile defense, as argued in subsequent chapters.

By the close of the 1990s, a number of stark security challenges were emphasized by military planners in Japan and the United States, and increasingly referenced by a general public becoming more sophisticated in its understanding of regional security issues. Among the greatest security challenges facing Japan by the late 1990s were the continued existence of the so-called divided states of North/South Korea and China/Taiwan, ongoing military modernization programs (particularly of rising-power China and "rogue-state" North Korea), outstanding territorial disputes (including minor disputes between Japan and several of its neighbors—Russia, South Korea, China, and Taiwan), and the proliferation of ballistic missiles and weapons of mass destruction among Japan's close neighbors, North Korea and China, as well as India and Pakistan in South Asia.[13]

A New Domestic Economic and Political Environment

In the late 1980s and early 1990s Japan was confident about its economic power, if not its purpose.[14] The general framework cast first by the Yoshida doctrine of emphasizing economic success and minimizing exposure on defense and military costs (both financial and political) had served Japan extremely well and had helped nourish Japan's high-growth economy, which cultivated powerhouse manufacturers and globally engaged trading firms that integrated aid, trade, financial flows, and diplomacy to great success. By the early 1990s, real estate and stock valuations in Japan reached phenomenal levels, driven not by culture or by unusually efficient workers, as some have argued, but by system-level deal-making that benefited Japan—a deal that was about to sour.[15]

The collapse of Japan's bubble economy in 1991 was swift and painful—both financially and psychologically. Addicted to the asset inflation Japan had experienced in the late 1980s, and combined with the need to balance the shock of the stronger yen on Japan's export industries, the Bank of Japan had pushed down the cost of capital to provide nearly cost-free funds for Japanese banks, trading houses, manufacturers, and even small businesses to move portions of their operations overseas, and also to continue to spur ongoing low-cost development in Japan. This practice further inflated asset values, continuing the spiral of high-leverage investment across borders that made Japan seem like a truly formidable economic heavyweight that had become too big to fail. These practices continued until the model became unsustainable.[16]

Japan's domestic economic problems caused a definitive crisis in domestic confidence of citizens in their basic financial and government institutions. These include such long-standing business practices as lifetime employment and seniority-based salaries as well as government institutions such as the revered bureaucratic planning and their *amakudari* ("descent from heaven") relationship with industry actors. As the cost of capital rises, these practices—often described as cultural determinants of Japan's economic success—become harder to maintain. By the late 1990s, although Japan certainly had not moved entirely toward the minimalist social safety net model of U.S.-style capitalism, it had allowed some of its prize firms—like the former Long Term Credit Bank and Nissan Motor Corporation—to be taken over by foreigners and had moved away from other core practices of the "Japanese model" such as seniority-based promotion, lifetime employment, and *keiretsu* networks.

Lack of confidence in long-standing institutions was not limited to the economic sphere, but rather naturally extended into domestic politics. The end of the Cold War internationally and the collapse of the bubble economy domestically presented a serious challenge to the long-ruling LDP, which had based its nearly forty years in power on a platform of anticommunism and economic growth.[17] Without the anchor of the LDP to guide security policy making in the new post–Cold War era, Japan lacked the ability to move in any single new direction to respond to changes abroad and at home. While a wide range of proposals were put forth from across the political spectrum regarding Japan's next international role,[18] in great contrast to the time of Japan's last major political renegotiation on security issues, this time there was a default position of staying the course. With the conflicting pulls of the first years of the post–Cold War international system compounded by political and economic reform at home, the security identity of domestic antimilitarism continued to shape Japan's responses to pressing security concerns.

The mid-1990s was a period of great turmoil in Japan's party politics, leading to the rise of the first non–LDP government in thirty-eight years briefly in 1993 under Prime Minister Morihiro Hosokawa, and then Prime Minister Tsutomu Hata in 1994. The selection of a Socialist prime minister, Tomiichi Murayama, in coalition with the LDP in June 1994, symbolized the fluidity of party alignment in a Japan wracked by systemic changes both internationally and domestically. T. J. Pempel (1998) writes: "After twenty-five years of exceptional electoral stability and party stability, parties split and recombined with the speed and unpredictability of amoebae, but totally without policy or socioeconomic logic" (p. 1).

Nowhere was this lack of policy logic clearer than with the ascension of Toichi Murayama to the prime ministership with LDP support, requiring Murayama to reverse over forty years of standing policy of the JSP/DSP (Japan Socialist Party/Democratic Socialist Party) against the U.S.-Japan Security Treaty and alliance with the United States in general, dating back to their "three principles of peace" platform adopted in 1949.[19] The idea of neutrality embodied in the JSP/DSP foreign policy position, however, no longer made sense after the end of the Cold War. Thus, even more than the LDP, the JSP/DSP had lost its raison d'être with the dissolution of the Soviet Union. In fact, as Michael Green and Richard Samuels (1994a) note, although the LDP suffered major losses due to large-scale defections from the party in the mid-1990s (particularly in the 1993 House of Representatives election), the total number of conservative politicians elected in 1993 *increased*, while the number of socialists elected dropped by half (p. 4).

Given this dramatic change in Japan's party politics, particularly the near demise of the one party, the JSP/DSP, which had consistently sought to limit the redevelopment of Japan's military capacity—one might expect that Japan's security policy would move equally dramatically to the right. That this did not take place is best explained by the continued power of the postwar security identity of domestic antimilitarism, reinforced by weakened opposition parties that continued to lobby in support of its central tenets for their own electoral advantage.

The Democratic Party of Japan (DPJ), the primary opposition party to emerge, was divided roughly into two camps on foreign policy that mirror the wings of the political spectrum of those who collaborated to form the party. On one end of the party are former socialists who continued generally to oppose the U.S.-Japan Security Treaty, despite the JSP's acknowledgment and acceptance of the security treaty and the SDF at the time of Prime Minister Murayama's ascendancy to the prime ministership. On the other end is a more conservative wing of the DPJ that embraced the treaty and sought to maintain and even strengthen the U.S.-Japan alliance while achieving more flexibility from the United States and empowerment of Japan in the security relationship. In his political tome, for example, then-DPJ leader Yukio Hatoyama (1996) both publicly called for constitutional revision—including of Article Nine—and publicly speculated about whether a strong, healthy alliance with the United States would not be better served by a mutual defense treaty in which there were no forward-based U.S. troops in Japan.

Ultimately, it continued to be the LDP that was the most supportive of incremental steps toward a greater security role for Japan—using each crisis as a way to move a step closer to that ultimate objective: the tried and true strategy of "reach, reconcile, reassure." However, the more dovish elements of the LDP—supported by an only slowly growing public awareness of the evolving security discussions centered on questions of national interest—served as significant constraints on LDP action, even without the opposition parties who also opposed most moves in this direction. In addition, although the New Komei Party (NKP, the former Komeitō), the LDP's coalition partner, had become much more accepting of the LDP's drive for more capacity for the Japan Defense Agency (JDA)/SDF and a bolder Japan in international affairs in general, it also served as a moderating influence on strident LDP policy proposals throughout this period, as it had in the past and did in the post-1998 period as well.

An Evolving Relationship with the United States

The end of the Cold War and the reminder of the first Gulf War that the previous clarity and relative order of the superpower rivalry had been superseded by a less predictable set of messy, hot conflicts raised anxiety levels in Japan about U.S. military forces stationed in Japan. For many, the threat to Japan from the Soviet Union was the sole reason that justified the forward-based deployment of U.S. forces. When the Soviet Union fell, the next most oft-cited threat in the mid-1990s was the paranoid, failed regime of inherited-leadership communism in North Korea. More recently, China has more clearly become the underlying focus of concern of both economic and security strategists thinking about future outcomes in the Asia Pacific region. Still, many Japanese citizens hoped for a U.S. withdrawal and yearned for Japan to become a neutral player in Asia unencumbered by the presence of a foreign military on its soil.

Others in Japan thought the end of the Cold War meant that the departure of U.S. forces from Japan would allow Japan to step forward as a "normal" nation, with normal military forces, and normal international responsibilities—relegating the past into the past once and for all. This group sought roles for Japan in the United Nations Peacekeeping Operations (UNPKO), in which Japanese played valuable roles in such places as Cambodia and Bosnia.[20] But beyond this effort to be seen as making a solid "international contribution," many thought that the time had come for Japan to define itself as a "normal" nation by shedding the political compromise of domestic antimilitarism that had preempted military organization and development on the international stage. LDP power broker-turned-renegade Ichiro Ozawa became the most visible advocate in the early to mid-1990s that Japan needed to redefine itself with the publication of his political tome which called, literally, for Japan to become a "normal nation" (futsu no kuni).[21]

The stress on Japan's security identity, already aggravated by the confusion of priorities and direction evident in U.S. behavior after the fall of the Soviet Union and after the successful military action against Saddam Hussein's forces in the Gulf region, was worsened further by the uncertainty about the long-term intentions of the United States in the region.[22] To counter the fear of a U.S. withdrawal evident throughout Asian capitals, a group of defense-focused policy planners in the Clinton administration, led by Joseph Nye—who served first as chairman of the National Intelligence Council and then as the Pentagon's assistant secretary for International Security Affairs—expressed an intention not to draw down further forces from Asia but rather to maintain a long-term presence of one hundred thousand troops in both the Asian and European military theaters (Nye 1993). The so-called Nye Initiative, as expressed in the 1995 East Asia Strategy Report (also known as the Nye Report) published by the Office of the Secretary of Defense, confidently conveyed the notion of security deliverables, in part, as the quantitative number of troops to be maintained, mirroring the Clinton administration's economic policy effort of trying to achieve "results-oriented" trade using similar numeric indicators.

For the United States, the most serious question facing its relationship with Japan in the 1990s was how to preserve the extraordinarily close bilateral relationship enjoyed during most of the Cold War.[23] For Japan, the long-term presence of American troops in Japan—continuously stationed there since the end of the Second World War—grated on many Japanese as a limit on national sovereignty and identity, fueling growing nationalist discourse in some quarters, and a more moderate push to Asia and "Asian values" in other quarters. Many articulations in the 1990s of Japan's future as a "normal nation" (*futsu no kuni*) used as a benchmark the degree of independence that Japan secures from the United States. Furthermore, Japanese independent technology development—as with surveillance satellites—was valued in part for its potential to disconnect Japan from American influence. If Japan were unfettered from U.S. leadership on defense planning and weapons system development, U.S. policy makers feared Japan could conceivably move in directions difficult for the United States to restrain. By contrast, joint development of an expensive and important new weapons system—as with the deepening of missile defense joint research currently in progress—would help lock Japan into its alliance with the United States by enmeshing the technological prowess and national security interests of both nations into a single system. Thus, the United States continued to act carefully and strategically in its efforts to "normalize" its close ally.

This strategy of enmeshing Japan into greater alliance cooperation appears to be the motivation for other cases of alliance deepening evident in the first decade of the post–Cold War period, such as the adoption of revised Guidelines for Japan-

U.S. defense cooperation in 1997 and the preceding joint statement on security by President Clinton and Prime Minister Hashimoto in 1996. The importance of the U.S.-Japan alliance to the United States is fundamental to U.S. military strategy in the Asia Pacific region. Indeed, the ability to maintain a robust presence of U.S. troops in Asia—particularly in Okinawa and at the U.S. military bases in Yokosuka, Yokota, and Misawa on the Japanese main island of Honshu—with the support of a dormant, but potent, Japanese military capability was viewed as the key security stabilizer in Asia (United States Department of Defense 1995). Many defense planners argue that the United States cannot maintain its current power projection capabilities without Japan as its strategic partner, even a partner that develops a more independent profile.

In September 1995, the brutal rape of a twelve-year-old girl by three American military personnel ignited the largest civil protests against the U.S. bases in Japan since 1960. Okinawa's governor, Masahide Ota, led the local prefecture in resolutions calling for the withdrawal of American troops and gathered the emotional sympathy of Japanese throughout Japan who may have felt guilty about the relative lack of economic gains that Okinawa had experienced in contrast to the rest of Japan as well as for leaving the Okinawans to shoulder nearly 80 percent of the United States military presence in Japan. Ota forced a Supreme Court showdown when he refused to sign renewal leases providing American forces the right to use the land they long had been leasing for bases and related facilities. While Ota lost the battle with the central government in Tokyo, it did inject new political forces into what had always been a very stable axiom—that U.S. forces were in Japan (and Okinawa) indefinitely. That axiom was called into question at the end of the Cold War, which captured the attention and imagination of many Japanese, including former Prime Minister Hosokawa and Democratic Party leader Yukio Hatoyama, both of whom have called for an alliance with the United States without a permanent U.S. presence in Japan (Hosokawa 1998, Hatoyama 1996).

Two examples of the leverage that the United States maintained over Japan's security policy apparatus show a change in Japan's security response between the decade of the 1990s discussed in this chapter and that of the twenty-first century discussed in Chapter 7. The first, the international coalition led by the United States against Saddam Hussein and Iraq at the beginning of the 1990s, is discussed below. The second, the international coalition against terror a decade later in response to the September 11, 2001, attacks on the United States, is discussed in Chapter 7. In the first case, Prime Minister Toshiki Kaifu's inability to rearticulate or renegotiate the security identity of domestic antimilitarism in order to make decisive commitments to send troops, medics, or other resources immediately to the Gulf haunted many Japanese security planners into the twenty-first century.

From the U.S. perspective, however, it is not clear that the United States ever wanted Japanese materials or soldiers on the front lines of conflict, or even on the back lines. Problems of joint coordination, command, and control between U.S. and other national forces were already overwhelming U.S. logistical planners; the United States did not need to further add the untested and uncoordinated Japanese personnel who might be sent into the field. By contrast, the United States did need money to support the massive deployment of troops in the region, a deployment of nearly half a million personnel. The security identity of domestic antimilitarism alone should have been sufficient to constrain the government's early, relatively eager, self-initiated response to participate in the Gulf War (as discussed below), but the additional factor of U.S. preferences in this direction ensured the final outcome of only financial support during the time of combat operations.

Adapting to New Challenges and Reaffirming Core Principles

Japanese political leadership evidently faced many challenges at home and abroad in the first decade of the post–Cold War period, many demanding an alteration of existing security practices. That the postwar security identity of domestic antimilitarism remained as resilient as it did is somewhat surprising. In particular, four areas of new security demands challenged the three tenets of the hegemonic security identity (see summary in Table 6). Increased military roles and capabilities for the SDF called into question each of the three central tenets of the postwar security identity: no military role in policy making, no use of force to resolve international disputes except in self-defense, and no Japanese participation in foreign wars. A deepening military alliance with the United States called into question the third tenet in particular. Pressure to respond to the 1990–91 Gulf War by sending SDF forces to Kuwait or Iraq challenged Japan's commitment to tenets two and three, and its subsequent decision to allow the SDF to participate in UNPKO especially threatened the commitment to tenet three. Despite the fears of many, however, compromises were ultimately reached which served more to further reify the existing security identity than to challenge it in a fundamental way. In this way, the long-standing central tenets of the security identity were reproduced and reified in this new era even more than they were altered.

Increased Military Roles and the First Tenet of Domestic Antimilitarism

Of the three tenets of domestic antimilitarism that have embodied Japan's postwar security identity, it is the first—the proscription on the establishment of traditional armed forces—that is under the most pressure in the post–Cold War

TABLE 6

Post-Cold War Pressure on Japan's Postwar Security Identity

Pressure on Tenet 1: Increasing military roles and missions of the SDF
Pressure on Tenet 2: Dispatch of SDF abroad
Pressure on Tenet 3: Deepening military cooperation with the United States

period. The first decade after the end of the U.S. superpower rivalry with the Soviet Union saw a continued increase in Japan's indigenous defense capability and increasing participation of the JDA and SDF in formulating strategy and aspects of Japan's broader foreign policy. The 1990s also witnessed greater defense cooperation between Japan and its close military ally, the United States. Both trends continued from early in the Cold War period but appeared to intensify in the 1990s. The major change, of course, between these two periods was the collapse of the principal adversary designated in Japan's defense-planning documents—the Soviet Union. Since its founding, the SDF's primary objective was to protect Japan from a large-scale invasion coming from the Soviet Union. For this reason, Japan's Ground Self-Defense Force (GSDF) was designed and sized to repel such an attack from the north. Although the possibility of such an invasion clearly declined in the 1990s with the collapse of the Soviet Union—a stark contrast to the mock invasion training exercise conducted by the Soviet Union in 1985, interpreted as a response to Prime Minister Nakasone's focus on increasing Japan's defense capabilities (Lind 2004)—Japan's defense posture retained a counterinvasion focus through the 1990s. It would not be until the middle of the first decade of the twenty-first century that such strategic planning would formally be altered in a fundamental way.[24]

The issue in the 1990s regarding the increasing stature of Japan's military is not that many politicians and policy makers were advocating a renaming of the Self-Defense Forces to the more traditional army, navy, and air force monikers (though some were), but that the mission of the SDF and its development as an independent state actor is steadily (and has been) increasing. This mission creep is not unique to the post–Cold War era, but it continued and further intensified in the 1990s. In the area of SDF mission, a significant expansion of military roles took place when the Maritime Self-Defense Forces (MSDF) sent minesweepers to the Persian Gulf in 1991 and the GSDF participated in UNPKO in Cambodia in 1992. In the area of an increased policy-making role, institutional enhancements of the JDA, such as the founding of the centralized Defense Intelligence Headquarters in 1997, the creation of a strategic planning unit in 1998, and the training and analysis role delegated to the JDA for the operation of surveillance satellites, all point toward greater legitimacy for the JDA and SDF as government actors.[25] In diplomatic circles as well, JDA and SDF participation is increasing, as evidenced by the growing number of defense-specific diplomatic forums and exchanges, and the increased number of defense attachés posted to Japanese embassies abroad (Oros 2002, JDA 2005). To a great extent, Japan's military—in image, at least—had been "normalized."

The continuing constraints of Japan's postwar security identity remain evident even as the capabilities of the SDF and JDA increase, however. For example, Japan's enhanced crisis management capabilities—developed in response to increased threat perceptions both domestically (the sarin gas attacks in Tokyo in 1995 and the Kobe earthquake also in 1995) and internationally (the takeover the Japanese ambassador's residence in Lima, Peru, in 1996, repeated intrusions of "suspicious ships" into Japanese waters, and regular North Korean missile testing)—served to deepen Japan's defensive posture and reinforced the principle of civilian control in practice. Moreover, specifically regarding the issue of surveillance satellites (discussed in further detail in Chapter 5), the JDA/SDF did not succeed in securing formal control of the satellites, which resides instead in the Cabinet Intelligence Research Office (CIRO).[26]

Moreover, despite the new roles and capabilities of Japan's SDF, debate over the constitutionality of the SDF continued in this post–Cold War period, with extensive public opinion polling over the past fifty years showing anywhere from a majority to a sizable minority believing that these forces are *not* constitutional, that is, that they violate Article Nine of Japan's postwar constitution which renounces the sovereign right of the exercise of military power—despite the JSP/DSP flip-flop on this issue, a new policy stance that arguably did the most to lead to its decline in popularity among voters. Still, Japan's Self-Defense Forces in this period boasted an annual budget second in the world only to that of the United States, or fourth in terms of purchasing power parity.[27] Security analysts actively debate the capability of these forces, but there is no doubt that they rank among the largest and most powerful armed forces in the world. Equally important, however, is that strict rules and norms limit their effective deployment and power projection capabilities—reinforced by the continuing influence of Japan's postwar security identity.

Another example of the continuing constraints of domestic antimilitarism, on the rhetorical front at least, is that the JDA remained a mere "agency" (*cho*) and was not (yet) uplifted to "ministry" (*sho*) status, despite the opportunity presented through the large-scale central government reorganization that took effect on January 1, 2001—and despite, as well, calls by a vocal minority for an upgrading of the agency's institutional status. In this latter example, however, bureaucratic politics among the ministries that faced diminished power as a result of potential JDA elevation in status also undoubtedly played a supporting role to the continuing influence of the postwar security identity on this security practice; and as discussed in Chapter 7, this continued restraint in the 1990s.

Another related area of policy innovation regarding the expanding capabilities of the JDA/SDF in the first post–Cold War decade is in the area of expanded military cooperation with the United States under the framework of the U.S.-Japan alliance, activities that additionally challenged the third tenet of domestic antimilitarism prohibiting Japanese participation in conflict abroad. In 1995 the issue of collective defense within the context of the alliance again was brought to the fore with the revision of Japan's National Defense Program Outline (NDPO), which expanded the mission of the SDF from defense against a "small-scale invasion" to a defense role in "situations in the area surrounding Japan that have a direct impact on the security of Japan"[28]—though legislation enabling the implementation of this new agreement was not passed until 1999, the period discussed in Chapter 7. At the same time the 1978 Guidelines for Defense Cooperation between the United States and Japan were in the process of being revised. At this time conservative politicians within the LDP and the opposition New Frontier Party publicly pushed for the government to explicitly recognize the right of collective self-defense. They were joined in their efforts by the conservative-leaning *Yomiuri Shimbun*, which included explicit language on the right of collective self-defense in the proposed draft constitution it published in support of constitutional revision (*Kempo Yomiuri Teigen* [The Yomiuri Constitution Proposal], www3.yomiuri.co.jp.). LDP coalition government with the JSP hindered strong support of constitutional revision or reinterpretation, however, and ultimately the new guidelines that were drafted relied on the traditional interpretation of Japan's role within the framework of individual self-defense. Even within this traditional interpretation, the SDF secured a greatly expanded role within the alliance that provided crucial operational support for U.S. forces involved in conflicts in East Asia.[29] Extensive discussion between the United States and Japan over post–Cold War defense roles culminated in 1997 in new "guidelines" for defense cooperation which expanded the role of the SDF in the alliance as well as the scope of joint U.S.-Japan military operations.[30] Supporting legislation necessary to implement the new guidelines was not approved by the Diet until 1999, however, and some remaining (and controversial) legislation was not passed until after the September 11, 2001, attacks on the United States, the nature of which limited to a large extent the usual influence of the security identity of domestic antimilitarism on policy debate on this latter development. Also within the rubric of greater defense cooperation with the United States in the post–Cold War period would be included greater cooperation on new weapons development and joint research on a theater missile defense system for East Asia discussed in Chapter 6.

The Persian Gulf War and the Second and Third Tenets of Domestic Antimilitarism

The first security shock to post–Cold War Japan, apart from the broad fear of a possible disengagement of the United States from Asia, was the expectation of Japan to contribute to the Persian Gulf War of 1990–91. This called into question Japan's commitment to the second and third tenets of domestic antimilitarism, regarding Japan's renunciation of the use of force to settle international disputes and its prohibition on participation in conflict abroad. This demand led to the first new nationwide debates over Japan's international security role in decades (as opposed to the long-simmering and increasingly stale JSP-led criticism of the constitutionality of the SDF and opposition to the security alliance with the United States), but the debates and resulting policy outcomes were plagued by conflicting demands on the political system and exceedingly slow action.[31] The final result, a significant monetary contribution to fund the war effort (but *not* weapons or soldiers themselves, nor funding for them)[32] and deployment of token MSDF vessels after active conflict had ceased upheld the long-standing tenets of domestic antimilitarism. Moreover, it should be noted, the stated objective of the later-deployed MSDF minesweepers was that potential mines represented environmental risks, rather than security hazards. Such a response closely mirrored Japan's response to demands to participate in the Korean and Vietnam wars led by the United States—providing only rhetorical support and, in general, action greatly limited by Japan's postwar security identity.

Multiple factors contributed to Japan's delayed and ultimately nonmilitary contribution to the first Gulf War—security identity alone did not determine that outcome, but it did offer a political solution and ultimately structured the policy response. Other domestic factors that contributed to the slow and mixed response to the crisis include, first, a characteristically slow political process in general, which at the time was especially bureaucracy-driven and not typically expected to make quick decisions over unexpected developments. Second, the nature of the response was affected by the LDP having only recently lost its control of the Diet, for the first time since its founding in 1955, due to the loss of its majority in the House of Councilors in the 1989 election. Unlike in more recent times, when the LDP has adjusted to this circumstance (it had not regained control of the Upper House as of 2007 and looks unlikely to even in the coming decade) by entering into a formal coalition with the minority KMT (Komeitō) party, in 1990 the LDP had no prenegotiated, stable ally, which greatly slowed the legislative process. A third domestic factor is the nature of the prime minister, Toshiki Kaifu, who has been described as less keen on SDF deployment abroad than many in his party and who himself was from one of the smaller and weaker factions within the LDP, further lessening his power within his own party to push for a controversial policy. This stands in contrast to Prime Minister Nakasone in the 1980s, or later Prime Minister Koizumi in the twenty-first century. In the roughly fourteen years between the five-year tenures of Nakasone and Koizumi, ten prime ministers would lead Japan, some for very short periods and with quite poor results, Kaifu among them. Finally, on the international level, the first dispatch of the SDF overseas generated significant concern especially among Japan's Asian neighbors, a factor many Japanese politicians and others cited as a reason to proceed with extreme caution (Midford 2003). As discussed in Chapter 7, when the next urgent request for SDF deployment would come from the United States, after September 11, 2001, Japan would have nearly ten years of experience of peaceful, humanitarian deployments of its SDF to build upon and use as reassurance to placate skeptical neighbors.

United Nations Peacekeeping Operations and the Third Tenet of Domestic Antimilitarism

The most dramatic and perhaps far-reaching policy evolution in the first post–Cold War decade was the tardy result of the many debates over Japan's contribution to the Persian Gulf War, the decision to allow the Self-Defense Forces to be deployed as part of the United Nations Peacekeeping Operations (UNPKO).[33] Legislation to allow Japanese SDF personnel to be deployed in UNPKO missions failed in the Diet during the period of Gulf War tension. However, the International Peace Cooperation Law was passed by the Diet in August 1992, permitting the first foreign deployment of the SDF since its creation, to Cambodia in September of that same year. SDF participation in UNPKO in Cambodia was followed by deployments to Mozambique (1993–95), Rwanda (1994), and the Golan Heights (1996–present) within the time period discussed in this chapter, through August 1998.[34] Although this development is widely viewed as the most dramatic departure in Japanese security policy in the post–Cold War period, this policy outcome again served to further codify the security identity of domestic antimilitarism rather than challenge it in a fundamental manner.

Arguably, the primary reason for Japan's lack of legislation to allow for SDF participation during the Gulf War—the ill-fated United Nations Peace Cooperation Corps (UNPCC) bill—was the Kaifu government's attempt to pass legislation that clearly would have exceeded the boundaries of the security identity of domestic antimilitarism. The Kaifu government attempt to force through legislation that specified not just a combat support role but potentially a combat role as well was unacceptable to both the Diet and the general public. Although stressing the external pressure limitations of the legislation, Paul Midford (2003) essentially makes this point:

> The PKO law enacted in 1992 essentially limited SDF participation to humanitarian relief and economic development assistance such as providing medical services, building roads, bridges, etc.—roles not altogether dissimilar from those the SDF has long played domestically as a de facto disaster relief corps.... Consequently, the PKO law represented less a shift in Japanese public opinion than a watering down of the more ambitious UNPCC bill, to bring it closer to the rather stable preferences of Japanese voters. (p. 340)

Even with a broadly more acceptable framework of a humanitarian mission embedded within a United Nations or other international organization, it took numerous successful deployments abroad before the public came to accept this extension of previous boundaries of the security identity as legitimate.

Looking Forward, Looking Backward

The process of reimagining and reconstructing Japanese security practices for a post–Cold War period continues today, with its final outcome uncertain. In tracing how debates over Japan's future role developed in the first ten years of the post–Cold War period, this chapter has sought to highlight the most important factors that must be monitored in the future, and which present the greatest challenges to the shape of Japan's long-held security identity of domestic antimilitarism. Among the most prominent domestic and international factors, two demand close attention on each front. On the domestic front these are the ongoing political realignment taking place related to the possible emergence of a true two-party system and Japan's continued economic challenges despite recent signs of a new economic vitality. On the international front these are future U.S. security policy in the region and the future actions of Japan's close neighbors, North Korea and China in particular.

There is no consensus among analysts about the direction of Japanese security policy suggested by the policy decisions of the 1990s. Several groups among analysts can be identified. One such cluster interprets recent expansion of Japan's security role as a rise of Japanese militarism, fueled by a rising nationalism— despite the successes of constraining forces noted above. Another group continues to focus on Japan's past preoccupation with economic power and thus interprets even new security moves as the minimum necessary response to pressure from the United States and changes in the international environment. Yet another group sees a rise of "realist" thinking in Japan that reflects a deepening of Japan's security alliance with the United States and a move toward a more equal partnership. Even those employing the same data and cases often come to different conclusions.

When a concerned public—domestic or foreign—speaks of fears of a rise of Japanese militarism, it is not clear exactly what they mean. Rising militarism can be signified by a number of varying factors, including a rise in militaristic attitudes among the Japanese public, a growth of the offensive (or defensive) military capability of the SDF, further integration with Japan's U.S. military superpower ally, and a growing independent defense capability among them. In the cases of arms exports, the use of outer space and surveillance satellites, and missile defense discussed in Chapters 4, 5, and 6 respectively, it is important to consider a definition of militarism that factors in a potential rise of a military-industrial complex that hitherto has not existed in postwar Japan. With the discussion of indigenous development (or joint development) of major defense systems, the question arises not only whether Japan's security infrastructure will change as a result of the end of the Cold War, but perhaps whether its supporting economic infrastructure will change as well. Once again, this issue returns focus to the question of security identity. From the outset, it is important to note that Japan has not suddenly developed a new technological or economic capacity to undertake such projects as missile defense or surveillance satellites, however, but rather a new will to do so. Japan long has possessed a technological base for missile development (as evidenced by its commercial rocket program), though its protection under the U.S. nuclear umbrella (and strong opposition from the United States) has acted as a disincentive for Japan to develop this technology for military purposes. Moreover, the security identity of domestic antimilitarism has made such activities politically costly.

It is because the decision to limit restrictions on arms exports, to deploy surveillance satellites, and to initiate development of missile defense could mark a beginning of a new era in Japanese defense production—or defense activity in general—that it is important to monitor such developments closely. Accordingly, one goal of the following chapters is to elucidate the areas of these policies to which careful attention should continue to be paid in the early twenty-first century. These chapters will analyze important Japanese security policy precedents to ascertain whether and how the security identity of domestic antimilitarism has in the past and continues in the post–Cold War period to influence security practice. After a consideration of these specific cases, Chapter 7 will return to the question of how best to monitor possible changes in Japan's security identity, and how Japan's security practice is likely to evolve in the early twenty-first century.

4

Limiting Conflict Through Arms Export Restrictions

The export of weapons—to friends, to enemies of enemies, or simply to those willing to pay—typifies to many what "normal" states do to further their foreign policy objectives. By this definition, Japan is not normal. Given Japan's status in the world as a leader among the most advanced manufacturing powers, its history of being a successful exporter in other areas, and the presence of a substantial domestic defense industry,[1] the question of why Japanese firms largely fail to export defense-related products deserves an explanation not readily provided by interest-based theories typically deployed to explain industrial policy in Japan (e.g., Johnson 1982, Uriu 1996). No Japanese firms are present in the top ten lists of major arms manufacturers; only one is present in the top twenty.[2] The explanation for this development lies not in a postwar culture of pacifism but rather in evolving postwar politics structured by the security identity of domestic antimilitarism.

The third tenet of Japan's postwar security identity—no participation in conflict abroad—in particular is brought into question by the idea of arms exports. Providing weapons to conflict areas might draw Japan into a military conflict and certainly undermines any principled pacifist stance held by the Japanese. More broadly, the first tenet of the postwar security identity—no traditional armed forces—also comes into play to the extent that arms exports can be seen as a military tool of foreign policy, as clearly they were during the Cold War as seen in the policies of not only the United States and the Soviet Union but also the United Kingdom, France, and even China, Cuba, and East Germany. Indeed, Japan's defense white papers regularly decry neighboring states' provision of weapons to other states—in particular Russia and China (e.g., JDA 2005, pp. 31, 58). Japan's arms export policies are only one of many areas where the effect of security identity is seen on Japanese security practice, but they are illustrative of how this interplay takes place in numerous policy areas. Despite a widespread view that Japan would "adjust" its restrictive export controls in the post–Cold War period, only a single limited exception to the broader policy has been proclaimed since the last exception in 1983. And while pressure continues to be placed on the policy despite the December 2004 exception, further change faces significant barriers imposed by this security identity of domestic antimilitarism.

Given the mixed security policy outcomes of the immediate postwar period, one must ask why arms export restrictions succeeded where other antimilitarist policy initiatives—such as the prohibition on all arms production—failed. Moreover, one must ask why it took until 1967 for arms export restrictions to be codified into a clear, publicly proclaimed government policy statement, and even then, why this policy position was not passed directly as legislation. Contrary to the many explanations of this policy rooted in domestic norms or culture, or in domestic politics, Japan's initial arms export ban—established at the time of its surrender in the Second World War—is unequivocally the result of *international* politics: it was imposed by the United States and its allies. Thus, the puzzle that must be explained is not how the ban arose initially, but why it was maintained after the Occupation and how it evolved over time as it did. A partial ban on arms exports was not declared as official Japanese government policy until 1967, when it was announced by Prime Minister Eisaku Satō. Later, the ban was strengthened by Prime Minister Takeo Miki in 1976 and then further codified into official government policy through a series of policy statements. It remains a policy declaration that can—and has—been altered by the prime minister to accommodate demands of powerful political actors at home and abroad.

Thus, the case of Japan's arms export "ban" is not as solid as is often portrayed. First, many of the restrictions in place are the result of international agreements, the same restrictions followed even by the United States. Second, a nominally comprehensive arms export ban dates only to 1976, over thirty years after Japan's defeat in the Second World War. And third, even this policy is riddled with exceptions in enforcement and by the significant practice of allowing dual-use exports, products or components that can be shown to have even a single civilian use, unless this is prohibited by a separate international agreement.[3] Moreover, a 1983 exception allowing technology exports to the United States, and the more recent December 2004 exception to allow for weapons component transfers related to missile defense to the United States, further reduces the de facto restrictions imposed by the Japanese state. The combination of exceptions for dual use and for the United States will undoubtedly allow for increased Japanese participation in weapons exports in future; it already has done so.

Still, Japan's arms export policies provide a good measure of Japan's normalization of security practice. A realization of unrestricted weapons exports by Japanese manufacturers or the provision of military aid by the Japanese state itself would signal a shift of Japan's security identity of domestic antimilitarism. As with many recent Japanese security policies, while there has been some movement in this direction, the scale of movement is small compared to what would have to take place to symbolize identity shift. Moreover, there is absolutely no indication that Japanese firms or the Japanese state is poised to begin large-scale export of weapons in the foreseeable future.

A number of factors contributed to the establishment and maintenance of Japan's arms export ban in the postwar period. Previous research has highlighted many of these, though no study of the policy has systematically evaluated them as competing explanations.[4] Often the arms export ban is mentioned in the general literature on Japanese foreign policy as one example of Japan's "pacifist" culture, though rarely is it pointed out that the effective domestic ban dates only from 1976 and that there are many exceptions to the policy.[5] Several excellent studies of Japan's defense industry in general (Green 1995, Samuels 1994, Chinworth 1992, Renwick 1995) also address arms export policies, but only briefly.[6] Richard Samuels provides the most thorough discussion of arms export restrictions within the context of political controversy surrounding defense production in general, though he too fails to problemize Japan's arms export policy independent of defense production issues in general. Despite this, Samuels's explanation for limited defense production provides a viable alternative, though complementary, identity-based explanation for Japan's arms export policies.[7] His explanation for the arms export ban is incomplete, however. First, on the economic level, it fails to account for why defense producers sought at times throughout the postwar period to export defense production, as Samuels himself details at various points in his text. Clearly they did see profit potential in arms export. Second, on the ideological level, Samuels's technonationalist framework does not systematically incorporate countervailing pressure on this ideology. Without appreciating the security identity of domestic antimilitarism, and the politics surrounding it, it is difficult to understand why "technonationalist" Japanese would oppose arms exports if such exports would help to further subsidize technological development and independence—an observation which clearly illustrates the need to acknowledge and conceptualize simultaneous and competing identities and the effect of this phenomenon on policy outcomes. Samuels does broadly address the effect of Japan's postwar security identity on Japan's arms export policies through his regular reference to limitations imposed by "public opinion," but it remains a puzzle within his framework why public opinion would so regularly conflict with the "ideology" of the elites, whom the public chooses to make national policy. A focus on the security identity of domestic antimilitarism provides such an explanation.

Consideration of three traditional solutions to the puzzle of Japan's lack of arms exports elucidates why a more sophisticated theoretical framework incorporating security identity is necessary to explain Japan's outlier status among advanced industrial democracies on this issue. The first traditional explanation to Japan's limited arms exports is that Japanese firms do not *want* to export defense-related production. This explanation is not as straightforward as it appears on the surface. To the extent that this is correct, one must ask, why not? Two factors in particular deserve attention. First, the defense-related production of most firms constitutes a small percentage of their total business and so is not the focus of their strategic planning. Second, and in a similar vein, these firms which specialize in other, usually consumer-focused products fear a domestic backlash if they become known as "merchants of death" (*shi no shonin*, in Japanese). Both of these factors, while based on economic logic, derive fundamentally from the political context surrounding Japan's postwar security identity of domestic antimilitarism.

The second simple solution to the puzzle of arms export restrictions is that potential arms exporters have been constrained by more powerful political actors. This explanation similarly contains the kernel of a complete explanation but is also not as straightforward as it appears. In Japan today, and in the immediate postwar period, firms engaged in defense-related production were among Japan's most powerful political actors. While counterfactual arguments are fraught with complexity, it seems clear that if the actors had been able to agree on a policy of arms exports, they should have succeeded in achieving this goal to at least some extent. So why did they not? Part of the answer refers back to the first solution offered above. There was no clear consensus on this goal. Powerful firms were forced to balance competing priorities within their operations, as well as their domestic reputations with the general public. Another important part of the explanation, however, is that in fact Japanese firms *have* exported defense-related production throughout the postwar period, particularly before a partial ban on such exports was finally declared in 1967 and later through the loophole of "dual-use" manufactures. Indeed, the boost to the Japanese economy created by weapons-related production during the Korean War was instrumental in Japan's economic recovery after the Second World War.[8]

Still, it is not the case that Japanese manufacturers got their way entirely. Again, while counterfactual logic must be employed to address this question, it does not appear that they even mostly achieved their goals vis-à-vis arms exports. The numerous exceptions to the arms export ban help to explain how the gap between two vastly different policy preferences—to export arms or not—was bridged. A focus on the security identity of domestic antimilitarism explains how the two divergent policy preferences were reconciled. To understand how the policy evolved over time, however, we must first consider the international origins of Japan's initial arms export ban—the subject of the next section—and then consider how such international factors interacted with domestic politics and the emergent security identity of domestic antimilitarism in crafting Japan's actual arms export policy over time.

The External Origins of the Arms Export Ban, 1945–1952

Japan's arms export ban was initially a by-product of the terms of Japan's unconditional surrender at the end of the Pacific War in 1945 under Directive 82, cited in Chapter 2: to "insure that Japan will not again become a menace to the peace and security of the world . . . the existing economic basis of Japan's military strength must be destroyed and not permitted to revive."[9] After the "reverse course" in Allied policy toward the Occupation of Japan, sparked by the outbreak of the Cold War, defense industries were promoted by the United States as a way of enlisting Japan into the emerging Cold War front against the Soviet Union. The existence of a domestic Japanese defense industry led to concern over potential exports to states not friendly to the United States, however—a fear the United States faced in other areas of the world as well. In November 1949 the precursor to the Coordinating Committee on Multilateral Strategic Export Controls (COCOM) was organized secretly by the United States and its primary European allies to restrict the export of arms and related technology to the Soviet Union and its allies.[10] Japan was not an initial participant in the COCOM regime, but as Japan was under Allied Occupation at the time, the United States was able to apply stricter controls over Japanese arms exports by banning them entirely under the Foreign Exchange and Foreign Trade Law (FEFTL) and Export Trade Control Ordinance (ETCO), both of which took effect on December 1, 1949, one month after COCOM was established. Such legal controls on Japanese exports were necessary despite the Occupation control over Japan because responsibility for foreign trade had been restored to the Japanese government in February 1949.

The outbreak of the Korean War in 1950 marks a fundamental turning point in the area of defense production in Japan and thus should be identified as a second international factor contributing to Japan's arms export policies. Through the United States government policy of "special procurement" (tokujū),[11] the United

States encouraged the redevelopment of manufacturing—including defense-related—industry within the Japanese economy. It is estimated that nearly 70 percent
of Japanese exports between 1950 and 1952 were the direct result of such special
procurement (Samuels 1994, p. 133). Much of these exports were not arms exports
but rather in general support of the war effort, but a sizable amount was directly
arms-related manufactures, particularly after March 1952, when the United States
government officially reversed its policy prohibiting Japanese arms production
and began to solicit Japanese manufacturers to produce artillery, explosives, and
other arms-related material. Civilian items used by military forces abroad—such
as the Jeeps Nissan produced for the United States military under license—initiated public discussion in Japan of the so-called dual-use doctrine, a doctrine that
would later allow for a significant number of exports of defense material that
would appear on the surface to violate a principled arms export ban.

The Allied Occupation of Japan ended soon after the U.S. decision to encourage arms production in Japan, in April 1952. This opened up political space for the
Japanese public and policy makers to participate more fully in security policy formulation, including that related to arms production and arms exports. Beginning
at this point it becomes necessary to carefully consider domestic political factors
in the continuation of the Occupation-imposed arms export ban and the critical
determining role of the emerging security identity of domestic antimilitarism.

The Post-Occupation Policy of Restricted
Arms Exports, 1952–1964

This first period of Japan's domestic arms export policy corresponds with the end
of the Allied Occupation at one end and the escalation of the American war in
Vietnam (using their bases in Japan as a staging ground) on the other. It is in the
early part of this period that the new postwar security identity of domestic antimilitarism is crafted and begins to be institutionalized—as discussed in Chapter
2. As this institutionalization takes place, the effect of the new security identity
on arms exports is evident. In this period, the Occupation-imposed ban on arms
exports is *not* formally maintained, though significant limitations on arms exports
continued in large part due to intense politicization of the issue domestically.
Importantly, it is in this period that Japan redeveloped defense production, giving
rise to the idea of exporting this production. This set the pattern for the roughly thirteen-year period in which the question of arms exports was inextricably
linked to the broader question of arms production, and the even broader question
of remilitarization. Limitations on arms exports were offered for political purposes
to allow for the more important conservative political objectives of redeveloping

domestic arms production and deepening redevelopment of military forces in alliance with the United States—the practice of reach, reassure, reconcile. Thus, as with much of Japanese security policy, it was a compromise policy among multiple political actors and not a first choice for any. It is not until the following period, 1965–79, that formal bans on arms exports are declared as official government policy.

At the same time as the domestic political situation regarding defense was evolving, important developments in the international arena were taking place as well that had a direct impact on Japan's arms export policies. It is useful to briefly consider Japan's international obligations related to the control of defense-related production before examining its domestically generated policies in further detail.

International Prohibitions and the Creation of a Domestic Export Control Regime

At the end of the Allied Occupation in April 1952, regulating control of international trade—including arms exports—became vested in Japan's Ministry of International Trade and Industry (MITI), ironically, the former Ministry of Munitions. The establishment of a legal and administrative framework for arms production and arms export control was enacted through the Aircraft Manufacturing Industry Law of 1952 and the Arms Manufacturing Industry Law of 1953. In August 1952 Japan became a member of COCOM. In addition, the Japanese government agreed to restrictions beyond those of other COCOM members with regard to trade with China (Yasuhara 1986, pp. 86–88). Membership in COCOM, and the general issue of international agreements on the export of arms and related technology, is an important factor in considering Japan's arms export policy. Given the emerging Cold War context and Japan's reliance on the United States for its security, Japan had little choice but to toe the line on refraining from exports to the communist bloc.[12] Due to requirements under international agreements such as COCOM, Japan was obligated to develop mechanisms by which arms-related manufactures could be categorized, tracked, and—where necessary—prohibited. While disputes did arise over how effectively Japan implemented this requirement during the Cold War, overall Japan managed to fulfill this obligation with few notable lapses. The infamous Toshiba scandal of 1987, in which the Japanese firm Toshiba Machine was found to have sold sensitive milling equipment to the Soviet Union (which was used to improve the stealth capabilities of its nuclear submarines), is the largest dispute between the United States and Japan arising from such a lapse, though there are other cases as well.[13]

The prohibitions that limited arms exports were enforced through the FEFTL and ETCO, which had come into effect during the Occupation. The terms of

TABLE 7

Current Ministry of the Economy, Trade, and Industry (METI) Categories
for Export via the Foreign Exchange Control Law

1. Arms	9. Communications-related
2. Nuclear power	10. Sensors, lasers
3. Chemical and biological weapon	11. Avionics-related
4. Missile	12. Maritime-related
5. Cutting-edge material	13. Engines
6. Manufactured material	14. Munitions
7. Electronics	15. Miscellaneous equipment
8. Computers	16. Subset of Items 1–4 above

Source: Center for Information on Strategic Trade Control (CISTEC).
Note: The numbering system of the sixteen categories above reflects current usage. At the time of their introduction, a different numbering scheme was used.

these orders required a potential exporter to receive permission from MITI for the export of arms or arms production-related equipment.[14] This regulation was in addition to the special permits that were necessary even to be engaged in arms production domestically, under the 1952 Aircraft Manufacturing Industry Law and the 1953 Arms Production Industry Law (Tomiyama 1981, p. 3). MITI served as final arbiter regarding an application for export. There was not—and still is not—an outright, legislated ban on arms exports but rather a process by which such exports must be approved. In 1967, the criteria for this process were declared in the Diet by Prime Minister Satō as the "Three Principles for Arms Exports." Before 1967, various prime ministers and government officials released vague statements of intent, but decisions on specific export requests were made on the basis of behind-the-scenes political negotiation and lobbying. This process was unwieldy and often led to public criticism of Liberal Democratic Party (LDP) policy, giving an inroad to the Japan Socialist Party (JSP), pacifists, and others to criticize broader LDP security policy.[15] In this way, arms export policy is broadly illustrative of the difficulty of managing security policy in Japan before the contours of the new security identity of domestic antimilitarism was institutionalized.

In order to determine whether an export would be allowed during this first period after the Occupation, MITI required the applicant to classify its goods using sixteen discrete categories such as "missile" or "engine" (see Table 7). Actual "arms" belonged to categories 1 through 4 (and later, 16[16]), while civilian-use products were divided among categories 5 through 15.

This system set the basis for MITI's "dual-use doctrine," whereby a potential export would not be seen as an arms export if it could be shown to have even a single civilian use. For example, the export of semiconductors would not violate a

TABLE 8

Annex List One of the Export Trade Control Ordinance

197	Firearms and cartridges to be used therefore (including those to be used for emitting light or smoke), as well as parts and accessories thereof (excluding rifle scopes)
198	Ammunition (excluding cartridges) and equipment for its dropping for launching, as well as parts and accessories thereof
199	Explosives (excluding ammunition) and jet fuel (limited to that where the whole calorific value of which is 13,000 calories or more per gram)
200	Explosive stabilizers
201	Military vehicles and parts thereof
201–2	Military vessels and the hulls thereof, as well as parts thereof
201–3	Military aircraft, as well as parts and accessories thereof
202	Antisubmarine nets and antitorpedo nets as well as buoyant electric cable for sweeping magnetic mines
203	Armor plates and military steel helmets, as well as bulletproof jackets and parts thereof
204	Military searchlights and control equipment thereof
205	Bacterial, chemical and radioactive agents for military use, as well as equipment for dissemination, protection, detection, or identification thereof

Source: Center for Information on Strategic Trade Control (CISTEC).

Note: In the 1990s, the numbering and division of these categories was changed to make sixteen subcategories on a new list.

policy against arms exports even if integrated into a weapon as long as it was not designed specifically for that weapon and did not have capabilities beyond those used in nonmilitary products.[17]

The ETCO Annex List One divides category one ("arms") further into nine categories, items 197 to 205 (see Table 8). Since approval for export of items from categories 1 through 4 involved political uncertainties, the law stood as a barrier to arms exports—and was understood by potential exporters as such. There were a number of exceptions, particularly in the immediate postwar period, however, while opposing political forces argued over the appropriate policy regarding arms exports. According to statistics collected by the Stockholm International Peace Research Institute (SIPRI), nearly every year from 1953 to 1978 (from shortly after the Japanese government regained complete control over Japanese government policy—minus Okinawa—to shortly after the 1976 "new Three Principles" effectively ended overt arms exports) Japanese manufacturers exported ships and aircraft to be used by the militaries of developing states, particularly in Asia.[18] Japanese firms also exported pistols, rifles, ammunition, hand grenades, and other small-scale weapons. Still, what exports did take place diverged sharply from the level sought by major arms manufacturers. These exceptions, limited as they may have been, illustrate the limits of policy proscription based on security identity alone—sometimes political factors necessitate policy beyond the bounds of what the security identity should allow.

The Initial Postwar Politics of Arms Exports

The creation of the Self-Defense Forces (SDF) and the signing of the Mutual Defense Assistance Agreement (MDAA) in 1954 led to the passing of legislation reinitiating domestic arms production, though under the strict regulations requiring special permits and other concessions not imposed on other industries. The SDF were originally equipped with weapons provided through United States military aid, but Japanese manufacturers soon actively sought to serve this market. In addition, they sought to make up for the drop in special procurement by the United States military after the Korean War by increasing arms exports elsewhere in Asia. Though successful in the former, they were largely stymied in the latter. At this point in time, international-level explanations no longer account for this policy outcome, nor do norms or culture-based explanations account for how domestic defense production was reinitiated.

As discussed in previous chapters, since its founding in 1955 the conservative ruling LDP advocated and pursued a security policy which combined a program of limited rearmament with alliance with the United States. This approach to providing for Japan's national security policy was fundamentally contested by opposition parties, particularly the rival JSP, during the first two decades of the postwar period. When the rearmament issue did surface in the Japanese press—as it often did—one way that policy decisions were justified was by pointing to the economic advantages of defense production, appealing to the "technonationalist" values described by Richard Samuels and Michael Green in their work on the subject (Samuels 1994, Green 1995; also see Arisawa 1953 and Asai 1953 on this point), and later appealing specifically to Ikeda's "economy first" initiative. Japanese firms—like their counterparts in the United States and elsewhere, only on a much smaller scale—used defense production under government contract as a way of developing a greater technological base, particularly through licensing agreements with U.S. defense contractors. These agreements themselves provide some explanation for Japanese firms' lack of significant export of arms, since export was often prohibited in licensing agreements with U.S. firms. It is not a complete explanation, however. In fact, defense producers in Japan actively sought to increase arms exports in the 1960s but were limited both by the LDP itself and by public opposition expressed through the mass media, opposition party platforms, and other political outlets.

In this sense, one might argue that it was in fact domestic public opinion that directly limited arms exports but which grudgingly permitted defense production for domestic use. This argument, while not incorrect, does not further analysis of the final policy outcome, because it fails to delineate how public opinion was codified around these issues and how stability in this opinion was maintained over time. By contrast, attention to the security identity of domestic antimilitarism allows one to understand that what is often mistakenly perceived simply as public opinion is in fact the result of a political negotiation among major domestic actors—in particular economic actors and political parties—that traded off contending security policy preferences.

In the arms export debate, the JSP argued that if arms were exported from Japan, this meant that Japan produced more arms than needed for self-defense. This would contravene Article Nine of the Constitution, which prohibits the maintenance of "war potential." More broadly, it potentially runs against the third tenet of the postwar security identity of Japanese participation in foreign war through Japanese firms providing weapons for combat. Further, the JSP argued, an increase in arms production capacity could distort the entire industrial structure of the fledgling postwar economy and threaten the political control over arms production and, even worse, over arms themselves (Hummel 1988, p. 8). Such rhetoric appealed to the first tenet of domestic antimilitarism, a suspicion of the military and significant restrictions placed upon it.

Continued restrictions on arms exports immediately after the Occupation can be understood as the result of a coalition of three powerful political actors in postwar Japan—the Ministry of Finance (MOF), non-defense-related big business (particularly *Keidanren*, the Federation of Economic Organizations),[19] and the politicians and intellectuals of the pacifist left (as well as many in the center and even center-right).[20] This is not to say that these actors participated in a coordinated, formal coalition, but rather that their independent actions together suggested a similar policy prescription: limited arms exports. Each of these powerful actors advocated a continuation of the Occupation policy regarding the ban on the export of arms—and more broadly, opposed the redevelopment of a major domestic arms industry—for its own reasons. What allowed these actors to work together was the legitimating rhetoric generated by the security identity of domestic antimilitarism.

First in the arms export–limiting troika, MOF opposed arms exports as a result of its general position against the redevelopment of a domestic arms manufacturing industry, not as a discrete export issue. In an economic environment of scarce foreign exchange, MOF sought to channel available foreign exchange and investment funds into nondefense industries, particularly light manufacturing. MOF's position against defense production was mirrored by the most politically powerful economic organization of the time, Keidanren.

While Keidanren's Defense Production Committee (DPC) naturally advocated the redevelopment of an indigenous arms industry with exporting goals,
the body as a whole argued for investment in non-defense-related industries. In
fact, the issue of defense production was so politically sensitive in the early 1950s
that when Keidanren established its DPC, it was afforded unusual independence
in order to distance the DPC from the views of Keidanren as a whole (Keidanren
DPC 1964, Asai 1953, Hisakawa 1953, Samuels 1994). This arrangement mirrored
the treatment of defense hawks within the ruling LDP: the LDP also took care to
keep controversial voices (particularly those with militarist overtones) outside of
mainstream LDP factions.

Finally, politicians and intellectuals of the political left argued for a continuation
of the Occupation-era policy against arms exports for a different reason—either
due to a genuine commitment to security policies that would reduce international violence or in order to appeal to voters who held such views or both.[21] More
broadly, one can understand the policy positions of the left on security issues as
a way to differentiate their views from political conservatives in the Liberal and
Democratic parties, later the Liberal Democratic Party (LDP). After the decision
to continue significant barriers to export—if not an outright ban—after the end
of the Occupation in 1952, it was the "pacifist"/antimilitarist arguments of the left
that tended to be used as the rhetorical justification for the ban, as the tumultuous
debates of the 1950s made way for the economic focus of the 1960s. This rhetoric surrounding arms exports should be distinguished from that surrounding the
broader issue of defense production. By 1956, Prime Minister Ichiro Hatoyama
declared in the Diet that arms exports "must be handled cautiously" in order to
prevent Japan's involvement in international conflicts, signaling restraints imposed
on defense manufacturers.

One area that was not restrained, however, was Japanese manufacturers' sales
of defense-related items to U.S. forces based in Japan, which were exempted from
any control by MITI through the FEFTL and ETCO, despite technically being
considered exports by standard economic accounting practice. As time passed the
issue of defense production was more often justified by reference to its contributions to Japan's technological base. Even in this area, however, the security identity
of domestic antimilitarism was important because it limited the extent to which
the "technonationalist" argument could be employed. Although Prime Minister
Ikeda—who succeeded the badly tainted Prime Minister Kishi (who rammed
ratification of the U.S.-Japan Security Treaty through the Diet despite violent
opposition)—advocated an "economy first" policy to help smooth over political
wounds, this new economy was not meant to be a defense-related one. In fact, the
issue of defense production in general was one that Ikeda sought to avoid due to

its divisiveness. In terms of restoring domestic political consensus, the LDP faced problems with its policy of national rearmament. When Prime Minister Eisaku Satō succeeded Ikeda in 1964, restrictions on arms exports were relaxed somewhat. This period of relaxation was brief, however, leading soon after to a reinstatement of a sort: the first official policy declaration on arms exports, the Three Principles doctrine in 1967 discussed in the next section.

Institutionalizing Arms Export Restrictions, 1965–1979

The 1960s and 1970s was a period of growing economic prosperity and movement toward further institutionalization of the new security identity of domestic antimilitarism after a decade of arguing and debating its establishment. In this period, one sees clear movement toward the type of policies on arms exports one would expect to result from Japan's postwar security identity—a reduction in provision of weapons to conflict areas. Following Kathryn Sikkink's (1991) formulation, the security identity moves from the implementation to consolidation phase. As with the previous decade, however, this period shows continued political disagreement over appropriate policy regarding arms exports. These disagreements regularly flared up in media coverage and led to demonstrable policy shifts.[22]

The formal institutionalization of arms export restrictions, in line with the postwar security identity, was first stated officially as government policy by way of the Three Principles on Arms Exports in 1967 and was later expanded in scope and scale by subsequent government policy statements in the late 1970s and early 1980s, including a Diet resolution on this matter. Despite the political momentum resulting from this series of policies prohibiting various aspects of arms exports, however, the Diet failed to enact a single law proscribing arms exports (though it was, of course, unlawful to violate a MITI order requiring an application for the export of weapons, as per publicly declared government procedures). Important government policy statements of this time period include Prime Minister Satō's and Miki's Three Principles statements of 1967 and 1976 (respectively) as well as later government statements which refined the above, such as MITI minister Toshio Komoto's 1976 statement that the export of arms-manufacturing technology must comply with the Three Principles and Prime Minister Takeo Fukuda's 1977 statement that Japanese foreign direct investment abroad must also adhere to the spirit of the Three Principles (JDA 1998, *Defense of Japan*, pp. 397–99; Sato 2000, p. 7) (see Appendix 5 for the text of these statements). This collection of government policy statements served to institutionalize the more haphazard and de facto policy from the 1940s and 1950s as well as to provide more specific delineation of the policies regarding arms exports. These moves thus should be understood both as progress toward codifying an effective arms export ban and as evidence of the effect of the new postwar security identity on postwar security practice.

A Changing International Context: The Vietnam War, Okinawa Reversion, and the U.S.-Japan Security Relationship

The timing of Prime Minister Satō's official declaration of the Three Principles on Arms Exports in April 1967 must be understood within the larger domestic political context together with the broader international security environment. Within Japan, increasing American involvement in Vietnam brought back memories of American involvement on the Korean peninsula in the previous decade, as well as demands the U.S. government placed on Japan to support American foreign policy objectives at that time. Such issues were beginning to resurface in the context of Japan's potential support for American forces in Vietnam, most of whom would be routed through American bases on the Japanese mainland or in Okinawa.

As in the United States, the war in Vietnam was deeply unpopular among many Japanese who, like their American counterparts, protested American participation in the conflict loudly and often. One influential public relations stunt specifically sought to draw public attention to Japan's arms exports to the region. Held in Tokyo from August 28–30, 1967, by political agitators closely tied to the Japanese Communist Party (JCP), a war crimes "trial" modeled on a similar mock trial held in Stockholm earlier in the year pointed in particular to the role Japan played as a staging ground for U.S. forces, to Japanese government assistance in recruiting land-sea transport (LST) crews in Japan (who worked together with the American military around Vietnam), and to Japan's arms sales to U.S. forces and directly to countries in Southeast Asia (Havens 1987, pp. 127–29). Also in 1967, a train wreck at Shinjuku station, one of Tokyo's busiest rail commuting hubs, between a freight train and tank cars filled with jet fuel—nearly 5 million gallons of which passed through central Tokyo each day in support of the American war effort—reminded average Japanese of the extent of their involvement in a foreign war. This involvement violated the third tenet of the postwar security identity which proscribed involvement by Japanese in conflicts abroad. Growing public awareness of this issue forced a government response which came by way of the Three Principles for Arms Exports discussed below.

Deepening American involvement in the Vietnam conflict in the mid-1960s began to generate greater demand for Japanese exports in general, similar to the boost in demand created by the American military during the Korean War of the previous decade—"everything from lettuce to Sonys" in the words of one observer (Havens 1987, p. 84). While, as with the Korean War effort, much of this new demand was for nonmilitary goods, even the "Sonys" which had become so popular were not always completely benign. One shock to many Japanese, featured prominently in the press, was that Sony video cameras were being used to guide American-made missiles in the war. Sony president Akio Morita publicly apologized for this when it was exposed in the press and claimed that Sony knew nothing about this use of its product. Such incidents underscored the need for a specific government policy statement regarding arms exports.[23] Absent such a statement it seemed likely that the third tenet of domestic antimilitarism would erode.

By the early 1970s, despite the domestic political moves discussed below, once again Japanese business was playing an integral support role for American military activity abroad. The end result was succinctly stated by Thomas Havens (1987): "America's great pacifist ally earned several billions of dollars through direct and indirect procurement and advanced into the markets of Southeast Asia because of the war" (p. 84). According to Havens's calculations, Japanese business earned at least 1 billion dollars per year from direct and indirect procurement during the war. While Prime Minister Satō's "Three Principles" statement played to those who opposed Japanese involvement in the growing Vietnam conflict, ostensibly codifying the third tenet of domestic antimilitarism more concretely into government policy, the concrete effect of the Three Principles on Japanese industry was limited. At the same time the Japanese government did little to limit the use of essential American bases in Japan to support American objectives in Vietnam. Thus, once again the tension between Japan's alliance obligations and its postwar security identity was exposed, and the traditional three Rs of Japanese security policy formulation—reaching for expanded arms-related exports and expanded use of U.S. military bases in Japan, then reassuring the public through the twin "three principles" declarations related to arms exports and to nuclear weapons, and reconciling these positions in line with the security identity of domestic antimilitarism—were evident.

The war in Vietnam was not the only significant international event of relevance to the arms export ban. Another important process that was unfolding was the behind-the-scenes discussions between U.S. and Japanese policy makers over the "reversion" of the Japanese islands of Okinawa back to Japanese administrative control, the final part of Japanese territory occupied by the United States since the end of the Second World War. As Okinawa was the primary staging ground for the Vietnam War, these discussions were inextricably linked to the war, but an equally important factor was broader discussion of the Japanese security role in East Asia in the medium term.

A principal policy objective of the United States at this time was to ensure continued American access to its bases in Okinawa (and elsewhere in Japan) as

well as to further deepen its alliance relationship with Japan. This objective was
not lost on average Japanese, who feared that the scope of any new "post-Occupation" commitment by Japanese policy makers would erode the central tenets
of domestic antimilitarism. It is this fear which brought to the fore issues such as
Japan's arms export policy as well as its nuclear policy (the other "Three Principles"—no manufacture, no possession, no introduction) and the policy regarding
the use of outer space (discussed in Chapter 5). These fears were exacerbated by
deepening U.S.—and Japanese—involvement in Vietnam.

The Shifting Domestic Politics of Arms Exports and
Declaration of the "Three Principles"

On the domestic political front, broad foreign policy questions continued to char-
acterize the political divide between left and right, with the JSP and JCP—and its
sympathizers in such media outlets as the *Asahi Shimbun*—using every opportunity to embarrass the LDP on the issue of arms exports and arms production in
general. Arms production posed a policy quagmire for the JSP, however, because
the union workers who supported the party were the same workers assembling
rifles and other equipment for export to Southeast Asia and elsewhere.

On the other side of the political spectrum, the LDP—under Prime Minister
Satō's skillful leadership—managed to continue to support the U.S. effort in Vietnam but strategically endeavored to maintain the appearance of noninvolvement
by the Japanese. Havens (1987) argues: "Satō correctly calculated that the LDP's
conservative electorate would pay Vietnam little heed unless Japanese became
embroiled in combat" (p. 259). In this sense the LDP correctly judged that the
third tenet of domestic antimilitarism could be finessed to some extent by dis-
tinguishing various levels of Japanese involvement in international conflict, from
individual Japanese involvement (such as piloting American ships or providing
mechanical assistance) to involvement of firms (through arms exports) to direct
state involvement (such as a support role for the SDF). To a large degree, it was
direct state involvement that appeared as the line that absolutely could not be
crossed—a judgment that would not shift until decades later, after the September
11, 2001, attacks on the United States.

The Lower House election in January 1967 must have given pause to proponents of this strategy, however, as the percentage of the LDP vote dropped
below 50 percent for the first time since the party's formation, resulting in a loss
of five seats in the Diet. Importantly, however, the JSP also lost ground in this
election, losing four seats despite a less than 1 percent drop in the popular vote
due to Japan's complex electoral system. The winners in this election were those
advocating the middle ground—the Democratic Socialist Party (DSP) which

gained seven seats (despite only a 0.1 percent increase in the popular vote) and the Komeitō (KMT) which secured twenty-five seats and over 5 percent of the vote in its first Lower House contest (see Appendix 4 for complete election results). At this time, the KMT—backed by the lay religious group Soka Gakkai—advocated a gradual, negotiated withdrawal from the U.S.-Japan Security Treaty, in contrast to the JSP's call for an immediate termination of the treaty. Moreover, the KMT's broader foreign policy platform called for concrete efforts to contribute to world peace, rather than simply following a policy of *domestic* antimilitarism. The enactment of the Three Principles only three months after the election must partially be understood as an appeal to middle voters by the LDP and as an effort to reassure nervous voters that the LDP could satisfy their concerns over security issues in line with the negotiated postwar security identity of domestic antimilitarism. This policy announcement thus demonstrates how the security identity structured politicians' understanding of the Japanese public, and conversely how Japanese public opinion was structured by the postwar security identity of domestic antimilitarism.

The barrier to arms exports in place since the end of the Allied Occupation in 1952 was codified into official Japanese government policy by Prime Minister Satō on April 21, 1967, as the "Three Principles for Restricting Arms Exports"— reprinted in Appendix 5.[24] These guidelines state that Japan shall not export arms (1) to communist countries, (2) to countries subject to an arms embargo authorized by the United Nations Security Council, or (3) to countries engaged in, or likely to be engaged in, international conflict. The "arms" subject to these principles are defined as "items employed by military forces and utilized for direct combat purposes" as specified by the Export Control Order Annex List 1, item 1 (reprinted in JDA 1998, *Defense of Japan*, p. 397, and in Table 8). This definition is slightly broader than that included in the Self-Defense Forces Law, which defines arms as "machines, apparatuses and equipment with purposes of directly killing or harming persons, or destroying materials as a means of armed conflict, such as firearms, explosives, and swords" (reprinted in JDA 1998, *Defense of Japan*, p. 397, and in Table 8).

Despite the widespread misunderstanding of the Three Principles in discussions today (which are often portrayed as a ban on arms exports), at the time it was clearly understood among the general public that the Three Principles did not represent a complete ban on arms exports. Thus, for example, the JCP organized the public "trial" discussed above in August 1967, *after* the Three Principles had been declared. Rather, it was understood largely as a codification of existing *barriers* to export that had been imposed without clearly published guidelines since

the end of the Allied Occupation in 1952. Moreover, only two of the three principles can be considered newly codified rules, since the first principle—banning
exports to communist countries—was already mandated by Japan's membership
in COCOM. What the Three Principles did clearly proscribe, however, was the
export of arms to Vietnam, a country "engaged in international conflict." This did
not keep Japanese arms manufacturers from exporting arms to Thailand, however,
for use in Vietnam.

In this sense the proscription of the security identity was upheld strictly speaking, though the continued acceptance of arms exports which would be used in
international conflicts exposed the continuing problem with arms exports vis-à-
vis the postwar security identity. The Three Principles also failed to proscribe arms
sales to U.S. forces based in Japan for use in Vietnam—despite the United States'
near continuous engagement in international conflict in the Cold War period.
Still, as detailed in data collected by the Japan Tariff Association and compiled by
Hartwig Hummel (1988), Japanese exports of revolvers dropped dramatically from
¥82.2 million to less than ¥5 million after 1968 as the Three Principles took effect.
On the other hand, exports of "bombs, grenades, and similar munitions of war"
skyrocketed in 1970–75, from just ¥17 million in 1967 to ¥2,332 million in 1975.[25]
By contrast, exports of "nonmilitary" guns underwent a continuous increase from
1967 until 1978, the year after the stronger "New Three Principles" (discussed
below) took effect. Despite the fact that the Three Principles did not ban arms
exports entirely, it did reflect the will of many Japanese to see arms exports curtailed (and eventually banned). In addition, it set in motion the process by which
arms exports would be banned completely—again, except for sales to U.S. forces
stationed in Japan—in the next decade, as figures such as the export of "bombs,
grenades, etc." become more widely known.

What should be patently clear from this extended discussion is that a ban on
the export of weapons did not follow directly from a shared pacifist belief generated from the shock of defeat in the Second World War. Further, the push and
pull over arms export restrictions are illustrative of similar movement on other
postwar security practices, from the establishment of the SDF itself discussed in
Chapter 2, to the use of outer space discussed in Chapter 5, and including other
related security practices such as those over nuclear weapons, defense spending,
and the level of SDF weapons capabilities.

More Movement on the Three Principles in the Context of LDP Decline

The end of the war in Vietnam coincided with a number of other important
domestic and international events of relevance to future movement on Japan's

arms export policy. Internationally, the rise in Japanese economic power led to new demands on Japan from the United States for "burden sharing" within the context of the U.S.-Japan alliance and also for a greater role in regional international relations from leaders in Southeast Asia. Domestically, the LDP was struggling to maintain its dominance in the face of economic challenges posed by the first oil crisis and Nixon shocks as well as politically by the rise of centrist political parties such as the KMT and the DSP which raised the possibility for the first time in decades of "parity" between the left and the right (Curtis 1988, pp. 20–21). These domestic factors influenced Japan's foreign policy outlook, including its arms export policy. Such movement also underscores a central line of argument advanced in this volume: while the security identity of domestic antimilitarism structured postwar security practices, domestic and international politics both allowed for—and at times required—flexibility on how the security identity would be respected at specific points in time.

Prime Minister Satō's ability to negotiate the reversion of Okinawa to Japanese control and to handle the Nixon administration's varied attempts to influence a new global role for Japan had been strengthened by the fact that he could rely on strong support from within the LDP. By contrast, the first half of the 1970s was a period of instability and transition within the party, as a new breed of LDP politicians began to accumulate power and take over the reins of the party. The predictability of party leadership that characterized the first decade of LDP rule gave way to a more contentious competition between factions for control over leadership positions (Curtis 1988, pp. 98–102). With a weaker LDP, political leadership on security issues was intermittent at best, and the party avoided confrontation with opposition parties as much as possible (Smith 1996, pp. 168–69). Such a pattern of avoidance of controversial security issues at a time of weakness, and advocacy of them at times of strength, is also evident more recently, as LDP Prime Minister Koizumi became more strident in his military activism as polls showed high support for the LDP in general, though not necessarily over the controversial security practices he advocated.

In November 1974, the Tanaka cabinet (the successor to Satō) was dissolved amidst a political bribery scandal. As a result, Takeo Miki became prime minister at a particularly vulnerable time for the LDP. Chosen largely for his reputation as "Mr. Clean," Miki was also known as a dove on security issues within the LDP and had been foreign minister under Prime Minister Satō when the Three Principles were declared in 1967. According to Sheila Anne Smith (1996): "Miki did not have a strong base of factional support, and was somewhat of a maverick within the LDP who gained recognition for advocating political reform within the party.

It was precisely this reputation for being 'clean' that was of value to the party leadership at a time when the Japanese public was still reeling from revelations of LDP corruption exemplified by Tanaka's money scandals" (pp. 178–79).

Although Miki's ascent to prime minister would not have been anticipated prior to the political scandals of the early 1970s, he and his cabinet managed to address and resolve many of the problems confronted by the LDP in implementing its security policy. During the two years of Miki's prime ministership, domestic politics were in such upheaval that many within the LDP feared that its future as a viable party was in serious jeopardy. The LDP had been badly damaged by political scandals over party financing that reached a crescendo in 1976 when revelations from the Lockheed scandal led to the arrest of former Prime Minister Kakuei Tanaka for taking bribes from American defense contractors. As a consequence of this as well as domestic economic troubles, the party suffered a major defeat in the general election held in December 1976, losing twenty-two seats and, technically, its Diet majority.[26]

The Miki government reaffirmed and strengthened the arms export ban set by Prime Minister Satō on February 27, 1976, announcing the new government policy guideline in the Diet. The strengthened policy maintains the specific prohibition on arms exports to the three types of states specified in the Three Principles declaration of 1967 but adds to this a blanket prohibition on exports, stating that "arms exports to other areas shall be avoided, in conformity with the spirit of the Japanese Constitution and the Foreign Exchange Control Law." Moreover, it adds: "exports of arms production-related equipment . . . shall be dealt with in the same manner as arms."[27] This policy development must also be considered vis-à-vis the broader domestic and international political context. The February 1976 strengthening of the arms export ban can be understood as a further appeal to middle voters before an upcoming Lower House election, which was called by the LDP later in the year in December. In addition, as argued by Gerald Curtis and others, the growing presence of the political opposition had resulted in a marked increase in the number of participants in the policy-making process in the 1970s. Curtis (1979) writes: "In the earlier years the LDP might have taken opposition views into consideration in the formulation of policy, but it was not necessary to involve opposition parties directly in arriving at a consensus view" (p. 50). In the case of the now complete ban on arms exports (apart from the continuing exceptions of sales to U.S. forces based in Japan and of dual-use products), the role of opposition voices in the formulation of this policy is clear from the regular stories in the popular press of its evolution. As well, the role of the security identity of domestic antimilitarism is especially evident in the evolution of policy over time.

New Challenges to Arms Export Restrictions, 1980–1989

One visible sign of continued conflict over the arms export ban can be seen in the events surrounding the JSP's efforts to pass a Diet resolution codifying the government's unified statement on the Three Principles as issued by Prime Minister Miki in 1976, and seeking further to extend it to include prohibitions on the export of materials later shown to be used by foreign armed forces and on Japanese firms acquiring an equity share of foreign arms manufacturers—an explicit challenge to MITI's dual-use doctrine.[28] The end result of the controversy over the JSP's attempts to codify existing policy into a Diet resolution was mixed, though it arguably served to *weaken* the ban. While the JSP did succeed in codifying the 1976 New Three Principles into a Diet resolution with some minor revisions (see Appendix 5), this tactic from the left provoked the counterresponse of the government arguing publicly that the U.S.-Japan Security Treaty of 1960—which provides for arms transfers between Japan and the United States—takes precedence over a mere Diet resolution.[29] This policy assertion set the stage for increased military cooperation between Japan and the United States in the 1980s, cooperation which continues to this day. In this sense, political balance was maintained among contending forces seeking to adapt the security identity to advance their goals.

LDP resurgence in the 1980 "double election," the continued rise of Japanese economic and technological status, and new demands placed on Japan to "normalize" its security practices and "burden share" more with the United States each contributed to a retrenchment of the steady institutionalization of arms export restrictions in the 1960s and 1970s.[30] The issue of dual-use manufactures and technology exports in particular became a central political issue domestically and internationally in the 1980s (see Fujishima 1992, Kinoshita 1989, Nagata 1987, and Okimoto 1981). This situation was rooted in a paradox of postwar Japanese economic development, and an ironic one as well. As noted by Samuels (1994), by the 1980s, "Despite its extremely low spending on defense, Japan is becoming a global leader in innovative products with military applications" (p. 1). This development was not due solely to developments in Japan, however, but also to developments in the role of technology in both the civilian and military arenas worldwide.[31] This development allowed Japanese manufacturers to some extent to have their cake and eat it too: they were able to use the arms export ban as a shield against forced participation in technology transfer schemes sought by the U.S. government, and they were able to substantially increase their export of components that would be integrated into weapons abroad.

Given the rise of the spin-on phenomenon, one would expect that the most important question for Japanese exporters—and the policy makers regulating them—would be the "end use" of the exported item. If the export is to become part of a weapon used directly in combat, then it would follow that it should not be allowed under the 1976 New Three Principles outlining Japan's domestically generated arms export ban. This is not how enforcement of the ban works in practice, however. Enforcement of the Three Principles departs from this conventional wisdom in two ways. First, the standard that MITI bureaucrats employ to consider requests for export licenses is whether the component in question has a commercial application (in addition to a military one). If even a single civilian application can be found, the item is labeled "dual-use" and export is permitted, provided that the exporter did not "know" that the product would be used in a weapons system.[32] Naturally, the question arises of how much a company should be expected to know, even if it is faithfully attempting to comply with the spirit of the New Three Principles. Designating functional parameters in the abstract is not easy in practice, however—a task which falls to often understaffed state bureaucracies. On the corporate side as well, Bates Gill, Kensuke Ebata, and Matthew Stephenson (1996) note: "Even large companies find it difficult to research and investigate all transactions. For example, Sumitomo Trading Corporation, one of the largest trading companies in Japan, deals in over 50,000 different items with 70,000 companies overseas" (p. 38). As a result of this peculiar enforcement of the arms export "ban," a significant amount of Japanese manufactures are used by militaries abroad, a situation that eases corporate resistance to the Three Principles regime in practice.

Following the declaration of the 1978 Japan-U.S. Guidelines for Defense Cooperation, the United States Department of Defense (DOD) began in 1980 to demand the establishment of a new regime for mutual technology exchanges—one that would allow for technology to be transferred from Japan to the United States, as well as the other way around. From this demand resulted the Japan-U.S. Systems and Technology Forum (STF). Green (1995) writes: "One signal to the Japanese side was clear—three decades of unquestioned one-way technology transfers were over" (p. 83). This pressure had been brewing since the 1970s, but it reached a critical mass in the 1980s as trade tensions escalated and Japanese economic power continued to grow.

The United States did not advocate the repeal of Japan's new blanket arms export ban (the 1976 "New Three Principles") but instead argued for exemptions for technology transfer only to the United States. The ban was arguably congruent with both U.S. economic and strategic interests, so there was no need to oppose it in principle. Economically, it kept rising Japanese corporations out of a lucrative market for American firms. Strategically, it gave greater control to the United States in containing international conflict within the Cold War world. The one area where it was inconvenient was that it restricted American access to Japanese technology—or at least tough MITI negotiators argued that it did. Thus, it was only in this latter area that the United States sought to alter Japanese policy.

In addition to American pressure, in Japan as well there were demands for change to Japan's arms export policy. Keidanren's DPC welcomed the initiative of the DOD to reexamine the U.S.-Japan defense production relationship in order to push its own agenda for change. For the DPC, the primary complaint was the long-standing Foreign Military Sales (FMS) regime, the United States government program of assistance in defense hardware. A report from the DPC in 1982 announced: "Given the variety of problems in price, delivery and quality, the committee thinks that procurement based on FMS should be reexamined" (Keidanren DPC 1982, as cited in Green 1995, p. 173). In addition to the DPC, MITI was also anxious to develop a new system beyond the traditional FMS regime, speaking against a regime which "lock[s] Japan into a pattern in which the United States would sell Japan weapons but black-box the technology, while Japan would have to give the U.S. technology without being able to sell hardware" (Green 1995, p. 84). Thus, both actors sought to achieve new policies that would allow Japan to exploit its growing technological prowess for military applications. Once again, it was not just foreigners but also domestic groups seeking to "normalize" Japan's security practices. Despite the widespread institutionalization of the postwar security identity, even a generation after the codification of this new security identity it still had not resulted in a uniform culture of shared belief.

The arms export ban served as a sort of double-edged sword for the Japanese government and industry during this period. On the one edge, it served as a nuisance (if not exactly a barrier) to the export of dual-use technology and manufactures. Japanese manufacturers had become irritated at having to segregate increasingly complex and ambiguous-use products—particularly in the area of high technology—into military and civilian use categories. On the other edge, however, it provided a convenient justification for MITI within the government and for private manufacturers not to share cutting-edge technology with the United States. Thus, in this period one sees some actors supporting the security identity of domestic antimilitarism for the instrumental reason of protecting Japanese industry. The rhetoric of domestic antimilitarism was convenient to actors who had previously sought—and were still seeking—to export arms.

By the 1980s, the de facto coalition that originally supported the maintenance of the occupation-era arms export ban had changed considerably. MOF, which originally supported the ban as a means of conserving foreign exchange, was no longer concerned with the balance payments for economic superpower Japan. Many business leaders—not just those involved in defense-related production and represented by Keidanren's Defense Production Committee—reversed their position on the ban in the 1980s, coming out in *favor* of arms exports as a boon for Japanese industry.[33] Only the pacifist left continued its support for the ban for the original reasons, joined ideologically by the rising political force of the Kōmeitō. Having been institutionalized into numerous policy statements and reflected in mass discourse, however, this change in political support had less effect than otherwise would be expected.

The ultimate achievement of employing the third tenet of domestic antimilitarism to codify arms export restrictions through the New Three Principles was threatened by the appointment of Yasuhiro Nakasone as prime minister in October 1982. Unlike previous prime ministers such as Miki and Fukuda, Nakasone became known almost immediately for his direct, action-oriented style, acting more like a U.S. president than a behind-the-scenes deal maker more in line with his predecessors. In addition, Nakasone long had been known as a hawk on defense issues, and he lived up to this reputation as prime minister by formally removing the 1 percent of GDP ceiling on defense spending (although spending only once, and then only barely, exceeded this threshold despite the lifting of the ceiling), agreeing to participation in the U.S. Strategic Defense Initiative (the precursor to missile defense, discussed in Chapter 6), and seeking to loosen the Three Principles on Arms Exports after decades of movement in the opposite direction codifying a ban on such exports (including under Nakasone's own directorship of the Japan Defense Agency under Prime Minister Satō). Nakasone's limited success in achieving changes in Japan's security policies demonstrates the political power and level of institutionalization of the security identity over the twenty years since the revision of the security treaty, however. In addition, it demonstrates the continued contestation over this compromise identity in the postwar period. Nakasone's push for change challenged not only the third tenet of domestic antimilitarism—which relates directly to the issue of arms exports—but the first as well. He actively sought to enhance the role of the Japan Defense Agency (JDA) and the SDF in security policy making within the state. Arguably he had more success in this area, though the political capital he expended to achieve such changes limited his ability to achieve his agenda in other areas. Once again, the long-standing expectation of "reach, reconcile, reassure" limited how far Nakasone could reach without reconciling and reassuring.

All of the above pressures on the arms export ban produced a marked shift in Japanese policy on January 14, 1983, when the Japanese government issued new policy guidelines related to arms exports that allowed the transfer of technology to the United States to be exempted from the Three Principles policies.[34] The policy was announced by Chief Cabinet Secretary Masaharu Gotoda:

> The Mutual Defense Assistance Agreement between Japan and the United States (MDAA, 1954) provides the framework for mutual cooperation in the area of defense between the two countries. Pursuant to the principle of mutual cooperation, Japan should positively promote cooperation with the United States in matters relating to equipment and technology, while paying due attention to the maintenance of its technological and production base. (JDA 1998, *Defense of Japan*)

In November 1983 both countries signed the Military Technology Transfer Agreement, setting the stage for the establishment of the Joint Military Technology Commission (JMTC) the following November. In December 1985, detailed rules attached to the agreement were fixed.[35] This agreement set the stage for a number of joint projects between the United States and Japan centered around advanced technology related to defense with diverse applications such as shipbuilding production techniques, advanced ceramics and carbon fibers for aerospace, and glass fiber cables and displays for weapons applications.[36]

The wording of the 1983 statement by the chief cabinet secretary explaining the exception—and the scope of the exception in general—is interesting for a number of reasons. First, setting the stage for future policy change, it roots U.S.-Japan security cooperation firmly in the MDAA—a precursor to the security treaty currently in effect between the two states after the Occupation signed in 1954. Second, it situates the question of technology exports not just in the security realm—the concern of the United States—but in the economic realm as well, making clear that "maintenance of [Japan's] technological and production base" was a key concern of the Japanese state. Third, as with nearly all policy changes apparent in the security realm which would follow in the next two decades, the change was narrowly framed to fit largely within the existing security identity (if with some new interpretation and explanation) and was justified in part by pressure from the United States and the demands of a new international environment. Thus, it was not at all a repudiation or reversal of existing security practice; rather, it was a shift within the existing framework, the security identity of domestic antimilitarism.

In 1987, after the United States successfully lobbied Japan to introduce an exception to the three principles to allow for technology transfer to the United States, the complexity and potential threat to the United States of Japanese dual-use technology entered the mass media in both countries due to the Toshiba Machine incident. Given the major public relations nightmare the incident caused not only to the Toshiba group specifically but to Japanese industry in general—immortalized by the picture of American congressmen smashing Japanese electronics on the steps of the U.S. Capitol building—it deserves mention. In neither country, however, was this incident framed in terms of Japan's domestic arms export ban but rather in terms of Japan's failure to abide by international agreements under COCOM and also domestic export regulations set by MITI. The offending incident itself had taken place five years earlier, in 1982, when the Toshiba Machine Corporation (a member of the Toshiba group) sold nine-axis and five-axis computer-controlled milling machines to the Soviet Union. Employing software developed in Norway, the Soviets were able to use the equipment to develop quieter submarine propellers which were used in both new and older submarines, requiring the United States and its allies to spend a considerable sum to redetermine the noise signature of the Soviet submarine fleet.[37]

The controversy surrounding this sale—in Japan at least—had much to do with the clearly illegal nature of the sale, *not* any ambiguity or policy disagreement about its appropriateness. There was consensus that it was not appropriate. Apart from any normatively derived policy against arms exports, exports of such high-performance milling equipment required an export license from MITI under the international COCOM regime. Such an application would have been denied given the destination of the equipment. Interestingly, it is unlikely that the incident violated the newly strengthened 1976 New Three Principles declared by Prime Minister Miki, given that the equipment itself was certainly not used in direct combat and that the equipment also had civilian uses (and thus was a dual-use product by Japanese definitions).

Among mainstream commentary in Japan, the primary issue was not the possible export of arms-related production equipment but rather the harm the sale inflicted on the reputation of Japan and its international firms, and the indignation over Toshiba Machine's blatant violation of the law. As the perceived protector of the interests of Japanese industry, MITI implemented wide-ranging corrective action in response to criticism of its oversight, including the creation of a new institution, the Center for Information on Security (now, Strategic) Trade Control (CISTEC), in 1989 (see Gill, Ebata, and Stephenson 1996, pp. 36–40, for further details). In the United States, by contrast, the incident provoked widespread indignation and unleashed a range of simmering resentment toward Japan. Most relevant to this study, it reaffirmed in the minds of American policy makers the critical need to take advantage of Japanese technology for use by *Western* military forces, vindicating the push for the technology transfer export exemption for the United States passed in 1983.[38]

No discussion of the heated debates of the 1980s surrounding the arms export ban and the issue of technology transfer would be complete without mention of the major concrete outcome of these agreements—the codevelopment and production of the "FSX" fighter plane, now called the F-2 fighter. In the midst of continuing discussion between the United States and Japan on programs to achieve two-way technology transfers on weapons systems, MITI and the JDA made the decision to develop Japan's first indigenous fighter plane—planes which until that time had been designed and manufactured in Japan based on U.S. engine and airframe designs. Confrontation over Japanese plans to develop an indigenous jet support fighter, the FSX, was perceived as a slap in the face to U.S. pleas for greater cooperation in advanced weapon development, further exacerbated by the volatile environment surrounding U.S. perceptions of a growing economic threat from Japan. Detailed reexamination of this controversial project—beyond the scope of this chapter—provides fascinating insight into the complex interaction among domestic and international political and economic forces in addition to international systemic factors such as rising and declining states epitomized by the end of the Cold War.[39] The FSX case is of particular importance to this study in relation to a later instance of joint research between the United States and Japan on missile defense in addition to its impact on initial U.S. reaction to Japan's plan to develop surveillance satellites.

The acrimony created by repeated negotiations and complaints about lack of parity in technology transfer in the FSX project, as well as the more mundane issue of the ratio of coproduction, was at a level not likely experienced before in the security relationship between the United States and Japan. Although surely exacerbated by the severe trade tensions of the time, as well as by the Toshiba Machine incident, the fundamental problem with the program was over the core issue of technology transfer, in particular the ability—or the willingness, in the eyes of U.S. officials—for the Japanese government to require Japanese firms to participate. The result of this bitter exercise was an extreme reluctance to attempt such a program again, thus effectively ending for a time further discussions of parity in technology transfer—only actively resurrected again in the context of missile defense, discussed in Chapter 6.

The end of the 1980s and the FSX experience illustrate the changing nature of arms production at the end of the twentieth century, a trend that is deepening in the first years of the twenty-first century (Brooks 2005). These changes push Japan toward greater cooperation with foreign defense producers, countering indigenous defense production goals evident throughout the postwar period. Surveys conducted of Japanese defense producers in the early 1990s indicate that Japanese firms expect their shortcomings in systems-level production to worsen, suggesting the necessity of further efforts at joint development and production—despite the problems faced in the FSX case (surveys cited by Green 1994, p. 28).

The Limited Post–Cold War Evolution of
Arms Export Restrictions

The 1990s presented an opportunity for Japanese industry and the Japanese defense establishment to address some of the trends in global defense production apparent in the 1980s in a new international and domestic political context. The end of the Cold War, lessening of the U.S.-Japan trade rivalry due in part to the collapse of the bubble economy and subsequent extended period of economic stagnation, and shifting domestic party politics presented—in theory—a range of new opportunities. Given the large number of "crisis" issues faced in the early 1990s, however, the issue of arms exports and possible joint U.S.-Japan weapons production did not enter into an active political agenda until the mid-1990s—after a cooling-off period had elapsed post-FSX, the first Persian Gulf War crisis was resolved, and most importantly, the post–Cold War nature of U.S.-Japan defense cooperation more broadly (i.e., a deepening defense alliance) had become clearer by progress in negotiations leading to the 1996 Clinton-Hashimoto Joint Statement and the 1997 Revised Defense Guidelines.

As discussed further in Chapter 6, one objective of renewed interest in joint weapons development with Japan was cooperation in technology related to missile defense, an objective first pursued without much success under the "Ron-Yasu" relationship of the mid-1980s and first given some limited achievement by the September 1993 establishment of a private, industry-led theater missile defense (TMD) working group. A formal agreement to pursue joint research on missile defense would be preceded by several other formal agreements for joint research (see Table 9). None of these earlier projects would ultimately lead to any substantial industry cooperation at the production level, however. Still, the potential for success at developing a reason for cross-national production required industry to anticipate a potential problem to this development by way of continuing arms export restrictions. Industry efforts to secure a relaxation of such restrictions prior to any concrete plan for export (or joint production, which is considered an export under existing guidelines) were unsuccessful, however. As discussed below, and also argued in Chapter 3, the continued strength of the postwar security identity of domestic antimilitarism continued to exercise considerable force even in the new post–Cold War environment.

As with previous periods, international factors continued to shape Japan's arms export restrictions in the new post–Cold War era, including the way that Japan would categorize and track such exports as well as the nature of formal international agreements to limit certain exports. The conclusion of the Cold War led to

TABLE 9

Japan-U.S. Joint Research Projects, 1992–2005

Project	Formal initiation date	Date of completion
Ducted rocket engine	Sept. 1992	Jan. 1999
Advanced steel technology	Oct. 1995	Jan. 2002
Fighting vehicle propulsion technology using ceramic materials	Oct. 1995	Oct. 2002
Eye-safe laser radar	Sept. 1995	Sept. 2001
Ejection seat	Mar. 1998	Mar. 2003
Advance hybrid propulsion technology	May 1998	Ongoing
Shallow water acoustic technology	June 1999	Feb. 2003
Ballistic missile defense technology	Aug. 1999	Jan. 2004
Low vulnerability gun propellant for field artillery	Mar. 2000	Ongoing
Avionics aboard the follow-on aircraft to the P-3C	Mar. 2002	Ongoing
Software radio	Mar. 2002	Ongoing
Advanced hull material/structural technology	Apr. 2005	Ongoing

Source: Adapted from JDA (2005), pp. 175–76.
Note: 1992 was the first year of such projects; therefore this table includes all projects to date.

the disbanding of COCOM in March 1994, an institution dedicated largely to restricting arms exports to the Soviet bloc. The issue of the danger of weapons trade to certain states did not disappear in the post–Cold War world, however, and in some ways intensified due to the proliferation of new security threats, increasingly dangerous dual-use technologies, and the broadening of the number of states that possessed such technology. As a result, the Wassenaar Agreement on Export Control for Conventional Arms and Dual Use Goods and Technologies (Wassenaar Agreement) immediately filled the gap created by the disbanding of COCOM the same year. Under this new regime, as a result of the aforementioned new challenges, Japan's obligations to control categories of exports actually increased.

At the same time, the difficulty of achieving such control—as evidenced in the previous decade by the Toshiba Machine scandal—continued to be evident. The cavalier attitude of the Aum Shinrikyo religious cult—the group responsible for the deadly sarin gas attack on a Tokyo subway in 1995—to flouting export controls shocked average Japanese by its sheer audacity, exporting and importing advanced chemicals and avionics apparently with ease. More recently, despite increased tensions between Japan and China, Japanese manufacturer Yamaha managed to circumvent controls on unmanned aerial vehicles (UAVs) and successfully sell several to a firm associated with China's People's Liberation Army (PLA). As with the earlier case of Toshiba Machine, however, such high-profile scandals were not the result of unclear guidelines or weak public will, but rather exposed problems of enforcement.

In terms of domestic politics, little had changed by way of public attitudes or party support regarding arms export restrictions, despite a vastly altered international and domestic political environment. Industry actors led by Keidanren's DPC still sought relaxation of existing restrictions, supported by some conservative politicians within the LDP. The KMT continued to oppose such relaxation and was newly empowered to achieve its views due to its coalition position with the LDP for most of the 1990s and all of the twenty-first century to date. The Democratic Party of Japan (DPJ), at least initially, played the role of the Cold War–era JSP in strongly opposing any reconsideration of the policy. Moreover, the policy was not a forgotten relic of an earlier period, but rather was often evoked both by those opposing broader government security policy initiatives and by a government seeking to reassure the public that the security identity of domestic antimilitarism remained in tact.

It would be the specific issue of missile defense that would lead to renewed consideration of arms export restrictions. As discussed in Chapter 6, joint U.S.-Japan research on missile defense led to inevitable questions about what the result of such costly research would be—presumably some sort of system to be manufactured jointly. Such a perceived inevitability—also in the context of several other joint research projects that had been initiated—led to public and politician concern over possible revision of arms export restrictions beyond the technology exemption declared by the Nakasone cabinet in 1983.

Conclusions: Security Identity and Evolving Arms Export Restrictions

While Japan's arms export "ban" is one of the most-cited examples offered by those describing Japan's "pacifist" or "antimilitarist" foreign policy—together with other policies such as refraining from foreign deployment of its troops, antinuclear policies, and limits on defense spending—like these other cases, a closer look at the evolution of this policy over time shows a pattern common to the cases examined in this volume of the United States and other international factors setting significant parameters for policy outcomes, but then domestic political factors playing an important role in the ultimate shape of the resulting policy. It is not the case that an antimilitarist culture resulted in the natural appearance of export restrictions. Rather, the compromise security identity of domestic antimilitarism that would emerge in the contentious fifteen years of immediate postwar politics suggested a direction for arms production and export that would lead to increasing (and increasingly institutionalized) restrictions on arms exports over time.

The continuation of the ban on arms exports after the end of the Allied Occupation was a result of the interaction of the new security identity of domestic antimilitarism with powerful political actors in this arena. Recast in a more traditional explanatory framework, the new security identity lent additional power to those actors espousing the principles of domestic antimilitarism which resulted in an alteration of the preference ordering of the major political actors that made some actions—such as abolition of the ban—more costly than they would have been absent the security identity. The independent power of the security identity has its limits, however. Thus, while the rhetoric of the arms export ban was maintained, significant concessions were made at various times during this period at the policy implementation level. These concessions reflect shifting political power resources operating within the limits set by the security identity.

Careful examination of two decades of political wrangling which led to the 1967 codification of a partial ban on arms exports illustrates how the security identity of domestic antimilitarism limited the development of an apparently appealing export industry and affected the broader character of postwar Japanese security policy. However, careful attention to the postwar economic situation and the sustained bargaining among powerful domestic and international political actors—particularly in the immediate postwar period—is necessary to understand the timing and character of the ban. It was not a matter of the security identity leading to an immediate and predictable policy outcome, but rather a case of identity and politics interacting for over twenty-five years until an acceptable compromise could be reached among political actors.

The security identity of domestic antimilitarism played a crucial role in the final policy outcome of a ban on the export of arms through its influence on political rhetoric, its enabling of political coalition-building, and the clear policy proscriptions it emphasized. It cannot be argued, however, that it led directly to the policy outcome. Rather, one aspect of the formation and construction of the ban over time is how societal forces managed to use an appeal to the negotiated security identity to advocate adherence to policy compromises over time, how the language of domestic antimilitarism pervaded politics in this period, and how domestic antimilitarism became institutionalized into the policy-making process. Another important aspect is the distribution of political power at key decision points, and how well these actors were able to articulate their policy goals in terms of the hegemonic security identity.

The ban on arms exports was not a one-time decision, nor was it even resolved after over twenty-five years of political wrangling leading to the codification of a partial ban through a government policy declaration in 1967. Rather, despite the pressure of the security identity on sustaining the policy, continued assaults were made even after the policy's codification, resulting in an erosion of the ban in the mid-1980s and sustained assaults on the ban that continue to this day. More broadly, changes in the nature of defense production, as well as the larger revolution in military affairs (RMA) that in part is driving these changes, will continue to exert pressure on Japan's security identity. Japan faces greater pressure in the post–Cold War period to cooperate with other states to provide for its defense, which challenges each tenet of the domestic antimilitarist security identity—in its demand for more active armed forces that play a greater role in alliance coordination, in growing demands for Japanese SDF participation in international peacekeeping, and in pressure to coordinate the manufacture of weapons across national boundaries. Finally, the greater incorporation of advanced technology into weapons systems has pushed military activity into the final frontier—outer space—the subject of Chapter 5.

The Next Frontier

Keeping Outer Space "Peaceful"

Outer space policy may not appear to be a central area of defense policy, but in fact research into both the militarization of outer space and the link between military and civilian space exploration has quite deeply affected the development of military capabilities. Such linkages will only deepen in the twenty-first century as more states embark on outer space research and as the technological capabilities of militaries continue to increase. These linkages posed significant barriers to Japan's development of outer space technology by putting the security identity of domestic antimilitarism into direct conflict not only with the maintenance of an able defensive force but with other state goals of economic and technological development. The effect of the security identity of domestic antimilitarism on Japan's defense-related use of outer space therefore provides an excellent case to consider competing explanations for the evolution of Japanese security policy in general, as well as being an important area of study of Japan's expanding military capabilities in particular.

Japanese space policy stands out from the other world space powers due to the nearly complete separation of space policy from military planning. Japan's status in the world today as a leader in technologies and manufacturing processes useful in outer space development was gained without substantial military funds devoted to outer space research. The best explanation for this remarkable departure is rooted in Japan's security identity of domestic antimilitarism. While Japan's policy regarding the peaceful use of outer space cannot be viewed as one of the central limitations on military development in postwar Japan, it is important due to the limitations it placed both on Japan's strong commitment to pursue technological strength and autonomy[1] and on the extent of military cooperation that could be pursued with the United States. The politics of outer space development are inextricably linked to discussions of Japan's controversial military alliance with the United States, a subject particularly volatile in the 1960s, a time of high Cold War tension exacerbated by U.S. military activities in Vietnam.

Japan's peaceful-use-of-space policy—symbolized by a 1969 Diet resolution affirming this intent[2]—is a frequently cited example of Japan's pacifist or antimilitarist foreign policy. Closer examination of Japan's actual outer space policy—in particular in regard to the military use of outer space—shows a more mixed picture. As with arms export restrictions examined in Chapter 4, the security identity of domestic antimilitarism has played an important role in the emergence of a policy restricting Japan's use of outer space through its influence on political rhetoric, its enabling of political coalition building, and the clear policy proscriptions it emphasized. To the extent that outer space development could be viewed as an increase in Japan's "war potential"—prohibited by Article Nine of Japan's postwar constitution and the second tenet of domestic antimilitarism, which limits the use of force by Japan to resolve international disputes—nonpeaceful uses of outer space were prohibited by Japan's postwar security identity. Moreover, the development of outer space capabilities together with the United States threatened to entangle Japan in third-party conflicts abroad, a practice proscribed by the third tenet of domestic antimilitarism.

It cannot be argued, however, that Japan's postwar security identity alone set the framework for Japan's peaceful-use-of-space policy. Rather, one aspect of the formation and construction of the policy is how societal forces managed to use an appeal to the security identity of domestic antimilitarism to advocate the creation of and adherence to the peaceful-use-of-space policy over time, how the language of domestic antimilitarism pervaded political discussion of this question, and how this security identity became institutionalized into the policy-making process. Another important aspect—which often limited the ideational coherence of the actual policy—is the distribution of political power domestically and internationally at key decision points, and how well these actors were able to articulate their policy goals in terms of the hegemonic security identity. Finally, it must be emphasized from the outset that, as the state that possessed far more resources and technology than any other, the United States played a crucial role in establishing Japan's outer space policy at each stage of its development.

As with arms export restrictions, the peaceful-use-of-space policy was formally adopted decades into the postwar period, in this case with the 1969 establishment of a government body to oversee outer space activities and a Diet resolution regarding such activities the same year. Previously, in 1960, the Japanese government had created the National Space Activities Council (NSAC) as an advisory body to the prime minister. In its very first report, submitted to the prime minister in the same year, the idea that outer space should be used for peaceful purposes only was included among a long list of preliminary national objectives, which also stressed another hallmark of Japanese space policy—the commercial and technological potential in outer space development (Yatō 1983). Unlike the case of arms export restrictions, however, the policy limiting the use of outer space to peaceful purposes had little practical effect on Japan's outer space development in the short term because Japan did not possess competitive technology in space industries as it did in the area of arms manufacturing. Moreover, areas where the declared peaceful-use-of-space policy conflicted with defense or industry objectives were regularly sacrificed in the pursuit of these goals, a practice particularly evident in the 1980s, further advanced in the 1990s, and a continuing subject of further relaxation today. Arguably the biggest anomaly (from a realist perspective) generated by the policy regarding the peaceful use of outer space—the prohibition on the use of outer space to collect military intelligence to support Japan's defensive military posture—was largely resolved in 1998 when Japan decided to overlook the apparent proscription of such a use of outer space and to develop a network of surveillance satellites that would be used, in part, for military purposes. Careful consideration of this recent evolution of security practice sheds light on the general trends in shifting security practices in recent years, practices which depart from earlier restrictions yet still remain rooted in the long-standing tenets of Japan's postwar security identity.

Military strategists have dreamed of using outer space for military advantage for at least a century, long before technology existed to make this a reality.[3] Beginning with the launch of the Soviet Sputnik satellite in October 1957, however, lofty dreams of the militarization of outer space were replaced with ambitious projects to translate such dreams into reality. By the turn of the century, more than four thousand satellites had been launched from earth (Burrows 1990); planetary probes had visited every planet in our solar system; and men had walked on the moon. The exploration of outer space and the development of space-related technologies cannot be analytically separated from military competition. While the general public—especially in the United States and the Soviet Union—was fed a steady diet of lofty goals for the pursuit of "pure science" applications through outer space programs, in reality the vast majority of development costs for such programs were borne by military budgets with military applications in mind.[4] This practice posed a significant challenge to Japanese space researchers saddled with Japan's postwar security identity of domestic antimilitarism.

Three areas of defense planning have been the focus of outer space exploration. First, missile technology was perfected in a series of programs designed to lift ever-heavier payload into orbit, and beyond. Second, orbiting satellites were envisioned to aid in military surveillance of hostile states (and later, to aid in military communications and weapons targeting). Third, outer space was seen as the "final frontier" for basing weapons directed at targets on earth. This latter category included space-based missiles and also giant space-based lasers, which were envisioned to be able to incinerate enemy weapons from great distances. Although even today, in the early twenty-first century, skeptics argue that technology is still decades away from enabling a workable system that would allow the targeting and interception of missiles from outer space, the military planners of the 1960s already possessed such ambitions (Mowthorpe 2004).

Although the reality of utilizing outer space for military purposes was far beyond Japan's capabilities at the time (and, not incidentally, its political will), the possibility of this happening—especially together with the United States—led to the adoption of a Lower House Diet resolution in 1969 declaring Japan's dedication to the use of outer space only for peaceful purposes (*heiwa no mokuteki*)[5] as well as the institutionalization of the idea of "peaceful use" into fundamental policy documents related to Japan's outer space policy and overseeing bodies. The Peaceful Use of Space resolution was not directed only at the potential development of surveillance satellites, but this use of space was one of the primary concerns of those opposed to the militarization of space—contrary to what many current politicians and commentators have recently claimed about the intention of the resolution. The issue first caught the attention of the Japanese public and mass media when an American U-2 spy plane, which had been launched from Japan, was shot down over the Soviet Union in May 1960. Many Japanese feared that such actions needlessly provoked the Soviet Union, further fueling opposition to the U.S.-Japan Security Treaty. The Diet resolution, and its political foundation, presented an institutionalized barrier to Japanese corporate and military use of space, rooted in the security identity of domestic antimilitarism.

A series of modifications to the peaceful-use-of-space policy significantly blunted the policy's impact in the years after it was formally adopted. First, in 1985 it was decided after much controversy and heated debate that the Self-Defense Forces (SDF) could use communications satellites for military communication. Also in the 1980s, it was decided again after much controversy and heated debate that the Japan Defense Agency (JDA) could purchase satellite imagery from abroad for use in military intelligence.[6] Once this latter precedent was set, it did not take long for Japanese military and corporate leaders to argue that there was no real difference between buying satellite imagery from abroad or producing it oneself—and, moreover, that the latter approach had the advantage of furthering other state goals. Surprisingly, though, the leap to development of such a system was not made until well into the post–Cold War period (December 25, 1998), several months after a North Korean Taepodong missile overflew the Japanese main island of Honshu. This delay—and the overall limitations and slowed development of Japan space technology—can be explained through the use of a framework based on security identity.

Even more than in the case of arms export restrictions, debates over the use of outer space were deeply rooted in ideational convictions over the appropriate role of Japan's military establishment in domestic political debate and policy making. The potential militarization of outer space strongly challenged the first tenet of domestic antimilitarism, which prohibited a full role for military actors in domestic political decision making. The threat of joint development of space-based weapons with the United States—effectively deepening the contested military relationship that was already vocally criticized by many—challenged the second tenet of domestic antimilitarism: it far exceeded the minimum capability necessary to provide for the defense of Japan, a fundamental limitation imposed on the SDF by the postwar security identity.[7] Finally, the militarization of outer space threatened to involve Japanese in conflict abroad, violating the third tenet of domestic antimilitarism. The controversy generated with the Soviet Union over the U-2 spy plane launched from Japan introduced to many Japanese the complications that could arise from expanding defense cooperation with the United States to include development of space-based defense systems.

As with the case of arms export restrictions, Japan's peaceful-use-of-space policy is rooted in *international* politics. In the case of the peaceful-use-of-space declaration in the Diet, the precedent for this policy comes from discussions in the United Nations which took place throughout the 1960s. In this case, two puzzles must be explained. First, why was the resolution passed in the Diet when it was, and not earlier or later? Second, why and how did the policy evolve over time? The following sections of this chapter will address these two puzzles by examining the development of Japan's outer space policy from the time of the creation of its first advisory council on outer space activities in 1960, through the launch of Japan's first satellites and rockets in the 1970s, and ending with more active attempts at the commercialization of outer space beginning in the 1980s, and further advanced by the domestic production and launch of surveillance satellites in the early twenty-first century. As with other cases considered in this volume, scrutiny of this case shows how the core principles of the security identity of domestic antimilitarism were reflected in Japan's outer space use policy in new ways as new pressures were placed on those who crafted Japanese space policy and as Japan faced an evolving security and economic environment. Moreover, the role of sustained opposition to strict enforcement of the peaceful-use-of-space policy—in particular by commercial actors—is evident upon further scrutiny.

International and Alliance Politics in Japan's
Early Outer Space Policy

Aside from general interest in the exploration of outer space among the Japanese public, it was international factors that drove Japan's early moves to develop a national space policy.[8] Four deserve specific mention. Foremost among these was the intense "space race" that had emerged between the United States and the Soviet Union after the Soviet launch of Sputnik in 1957. U.S. president John F. Kennedy had set a national goal of landing a man on the moon by the end of the 1960s; several major European states and Canada were also embarking on ambitious programs to explore outer space.[9] Japan, motivated strongly by the goal of "catching up to the West," could not fail to join this important area of technology development.

A second important international factor driving Japan's early space policy was heated discussions in the United Nations over the future course of space development, which led to the Treaty on the Principles Governing the Activities of States in the Exploration and Use of Outer Space (the Outer Space Treaty) that put forth the restriction on the use of outer space to peaceful purposes only. The Japanese pacifist movement of the 1960s was deeply informed by international discourse on antiwar topics, including the possible militarization of outer space. Alarmed by the developing "space race" between the United States and the Soviet Union within the context of the Cold War, a number of countries including Japan took their concerns to the United Nations to deliberate on possible restrictions of the use of outer space to peaceful purposes. It was in response to the international demand that states utilize outer space only for peaceful purposes that the Japanese government was pushed to create an institution within the government which could oversee Japan's space policy. The U.S. creation of the National Aeronautics and Space Agency (NASA) in 1958, over ten years before the establishment of a similar body in Japan, also undoubtedly led to pressure for a counterpart institution to exist in Japan, in part to allow Japan to better benefit from technology transfer and general assistance offered generously by the United States to its close Cold War ally at the time. Based on the final report of the NSAC (established in 1960), the Japanese government submitted legislation to the Diet to create the Space Activities Commission (SAC) in 1968 via the Space Activities Establishment Act and the National Space Development Agency (NASDA), Japan's equivalent of NASA, in 1969.[10]

A third important international factor driving Japan's early space policy was the opening of the international conference for a Permanent Agreement for INTELSAT, the International Telecommunications Satellite Organization, first proposed by the United States in 1963. As with the United Nations' Outer Space Treaty, the Japanese government perceived a need to establish an institution that could effectively determine national priorities in outer space before agreeing to limits on future space policy. The negotiations over the Permanent Agreement of INTELSAT were concluded and opened for signature in 1971 and entered into effect in 1973.

A fourth factor, one which best explains the specific timing of Japanese government institutionalization of its space program, is the desire of the Japanese government to benefit from superior U.S. technology in the space industry. On January 17, 1968, the U.S. ambassador to Japan, U. Alexis Johnson, officially proposed U.S.-Japan technology cooperation in space, following Prime Minister Satō's visit to the United States in November 1967. At the time of the U.S. proposal for formal cooperation with Japan on space development, the Japanese government had no institution devoted to long-term planning of Japan's space policy. Given the controversial nature of the U.S.-Japan alliance in the context of the ongoing U.S. fighting in Vietnam—waged in large part from the string of bases in Japan—Japan could not conclude formal cooperation with the United States on outer space activities prior to the development of a national consensus on Japan's objectives in outer space activities. Only after the passing of the Diet resolution on the peaceful use of space in May 1969 was the Japanese government able to conclude a formal agreement with the United States regarding technology assistance in the development of space industry, signed in July 1969.

The timing of the 1969 Diet resolution on the peaceful use of outer space must also be understood within the context of the broader international security environment. As noted in Chapter 4, increasing U.S. involvement in Vietnam (which was particularly evident in Japan beginning in 1965 and reached its peak in 1968) evoked Japanese memories of U.S. involvement on the Korean peninsula in the previous decade, as well as demands the U.S. government placed on Japan to support American foreign policy objectives at that time. Such issues were beginning to resurface in the context of Japan's potential support for the U.S. war effort in Vietnam, much of which was staged from U.S. bases on the Japanese main islands (including areas surrounding Tokyo, Japan's most populous region) and especially in Okinawa (which remained under U.S. administrative control after the occupation of the rest of Japan ended in 1952). As in the United States, the war in Vietnam was the target of sustained public protest in Japan. Diplomatic negotiations between U.S. and Japanese policy makers over the "reversion" of the Japanese islands of Okinawa back to Japanese administrative control, the final part of Japanese territory occupied by the United States since the end of the Second World War, also created concerns that the scope of any new "post-Occupation" commitment by Japanese policy makers would significantly erode the central tenets of domestic antimilitarism.

Growing public discontent with the situation—discussed further in the next section—forced the ruling Liberal Democratic Party (LDP) to respond to charges that Japan was being too complicit in the U.S. war effort, leading Prime Minister Satō (who in 1974 would be awarded the Nobel Peace Prize for his antinuclear policies) to engage in a flurry of policy initiatives including the Three Principles on Arms Exports discussed in Chapter 4 and the Three Nonnuclear Principles (no manufacture, no possession, no introduction[11]) in December 1967. The peaceful-use-of-space policy declared in the Diet in 1969 should also be understood in this context—as an effort to "reassure" after a "reach" of deepening military cooperation with the United States in the context of the growing conflict in Vietnam. Numerous incidents that exposed the extent of Japanese complicity in the U.S. war effort—such as the media coverage of Sony video cameras being used in U.S. guided missiles discussed in Chapter 4—underscored the need to limit the extent of coordination with the U.S. military, including joint research and development of outer space. Absent such a statement, it seemed likely that the third tenet of domestic antimilitarism would erode.

In the area of outer space use, Japan adopted a more restrictive definition of the word *peaceful* in its declared policy on outer space use than did other space powers such as the United States and the Soviet Union. The Japanese government interpreted *peaceful* to mean *nonmilitary*, while the United States and the Soviet Union defined the word as *nonaggressive*. This more restrictive Japanese definition—an effort to reassure a public skeptical about cooperation with the United States—was soon to change, however, as Japanese technological capabilities increased in the 1970s and 1980s, putting new pressure on this different initial Japanese interpretation. Moreover, as was evident in the broader area of defense production, the expansion of dual-use applications presented added complications to the enforcement of the "peaceful use" provision over time.

Domestic Political Issues Raised by Possible Japanese Activities in Outer Space

Japan's first government space body, the NSAC, consisted of twenty-nine members, including eight ministry bureau chiefs. This group sent its first, five-member mission abroad to study the space agencies of other Western allies in January 1961. After this initial foray abroad, the composition of the NSAC changed, adding six new members from industry (from a start of only two, both of whom were sent from Keidanren, the Federation of Economic Organizations) and replacing the bureau chief level ministry officials with vice-minister-level representatives (Yatō 1983). This upgrading of ties with industry actors and the government bureaucracy indicates that Japanese leaders were taking the development of outer space more seriously. By the mid-1960s, the NSAC was stressing the importance of space activities to national development goals and urging long-term planning for space development as a so-called national project (Science and Technology Agency 1978).

Early industry actor participation in planning for Japan's space program also led to the establishment of the Space Activities Promotion Council (SAPC) by Keidanren in 1968. This council provided an institutionalized channel for industry to express its views to government regarding the future of space development in Japan. Reports of the time list the following as its three primary objectives: (1) to review the current level of space development in Japan; (2) to improve indigenous technological development capability and promote domestic production; and (3) to further engage in international cooperation with advanced and developing states (Chiku 1992, p. 14).

Given Japan's limited technological development in the 1960s, together with a military budget far smaller than those of similarly positioned states, the pursuit of an independent military use of space was not a viable option. What was possible was joint research on military space applications together with the United States, a program advocated by U.S. policy makers. This is exactly the situation that many Japanese feared—a deepening of the security relationship with the United States, one which potentially could draw Japan into outside conflict—and was brought to the fore by the January 1968 U.S. proposal for institutionalized cooperation between the United States and Japan on outer space development. In the debate over the use of outer space, the Japan Socialist Party (JSP) and its allies offered an argument similar to their opposition to arms exports, one rooted in the constitutional prohibition on the maintenance of "war potential." Furthering the general argument against defense production, the JSP spoke strongly against military involvement in space development—evoking the popular buzzword of "civilian control."[12] The left and dovish politicians of the right were against unchecked exploration of outer space for a number of reasons relating to their principled antimilitarist beliefs. For the left, joint U.S.-Japan development of space technologies represented a further deepening of the U.S.-Japan alliance and further exposed Japan to the possibility of a deepening rift with the Soviet Union. Moreover, proposed space cooperation with the United States potentially challenged recent gains made in the area of arms export restrictions declared in the Three Principles declaration of 1967 and could lead to the militarization of a hitherto nonmilitarized region, outer space.

The Lower House election in January 1967 marked a potential turning point for the LDP—as noted in Chapter 4 in the context of arms export restrictions—as the percentage of the LDP vote dropped below 50 percent for the first time since the party's formation in 1955. Importantly, however, the JSP also lost ground in this election, while those advocating the middle ground—the Democratic Social- ist Party (DSP), which gained seven seats, and the Kōmeitō (KMT), which secured twenty-five seats in its first Lower House contest—gained ground. (See Appendix 4 for complete election results.) At this time, the KMT advocated a gradual, nego- tiated withdrawal from the U.S.-Japan Security Treaty, not a deepening of ties on outer space development. Moreover, the KMT's broader foreign policy platform called for concrete efforts to contribute to world peace, rather than simply follow- ing a policy of *domestic* antimilitarism. The declared peaceful-use-of-space policy played to this sentiment, stressing the international contribution space develop- ment could make to all humankind. Thus, the passing of the resolution on the peaceful use of outer space can be seen as a further attempt by the LDP to build on the political appeal of the 1967 Three Principles declaration on arms exports in an effort to reach centrist voters. What guided the shape of this policy declara- tion—the language and its scope—was the codified security identity of domestic antimilitarism.

Space policy was a relatively easy area for the LDP to appeal to opposition party supporters—and doves within their own party—while still retaining sup- port from their core business constituencies, because Japan did not possess the technology to achieve a military use of outer space; moreover, industry actors were not anxious to devote significant funds for an area of research with unproven and unclear commercial potential (Chiku 1992). Space policy also enjoyed the advantage of being able to be delinked from the perception of military applica- tions in a way that arms production could not be. In the area of arms produc- tion, the best argument that could be made to justify the practice was the need for Japan to possess the capability of self-defense and simultaneously to stress the technological spin-off from such production, while emphasizing the limits on the scale of domestic production. In the area of outer space development, however, research and development could be presented in an entirely peaceful light, with an emphasis on the commercial applications of the technology and the contribu- tions of space industries to domestic and international well-being—exactly the principles set out in the opposition-sponsored Peaceful Use of Space Diet resolu- tion, and evident in every major policy statement on the use of outer space issued by the Japanese government. As seen in the text of this resolution (reprinted in Appendix 6), although "peaceful purposes" is stressed in the first clause of the not lengthy resolution, equally evident is the potential commercial, technological, and social benefit of outer space activities.

Even after the 1969 establishment of NASDA to guide Japanese space policy under clear limits and the adoption of the resolution over the peaceful use of outer space in the Diet, however, public concern over deepening military relations with the United States vis-à-vis space cooperation were not quelled entirely. When Thomas Paine, the chief administrator of NASA, visited Japan in 1970 to propose joint development of the U.S. space shuttle concept, Japanese leaders demurred on this issue. It was not until 1974, after the conclusion of fighting in Vietnam, that Japan expressed interest in cooperating with the United States more fully in the space shuttle project, by which time the United States had already decided to pursue the project independently (Chiku 1992).

Broad policy questions were not the only concern of political actors, of course. Japanese firms—like their counterparts in the United States and elsewhere, only on a much smaller scale—sought to use government-sponsored outer space research and development as a way of developing a greater technological base, including through licensing agreements with U.S. space contractors. Such collaborative agreements with U.S. producers provide another explanation for Japanese firms' limitation of outer space development to peaceful purposes, since military—and even large-scale commercial—applications were generally prohibited in licensing agreements. Thus, support for an active development of outer space was lacking even from industry actors at this time, quite apart from any constraints imposed by the security identity of domestic antimilitarism. In addition, the Ministry of Finance (MOF) did not support the initiation of a costly new space program from a budgetary perspective. Also on the bureaucratic front, the Ministry of International Trade and Industry (MITI) feared that since Japan did not possess the technology to develop outer space industries at a reasonable pace on its own, the United States would dominate the development process and reap most of the benefits. Both ministries feared increasing power to the JDA were it to control any resulting satellites. The cross-industry actor, Keidanren's SAPC, also did not actively support substantial investments in outer space industries for reasons similar to that of MITI—namely, that Japanese companies stood to gain little from the production of a costly technology they had not yet mastered.[13] Thus, while domestic antimilitarist opposition to the military use of outer space was apparent in this period, it cannot be seen as trumping other important political forces but rather complementing them. This congruence of interests would not continue in the next period of Japan's outer space activities, however.

Japan orbited its first satellite, Ōsumi, in February 1970, largely due to technology provided by the United States. Japan would not launch a 100 percent domestically produced satellite, the ETS-4, until 1981, and it continued to rely on foreign (mostly U.S.) technology throughout the 1980s and into the 1990s.[14] The accomplishment of orbiting Ōsumi also underscored Japan's continued dependence on the United States in a second way in that Japan did not possess the capability to launch the satellite by itself—another service provided by Japan's Cold War ally. A general agreement between the United States and Japan over the launch of Japanese satellites on U.S. rockets was concluded on May 23, 1975, but by that time Japan had successfully developed the M and N class rockets capable of launching lighter-weight satellites and the United States was pushing Japan and its European allies to cooperate further in the so-called Post-Apollo project.

In sum, this period of Japan's early outer space policy shows the security identity of domestic antimilitarism informing policy debate, being institutionalized into policy bodies and statements, and linking the question of outer space policy with other defense questions. However, unlike some other areas of defense policy at the time, the prescription of the security identity did not face substantial opposition. Thus, the explanation of the policy outcome cannot be ascribed solely to the power of the postwar security identity.

Growing Enthusiasm for Outer Space Activities

By the late 1970s, the time was ripe for Japan to reevaluate the practices it had been following to promote outer space development—one based on peaceful use, close cooperation with the United States, and on limited government investment—and instead to consider in particular how to further an initial goal of its space program: the use of outer space for commercial purposes. After some deliberation, the SAC decided that a new national space policy was required, and it established the Long-Term Vision Panel to draft a new Fundamental Policy of Space Development, which ultimately was ratified in 1978—not coincidentally the same year that the first defense cooperation "guidelines" were declared as part of an enhanced U.S.-Japan military alliance.[15] At a time when defense cooperation with the United States was intensifying in one area, the Fundamental Policy of Space Development, or Fundamental Policy, further served to institutionalize the principles of domestic antimilitarism into government policy, setting out three "fundamental principles" to Japanese space policy.[16] This institutionalization is important because it codified the 1969 Diet resolution on the peaceful use of space—which did not itself have the force of law—into a government-promulgated, cabinet-adopted policy which all government bodies that engage in space activities were required to follow. This process illustrates, once again, Kathryn Sikkink's (1991) framework of stages of identity adoption, from initial adoption through implementation to consolidation. The policy opens with a first principle reaffirming Japan's commitment that all Japanese space activities should be designed only for peaceful purposes, and more broadly should serve to contribute to the economic and social development of all mankind (at home and abroad).[17] The second principle further reaffirms Japanese practice, that securing and developing indigenous technology should be a priority of space activities. Finally, an objective of harmony with international activities and a broader international contribution was declared.[18]

On December 3, 1980—once the peaceful nature of Japan's space policy had been further institutionalized—a new agreement on space cooperation was concluded between Japan and the United States, allowing U.S. industry to assist Japan in developing a next generation of launch vehicles capable of lifting a much heavier payload into outer space. Such timing once again follows the long-standing practice of "reach, reconcile, reassure"—although in this case the reassurance (in terms of the new Fundamental Policy) came first. At this point, however, the United States had begun to see Japan as a potential future competitor in the area of space industries. To check this development, the United States insisted on two significant restrictions on the use of U.S.-provided technology regarding launch vehicles. First, it sought to prohibit Japan from launching satellites that might compete with the INTELSAT virtual monopoly; second, it prohibited Japan from using any newly acquired rocket technology to launch payload from third countries.[19] Such a development, in 1980, is somewhat ironic given that just over a decade earlier there had been great concern among the Japanese public that cooperation with the United States on space development would lead to the militarization of Japan's space policies. Arguably, U.S. restrictions on the use of transferred technology had the reverse effect: pursuant to licensing agreements with the U.S. government and U.S. manufacturers, Japan was not allowed to utilize received technology for military purposes, nor to transfer proprietary technology to other states (in order to control possible military applications). Thus, and again contrary to commonly seen explanations of Japanese policy, Japan's policy regarding the peaceful use of outer space was institutionalized to a significant degree by *international* obligations. This mirrors the case of arms exports, discussed in Chapter 4, where Japanese limitations were imposed to a large degree by its obligations to the Coordinating Committee on Multilateral Strategic Export Controls (COCOM).

New International Forces Influencing Japan's Evolving Space Policy

The 1980s witnessed a significant worsening of Japan's relationship with the United States in the economic arena, fueled by the crosscutting phenomena of the rising economic competitiveness of Japan with the declining economic competitiveness of the United States. Although major changes in the international system took place in 1989 with the fall of the Berlin Wall and in 1991 with the collapse of the bubble economy, the 1980s were already showing signs of another major change in the international environment—the continued rise of Japanese economic power and the challenge this posed to U.S. leadership in the world. This period of Japan's space development was also one of intense commercial friction between Japan and the United States, both in general and also on the specific issue of satellites. A wire service headline in November 1983 signals the trouble to come: "U.S.-Japan Satellite War?" (*Jiji Press,* November 9, 1983). Subsequent headlines convey important developments that followed: "Big Money Is Riding on Success of Satellites" (*Nihon Keizai Shimbun,* September 30, 1989); "[United States Trade Representative] Hills Urges Japan to Open Satellite Market" (*Jiji Press,* October 13, 1989); "U.S. in Sanctions Threat on Japanese Satellite Market";[20] "Japan May Scrap Satellite to Avoid U.S. Trade Clash";[21] "Satellite Accord Historic: U.S. Official" (*Jiji Press,* April 3, 1990); and finally, "Satellite Program Heads for Major Cuts after Trade Talks" (Kyodo News Service, April 4, 1990). Thus, the 1980s marks economic and technological superpower Japan's entry into the competitive world of commercial satellites. This important development vastly altered the policy-making environment and put new pressure on the dated Diet resolution regarding acceptable uses of outer space.

An important development in Japan's "rising hegemon" status was the Plaza Accord of 1985, which greatly increased the value of the yen vis-à-vis the dollar and the major European currencies and fueled the explosion of Japanese foreign direct investment in the United States and elsewhere in the world. Concurrent with American fears of Japan "buying up the United States" was growing criticism of the perceived "unfairness" of Japanese trade practices.[22] These concerns were reflected in new legislation in the U.S. Congress to force Japan to change a number of government-led support programs for Japanese (and other states') industry, epitomized by the powerful new "Super 301" trade sanctions passed as part of the Omnibus Trade and Competitiveness Act of 1988. Among the first sectors targeted by Super 301 in the case of Japan was the nascent Japanese satellite industry, where the United States Trade Representative (USTR) accused the Japanese government of exclusionary government procurement. At that time the Japanese government had been purchasing roughly two satellites per year from Japanese industry and was not open to substituting such purchases with satellites produced by U.S. manufacturers—despite the U.S. satellites being less expensive and more powerful (Chiku 1992, p. 67). The Japanese government initially responded that such support for an essential industry was comparable to support provided to the U.S. space industry through the massive U.S. defense budget, but Japanese negotiators quickly retreated on this point and agreed to stop the practice of favoring domestic satellite producers, much to the consternation of the three primary domestic manufacturers, Nippon Electric Company (NEC), Toshiba, and Mitsubishi Electric. Thus, conceding to U.S. pressure on this issue is arguably at least as powerful an explanation for why development of satellites using government support was put off in the 1980s; a change in this factor by the mid-1990s (at which time it was Japan that faced a stagnant economy and high budget deficit) counterfactually provides a strong alternative explanation for a change in Japanese policy regarding satellite development apart from one rooted in the claim of a changing security identity.

It is ironic that Japan's peaceful-use-of-space policy suffered its greatest setbacks at a time when its cooperation with the United States in the area of space development was waning, given that one of the initial domestic motivations for the 1969 Diet resolution on the peaceful use of outer space was the fear of increased cooperation with the United States. Despite this irony, however, it was Japan's own drive to derive commercial benefit from outer space that competed with its commitment to limiting its use of outer space to purely nonmilitary purposes—further illustrating the need to better conceptualize how different identity discourses interact to shape policy outcomes. More theorizing in this area is required, but in this case one can clearly see the effect of opposition to the hegemonic security identity on actual security practice, in particular in the area of industry pressure, building on an alternative identity narrative of technonationalism. As with arms export restrictions, the United States had no interest in advocating for the repeal of Japan's peaceful-use-of-space policy. The policy was congruent with both U.S. economic and strategic interests, so there was no need to oppose it in principle. Economically, Japan's "antimilitarist" policy kept rising Japanese corporations out of a lucrative market for U.S. firms. Strategically, it gave greater control to the United States in marketing its view of international conflicts within the Cold War world due to the U.S. monopoly on intelligence gathered from its extensive network of surveillance satellites. In the following decade, Japanese challenges to the U.S. information monopoly would engender a strong negative reaction from defense policy makers in the United States.

Reconsidering "Peaceful Principles" in a New Domestic Political Environment

As with the restrictions on arms exports, Japan's peaceful-use-of-space policy was subject to reinterpretation and changing political support over time. The first major erosions of the policy regarding the peaceful use of outer space took place in 1985 under the prime ministership of Yasuhiro Nakasone, who began his term in 1982. Unlike previous prime ministers such as Miki and Fukuda, Nakasone became known almost immediately for his direct, action-oriented style, an excellent counterpart to the popular U.S. president Ronald Reagan. Moreover, like

Reagan, Nakasone had long been known as a hawk on defense issues and lived up to this reputation as prime minister by removing the 1 percent of GDP ceiling on defense spending,[23] agreeing to participation in the U.S. Strategic Defense Initiative (SDI),[24] and seeking to loosen the Three Principles on Arms Exports after decades of movement in the opposite direction codifying a ban on such exports.[25]

Under Nakasone, two important modifications to Japan's space use policy were enacted. First, it was determined that the purchase of satellite images *from abroad* for use as military intelligence did not violate the ban on Japan's military use of space.[26] This decision created an uproar in the media and by the left, who argued that the nationality of the satellites was irrelevant to the question of what the images would be used for—that is, if the images were not to be used for "peaceful purposes" in Japan, the fact that they originated abroad was irrelevant. By contrast, it should be stressed, the Diet resolution explicitly allows for (and even encourages) the use of satellite imagery for nonmilitary purposes, such as weather forecasting. Second, and more damaging to the previous interpretation of peaceful use, the Nakasone administration maintained that the use of domestic satellites for military *communications* purposes did not violate the peaceful-use-of-space policy. This decision not only allowed for foreign (in particular, U.S. military) satellites to be used to support the Self-Defense Forces, but also—and more importantly—for *domestic* firms to operate and/or produce satellites for the JDA.[27] Both types of satellites (foreign and domestic) began to be used by the JDA and the SDF beginning in 1985, as per a government "clarification"—provided at a Budget Committee meeting of the Lower House of the Diet on February 6 (reprinted in Appendix 6).

Nakasone's push for change challenged both the first tenet of domestic antimilitarism, by actively seeking to enhance the role of the JDA and the SDF in security policy making within the state, and the third tenet of the security identity, by more closely linking the United States and Japan into a common security framework. Clearly Nakasone achieved some success in this area, though the political capital he expended to make such changes limited his ability to fulfill his objectives in other areas. Nakasone's limited success in achieving changes in Japan's overall security policies demonstrates the permeation of the security identity of domestic antimilitarism into the policy-making process over the twenty years since the revision of the U.S.-Japan Security Treaty in 1960. In addition, it demonstrates the continued contestation over the political compromise of domestic antimilitarism.

Apart from Nakasone's agenda, new interest from domestic economic actors within Japan in both industry and government in satellite development drove a change in policy. Moreover, the increasing difficulty of separating dual-use, in particular high-technology, manufactures into military and civilian categories eroded the simple ideational power of the peaceful-use-of-space policy at the rhetorical level, a phenomenon also evident in the case of arms export restrictions discussed in Chapter 4, and in a wide array of technologies which proliferated in the early twenty-first century discussed in later chapters. Despite a great enthusiasm for space exploration among the general public,[28] Japanese government and industry officials did not aggressively pursue the development of space-related activities until the late 1980s. Only after the 1985 Plaza Accord–generated exchange rate revaluations greatly increased the wealth of Japanese companies, and Japanese technology had risen to a level competitive with (and even beyond) that of the United States on many levels, did Japanese government and industry leaders seriously consider the development of outer space industries. Before this point, Japan primarily engaged in space industries at a minimal level necessary to stay informed of major developments in the field and to benefit from generous technology transfers offered by the United States, its close Cold War ally. The Japanese space budget never reached more than 10 percent of that of NASA in the United States (Science and Technology Agency 1991); moreover, this comparison does not figure in the vast additional (and classified) outer space–related budgets of U.S. military programs funded by the Pentagon, the CIA, and the NSA, among other agencies. Japan's increasing technological capability, its sense of confidence in its economy and general know-how, and—importantly—new government support for satellite development due to Prime Minister Nakasone's announcement that the JDA could utilize satellites for military communications each contributed to a growing interest in outer space development in the 1980s.

By the mid-1980s—when pressure to lessen restrictions on arms exports was also being generated by important industry actors—Japanese firms became convinced that successful development of space-related technology was imperative to a number of technologies that would be important in the twenty-first century. Pursuant to this interest, business groups successfully lobbied for government support of research and development into satellite technologies, beginning with communications satellites that had both commercial and military applications. In addition to general communications satellites, the three major firms that were developing satellite technology (Mitsubishi, NEC, and Toshiba) were also interested in expanding their market—and securing additional government support—by developing technologies relevant to surveillance satellites. Thus, consistent with the growing rhetoric of indigenization (Samuels 1994), discussion could be heard within certain LDP circles and in the Keidanren SAPC and Defense Production Committee (DPC) for Japan to develop its own surveillance satellites, rather than to continue to rely on foreign satellites for military intelligence.

Particularly galling to proponents of the peaceful-use-of-space policy was that proponents of the domestic production of satellite imagery adopted exactly the earlier argument of their opponents, though twisting the message to suit their own purposes. In stark contrast to their previous claims, opponents of a strict interpretation of the peaceful-use-of-space policy now concurred with supporters of the policy that there was no effective difference between purchasing satellite images from abroad or acquiring them from domestically owned (and produced) satellites. Thus, by trumpeting the earlier-secured precedent of allowing the purchase of satellite images from abroad, opponents of the peaceful-use-of-space policy were able to push their case for the policy's further erosion by demanding the ability to build and operate surveillance satellites domestically. While no one could say whether this was their strategy all along, if it had been it was a very clever one in that it appealed to the growing rhetoric in other policy areas of Japanese government policy of *kokusanka*, or indigenization. However, though clever, this strategy did not lead to a successful outcome. The push for domestically produced and operated surveillance satellites would not yield concrete results for another decade, due in large part to the continued power of Japan's domestic antimilitarist security identity (which was also instrumental in checking other Nakasone initiatives), as well as to the pressure from the United States noted above. Still, at this period of time, the role of the hegemonic security identity of domestic antimilitarism as well as actors working against this hegemonic force is plainly evident, and moreover, exercised a clear effect on policy outcomes.

Identity Shift? The Decision to Deploy Surveillance Satellites

On December 25, 1998, the long-standing policy against the use of outer space for military intelligence purposes was reframed yet again when the government announced its intention to develop a network of domestically produced and deployed "information-gathering" satellites (IGS) to be utilized primarily by the JDA and the SDF in response to new security threats.[29] This decision marks one of the biggest changes in interpretation of Japan's peaceful-use-of-space policy to date, a departure not fully acknowledged by key decision makers, who insist that because any deployed satellites will be used to support the peaceful, *defensive* mission of the Self-Defense Forces, such activities will not contravene the peaceful-use-of-space policy established in 1969. This is one reason why the government-preferred terminology for these satellites is IGS rather than surveillance or spy satellites. Though certainly the decision calls into question the staying power of Japan's postwar security identity of domestic antimilitarism in the twenty-first century, as with nearly all security decisions in recent years, political leaders worked hard to fit a new policy objective within the contours of the security identity, sacrificing some efficiency and broader objectives of the satellite program in the process.[30] Moreover, as illustrated above, this was by no means the first time that Japan's policy regarding the use of outer space had to be adjusted to a new domestic and international environment.

Clearly Japan's security environment had changed since the end of the Cold War, as discussed in Chapter 3. This point was driven home particularly starkly by the so-called Taepodong Incident of August 1998, when a North Korean missile unexpectedly overflew the Japanese main island of Honshu before splashing down in the Pacific Ocean nearby. The launch was later claimed by North Korea to be a research satellite, but it was perceived by Japan and the United States as another test of North Korea's ballistic missile capability. Despite the clear spark toward policy shift instigated by the Taepodong Incident, which built on long-brewing security concerns that Japan needed an independent intelligence capacity, understanding of Japan's security identity of domestic antimilitarism best accounts for the delayed implementation and ultimate nature of the 1998 decision to develop a network of surveillance satellites. Failure to incorporate this factor leaves inexplicable the nature of the ultimate policy decision as well as its delayed implementation.

The security identity of domestic antimilitarism structured the final policy outcome regarding IGS in three ways. First, the security identity provided an acceptable language with which to discuss the issue. It diffused discussion of controversial "spy," "military," or "surveillance" satellites by offering instead the idea of "information-gathering" (joho eisei) and "multipurpose" (tamokuteki) satellites. This allowed the issue to enter public discourse on terms acceptable to a majority.[31] While the point may seem trivial, knowledge of the long-standing constraints imposed by the security identity allowed decision makers to avoid a misstep over the issue of surveillance satellites from which they may not have been able to recover. Had they proposed the development of military spy satellites up front, they may not have been able to backtrack to "information-gathering" satellites later.

The terms information-gathering and multipurpose were not just rhetorical. They affected the mission of the satellites as well. Thus, a second way that the security identity continued to influence the policy outcome is that it removed certain policy options from discussion from the start—a "logic of appropriateness" or a commonsense screening mechanism (March and Olsen 1989, Weldes et al. 1999). Pursuant with the first tenet of domestic antimilitarism—that Japan would possess no standard armed forces that played a central role in formulating security policy—surveillance satellites could not be controlled by the JDA or the SDF alone. This was seen as too empowering of military decision makers at the expense of civilian control. The idea of multipurpose satellites allowed the military to benefit from the satellites, but only (at least nominally) as would other government ministries and agencies.

A third way that Japan's postwar security identity structured the policy outcome was that, due largely to the above two points, it focused public opinion around acceptable boundaries for satellite development, allowing a consensus to emerge on the issue. This point is particularly important given the speed with which the final decision to develop the satellites was made—less than four months after the North Korean Taepodong I missile overflight in August 1998, despite literally decades of previous lobbying to enact such programs.

What is it that led to the decision to develop surveillance satellites in 1998, and not earlier? This question gets to the core of contending explanations for Japanese foreign policy outcomes. In the case of surveillance satellites, three factors contributed to the decision, two in the security sphere and one economic. First, a specific security threat—the Taepodong missile overflight of Japan in August 1998—pushed simmering broad security concerns to the forefront of Japanese discussions of security preparedness. Without this spark, it is unlikely that surveillance satellites would have gained a place on the government's policy agenda. Second, on the broader security front, Japanese defense planners and conservative politicians had long lamented Japan's lack of adequate intelligence resources and its dependence on the United States in this area, particularly given Japan's expanded international role in the 1990s. In the post–Cold War period, Japanese defense planners had marked success in filling this intelligence gap on a variety of fronts, though not in the area of domestically controlled surveillance satellites.[32] Third, and equally important, the sudden desire to better guard against the North Korean threat would not have led to lightning-speed policy outcomes had business actors not been prepared to capitalize on the moment. Thus, the role of economic actors in this security policy decision must be given serious consideration. Each of these three factors is briefly discussed below, noting the parallels between this policy change and previous instances of change in the restrictions on the use of outer space discussed above—changes all structured by Japan's postwar security identity.

A Response to the Taepodong Incident of 1998. On August 31, 1998, North Korea launched a Taepodong I missile over the main Japanese island of Honshu that splashed down in the Pacific Ocean. While the North Korean missile was tracked by a Japanese Aegis destroyer, the attack reinforced the perception that Japan would be defenseless in a ballistic missile attack, leading to new prescriptions such as the deployment of domestically controlled surveillance satellites and the

development of a ballistic missile defense (BMD) system.[33] Just one week after the
North Korean Taepodong missile overflight of Honshu, on September 7, the Japanese government and the LDP "liaison council" began looking into the option
of acquiring "multipurpose satellites" (*tamokuteki eisei*)—adopting a terminology proposed by industry advocates careful to frame a proposal in line with the
requirements of domestic antimilitarism. Just over two months after the incident,
on November 6, the cabinet adopted a plan to launch four "information-gathering" satellites in fiscal 2002.[34] This was the second incident in which North Korea
in effect aimed missiles or their equivalents at Japan, the first being the Nodong
missile test in 1993 and, moreover, created a perception among many Japanese that
Japan was being coerced by North Korea. Japanese politicians were unprepared to
react to the Taepodong overflight. In the aftermath of the launch, Japanese politicians and the public suffered what one report called a "Sputnik flinch,"[35] alluding
to the reaction of the United States to the launch of the Soviet satellite in 1957. As
a result of the Taepodong Incident, some argued, there was a quick reconsideration in Japan about what is acceptable and desirable in the realm of military space
activity.

Such a reconsideration did not take place in a vacuum, however. As discussed
below, powerful economic actors stood poised to exploit this new opportunity.
Moreover, the reconsideration of the limits on Japan's use of outer space did not
result in the flouting of domestic antimilitarism. While the decision to develop
and deploy surveillance satellites marks another step in the evolution of the peaceful-use-of-space policy, the final policy outcome was still substantially affected by
Japan's long-standing security identity.

The Broad Security Argument. Many in the Japanese political and defense communities question possible bias in U.S. intelligence provided as part of the security
alliance.[36] They fear that the United States provides only the type of information
and intelligence that it finds convenient to share in order to manipulate Japan. As
one Ministry of Foreign Affairs (MOFA) official commented anonymously: "The
U.S. will not supply Japan with information or intelligence if it deems that Japan's
measures are disagreeable to the U.S. policy direction. Being self-sufficient in
information gathering can be translated into having a greater freehand. That's how
things work in the post–Cold War period."[37] Several important politicians share
this view. Tomoharu Yoda, former administrative defense vice-minister, has stated,
"Japan has a defense-only security policy, so for that purpose, we have to have
intelligence. We can get intelligence from the U.S., but from the points of view
of security and crisis management, we need to have our own intelligence-gather-
ing satellites."[38] Mitsubishi Electric (MELCO)—the firm with the most interest

in supporting surveillance satellite development—plays on these fears in its promotional literature, emphasizing "accomplishing independence unsusceptible to manipulation of information by other countries."[39]

Pressure from Industry. Military security issues provide only a partial explanation for the decision to deploy surveillance satellites. Economic issues have also played an important role in the development of security policy decisions. The case of surveillance satellites is no exception. The commercial use of outer space is expanding exponentially in the twenty-first century, leading to the entry of a larger number of players from a greater number of countries. While satellite production and operation is only one aspect of this market, it is one of the largest parts. More than one thousand satellites are projected to be launched in the first decade of the twenty-first century (National Defense Panel 1997, p. 38). Moreover, for the first time in history, the number of commercial launches exceeded government launches in 1996. Growth in the commercial satellite market is expected to continue to increase in the twenty-first century from $7.5 billion in 1995 to a projected $13.69 billion in 2004 (Frost and Sullivan 1999). Thus, it is not surprising that Japanese firms have continued to aggressively push for relaxed restrictions on their activities at home and abroad in the 1990s.[40]

While ostensibly the decision to deploy surveillance satellites is a national security issue, the enormous cost of an effective system—estimated at over 1 trillion yen ($10 billion) over ten years—requires one to carefully consider the potential commercial benefits to the producer of such a system. Japan's major defense producers are keenly aware of this benefit—both for the profits of building such a system by itself as well as for the spin-off benefit of expertise that could be applied to commercial satellite development and production. Japanese national security policy explicitly rejected the use of outer space for direct military purposes through its "peaceful-use-of-space policy" declared in the Diet in May 1969. However, one could argue that Japan has been engaged in developing military space capabilities from the onset of its independent space program because of the common technologies basic to many civil and military space systems—a point also pertinent to the arms export issue. In the world of twenty-first-century technology, the U.S. Global Positioning System (GPS) satellites widely used in Japan, reconnaissance satellites, and satellite communication systems all represent utilization of passive military space systems. The ability to rationalize their justification and legality is far more palpable than explicitly acknowledging the development of overt space-based weapons systems—even if the weapons are defensive in nature, such as in the case of ballistic missile defense (BMD) considered in the next chapter.

In an effort to take advantage of this commercially promising field, the Space Activities Promotion Council, a special committee of Keidanren, issued a report in July 1999 entitled "Proposal for the Establishment of a Comprehensive Policy on Space Activities and for the Strengthening and Industrialization of Space Industries," which was widely distributed to leading government officials.[41] Later in the same year, Keidanren's Industrial Affairs Bureau issued an even more forceful opinion on the need to capitalize on the space market:

> The Western countries are pushing forward money-making projects to redouble their efforts to commercialize space industries and increasing their competency.... Now is the time, and it is essential for Japan, to establish a national strategy to strengthen the basis of cutting-edge technology and to promote in a timely manner ongoing space projects so that we can succeed in global competition.[42]

In this report, there is no explicit mention of military satellite applications, though it is reasonable to expect that Japanese firms will actively seek out military-use applications for their satellite business, especially given the government's recent signal that BMD research is not seen to violate the Diet resolution on the peaceful use of space.

The enthusiasm of government ministries, agencies, and politicians helped MELCO and NEC to actively promote their products. NEC had been promoting its version of a satellite system, though it was hindered by a JDA procurement scandal in which NEC was implicated. According to the *Asahi Shimbun*, NEC was the first corporation to formally present a surveillance satellite project to the LDP, in 1997.[43] At this time NEC proposed a system consisting of one optical and one radar satellite, with the optical satellite capable of a resolution of 0.4 meters, a level far superior to the system ultimately contracted and one used today only by military satellites.[44] On August 25, six days before North Korea fired the Taepodong missile, MELCO president Ichiro Taniguchi attended an LDP Science and Technology Council meeting to make an in-depth presentation on "multipurpose precision observation satellites." In the session, Taniguchi stressed the importance and advantages of possessing surveillance satellites. The MELCO presentation on surveillance satellites could not have come at a more fortuitous time, as it must have been fresh on several legislators' minds when they heard of the Taepodong overflight on August 31.

In sum, although news reports of the time frequently stated that the idea of Japan owning multipurpose satellites emerged after the Taepodong Incident, this claim is patently false. Major Japanese defense producers—namely MELCO, NEC, and Toshiba—had sought for years to secure government support for national satellite development in a variety of forms. Japan had long been a space participant, but only in the realm of civil and commercial activity. The Taepodong Incident provided the spark to justify taking these activities to the next level, to allow further Japanese corporate cooperation with the JDA in the use of outer space. The Taepodong Incident provided the final push needed by those advocating that Japan acquire surveillance satellites to empower a recrafting of the security identity of domestic antimilitarism to allow for this new policy outcome.

Security Identity and the Limited Scope of the Surveillance Satellite Program

By mid-September 1998, it appeared clear that government and industry at last would be able to move ahead with plans to develop Japan's satellite intelligence capabilities. What was not clear was the scope of the system that would be built and whether it would be produced 100 percent domestically or whether components would be imported from abroad. From the earliest stages, the government took care to employ the rhetoric of domestic antimilitarism in any discussion of surveillance satellites, which affected the question of the scope and capabilities of the system ultimately approved. Efforts by the United States to block and then to shape the nature of the surveillance satellite system also structured the nature and timing of the final outcome.

The Taepodong Incident provided an opportunity for the government to justify and implement long-brewing plans for the domestic development of surveillance satellites. Still, LDP and industry leaders proceeded cautiously. Even in the near hysterical domestic environment of the days immediately following the Taepodong Incident, government declarations regarding surveillance satellites provided information on the true nature of the potential new satellites only sparingly.[45] According to one of the first government reports on the decision, Japan would use the satellites for national security purposes, to watch for natural disasters, and to fight smuggling and illegal immigration.[46] The government also explicitly stated its view that such satellites would be consistent with the 1969 Diet resolution on the peaceful use of outer space. Accordingly, data gathered from the satellites would not be sent to defense authorities for analysis and rather would be based in the Cabinet Information Research Office (CIRO).[47]

Although the Diet resolution on the peaceful use of space posed one obstacle to domestic surveillance satellite development, it was by no means the only obstacle. As the plan for developing such a system gained momentum, other issues such as which agency would administer the system, which would pay for it (and in what share), the reaction of the United States, and the reaction of Japan's neighbors all exerted considerable influence on decision making. After the public had a little more time to digest the significant change in Japanese policy, the *Nihon*

Keizai Shimbun editorialized explicitly against the satellite plan as it was developing, under the banner "Focus on intelligence satellites should be placed on natural disasters,"[48] and did not include reference to the Diet resolution on the peaceful use of space, rather focusing on a number of technical difficulties of the plan, including the lack of sufficiently trained imagery analysts, the fact that the proposal would not include early-warning capabilities, and that imagery of equal resolution would soon be available to the JDA from commercial sources. Moreover, concern was expressed regarding the impact of such a program on Japan's international reputation. Opines the *Nihon Keizai Shimbun*: "The project poses an array of questions over the specifics of its implementation, as well as the sensitive issue of winning the understanding of neighboring nations."[49]

Although public concern over the possible military nature of the surveillance satellites proved less important than the perceived security threat from North Korea and the need for adequate preparations for future missile development on the part of North Korea,[50] the ultimate scope and nature of the surveillance satellite program was clearly shaped by the long-standing security identity—beginning with its very name, IGS. Under the MELCO-proposed multipurpose satellite system, satellite-collected visual data would be utilized for such purposes as forecasting weather conditions, probing mineral resources, creating maps, and preventing disasters, in addition to less-discussed military applications. In practice, however, the four satellites currently in operation are used almost exclusively (and some suspect entirely) for military purposes—a subject closely followed by the left-leaning *Asahi Shimbun* and other intelligence watchdogs. The ultimate plan is to have two 1-ton optical satellites and two 1.5-ton radar satellites, initially expected to be operational by 2003 but only realized in February 2007. The optical satellites are capable of producing images at a one-meter resolution, covering areas up to fourteen kilometers, while the best of the two radar satellites produce images between one and three meters of resolution. A one-meter resolution standard marks a dramatic improvement over the ten-meter resolution that the JDA had been previously purchasing from private sources,[51] and it will allow for differentiation between types of ballistic missiles and fighter aircraft—but, due to limits imposed by the postwar security identity, it is not as high a resolution as typically used by military intelligence satellites.[52] Moreover, the satellite system is controlled by a new Cabinet Satellite Intelligence Center (CSICE) within the CIRO, which processes requests from the various governmental ministries and agencies for imagery and analysis—fulfilling another prescription of domestic antimilitarism that the satellites not be directly controlled by the military.

Conclusions: Security Identity and the
Evolving Use of Outer Space

The evolution of Japan's policies on the peaceful use of outer space illustrates the continuing effect of Japan's postwar security identity on actual security practice, but it also exposes the limits of an explanation based on this factor alone. As Japan's technological capabilities rose, and its sense of external threat and power in the international system increased, a series of decisions were negotiated by key political actors to reinterpret policy to allow the use of satellite imagery for military purposes—a significant concession to the original intent of the 1969 Diet resolution. Attention to the ideational arena as well as international systemic and domestic political pressures is necessary to explain this policy evolution. More-over, a commitment both to the peaceful use of outer space and to the indigenous development of technology have been facets of Japanese policy toward outer space activities from the very beginning of its space policy. Thus, this case illustrates how multiple identities interact in the formation of actual policy. Such a conclusion is consistent with Japanese policy in other areas of security and economic develop-ment as well (Samuels 1994, Green 1995). Both factors served to legitimate Japan's close cooperation with the United States in the area of space development in the 1960s and 1970s, but as the two principles increasingly came into conflict with each other, it was more often the former that was sacrificed to the latter.

It was not only a commitment to its core security identity that drove Japan's decisions vis-à-vis outer space; rather, it was economic and technical realities, together with alliance politics *and* a continuing concern about possible resurgence of militarism within the postwar Japanese state. Any precedence of the principle of indigenous production and the commercialization of outer space over the principle of the peaceful use of space is not the result of a shift in "norms" or security identity in Japan. Rather, it is indicative of a shifting political and material (especially technological) environment at home and abroad. At a time when Japan possessed neither the technology nor the funds to develop outer space industries that would challenge the peaceful-use-of-space principle, the LDP was content to endorse the peaceful-use-of-space policy for electoral advantage. However, when this policy presented a challenge to core LDP constituencies, in particular the wishes of Keidanren's Space Activities Promotion Council and its core industry members, the policy was significantly relaxed to reflect the preferences of these influential political actors. Thus, while the security identity of domestic antimilita-rism shaped the evolution of the policy over time, it did not nearly determine the final policy outcome by itself. Moreover, instances of sacrificing to some extent the ideational aspirations of the security identity is not new to the post–Cold War period.

As in the case of arms production, early restrictions on the scope of outer space use had a lasting effect on the development of the industry overall. The security identity of domestic antimilitarism did play some role in shaping the ultimate policy trajectory but not just through the peaceful-use-of-space policy. Rather, without a significant defense budget devoted to space industries or a national consensus on the need for significant civilian spending on space industries, industry actors did not aggressively pursue outer space development. Only in the 1980s, when Prime Minister Nakasone successfully relaxed a number of restrictions related to defense cooperation with the United States and when Japanese indigenous technology had increased substantially did industry actors become motivated to pursue commercial applications in outer space development. Since this time, Cold War–era policies largely banning the export of weapons and the military use of outer space have been pushed to their limits due to changes in technology, Japan's international status, and domestic political change that have led to debate over the development of new military capabilities apart from surveillance satellites—in particular the decision to develop effective ballistic missile defense together with the United States, the subject of Chapter 6. Upon examination of this second post–Cold War case, a concluding chapter will link these cases to broader developments in recent Japanese security policy in order to draw conclusions about the continuing resilience of security identity for structuring security practices in twenty-first-century Japan.

6

Missile Defense, Alliance Politics, and Security Identity

The December 1998 decision by the Japanese government to embark on joint research with the United States on the development of a missile defense system and the subsequent December 2003 decision by Japan to develop a related, individually operated missile defense system provide another important case for examining the continued influence and resilience of Japan's postwar security identity in the post–Cold War period, as well as an opportunity to consider other factors which help to determine Japanese security practice.[1] The decision to intensify joint research and move to the development phase in fiscal 2006 deepens interest in this question. This case provides an illuminating example of how the politics surrounding the security identity of domestic antimilitarism have been altered in the post–Cold War period, yet how the central tenets of Japan's security identity remain entrenched—at least for now.

Missile defense is not a policy option considered by Japan independently of U.S. policy planning. It is a direct response by Japan to U.S. initiative, U.S. planning, and U.S. pressure. Despite the external initiation of the policy, Japan's existing security identity is an important component of the tepid initial Japanese response to the U.S. initiative and continued limitations on the program to date. Although some obstacles to development of missile defense appear to have been overcome (as evidenced by the deployment of an initial system), further moves toward deployment of a jointly developed system are bound to raise additional issues related to Japan's security identity and may play a major role in reshaping this identity in the process. Indeed, in interviews with Japan Defense Agency (JDA) officials (December 2005 and January 2006), missile defense was repeatedly referred to as an "engine of change" for Japanese defense policy as well as for Japan's alliance relations with the United States.

The role of the United States in the codification of Japan's security identity of domestic antimilitarism, and on the evolution of specific policy issues such as arms export restrictions and outer space use, is apparent in earlier chapters that focused in particular on the domestic politics of Japan's postwar security identity and security practice. This chapter moves the role of external actors on the shaping of Japan's security practice to the center of analysis, focusing especially on the United States' role in the development of Japan's missile defense policy. U.S. pressure on Japan to share development costs and technical hurdles of missile defense not only led to Japan's adoption of missile defense as an important new capability for the Self-Defense-Forces (SDF) but also led to a rearticulation of core security practices in early twenty-first-century Japan, including such issues as preemption, the exercise of the right of collective self-defense, the use of outer space, the export of weapons technology and components, and the interoperability of U.S. and Japanese forces and equipment. Thus, as with earlier cases examined in this study, the adoption of a new security policy resulted not only in new security practices but also in a new articulation of Japan's security identity itself.

Two separate issues face Japan regarding missile defense. First are Japan's own strategic concerns based on the new post–Cold War international environment. These concerns differ from those of the United States because Japan's security environment and interests differ from those of its superpower ally, despite efforts of elites to play up the "common agenda" of the two states.[2] The second issue facing Japan is the limitations imposed by its security identity, as well as other domestic factors such as bureaucratic politics, industry pressure, and budgetary concerns on responding to U.S. initiatives on missile defense in particular, and broader strategic concerns in general. Several detailed studies of Japan's initial response to missile defense initiatives by the United States examine an impressive range of factors that influenced the initial policy decision to pursue joint research.[3] This chapter reframes some of the evidence presented in these studies into a theoretical context focusing on the central role of Japan's security identity on the policy outcome and additionally updates the narrative based on important developments in U.S.-Japan cooperation on missile defense in recent years as well as Japan's decision to pursue a separate type of missile defense independently.

Japan's joint development of missile defense with the United States was constrained from the start by each of the central tenets of domestic antimilitarism. Regarding the first tenet—prohibiting traditional armed forces with full domestic standing to formulate policy—the concept of a functional missile defense system threatens to extend too much authority to the JDA/Ministry of Defense (MOD) and/or the SDF vis-à-vis other government ministries and agencies. In particular, the issue of control of the system is problematic for Japan's existing security identity. This issue was also present in the debate over surveillance satellites, but in that case it was resolved in two ways consonant with the domestic antimilitarist security identity: first, the mission of the satellites was expanded from a purely military application to one shared by many ministries and agencies—thus, the formal name "information-gathering" satellites, and their cost not drawing from the JDA budget but rather from the Cabinet Office. Second, operational control of the satellites was placed within the Cabinet Intelligence Research Office (CIRO), not the JDA. In the case of missile defense, similar solutions are limited by the purely military nature of the system. As discussed further below, the issue of control poses a significant stumbling block both domestically and with the United States. This issue has partially been resolved, for the case of the Japan-operated system, but remains outstanding for a possible joint U.S.-Japan system. The resolution of the issue for the domestic system raises questions about the recent evolution of Japan's security identity as well as the resulting practice.

The second tenet of domestic antimilitarism—prohibition of the use of force to settle international disputes—is not directly challenged by the defensive nature of missile defense but is still present in discussions of missile defense in Japan simply because missile defense acquisition would continue the trend of increasing the capabilities of the SDF, whose mission is limited to the minimum necessary for the defense of Japan. Each time the SDF increases its capabilities, discussions ensue over the necessity of the increase. The defensive nature of missile defense helps to ameliorate criticism but does not erase it entirely. In particular, the fact that a system may be deployed together with the United States obscures the purely defensive nature of the system because the United States, unlike Japan, does possess offensive weapons—many based in Japan itself—that would be protected by the defensive shield. In this sense, criticism of Japan may be lessened if it were to continue to pursue missile defense independently—an unlikely option due to cost and lack of sufficient technical knowledge.

It is the third tenet of domestic antimilitarism—Japanese nonparticipation in third-party conflict—that is threatened most directly by the idea of a joint missile defense system. This is primarily due to the joint nature of the project: since the system will be developed and, presumably, operated jointly with the United States, it is easy to imagine that it may be used by the United States in a conflict in East Asia outside of Japan—such as on the Korean peninsula or between Taiwan and China.[4] An analogous issue developed in the wake of the September 11 terrorist attacks on the United States in 2001, when Japan considered deploying Aegis-equipped destroyers to aid in the American "war on terrorism." In addition, joint production of the system challenges a long-standing institutionalization of Japan's security identity, the restrictions on arms exports. Already joint research on missile defense has instigated a change in Japan's arms export restrictions—declared on December 10, 2004—but further pressure for greater change continues.

Overall, U.S.-Japan cooperation on missile defense poses one of the biggest challenges to the maintenance of Japan's long-standing security identity of domestic antimilitarism. Already such cooperation has resulted in the reinterpretation of several policies previously restricted by Japan's security identity. A number of additional reinterpretations are pending. Still more will likely be necessary if a robust joint missile defense system is ultimately developed and deployed. Before the implications of missile defense for the U.S.-Japan relationship can be examined further, it is necessary to explain the basics of this envisioned type of defense. Technical specifications, the number of different systems subsumed by the blanket term *missile defense,* and the different legal implications of each require more than a superficial overview. Then, several traditional explanations for Japanese security policy will be considered vis-à-vis the pattern pursued to date for missile defense: those based on international relations realism, domestic interest group and bureaucratic politics, domestic norms, and external pressure (*gaiatsu*). Each of these traditional explanations is found lacking absent the overall frame provided by Japan's postwar security identity. Thus, the following section describes how an explanation rooted in security identity best explains the policy course Japan has followed, but additionally how this course itself threatens the future viability of Japan's long-standing security identity. The final section of this chapter further develops this latter point as a transition to the Chapter 7 discussion of the likely staying power of Japan's postwar security identity and the likely future direction of the U.S.-Japan alliance and Japanese security policy more broadly.

U.S.-Japan Cooperation on Missile Defense: Past, Present . . . and Future?

Missile defense is based on the idea that it should be technologically possible to ameliorate the threat of incoming hostile missiles by destroying them midflight, before they reach their intended targets, either with an intercepting missile or by the use of a laser-based system. This idea was first translated into a policy initiative by U.S. president Ronald Reagan under the Strategic Defense Initiative (SDI) in the early 1980s. The Reagan administration, seeking to develop reliable protection against the sizable Soviet missile capability, envisioned a large-scale missile defense system capable of shielding the United States from a Soviet missile attack—what today is referred to as national missile defense (NMD). This approach has been abandoned both because of technical difficulties with intercepting a large number of incoming missiles and because of the reduced threat from Soviet, now Russian, missiles.[5] Instead, the focus of missile defense research today is on the interception of a limited number of rogue missiles, whether over an entire national territory, NMD, or over a limited military theater (theater missile defense, or TMD)[6]— both of which are examples of ballistic missile defense (BMD), or simply missile defense (MD).

An operational missile defense system theoretically requires a number of different advanced technical systems: satellite-based infrared sensors to detect missiles, a radar system to track them and to guide an intercepting missile (or other destructive force) to their positions, and the intercepting instrument itself (whether missile or laser-based). One application of a missile defense system—a "lower-tier" land- or sea-based system—was tested in the Gulf War in 1991, when U.S. Patriot missiles were used to intercept airborne Scud missiles launched from Iraq. During the course of the war, the Patriot system suffered a high failure rate, but since the early 1990s the technology has improved significantly after various upgrades. The Patriot PAC-3, the latest iteration of a "lower-tier" missile defense, is currently under production for deployment in Japan in 2008.[7] Additionally, an "upper-tier" system—formerly called Navy Theater Wide (NTW) and now referred to as Sea-Based Midcourse Defense System (SMDS)—is also being researched by the United States and Japan jointly.[8] On December 19, 2003, Japan's chief cabinet secretary announced that Japan would deploy versions of both of these types of missile defense beginning in 2004: PAC-2 (and, when available, PAC-3) ground-based interceptor missiles and Aegis-based upper-tier interceptor missiles.

On August 16, 1999, Japan and the United States signed a Memorandum of Understanding (MOU) on the subject of joint technology research for NTW Theater Ballistic Missile Defense, currently referred to as SMDS. Although the full text of the MOU remains classified, the following summary was released to the public:

> The agreement calls for the two countries to conduct analysis, preliminary design, and certain risk reduction experiments. This would lead to the design specification and technology selection for the four agreed missile sub-components due to be integrated into the STANDARD Missile's latest derivative, the SM3.... The Agreement covers a Requirements Analysis and Design (RA&D) effort which will apply advanced Japanese and U.S. technology to improve the capabilities of four major guided missile components: sensor, advanced kinetic warhead, second stage propulsion, and lightweight nose cone.[9]

Thus, Japanese researchers will work together with their U.S. counterparts to develop four components of a potential missile defense system for use in East

Asia. The Japanese government initially budgeted ¥22 billion (over $204 million) through fiscal 2003 on this joint research,[10] with actual spending from fiscal years 1999–2004 totaling ¥25.3 billion (JDA 2005, p. 196).[11] The fiscal 2005 budget allocates a further ¥900 million to cover testing costs (JDA 2005, p. 196). The total cost of the envisioned system is expected to exceed ¥1 trillion—a cost to be shared between the United States and Japan.[12] By contrast, the *yearly* expenditure for *total* equipment purchases by the JDA has not exceeded 1 trillion yen since 1994 (Umemoto 2003, p. 203). To date, the Japanese government has agreed only to participate in joint collaborative research on the SMDS missile defense system and to acquire ground-based PAC-3 (the first of which were deployed outside Tokyo in March 2007)[13] and sea-based Standard SM-3 missiles to be deployed aboard six Japanese Aegis-equipped air-warfare destroyers from around 2011.[14] The government has asserted that a potential missile defense system would not violate Japan's existing arms exports or peaceful-use-of-space policies,[15] while at the same time introducing a change to Japan's long-standing arms export restrictions to allow for weapons components related to missile defense to be transferred to the United States. Even this change does not fully address the issues that missile defense raises vis-à-vis Japan's existing arms export restrictions, though it is the first change in policy regarding these restrictions since the 1983 exception to allow technology (but not components) to be transferred to the United States.

Contending Explanations for Japan's Missile Defense Policy

Realist theory, the interplay among domestic actors, norms, and foreign pressure can each be used to explain part of Japan's missile defense policy. The security identity of domestic antimilitarism, the changing nature of foreign pressure, and the interaction between these two provide the best explanation, however. This section considers three popular explanations for Japan's security policy—realist theory, domestic interest group and bureaucratic politics, and normative constraints. The next sections consider in greater detail the role of foreign pressure, particularly by the United States, and then the role of Japan's security identity in the policy outcomes.

Realist Theory and Missile Defense

Cooperation with the United States on developing an effective "missile shield" against perceived security threats in the region—particularly North Korea and China—follows the type of policy expected by alliance theorists such as Steven Walt (1987). Under Walt's balance-of-threat theory, one would expect Japan to bandwagon with a stronger external power (the United States) against a neighbor with rising threat potential (China). Effectively this is what one sees in the case of cooperative missile defense research, though Japan's policy is typically explained as directed at North Korea rather than at China (Hughes 1996, Swaine, Swanger, and Kawakami 2001). Realist theories do not offer a clear explanation for Japan's great reluctance to commit to joint development of missile defense with the United States, however; nor do they explain the limited initial scope of the joint project.[16] Ten years after formal agreement to work together with the United States on a missile defense system, Japan had agreed to joint research on only four components of one part of the system (the interceptor missile)—and this only after North Korea had test-fired two missiles directly at Japan (in 1993 and 1998) and declared its intention in 2003 to develop nuclear weapons. Nor does realist theory explain the many qualifications Japan has placed on its cooperation with the United States, as well as the uncertainty involved in deeper cooperation on production and deployment of any realized system in future.[17] Moreover, strictly following realist logic one would expect Japan to possess ballistic missiles and other offensive weaponry itself to deter potential aggression by its neighbors such as North Korea and China. However, some realists would rebut these arguments with two counterpoints. First, while Japan has not robustly committed to missile defense with the United States, such a development does indeed look quite likely in the near term. More importantly, Japan *has* developed its own limited missile defense capability in the meantime, apparently making such a decision as a result of close monitoring of the regional security environment (Kliman 2006, chap. 5). Second, some newer strands of realist theory such as "defensive realism" (Schweller 1998, Green 2001, Kliman 2006) do seek to account for states that follow a defense security posture in an attempt to ameliorate an emerging security dilemma. Still, these anomalies to realist theory—or the new versions of realism they require—are better explained by a framework based on Japan's security identity, rather than ad hoc changes to core aspects of classical realist theory.

Domestic Interest Group and Bureaucratic Politics

Because the policy of joint research on missile defense was initiated by the United States, it is difficult to root an explanation for this outcome at the domestic level. However, as with the other cases of defense policy considered in earlier chapters, the role of bureaucratic and industry actors in the evolution of the policy process should be considered.

Prior to the Taepodong missile overflight in August 1998, the JDA was the most active supporter of missile defense cooperation with the United States. The JDA's position was greatly boosted within the government as well as among Diet members and the general public after the Taepodong Incident, given the perceived rising security threat from North Korea. As with the issue of surveillance satellites, the position of different JDA officials regarding missile defense is often a result of their individual institutional responsibilities. Among JDA policy makers, missile defense is seen as a way to strengthen ties with the United States and its individual armed forces and as a way to further deepen Japan's military technology base. Conversely, the issue of the cost of the system raises concerns among a number of policy planners and threatens to upset the delicate interservice balance among the three branches of the SDF.[18] As the security situation in the areas surrounding Japan worsened, however, particularly in regard to China and North Korea, JDA officials together with politicians and even the general public appeared to converge in their view of a need for missile defense of some sort.

The Ministry of Foreign Affairs (MOFA) has been less supportive of the missile defense initiative overall, especially given concerns over the effect of the program on Japan-China relations, but MOFA supports the missile defense project because of the perceived benefit of joint missile defense research on the U.S.-Japan alliance overall. Given the multiple interests of Japan's diplomacy, often neatly divided by MOFA's own internal organization, it is not surprising to find a diversity of views regarding missile defense within MOFA. China hands worry about their area, while specialists on nonproliferation worry about theirs. Currently it appears that the North American bureau and its U.S.-Japan Security Treaty Office, the internal organizations responsible for missile defense, have exercised the greatest power in the existing policy outcome—but a lack of consensus on this issue in the mid- to late 1990s partly explains the delays in policy implementation.

As discussed in Chapter 4, U.S. pressure for reciprocal technology sharing at the end of the 1980s and the joint production experience of the FSX/F-2 fighter plane illustrate the changing nature of arms production at the end of the twentieth century, a trend sure to continue in this new century and one that further will erode Japan's indigenous defense production goals. Surveys conducted of Japanese defense producers in the early 1990s indicate that Japanese firms expect their lag in systems-level production to increase, suggesting the necessity of further efforts at joint development and production—despite the problems that were faced in the FSX case.[19] It is in this context that discussions over missile defense joint research take place. In 1995, Keidanren sought to create a more advantageous framework for joint research and development on defense products between U.S. and Japanese firms by proposing a new policy to allow transfer of defense-related subsystems to the United States and other countries.[20] The drive behind this initiative was to facilitate the design of Japanese subsystems and components into future U.S.-designed systems. However, such joint production would necessitate further revision of the Three Principles on Arms Export to allow not only for technology transfer to the United States but also the transfer of components and even subsystems. The expansion of any such exemptions to countries other than the United States would represent further erosion. The Keidanren proposal was aggressively attacked by members of the Japan Socialist Party (JSP), the Japanese Communist Party (JCP), and some members of the KMT, who rooted their criticism in the rhetoric of domestic antimilitarism. Although the Keidanren proposal enjoyed some support within the Liberal Democratic Party (LDP), it was not adopted at that time—but a diluted version was, later, in December 2004. A future move to the production phase of missile defense would require further change to the current arms export restrictions. Had Japanese industry actors—and their support organizations such as Keidanren and the Ministry of the Economy, Trade, and Industry (METI)—aggressively opposed participation in the project, it is unlikely that it would have proceeded.[21] Given Japanese industry enthusiasm for the project, and the purported power of industry in domestic decision making under interest-based theories in Japan, one would expect an earlier policy outcome and greater participation on the part of Japan. While cost issues and bureaucratic infighting provide some explanation for the lack of this outcome, it is the security identity of domestic antimilitarism that provides the best explanation for industry actors not securing the policy outcome they sought.

Cultural Norms and Missile Defense

A different domestically based alternative explanation is one based solely on pacifist or antimilitarist norms or culture. Future development and deployment of a missile defense system will challenge a number of long-standing antimilitarist norms, including arms export restrictions, the peaceful-use-of-space policy, and the prohibition of participation in collective defense activities. While Japanese government officials are quick to note that missile defense cooperation with the United States is only at the initial research stage and that no decisions on future development have been made, even this initial step suggests that the state is considering policies which would conflict with a norms or culture-based explanation. Such considerations are particularly problematic for explanations based on culture or norms, since violations of the norm should not even be considered among a population that shares these views widely. Thus, this approach cannot account for Japan's initiation of joint research with the United States on missile defense.

External Actors, Missile Defense, and the Evolution of Japan's Security Identity

Clearly in the case of a policy initiated by the United States, it is important to consider the role of external actors (or foreign pressure/*gaiatsu* to use the theoretical lingo) in the final Japanese policy outcome. Joint research on missile defense must be considered within the context of deepening alliance relations between Japan and the United States. As with the case of surveillance satellites, however, an explanation based on *gaiatsu* can explain neither the timing nor the limitations on the policy outcome to date. Japan partnered with the United States on the precursor to missile defense, the Strategic Defense Initiative, in 1983. In 1993, Japan joined a joint study group with the United States to examine cooperation on missile defense. By 2006, however, despite great pressure from the United States throughout the preceding twenty-six years, all that Japanese policy makers would commit to a jointly pursued missile defense was further research into only four components of one part of a future missile defense system, the interceptor missile, and cost sharing of about ¥26 billion of a total cost of over ¥10 *trillion* the United States has invested in missile defense to date (JDA 2005, pp. 196, 193). While U.S. policy and pressure on Japan regarding SDI/missile defense/NMD has varied in its character over the years, the United States has consistently pushed Japan to assume a larger role in development of a missile defense system, with substantial success only recently. The case of missile defense does, however, show how foreign pressure can not only result in some shift in individual security policies such as with missile defense, but also contribute to a broader reconsideration of the security practices themselves, and perhaps even to a reconsideration of core aspects of their underlying basis in security identity.

Pressure from the United States

The United States has pressured Japan to actively participate in the development of missile defense since the early 1980s, when President Reagan successfully convinced Prime Minister Nakasone to support the U.S. Strategic Defense Initiative. American planning and goals for missile defense in general have not remained constant since this time, however. The U.S.-envisioned system has evolved from a space-based missile shield designed to protect the United States from the Soviet Union (SDI), through one aimed at a more limited threat posed by "rogue states" to U.S. forces abroad (TMD), to the recent focus under President George W. Bush on larger-scale protection from errant missiles across the vast territory of the United States (NMD). Despite changes in the U.S. conception of missile defense over time, its goals vis-à-vis Japan have remained fairly constant.[22] First, the United States seeks a financial contribution to the development of missile defense, and to its eventual deployment (i.e., the JDA as funder and customer). Second, it seeks access to "spin-on" technologies that can be adapted from Japan's advanced commercial manufacturing base. Third, it seeks to deepen the nature of its alliance with Japan, securing future basing rights to whatever missile defense system may be developed, as well as a partner in operating such a system.

Due to the constraints imposed by Japan's security identity of domestic anti-militarism—in addition to other factors discussed in the previous section—the United States has enjoyed only limited success in each of its goals vis-à-vis Japan. In September 1993 the TMD Working Group was established jointly, and it met twelve times from December 1993 until replaced by Bilateral Study on Ballistic Missile Defense to determine the technological feasibility of a joint system. In total, between 1995 and 1998 the Japanese government devoted ¥560 million for study costs into TMD-related systems and technology (Hughes 2004b, p. 184), and substantially more between 1998 and 2005. The Japanese government approved joint research with the United States in December 1998, signing an exchange of notes in August 1999. It expressed its intention to upgrade to PAC-3 systems in 2003 and otherwise has focused research on NTW/SMDS defensive systems. The deepening of U.S. interest—and spending—in missile defense under President George W. Bush places further pressure on Japan to partner with the United States on missile defense. Under President Bush, missile defense has been explicitly linked to U.S. National Missile Defense (NMD). Missile defense development with Japan is now characterized (at least in the United States) as a stepping-stone to NMD and as one tier of a multitiered defense of the United States and its interests. The left-leaning *Asahi* newspaper in Japan has editorialized against U.S. development of an NMD system, though it grudgingly appears to accept joint U.S.-Japan missile defense research as long as these two programs remain separate,[23] a view shared and rigorously maintained both by MOFA and by the JDA/MOD.[24] The *Asahi* writes:

> The Japanese government has characterized TMD, primarily intended to defend America's allies and its forces stationed abroad, as "a purely defensive system that is in line with Japan's commitment to exclusively defensive defense policy." But the latest American plan would integrate NMD and TMD into one program. If the missile-defense system is projected globally and missile defense deployment were to become part of the U.S. global defense strategy, the position maintained by Japan would crumble at its foundation. TMD deployment would also raise a controversy involving Japan's right to exercise collective self-defense.[25]

Thus, increased linkage between a missile defense system for Japan and one for the United States developed in part by Japan threatens either to erode Japanese government support for joint research and development with the United States on missile defense or to call into question the resilience of the long-standing security identity of domestic antimilitarism. Even vis-à-vis U.S. pressure, the politics of domestic antimilitarism enter prominently into policy outcomes. Moreover, other international factors pose barriers to future missile defense development and deployment.

Pressure from Other External Actors

Potential international reaction to Japan's missile defense policy is considered carefully by policy makers in Japan. Reaction is not uniform across states in the region, however. Foremost among Japan's concerns is the reaction of China, the large and rising power in the region. Next come concerns of Japan's other neighbors, including South Korea and the countries of Southeast Asia. Finally, the concerns of Russia as well as general international concerns regarding missile defense and the policies it symbolizes are considered.

China's reaction to Japan's missile defense policy figures prominently in the calculations of policy makers in the JDA and the MOFA in particular.[26] In the case of China, reaction is gauged on a number of levels. First, Japan (and the United States) is involved in a realist, strategic interaction with China, attempting to balance rising Chinese power while not encouraging an arms race. In this sense, missile defense poses the risk inherent in the classic security dilemma.[27] Second, Japan seeks to protect itself against a concrete (and rising) ballistic missile threat from North Korea and China[28]—though typically it couches such concerns by emphasizing the threat from North Korea. Third, Japan seeks to present to China and its East Asian neighbors an acceptable image of a military which has reformed since the end of the Second World War.

Japan is sensitive to fears among its neighbors over the SDF's increasing military role in the region, particularly among those who experienced harsh Japanese military occupation during the Second World War.[29] Consideration of this issue permeates discussion of Japanese security policy, though it acts more as a general brake on an increased military role in the region than as an overall structure to security policy provided by the security identity of domestic antimilitarism. In contrast to the issues raised vis-à-vis collective defense and arms exports, however, joint development of missile defense with the United States is likely to be the best course of action to assuage the fears of Japan's neighbors regarding missile defense.

Finally, broader international reaction is also important to Japan regarding how missile defense relates to Japan's larger foreign policy objectives. Seeking to build on its security identity of domestic antimilitarism, Japan's "international contribution" to date has focused in particular on the areas of arms control and nonproliferation. It has been argued that missile defense stands to contribute to these areas by reducing the effectiveness of—and thus the motivation to develop—a limited number of ballistic missiles as offensive, first-strike weapons.[30] This assertion is based largely on an intersubjective perception, however. One could equally argue, under the classic security dilemma, that a marginally effective missile defense system will encourage greater proliferation of ballistic missiles in order to ensure that some missiles will reach their targets. Japan must therefore pay close attention to the effect of missile defense development on its nonproliferation efforts.

Missile Defense and the Politics of Security Identity

As with other policy areas considered, Japan's domestic antimilitarist security identity affects the policy outcome on missile defense through three mechanisms. It dictates the rhetoric of missile defense and provides a focal point for political debate on this issue—as seen in the case of surveillance satellites. On the first point, the issue of rhetoric, however, the language of domestic antimilitarism is already largely reflected in the nature of a missile defense system—that it is defensive by nature, and only poses a threat to those who have offensive aspirations. In this sense, there is no need for new rhetoric for this program; the language used in Japan is similar to that used in the United States and elsewhere—in contrast to the case of military surveillance satellites becoming "information-gathering" satellites as discussed in Chapter 5. A similar point can be made regarding the role of domestic antimilitarism in providing a focal point for public opinion: in the abstract, missile defense fulfills the criteria for domestic antimilitarism without any substantial alteration. What stands in the way of missile defense congruence with domestic antimilitarism is the outside partner, the United States.

The third way that domestic antimilitarism has dictated the policy outcome on missile defense is the most substantial: through the prior institutionalization of the security identity into the security policy-making process. In particular, three existing policies serve as barriers to the development and deployment of an operational missile defense system, two of which are central subjects of this larger study. First, future joint missile defense production and deployment challenges Japan's long-standing restrictive arms export policies. Second, the conception of missile defense being jointly researched—the upper-tier SMDS—threatens Japan's policy regarding the peaceful use of outer space. Finally, deployment of missile defense jointly with the United States challenges Japan's long-standing prohibition on the exercise of its right of collective self-defense. Moreover, missile defense raises a large number of operational questions linked to Japan's security identity, such as who specifically would control the system, questions which have partly been resolved in order to introduce a first-stage domestically operated system, but which in themselves already challenge long-standing notions of civilian control. In this case, careful study of the evolution of Japan's missile defense policy provides an excellent bellwether of Japan's evolving security identity. These three areas are each considered further below.

The Altering of Arms Export Restrictions

Japan's restrictive arms export policies were one of the first manifestations of its new security identity in the immediate postwar period, as discussed in Chapters 2 and 4. Although the exact nature of its enforcement has varied over time, it has been fully institutionalized into Japan's security policy-making process. Among the central issues posed by missile defense to Japan's current arms export policies, two feature prominently. First is whether Japanese technology incorporated into the system could be transferred by the United States to third parties (such as South Korea or Taiwan, or even elsewhere in the world: Spain and Israel are two likely contenders). Second is where the system, if developed, would be manufactured: in particular, controversy surrounds whether components of the system would be exported from Japan, which would constitute a violation of existing Japanese policy regarding arms exports.

The first issue, the question of third-party transfer of a jointly developed missile defense system, raises a number of problems for current Japanese policy. Regarding the arms export ban in particular, currently military technology can be transferred from Japan to the United States under the exception to the Three Principles on Arms Exports declared by Prime Minister Nakasone in 1983.[31] An additional exception would be required for transfer of technology to states other than the United States. At the time the exception for technology transfer was made for the United States, the Japanese government entered into discussions with several European states regarding exceptions for them as well, but no progress was made on this issue at the time. In the case of missile defense, however, it is not the issue of transfer to European NATO allies that is of primary concern. Instead, it is the transfer of missile defense technology to Taiwan that generates the greatest concern. Ballistic missile defense of Taiwan from China could take place in two ways. First, a jointly developed Japan-U.S. missile defense system could be used to protect Taiwan in case of attack. This option is problematic apart from the issue of arms exports because it would involve Japan in a third-party conflict, in explicit violation of the third tenet of domestic antimilitarism. Moreover, it would violate the current prohibition on the exercise of collective self-defense, discussed later in this chapter. Thus, a second option would appear less problematic—allowing Taiwan to acquire its own missile defense system to provide for its protection against China. It is this option that would violate Japan's current arms export policies, despite the chief cabinet secretary's assurances that missile defense policy would respect Japan's existing arms export policies—a statement already contradicted by the subsequent policy exception for component transfer to the United States issued in December 2004. Amending current arms export policies to allow for the transfer of missile defense technology to Taiwan would be politically problematic both for domestic reasons rooted in Japan's security identity and for international reasons, because it certainly would create a major policy confrontation between Japan and China.[32] Such a standoff was already witnessed on a small scale in February 2005, when Japan insisted that a joint U.S.-Japan declaration of the Security Consultative Committee (SCC) explicitly state that Japan is committed to the peaceful resolution of China's dispute with Taiwan—not a new position, but new in its explicitness, which generated significant media attention in Japan, China, and elsewhere.

The second challenge of missile defense to Japan's current arms export policies is the question of where the system would be manufactured. While the aforementioned 1983 exception to the Three Principles allows for *technology* transfer to the United States, it does not allow for weapons *components* to be transferred. This issue is critical because such transfers would be required if Japan were to manufacture part of a missile defense system to be completed in the United States—the most likely scenario for missile defense production, if Japan-U.S. cooperation moves forward as expected. Although the Japanese government has stated that military technology transfer deriving from joint research on missile defense would take place within the current policy framework allowing military technology transfer to the United States,[33] consideration of previous cases of joint U.S.-Japan technology cooperation strongly suggests that any product that reaches a manufacturing stage would at least partially be manufactured in Japan, giving rise to concerns about how arms export restrictions would be implemented in this case in future. As early as 2001, LDP Diet members with defense industry ties called for a change in Japan's current arms export policy in order to ensure that Japanese defense contractors would be able to participate in the production of missile defense components for export to the United States.[34] And, indeed, in December 2004, the cabinet issued a further exception to the United States to allow for missile defense-related components to be exported to the United States (though not other weapons components, and not to other countries—as yet).

The issue of third-party transfer poses an obstacle to any likely compromise in this area as well. For example, if the Japanese government were to pass an additional exception to the Three Principles allowing general military product transfers to the United States, the final product of any collaboration would presumably be prohibited from sales or transfer to another state—a condition the United States is likely to honor only in the breach.[35] The overlapping barriers of Japan's security identity would therefore seem to pose insurmountable barriers to future missile defense deployment—requiring a shift either in the security identity (or its interpretation, if possible) or to the policy of missile defense cooperation.

Further Dilutions of the Policy Regarding the Peaceful Use of Outer Space

A second long-standing policy generated from the security identity of domestic antimilitarism that is challenged by missile defense is Japan's policy regarding the peaceful use of outer space. The 1969 Diet resolution on the peaceful use of space—reprinted in Appendix 6—delineates the areas in which Japan can utilize outer space. These uses are explicitly "confined to peaceful purposes." As discussed in Chapter 5, the central issue in the decades of debates over the extent of limitations imposed by this policy is how to interpret the term *peaceful*—whether it precludes all military use (i.e., it means *nonmilitary*) or it can be understood as synonymous with terms such as *nonaggressive* or *defensive*. Previous uses of outer space by the SDF—specifically, the use of satellites for military communications and the use of satellite imagery for military intelligence—have generated significant debate and have led to only limited incremental shifts in policy. Unlike surveillance satellites, however, missile defense is exclusively a military system. There is no obscuring this fact, though the defensive mission of missile defense is stressed at every opportunity. Since a feasible system has not yet been developed, it cannot be said for certain what use of outer space a future missile defense system will entail. Although possible in principle, it is unlikely that Japan would pursue development of a system utilizing space-based lasers to target missiles, as this would constitute the positioning of a likely offensively capable weapon in space.[36] The most likely outcome is that space-based satellites will be employed to direct interceptor missiles launched from land-based (THAAD) or sea-based (SMDS) stations to incoming hostile ballistic missiles. Japan does not possess the early-warning satellites necessary to track incoming ballistic missiles. It is possible, however, that by the time of future missile defense deployment—considered to be at least a decade from now—Japan will possess the capability to build and deploy such satellites, or even that Japan will already possess such satellites.[37]

The Japanese government has officially stated that the missile defense system envisioned by researchers falls within acceptable parameters of the Diet resolution on the peaceful use of outer space. The announcement made by the chief cabinet secretary on December 25, 1998 (reprinted in Appendix 7), says in effect that space use for missile defense is peaceful use, in particular because missile defense is "a purely defensive measure." According to Masamitsu Yamashita, Susumu Takai, and Shuichiro Wada (1994), however, the words "peaceful purposes" in the 1967 Outer Space Treaty, upon which the 1969 Diet resolution is modeled, is in the United States and Soviet Union accepted as "nonaggressive purpose" in the attempt to preserve the states' self-defense right in space. They note that the Japanese interpretation of *peaceful* as *nonmilitary* is contrary to the interpretation accepted in international discourse.[38] Another approach to this problem would be to rescind or to modify the Diet resolution itself, as reportedly proposed by a crisis management team in the Diet led by LDP Diet member Fukushiro Nukaga[39] and currently being considered by two different Diet study groups.[40] A continuation of the long-standing strategy of reinterpretation of existing policy is more likely than an outright modification of it.

Assuming a workable missile defense system is developed along the lines discussed above, Japanese policy makers would choose between two options over the use of outer space in a missile defense system. First, Japan could rely on U.S. early-warning satellites to target incoming missiles; second, Japan could maintain its own early-warning satellites to be used in targeting. Both options are problematic vis-à-vis existing policy and the security identity of domestic antimilitarism. The first would appear the better option regarding Japan's peaceful-use-of-space policy. Although objectively speaking there should be no difference between utilizing U.S. or Japanese satellites for targeting, previous precedent regarding the use of outer space for military satellite imagery makes a distinction between foreign-owned and domestic-owned satellites. For example, the JDA was allowed to analyze U.S. satellite images for military purposes in the 1980s. Following this precedent, one could expect the JDA to argue that the use of U.S. satellites for targeting also would not violate *Japan's* peaceful use of space. Critics may draw a distinction between satellite images that are transferred to Japan and satellite targeting that would be integrated into a Japanese (or joint U.S.-Japan) system, however, arguing that system integration effectively extends the use of outer space to Japan. The drawback of such a solution would be that Japan's missile defense system would be linked inextricably to the United States, but this likely will be the situation in any case given the proposed joint development of the system.

The second option for Japan's use of outer space for missile defense would be Japan's own deployment of early-warning satellites to target incoming hostile missiles. In principle it is imaginable that a jointly developed and operated system between the United States and Japan could involve separate command and control functions (including targeting satellites) for each country. In this case, the declaration by the chief cabinet secretary that the government views missile defense as compatible with the policy regarding the peaceful use of outer space is the best indicator of future government policy intentions. At the time of approval of such a system, however, the Diet may not agree to accept such an interpretation.

In the view of some (e.g., Handberg and Johnson-Freese 2001), Japan's peaceful-use-of-space policy has been enforced strictly, as evidenced by the need of the SDF to receive permission to use satellites for military communications and for reconnaissance. The fact that these permissions were granted, however, indicates that the policy is not applied strictly. Rather, the determining factor—as with arms exports in general—is not military use but rather the "dual-use" doctrine.[41] In the world of twenty-first-century technology, the U.S. Global Positioning System (GPS) satellites widely used in Japan both by the JDA/SDF and by private cars for *ka-nabi* (car navigation), surveillance satellite imagery shared by the United States (and now being developed by Japan), and satellite communication systems all represent utilization of passive military space systems. Justification for the use of such systems is far easier than for possible weapons systems, however—even if the weapons are defensive in nature, such as missile defense.

The distinction between the use of outer space by surveillance satellites and by a future missile defense system seems clear to the Japanese public. A November 1998 poll by the U.S. Information Agency found that 54 percent of respondents favored Japan's development of independent "information-gathering" satellites, but only 43 percent favored cooperation with the United States to develop missile defense (USIA 1998, p. 2). While a number of factors could explain the difference in support for the two systems—such as the divergent economic benefit likely to be derived from the two systems or the issue of domestic versus shared control—the best explanation for this difference is rooted in the security identity of domestic antimilitarism: the use of surveillance satellites as reconstituted during debate over the policy largely upholds the security identity of domestic antimilitarism while missile defense does not.

The Next Target: Exercise of the Right of Collective Defense?

A third critical issue to future missile defense deployment vis-à-vis existing security policies rooted in the security identity of domestic antimilitarism is the issue of collective defense.[42] A central question in any future missile defense system is whether the likely utilization of a joint system would violate the current prohibition on Japan's participation in collective defense arrangements. Under an interpretation pronounced by the Cabinet Legislative Affairs Bureau in 1981, Japan acknowledges that it possesses the right of collective defense under international law, but it cannot exercise this right due to constitutional limitations on defense activities to the minimum necessary to defend Japanese territory.[43] The terms of Japan's security alliance with the United States satisfy this requirement because Japan's responsibilities under the 1960 Security Treaty are limited to the defense of Japan: Japan is not obligated under the treaty to aid in the defense of the United States or even of U.S. forces based in Japan, nor to participate in U.S. military efforts elsewhere in Asia. Daniel Kliman (2006, p. 107) also stresses the January 2004 pronouncement by the Cabinet Legislation Bureau (CLB) that intelligence sharing of sensor data related to missile defense would not be considered an example of collective self-defense as another case of Japan's incremental shift in security practice. This interpretation clearly falls within accepted boundaries of domestic antimilitarism to the extent that such data are shared for the purpose of protecting Japan, following other recent decisions related to surveillance satellites and the 1997 Defense Guidelines. Were Japan to share such sensor data to assist the United States in an offensive military operation in the region to which Japan was not a party, the argument developed in this study would predict a fierce reaction on the part of the Japanese public due to a perceived violation of the central tenets of Japan's postwar security identity.

A number of problematic scenarios can be envisioned regarding a future joint missile defense deployment under the current ban on collective self-defense. Naturally, how these scenarios would play out in practice would depend on the nature of the system developed and deployed. Most basic to this question is whether the system will be operated solely by Japan, or whether it will be a jointly operated U.S.-Japan system. The first step of missile defense in Japan, enacted in fiscal 2004, is for Japan to possess an independent capability. The direction of policy in future years, however, is clearly toward a jointly operated system.[44] Such a deployment strikes at the essence of the ban on collective self-defense. Under current restrictions, if a joint command and control system, or joint satellite and/or sensor system were deployed, the United States would only be able to use this system in the defense of Japan; any other use necessarily would involve Japan in a third-party conflict, which is explicitly prohibited by current policy guidelines as well as by the third tenet of Japan's postwar security identity. The alternative development possibility, while unlikely, would be for Japan to maintain its own command and control functions, and perhaps even its own sensors and satellites (though, as noted above, the CLB paved the way for shared sensors by its January 2004 ruling). This would be a high price to pay to uphold the principle prohibiting the exercise of the right of collective self-defense. Moreover, it would expose Japan to severe strains with its alliance partner if U.S. forces were to come under fire in the defense of Japan, or even elsewhere in areas surrounding Japan, since Japan still would be prohibited from using its missile defense system in the defense of U.S. forces.

Some analysts downplay this latter fear of leaving U.S. forces in Japan unprotected because arguably Japanese forces would be able to come to the assistance of U.S. forces in a number of possible scenarios. For example, U.S. forces on Japanese territory could arguably be protected from incoming missiles since they would be targeted at Japan itself; moreover, missiles aimed in the direction of Japan—even if at U.S. forces not on Japanese territory—could arguably be intercepted given that Japan was a plausible target.[45] Indeed, the CLB formally set out such an interpretation in January 2003, ruling that a missile "judged to have a significant probability of targeting Japan ... will be considered to have justified our right to self-defense."[46] Responding to such imaginable scenarios, the JDA announced on June 22, 2003, that the interception of ballistic missiles flying over Japanese airspace toward the United States does not violate Japan's restrictions on collective security. However, it also declared that the interception of missiles in air space not above Japan would violate current restrictions on collective security (Arima 2003, p. 15). This leaves U.S. forces exposed in a number of other possible circumstances. Moreover, it grants to the SDF a level of discretion not generally extended to the military under Japan's postwar security identity. Thus, the existing policy prohibition on collective self-defense would still appear to present a significant obstacle to missile defense deployment. In order for missile defense to move forward, yet another long-standing institutionalization of the state would need to be circumvented or otherwise modified.

Looking Forward: Missile Defense and Japan's Evolving Security Identity

Numerous factors have affected Japan's policy course over missile defense, but one factor has exercised an extraordinary influence: the security identity of domestic antimilitarism. Domestic antimilitarism structured the nature of missile defense policy even before concrete discussions with the United States began, and it continued to affect the development of policy through the recent decisions to embark on joint research with the United States on four components of a future missile defense interceptor missile and to deploy a more limited interim missile defense system independently. Moreover, this security identity promises to continue to play a central role in Japan's further development of missile defense policy. The politics of missile defense do not continue unabated or unaltered, however. Tetsuya Umemoto plainly discusses the possible direction in which further missile defense cooperation with the United States could lead:

> Joint development and production of antimissile systems could also draw the Japanese and U.S. defense industries closer. In the process, the Japanese would have the chance to contribute to U.S. homeland defense, because many of the technologies for defense against theater ballistic missiles could be applied to protection against long-range missiles. *Japan's role in the defense of the continental United States would become more evident, should Tokyo allow its defensive capabilities to be incorporated in a more comprehensive U.S. BMD architecture.* (Umemoto 2003, p. 201, emphasis added)

As noted by Christopher Hughes (2004b): "BMD may finally tip Japan toward collective self-defense, which would lead to a radical transformation in Japan's military security policy and participation in nearly all forms of military operations, especially in cooperation with the United States" (p. 206). Should such a threshold be crossed, one could plausibly argue that a shift in Japan's security identity was imminent or already taking place.

As with a number of analysts of the U.S.-Japan relationship and its likely future direction, however, Umemoto (2003, pp. 201–3) cautions that the deepening of alliance cooperation in the area of missile defense also runs risks: including the development of more cavalier attitudes among the American public about cooperation beyond missile defense, the need for "real consultation" to coordinate missile defense policy and the friction that might engender, and the pressure missile defense development would place on Japan to alter its current security prohibitions such as the ones discussed in the previous sections. This evolution of Japan's security identity, particularly evident in the early twenty-first century, is the subject of the final chapter of this volume.

Japan's Security Identity and Security Practice in a New Century

There is no doubt that both the tone of discussion and content of Japan's security policies have shifted considerably since the Cold War and early post–Cold War periods. Beginning shortly after the North Korean Taepodong overflight of Japanese territory in August 1998, a series of surprising policy outcomes were enacted, including the plans to develop missile defense and surveillance satellites and to relax arms export restrictions detailed in earlier chapters, as well as legislation enacting some controversial aspects of the 1997 revised U.S.-Japan Defense Guidelines and establishing constitutional research commissions in both houses of the Diet to devise concrete proposals for possible revision of Article Nine and other limits on Japanese military activities. Moreover, a number of pieces of domestic legislation suggesting a rising acceptance of symbols and actions of the state were also passed at this time after years of controversy, including legalizing the long-controversial national anthem and national flag and requiring them to be displayed in schools, and approval of wiretaps to be conducted by the national police—sparking concerns at home and abroad of a rising nationalism in Japan.

Further change is apparent even more recently. The involvement of the Self-Defense Forces (SDF) in United Nations Peacekeeping Operations (UNPKO) post–September 11, 2001, included the first participation of the SDF in an active combat operation (though in noncombat roles) since its creation—first the Maritime Self-Defense Forces (MSDF) in the Indian Ocean in support of U.S.-led coalition operations in Afghanistan in late 2001, and next all three services in support of U.S. operations in Iraq in 2004. So-called emergency legislation was passed to allow the SDF to operate domestically under a legal framework in times of conflict. New agreements with the United States further integrated the capabilities and interoperability of both states' military forces.[1] Japan's military capabilities and future weapons development also expanded in this period (Tatsumi 2007). Perhaps most dramatically, the Japan Defense Agency (JDA) was elevated to a ministry, the Ministry of Defense (MOD), in January 2007, a change that begins to call into question the long-term viability of at least one core principle of Japan's long-standing security identity regarding the role of the military in political decision making. As with other developments in recent years, however, the result of the elevation in status of the JDA *to date* has been limited.

Overall, despite the impression conveyed from the above examples, Japan's security practices have not become centered around fundamentally new principles even in this contemporary period, but rather have advanced along a course clearly framed by the long-standing security identity of domestic antimilitarism. Although this is perhaps counterintuitive, a careful examination of how security practices have evolved to date clearly supports this view. Japanese military forces are still focused on Japan's self-defense, still do not engage in combat activities abroad (even under UNPKO), and still face enormous obstacles to their actual deployment. Japan still refrains from exporting weapons or developing nuclear weapons. The new Ministry of Defense still lacks the resources to develop a national strategy beyond short-term targets (despite renewed interest and efforts to do so) and has seen its budget actually *decline* in recent years despite a rebounding economy.[2]

More broadly, despite increasing security awareness among the Japanese public and elites, increased evidence of strategic thinking and planning, and a broader scope of debate of once-taboo subjects, much debate is still consumed with legalistic questions such as whether Japan can exercise its inherent right of collective self-defense, or whether a particular dual-use function of a weapon is essentially offensive or defensive—and all despite greatly increased threat perception among both the general public and elites and an objectively more dangerous security environment. Finally, any action on revising the linchpin of Japan's postwar security identity—Article Nine of the postwar constitution—has now been foreclosed until 2010 at the earliest,[3] and even then serious hurdles remain. The constraining and framing effects of the security identity of domestic antimilitarism are still very much apparent in Japan today, though without a doubt there are many signs of stress.

In conclusion the question of interest is whether future security policy will continue further down this known path (and how far and at what pace), whether a new path will be forged under a substantially different security identity, or whether developments will slow in frequency while recent changes are codified and institutionalized. This chapter acknowledges the obvious: a new politics of security apparent in Japan today. It is a new politics of security because it is informed by new attitudes toward security by both elites and the general public, who increasingly challenge old constraints. Yet it is not an entirely new politics of security, because it continues to be fundamentally shaped by the now half-century-old central tenets of Japan's postwar security identity—even if the ultimate shape of resulting policy is to somewhat exceed the constraints of an earlier period.

This analysis is not meant to disregard the evident change in the nature of public discussion of security in Japan today—what it is tempting to call an identity shift—but as argued throughout this volume, it is important to separate public discussion and public opinion (which throughout the postwar period had ranged far beyond actual security practice) from a definition of security identity itself. Japan's security identity is the product of a decades-long negotiation among contending political forces whose descendants continue to influence policy in contemporary Japan. Contending political forces continue to argue for a new articulation of Japan's security identity but to date have been unsuccessful. Such interaction of rival political forces in the creation, maintenance, and reproduction of Japan's security identity underscores one of the central theoretical claims of this volume: that Japan's security identity (and "identity" in general) has always been a subject of great political interest and an object of extensive political interaction among diverse actors. Such a conceptualization of identity moves us beyond a common existing view of a fixed Japanese identity perhaps at the point of breaking, toward an understanding of an evolving security identity that responds to policy demands but yet is resilient and continues to shape evolving security practice.

A continued constrained security role for Japan is not a foregone conclusion, however. Major exogenous or endogenous shocks to the Japanese political system could result in a stark break from past practice. Three such sparks are considered in this chapter. After an overview of major recent developments in Japanese security practice in the last decade, this volume will conclude with some general theorizing about the sources of possible future identity shift in contemporary Japan, and it will outline a few areas of future research that would help to monitor this important question in the years to come. First, however, contemporary debates and developments in Japanese security policy are considered and contextualized vis-à-vis the security identity of domestic antimilitarism, and they are linked to earlier discussion of substantive change noted in the previous case chapters.

Moves Beyond the "Three Rs" of Japanese Security Policy Making

Beginning in the late 1990s, some saw the familiar postwar pattern of "reach, reconcile, and reassure"—discussed in Chapter 1—give way to a new pattern of extending the limits of the central tenets of domestic antimilitarism without compensating in other policy areas. To some critics, it was a new pattern of "reach, reach, and reach," or perhaps "reach, replace, and review." The reach remains the same, but rather than reconciling new policy with past practice, some now see a replacement of old policy precedents. Rather than reassuring the public after a new reach, today we often see a review once again of existing policy to identify areas of further reach. The 2001 dispatch of the MSDF to the Indian Ocean to play a rear-area support role to U.S. combat operations, followed in 2004 by both the MSDF and the Air Self-Defense Forces (ASDF) to play a similar role in Iraq (though not the prominent Ground Self-Defense Forces [GSDF] dispatch, which continued with the 1990s practice of offering only humanitarian and reconstruction assistance), is often cited as an example of reach, reach, and reach. To date, however, one could still also understand even such a dramatic evolution of security practice in terms of the old "3 Rs"—reach to dispatch the SDF abroad; reconcile this with SDF law by greatly limiting rear-area support scope and simultaneously stressing the humanitarian mission of the GSDF in Iraq; reassure the public by limiting the duration of the enabling legislation.

It is notable in this example of SDF deployment abroad that the GSDF operations—by far the more traditional-style SDF deployment, focusing on humanitarian relief—dominated government briefings and media coverage, and that the GSDF operation involved a substantially larger number of personnel (600 versus 200 for the ASDF operations based in Kuwait, or the 330 for MSDF operations in the Persian Gulf). Moreover, it is notable that the deployment has now ended, and no substantive progress has been made on achieving a new dispatch—despite much pressure to do so by those seeking a more "normal" Japan, such as some in the MOD, the Ministry of Foreign Affairs (MOFA), and the Liberal Democratic Party (LDP).

This greater reach can be explained to some extent by a changed international strategic environment and domestic political configuration, but new attitudes toward security that are increasingly apparent in recent public opinion polls should also be considered in an analysis of the staying power of Japan's current security identity. Indeed, the new domestic political configuration itself in part is the result of shifting public attitudes about security issues that contributed to a new domestic political environment—in Japan's democratic political system, voters choose among politicians advocating different security practices. Recent public opinion polling—such as the cross-national U.S.-Japan Study of Attitudes and Global Engagement (SAGE) survey, conducted in autumn 2004[4]—illustrates a shift in public perception of a number of security issues, some quite surprising when viewed in a historical context, while in other areas a marked continuity is apparent.

According to the SAGE survey, over 90 percent of Japanese considered the world a more dangerous place in 2004, compared to twenty-five years ago. Over half feared an attack on Japan from abroad. Nearly 80 percent believed Japan should play a more active role in international affairs, with three-quarters responding that Japan should exert more active international leadership. Such figures are consistent with polling conducted by the *Yomiuri Shimbun* in July 1999, which showed 56.5 percent of Japanese responding that Japan was very or somewhat likely to be attacked by a foreign country in the near future, and over 70 percent expecting a war or conflict in the near future in areas surrounding Japan that will threaten Japanese security (August 4, 1999, p. 15).

Yet, importantly, despite a clear sense of perceived threat, the conclusions a majority of Japanese draw regarding an appropriate policy response to such threats differ markedly from the responses of Americans polled under the same SAGE study, and from the prescriptions of realist international relations scholarship as well, and hearken back to the central tenets of the security identity of domestic antimilitarism. According to the 2004 SAGE poll, nearly half (47.7 percent) of Japanese view war as illegitimate *even if one's own state is attacked*. Far less than one-quarter (21.5 percent) believe that a strong defense will result in peace, while almost twice as many (42.3 percent) believe that disarmament will. Strikingly, Japanese overwhelmingly (85.9 percent) believe that war can be avoided through international cooperation (versus 41.9 percent of Americans, who view war as inevitable). When asked what is the most effective way of dealing with terrorism, nearly two-thirds (64.4 percent) of Japanese point to the United Nations, followed by over a third (38.6 percent) who encourage the fostering of new alliances using diplomacy (multiple responses were permitted). Given Japanese public opinion on security issues conveyed through such polling data, it is not surprising that the post–Cold War pattern of extending the boundaries of Cold War Japanese security practice is still moored in the postwar security identity of domestic antimilitarism. Despite a changed international environment—even one understood as such by the public—there is not support for a fundamental departure along the lines of what some view as "normal nation" conduct. In fact, even the author of the very phrase "normal nation," Democratic Party of Japan (DPJ) leader Ichiro Ozawa, today argues a position more in line with the conception of Japan as a "civilian power" than as a junior partner to the United States ramping up for a military rivalry with China and others.

Evidence of the continued reproduction and reification of existing principles while extending the limits to some degree can be seen in the limitations on Japanese forces in Iraq, weapons acquisition policies and long-term planning, even debate over constitutional revision—which now looks more likely to further entrench the core principles of Article Nine than to abandon them, much to the chagrin of hawkish conservatives, who are increasingly pessimistic about their prospects for change in the near term. Context, and the *interaction* among political actors—not just their relative power in a political system—plays a crucial role in the determination of policy. A state's security identity can set a framework for such interaction that serves to mitigate the otherwise straightforward power resources of different political actors, such as the rise to power of two successive prime ministers (Koizumi and Abe) with a clear preference for more robust Japanese military activity.

Chapter 3 and subsequent case chapters examined some of the most important shifts in Japanese security practices in the first decade after the end of the Cold War. These included the first dispatches of the SDF abroad, new defense cooperation "guidelines" with the United States leading to increased roles and missions for the SDF, and the decisions to pursue surveillance satellite and missile defense programs. It was argued that in each instance, the strong effect of Japan's postwar security identity was evident in the resulting new security practices. A more detailed examination of some of the most controversial new security legislation and practice in this most recent period, beginning after the North Korean Taepodong missile launch and continuing through the responses to the September 11, 2001, attacks on the United States, as well as subsequent U.S.-led military operations in Iraq in 2003, illustrate the continued melding of past practice with new strategic imperatives. First, however, it is important to note the mounting number of security challenges Japan has faced in this most recent period (as summarized in Table 10).

Security "shocks" to Japan did not begin with the 1998 Taepodong overflight, but they do seem to have increased in recent years—and in any case, the Japanese public certainly perceives them as having increased (Midford 2006). The mid-1990s also saw a series of security shocks to Japan, but these were largely perceived as "crisis management" (*kiki kanri*) issues—reflecting an unease with government response and responsiveness, but not necessarily of fundamental unease with security overall. The slow and inadequate response to the Kobe earthquake and sarin gas attack in 1995, and the siege of the Japanese ambassador's residence in Lima, Peru, in 1996 led to a number of improvements in crisis-management and intelligence capabilities.[5]

By contrast, beginning with the Taepodong overflight in August 1998, a new series of security shocks to Japan resulted in renewed questioning of the adequacy of Japan's current military strategy, capabilities, and posture, and ultimately, these led to a new strategy being adopted in the 2005 National Defense Program Guidelines (NDPG),[6] based on the report of a new security commission, the so-called Araki Report. Among the major security shocks to push Japanese forward in considering their security practices and overarching security identity would be included, of course, the September 11, 2001, terrorist attacks on the United States and the subsequent U.S. policy response to these attacks. As with the Gulf War of 1990–91, Japan was expected to contribute to the security initiative of its primary ally—in particular in the reprisal attacks on Afghanistan, and the later military operations in Iraq. Once Japan chose to participate in these operations, subsequent shocks included the fatal shooting of two Japanese diplomats in Iraq, the kidnapping of three Japanese aid workers, and later, two Japanese journalists—though, fortunately and importantly, no casualties among the SDF ultimately deployed to the region.

Regionally as well Japan faced a series of security shocks, one following soon after the Taepodong Incident when a suspected North Korean spy ship was detected off the Noto Peninsula in the Sea of Japan in March 1999, followed not long after by another suspicious ship incursion into Japanese waters in southern Japan in December 2001, and culminating (to date) in a Chinese nuclear submarine being detected in Japanese waters in November 2004. Along the same lines, a Japanese commercial vessel was attacked further afield in the Straits of Malacca in March 2005, an attack which also included the abduction of three crew members. Rising tensions with North Korea and China were also fueled by the North Korean revelation, in September 2002, of North Korea's previous abductions of Japanese citizens from Japanese territory and the continuing six-party negotiations over North Korea's nuclear program, and anti-Japanese demonstrations in China in August 2004 (after a Japan-China soccer match) and in April 2005 (in response to numerous emotional issues related to past history and territorial disputes), as well as trade tensions and continuing barbs over each nation's treatment of past history.

Apart from such discrete events, China's steady economic and military rise continues to concern Japanese security planners and is now noted with rising concern in Japanese defense white papers. In 2005, Japanese politicians (both

TABLE 10

Important Security-Related International Developments, 1999–2007

Date	Event
(Aug. 1998)	(North Korea launches Taepodong missile over Japan)
Mar. 1999	Spy ship off Noto Peninsula leads to Coast Guard intervention
Sept. 2001	Terrorist attacks on the United States
Dec. 2001	Suspicious boat intercepted by MSDF off coast of Kyushu
Sept. 2002	North Korea admits to past abductions of Japanese citizens
Jan. 2003	North Korea withdraws from Nuclear Non-Proliferation Treaty
Mar. 2003	U.S. and U.K. forces initiate military operations in Iraq
Aug. 2003	First round of "six-party talks" to solve North Korea nuclear issue
Oct. 2003	China becomes third country to achieve manned space flight
Oct. 2003	North Korea completes reprocessing of nuclear fuel rods
Nov. 2003	2 Japanese diplomats shot to death in Iraq
Mar. 2004	Jakarta, Indonesia terrorist bombings
Apr. 2004	3 Japanese taken hostage in Iraq
May 2004	2 Japanese journalists killed in Iraq
Sept. 2004	50th anniversary of the JDA/SDF
Nov. 2004	Chinese nuclear submarine detected in Japanese waters
Mar. 2005	Japanese ship attacked in Straits of Malacca, 3 crew abducted
Apr. 2005	Massive anti-Japanese demonstrations in Beijing and Shanghai
May 2005	North Korea announces unloading of 8,000 spent nuclear fuel rods
July 2006	North Korea conducts further missile tests
Oct. 2006	North Korea conducts a nuclear test
Jan. 2007	China successfully tests an antisatellite weapon

Source: Primarily excerpted from JDA (2005), pp. 588–605. Adapted from Oros and Tatsumi (2007), p. 16.

LDP and opposition DPJ) sought to capitalize on growing anti-China sentiment among Japanese voters by overtly referring to China as a "threat" in public
speeches.[7] Due to China's steady ascendance, its economic size is roughly triple
that of 1989, when Japan made its first steps into the post–Cold War period.
More starkly, China's military spending has increased at an even greater pace—as
Japan's 2005 Defense White Paper notes: "China has recorded a growth rate of
over 10% consecutively for 17 years in terms of initial defense budget and the
announced defense budget for FY2005 was almost doubled from that for FY2000,
and almost tripled from that for FY1997" (p. 59). China is now thought to have
exceeded Japan's overall defense spending, though official Chinese figures show a
substantially lower level of spending than that estimated by security analysts—due
both to presumed underreporting on the part of the Chinese government and
to adjustments for purchasing power parity. Like Japan, China has been seeking
to modernize its military forces by investing in better equipment and reducing
its vast manpower. China has a stated intention of developing a blue water navy,
which in the future will surely become a more visible presence in East Asia (and

perhaps beyond) in addition to Japanese, American, and Russian naval forces. In the same vein, at least in the minds of many Japanese, China's achievement of manned space flight in October 2003—only the third nation to do so, following the United States and the Soviet Union—created a stir in the defense and outer space industry as well as among defense planners overall. China's successful attack on and destruction of one of its own satellites in a January 2007 test has also fueled both serious concerns in Japan and the United States about Chinese militarized space capabilities and fears of a space-based arms race.

Such a security environment—characterized by a series of security shocks as well as a looming security threat from China—combined with continued fluidity in party politics at home would have been a natural context for renewed debate and negotiation over crafting a new security identity for twenty-first-century Japan. As with policy responses in the 1990s, however, instead the existing security identity of domestic antimilitarism evolved modestly to endure in the new international environment in which Japan finds itself. Without sufficient attention to the underlying basis of Japan's security identity, and the ways it is reproduced each generation (each year, actually), this outcome appears puzzling.

A Resilient Security Identity in Post-Taepodong and Post-9/11 Japan

Japan has modified its security practices in a number of ways, large and small, to respond to the new security threats outlined above, and the new security environment in East Asia and the world in general. The volume of recent changes naturally leads one to query whether something deeper is afoot. Table 11 provides a partial list of some of the most significant Japanese decisions regarding security practices since the Taepodong overflight stirred the Diet into action after August 1998—including so-called emergency legislation, the formal study of constitutional revision in both houses of the Diet, the decisions to deploy the SDF abroad for combat support missions to the Indian Ocean and Iraq, and greater defense cooperation with the United States. The number of changes to Japanese security policy in these past ten years, however, is much too great to include on one list, or even to examine fully in a single chapter. For example, the Diet has amended the Self-Defense Force Law over fifty times since 1989, compared to only once from its adoption in 1954 through the end of the Cold War.[8] Instead, the argument for why this degree of change—and how it still falls within the parameters of the existing security identity—is developed around three important areas of change in the following sections: (1) new legislation passed soon after the Taepodong over-

TABLE 11

Important Japanese Security Decisions, 1999–2007

Date	Event
(Dec. 1998)	(Cabinet announces decisions to develop surveillance satellites (IGS) and pursue joint research on missile defense with the United States)
Aug. 1999	New legislation on "situations in areas surrounding Japan" passes Diet
Dec. 1999	Security Council approves investigation into midair refueling
Jan. 2000	Constitutional research commissions set up in both Houses of the Diet
Nov. 2001	"Anti-terror Special Measures Law" passes Diet / MSDF to Indian Ocean
Dec. 2001	"International Peacekeeping Operations Law" revised to allow new activities
Oct. 2003	"Anti-terror Special Measures" Law extended for 2 years
Dec. 2003	3 measures on "armed attack situations" pass the Diet, expanding regional contingency area and cooperation with the U.S. beyond 1999 law BMD introduction announced by cabinet
June 2004	Cabinet announces decision to enable SDF dispatch to Iraq for one year 7 pieces of "contingency response measures" pass the Diet
Dec. 2004	New NDPG extend U.S.-Japan military cooperation and SDF capabilities
Apr. 2005	Diet Constitutional Research Commissions issue final reports
May 2005	SDF officially takes part in multilateral Cobra Gold exercise in Thailand
June 2006	GSDF withdraws from Iraq; ASDF remains in Kuwait
Jan. 2007	JDA elevated to MOD
May 2007	Diet passes legislation to allow for a referendum on constitutional revision in 2010 or later

Source: Primarily excerpted from JDA (2005), pp. 588–605. Adapted from Oros and Tatsumi (2007), p. 14.

flight; (2) the immediate policy response to the September 11, 2001, attacks on the United States; and (3) the decision to deploy the SDF to Iraq.

New Security Legislation Post-Taepodong and Its Effect on Security Practice

The Taepodong Incident of August 1998 triggered quick policy action in the areas of surveillance satellites and missile defense, as argued in Chapters 5 and 6, leading to decisions to proceed with development of the surveillance satellites and to increase the pace of research into missile defense in December 1998 (followed in December 2003 with a decision to actually deploy missile defense in Japan). In both of those cases, certain political actors had been waiting for such an opportunity; they were not new policy ideas. Similarly, legislation necessary to implement the renegotiated 1997 U.S.-Japan Defense Guidelines had also been waiting for an opportunity to pass an otherwise unenthusiastic and even skeptical Diet. Among the most controversial aspects of the new roles agreed upon under the new guidelines was the envisioned more active role of the SDF in the event of a military action under the U.S.-Japan Security Treaty, particularly in the areas of so-called rear-area support and Japan-conducted ship inspections.

Congruent with the negotiated security identity of domestic antimilitarism,

Japanese engagement in combat-related missions was strictly limited to the defense of Japan, and even then was meant to be conducted through the least aggressive means. That Japan would participate in its own self-defense was not particularly controversial (though a minority of Japanese still reject the legitimacy of the SDF), but the scope of this action in conjunction with the United States had potential to be politically divisive—particularly if this action was to take place outside of Japanese territory, as the new guidelines envisioned: activities in "areas surrounding Japan" (*shuhen jitai*). Here the LDP faced an uphill battle, one it probably would not have won without the spark of the Taepodong Incident (and thus had shelved from immediate consideration in the Diet after the new guidelines were declared in 1997).

As a result of the Surrounding Areas Emergency Measures Law, passed in August 1999, the SDF is permitted to provide noncombat logistical support to U.S. forces in areas "surrounding" Japan—but what precisely is meant by "surrounding" was not entirely resolved. It purposely was not resolved in the case of Taiwan in order not to anger China and also to preserve some uncertainty for China regarding Japan's possible contribution to a defense of Taiwan, but in questioning in the Diet, Prime Minister Obuchi did set some limit on how this could be interpreted by saying explicitly that it would not extend as far as the Indian Ocean (cited in Midford 2003, p. 332). As a result, after September 11, 2001, it was determined by Prime Minister Koizumi that expanded legislation should be passed to authorize dispatch of the MSDF to the Indian Ocean to support U.S.-led forces there in the war against Afghanistan, though it arguably would also have been possible to have the Cabinet Legislation Bureau (CLB) determine that new circumstances had led to a new definition of "surrounding areas."

The case of the MSDF's engagement of two suspicious ships in March 1999 underscores the continued constraints on Japan's military engagement imposed by domestic antimilitarism and codified in a wide body of law and regulations—an engagement that took place prior to the new security legislation outlined above and seemed to underscore the need for such changes. Although Japan's intelligence and surveillance capabilities allowed for early detection of three suspicious vessels and rapid confirmation of the rogue identities of two of them, the ships were allowed to proceed outside of Japan's territorial waters despite initial efforts by the MSDF to make the ships stop inside Japan's territorial waters. On March 23–24, 1999, PC-3 planes and three destroyers (*Myoko, Haruna,* and *Abukuma*) from the MSDF fired "warning shots" at two suspicious ships (over the top of the ship's bow and around the ships' perimeters), but the ships were allowed to escape without being forced to stop once they managed to sail out of Japan's territorial waters.[9]

Support for such restraint is seen in public opinion polling. When asked in a *Yomiuri Shimbun* poll in July 1999 (four months after the incident), more than one-third (36.1 percent) of Japanese responded that the MSDF should *not* fire live shots at foreign vessels intruding into Japanese territorial waters; just under one-third (32 percent) thought the MSDF *should* fire live shots in such circumstances; and over one-quarter (27.9 percent) could not say which view they held (August 4, 1999, p. 15). Thus, even in post-Taepodong Japan, and faced with a related security threat, a plurality of Japanese consider firing on a possibly hostile ship illegally in Japanese waters to be imprudent, and over a quarter of Japanese in addition are unable to express a view on this issue—far more than a majority of Japanese. Security analysts would be hard-pressed to describe this response as "normal"; and it does not offer evidence of security identity shift since the end of the Cold War, though a similar incident in December 2001 discussed in the following subsection suggests that the September 11 attacks on the United States may have shifted Japanese public opinion on this point.

Policy Responses to the September 11, 2001, Attacks and
the Effect on Security Practice

To illustrate the new reach of Japanese security policy as well as its continued mooring in the established security identity, it is useful to recount what has been Japan's policy response to the terrorist attacks on the United States—considered by many to be the spark for a dramatic shift in Japanese security policy.[10]

In large part, Japan's response has been much of what one would expect from a close ally of the United States. Prime Minister Koizumi was one of the first foreign leaders to offer condolences and disaster relief support to the United States, amounting to over $10 million. Japanese companies donated more than $34 million to relief charities in the United States. Japan contributed $40 million for refugee relief in Pakistan, and the ASDF delivered food directly to Pakistan on C-130 aircraft. Moreover, Japan suspended payment demands on $550 million in Pakistani debt to Japan.[11] It froze assets of those associated with Osama bin Laden. It expanded intelligence cooperation with the United States and its allies. Japan also strengthened security around U.S. bases in Japan—an extremely important staging ground for any U.S. military operations in Asia and the largest permanent foreign deployment of U.S. troops in the world today. None of these responses should be considered surprising or a departure from the tenets of domestic antimilitarism.

It is another policy response by Prime Minister Koizumi that made newspaper headlines across the United States and Japan. Two antiterrorism bills—the so-called Anti-Terrorism Special Measures Law—passed in the Diet allow the SDF, for the first time, (1) to defend U.S. bases in Japan, and (2) to provide logistical support to U.S. forces operating outside of Japan (and not just "areas surrounding Japan," as approved in the 1999 legislation discussed above).[12] Both of these functions had long been sought by the United States and defense hawks within Japan and had actually been agreed upon as part of the new defense guidelines between the United States and Japan concluded in 1997. The enabling legislation for the new level of defense cooperation had not been fully introduced to the Diet, however, and had been expected to take several years to pass in entirety. The passage of this legislation is one of several recent milestones in Japan's security evolution, a clear "reach" beyond previous practice.

Japan's MSDF is fully capable of playing such an expanded role, as the largest naval force in Asia after U.S. forces. Further, this advance is understood by many in the U.S. defense establishment and in Japan as a step toward greater U.S.-Japan cooperation for regional and global security in general—a troubling prospect for many in Japan and across Asia and the world. The opportunity presented to Prime Minister Koizumi to expand the reach of the SDF beyond the provision of humanitarian assistance was seized upon immediately after the attacks on the United States, and it was noted quickly by both supporters and opponents of such reach. By contrast, the dispatch of six C-130 ASDF military transports which landed at Chaklala Air Base in Pakistan to off-load relief supplies for refugees on October 9, 2001—one of the first such relief efforts—was uncontroversial, clearly falling within the boundaries of Japan's postwar security identity.

Although the dispatch of the SDF to participate in an active conflict abroad rightly dominated the headlines over Japan's response to the war on terrorism, what is more striking about Japan's response to U.S. demands is the continuing focus on humanitarian assistance and rear-area support for the United States rather than a true departure from past practice. This aspect of Japanese policy might be understood in terms of "reassure" by reinforcing past practice. The one exception to policies in line with Japan's long-standing security identity is the decision to allow the SDF to participate in an active international conflict (although in non-combat roles and areas), a violation of the third tenet of domestic antimilitarism. Even in this area, however, the SDF is not empowered to actually engage in international conflict but rather to support it from outside of Japan for the first time (and only from a safe distance). Moreover, the idea of a "war on terror" is carefully distinguished from traditional interstate warfare in Japanese discourse supporting the new security practice.

Numerous other restrictions were also included in the Anti-Terror Special Measures Law, which, while extending the boundaries of the security identity (literally), also served to further reify existing security practice in a new environment. For example, SDF forces were to be positioned well apart from areas of active combat (an issue in the later Iraq deployment); the SDF was prohibited from supplying weapons or ammunition, *or even transporting them within foreign territory,* and from refueling or serving combat vehicles, ships, or aircraft; and the prime minister is required to seek approval from the Diet for such a deployment within twenty days of the start of such an operation, or in the next Diet if the Diet is not in session at the time; and perhaps most important, the legislation included a sunset clause, and thus would "expire" unless reauthorized in two years. The opposition parties in the Diet asked for even further restrictions in line with the security identity, including *prior* approval by the Diet for such a dispatch (reinforcing the importance of civilian control) and the outright prohibition on the transport of weapons rather than restrictions on their transport only in foreign territory (which allowed, then, MSDF transport of weapons in international waters, though it required the transfer of such cargo midsea, since ports are in foreign territory).

Opposition to SDF action beyond support roles is shown in public opinion polls as well as through the limitations imposed in the enabling legislation. A July 1999 *Yomiuri Shimbun* poll shows 41.9 percent of Japanese against "unfreezing" Japan's participation in such activities as cease-fire surveillance and disarmament, while 26.2 percent say they support such a move. The high number of respondents who answered that they cannot decide (26.1 percent) is also interesting here, however—and perhaps important for understanding future movement toward greater SDF participation in Iraq, forthcoming four years later in 2003. Even in the wake of September 11, 2001, Japanese public opinion had not substantially shifted regarding the acceptable scope of operations for the SDF abroad: still less than a majority of Japanese (48.3 percent) supported the SDF participating in even *non*combat rear-area support roles, and only 8 percent supported the SDF participating in a combat role (cited in Shinoda 2001, p. 4). As a result, though Prime Minister Koizumi wisely avoided the problems suffered by Prime Minister Kaifu's overreaching for new SDF activities in 1990, still only 42 percent of the Japanese public supported his plan for dispatching the MSDF to the Indian Ocean to offer noncombat rear-area support, while 46 percent opposed it.[13] Arguably the astonishingly high support rate for the prime minister—at the time over 80 percent—allowed him to push through a policy that a weaker prime minister would not have accomplished, much like in the United States, where President Bush was able to pass new legislation such as the USA PATRIOT Act, which included provisions that had been rejected when the president was less popular.[14]

Without doubt this incremental policy shift of foreign SDF deployment continues a trend evident from the beginning of the post–Cold War period in response to the Persian Gulf War, and it provides further evidence for realist international relations theorists of Japan's predictable movement toward a military role in the international system congruent with its power resources. The important question for future Japanese policy, however, is whether the decision to deploy the SDF abroad represents a true departure from past policy—which would imply the possibility of a greatly increased pace for acquiring further military capabilities that depart from limits of the postwar security identity—or rather a continuation of the familiar politics of domestic antimilitarism within a changed domestic and international environment. This volume argues the latter, though it suggests in the following section three scenarios that might lead to a true security identity shift—rather than policy shift—in future.

Coming soon after the new antiterror and related legislation, the December 22, 2001, incident of a Japan Coast Guard vessel firing upon a "suspicious" and unidentified vessel after it fled Japanese territorial waters further raises the question of whether Japan's response to September 11 will mark a watershed in Japan's post–Cold War security practices.[15] As noted in the previous section, this was not the first time that Japanese naval forces engaged a suspected North Korean spy ship, but the outcome was quite different on this occasion. A new security activism and new legislation enacted to enable this activism have relaxed limitations placed on Japan's naval patrols after September 11, 2001, resulting in a dramatically different outcome for the December 22, 2001, engagement than the previous instance in March 1999 discussed above. In the case of the 2001 interception, the suspicious (and suspected North Korean) ship was first sighted in Japan's two-hundred-mile "exclusive economic zone," where Japan asserts the sole right to fish and mineral resources. The vessel refused to identify itself and to stop for inspection, fleeing over the next thirty hours into China's neighboring economic zone before being engaged by the Japan Coast Guard. It was in these waters—outside of Japan's sovereign territory—that the Japan Coast Guard fired over five hundred rounds of "warning shots" at the unidentified vessel, resulting in the sinking of the vessel and loss of life of a suspected fifteen crew members (the bodies of only two of whom were recovered).

The 2001 case differs from the 1999 interception in a number of important ways which signal important policy precedents. First, the Japan Coast Guard followed the suspicious ship outside of Japan's territorial waters. Second, it fired upon the ship outside of Japan's territory. Finally, it reportedly engaged the suspicious vessel through new empowering legislation rather than as a result of cabinet-level decision making, as was the case of the 1999 engagement.[16] Although Prime Minister Koizumi described the sinking of the ship as "an act of legal self-defense" that was further justifiable by new coast guard legislation passed in November 2001, many opposition lawmakers questioned both the conduct and the timing of engagement (so soon after the enabling legislation passed only a month earlier). Consonant with the expected domestic political reaction, both the SDP (the former Japan Socialist Party) and the Japanese Communist Party (JCP) have argued that the Coast Guard was "overly enthusiastic" in making use of new legislation allowing more active engagement of the Coast Guard to intercept suspicious ships,[17] which includes the right to fire upon suspicious ships in Japanese territorial waters but does not explicitly grant permission to the Coast Guard to follow ships outside of Japan's exclusive economic zone. The limited political power of these parties, in contrast to their power during most of the Cold War period, partly explains the muted reaction to their criticisms to date. A new security awareness on the part of the Japanese public also surely plays some role.

Future reaction by the Japan Coast Guard and the MSDF to inevitable unidentified incursions into Japanese waters will provide one barometer to the changing politics of domestic antimilitarism in the coming years. Such incursions are not at all a new phenomenon to Japanese coastal security patrols; they have been noted by defense analysts and in JDA defense white papers for decades. A 2002 release by the JDA of a list of twenty-seven "suspicious" ships sighted operating in the seas around Japan[18]—including North Korean, Chinese, and Russian vessels—and suspected of illegally entering Japanese territorial waters on a regular basis underscores the potential for an elevated Japanese response in this area in future.

SDF Deployment to Iraq

Although legally speaking the MSDF deployment to the Indian Ocean had crossed the barrier of SDF deployments abroad for nonhumanitarian missions in December 2001, the possibility of SDF deployment to Iraq in 2003 raised this issue anew to the Japanese public. Arguably the antimilitarist aspect of the security identity played an especially strong role here as Japanese envisioned their troops on foreign soil for the first time in a combat support role (a GSDF deployment, as opposed to the previous MSDF deployment) and sought to contrast this to the last time combat-ready ground troops were deployed abroad—across Asia in the 1940s. The fact that the GSDF provided by far the largest overseas contingent to Iraq in terms of number of personnel (about 600 compared to about 330 for the MSDF and about 200 for the ASDF; JDA 2005, p. 535) and that it had the least experience with cooperating with foreign militaries also surely contributed to widespread public concern. Potential loss of life among SDF members also featured highly in public discussions.

Despite these public and political concerns, however, the legal framework for GSDF deployment to Iraq already existed in the form of the 2001 Anti-Terrorism Special Measures Law, which had been extended to allow for continued MSDF activities in the Indian Ocean. A political constraint still remained, however, in that Diet approval eventually would be required for the Iraq deployment—either within twenty days of the deployment if the SDF were dispatched during a Diet session, or in the following Diet session. Likely due to the combination of a public opinion constraint and a legislative obstacle, Prime Minister Koizumi once again chose the safer course of choosing a role for the GSDF in Iraq that would clearly fall within accepted boundaries of the hegemonic postwar security identity—a humanitarian mission for the GSDF. By contrast, the ASDF was dispatched to neighboring Kuwait at around the same time, but to engage in the more controversial noncombat support role for the U.S.-led coalition; and soon after, the MSDF was dispatched to the Persian Gulf also to conduct rear-area support similar to the role it played in the Indian Ocean.

The Japanese concern with SDF deployment to Iraq was in marked contrast to the concerns of other Asian nations in this case, as opposed to the first time Japan debated sending its forces to the Persian Gulf. In the first instance, in 1990–91, the reaction of Japan's Asian neighbors against the possible deployment of the SDF (which at that time would have been for the *first* time) was equal to or even greater than Japanese domestic concern (Midford 2003). By contrast, in 2003 Japan's neighbors were largely resigned to limited Japanese SDF deployments abroad and expressed no strong concern over such activities. This contrast may lead one to reexamine the relative weights of the constraining effects of domestic and international concern expressed in the 1990–91 case, though a definitive answer to this question is probably not attainable (and in any case, it is clear that both domestic and international concern contributed to the slow and limited decision reached at that time).

Conceptualizing Change in Japan's Security Future

What is most likely to come after the next "reaches" of future Japanese security policy—reconciling and reassuring, or replacing and reviewing? Existing theory on identity shift is almost uniformly rooted in the idea of a collapse—a widespread discrediting of the existing order or growing awareness that the basic tenets of the identity no longer lead to the outcomes expected. As discussed in Chapter 2, in the context of Japan's overwhelming defeat in the Second World War, scholars have long noted cases of fundamental breaks with the past after catastrophic "shocks" to the system. Jeffrey Legro (2005) adds the useful corrective that a shock to the system alone will not necessarily lead to change if there is no clear and supported alternative identity available. He notes in one case study, for example, the contrast in the German response to defeat in the two successive world wars. Moreover, the shock to the state need not be negative, in the sense of defeat:

TABLE 12

Three Scenarios for Japan's Future Security Practices

---

1. Continued policy evolution in line with the existing security identity
2. New security practices resulting from an unexpected shock that discredits the security identity of domestic antimilitarism
3. New security practices resulting from a growing irrelevance and subsequent abandonment of the security identity of domestic antimilitarism

---

Legro also examines the case of shift in American identity after victories in the world wars.

Thus, "collapse" need not mean collapse of the state or of order in general, but rather can result from a more gradual awareness of a disconnect between expectations and results. This broader model of how a long-standing security identity might collapse and be replaced by a different security identity is useful when considering the case of Japan today and in the future since—obviously—Japan has not experienced a dramatic security crisis, apart from what Michael Green (1998) aptly titled a "crisis of expectations" and the general changes in Japan's international environment. Looking forward, then, this broader model for identity shift presents three possibilities for Japan's future security practice, as summarized on Table 12. First, security practice can continue to evolve in line with the central tenets of the existing security identity of domestic antimilitarism. As argued throughout this volume, policy change—sometimes even significant policy change—is possible within the existing security identity in response to changing domestic and international factors, including the preferences and initiatives of key political entrepreneurs.

Recently, Prime Minister Koizumi sought to press evolution of existing security practice, achieving a degree of success. Prime Minister Abe's early policy achievement of elevating the JDA to the MOD foretold his attempts to further such a "normalization" of Japanese security practice to the extent he was politically able, which proved to be not very much. He resigned in September 2007, when it become clear he would not be able to extend the "special measures" necessary even to maintain the security "reach" achieved by his predecessor, much less extend this reach further. Thus, although he sought to achieve a substantial revision of the present constitution to firmly establish the legitimacy of the SDF, to allow for its use at home and abroad in a wide array of circumstances, and to allow Japan to exercise its sovereign right of collective self-defense, what he was able to achieve was an incremental step forward toward the goal of constitutional revision by way of enabling legislation to take effect in 2010—a far cry from a substantial policy shift.

The goal of greater use of the SDF abroad can likely be achieved to a degree within the present constitutional framework and tenets of domestic antimilitarism, but an unrestricted realization of these goals will likely require constitutional revision and would certainly be evidence of the abandonment of core tenets of the existing security identity by contradicting tenets two and three related to the use of force and involvement of the SDF in foreign military conflict, and likely the first tenet as well, related to the role of the military in political decision-making. Thus, policy evolution within the existing security identity cannot proceed carte blanche—even if there is political support to do so. At some point, the pushing of the envelope results in the abandonment of the understood consensus on security principles.

The value of the approach advocated here—which divorces the specific practices from the underlying principles—is that it allows one to estimate a baseline from which one can judge this disjuncture. That said, this baseline is likely to be affected by a changing international environment, technological innovation, and perception of threat, as seen in the cases presented in previous chapters. For example, at one point the use of satellites for communications purposes seemed quite novel, and it appeared to impart a tactical advantage that could be unseemly for a constrained military force; today, satellite communications are commonplace. Similarly, cross-border manufacturing was also once rather novel; today, it is commonplace, creating new interpretations of joint weapons production. Here, Wedeen's (2002) point about the impact of context in political analysis of cases and "variables" is evident. Thus, it is problematic to attempt, a priori, to set a firm threshold over which reinterpretation of existing principles would represent an essential abandonment of the principles. Still, some attempt at designating such thresholds is useful to consider the current potential for identity shift in Japan's future—as set out in the introduction to this volume in Table 1.

The second and third possibilities for Japan's security future both include exactly such a wholesale shift away from the security identity of domestic antimilitarism. The difference between the two possibilities lies in the nature of the shift—whether sparked by an unexpected shock to the system (such as the 9/11 attacks on the United States created, as Legro writes) or through a more gradual acceptance among societal actors that the central tenets of Japan's existing security identity are no longer appropriate for Japan's future (perhaps sparked by continued tension over perceived security threats from North Korea, China, or terrorist incidents). What would such a shift look like in practice? And how would we know it when we saw it? The next sections consider these questions by way of conclusion.

The X Factor: Three Potential Shocks and Pressures
for Identity Shift in Japan Today

Within Japan's democratic institutions, a substantial change in the security identity of domestic antimilitarism can occur only through two routes: (1) an unusual popularity of a single political party which gains enough seats in both houses of the Diet to enact changes in major legislation and to initiate constitutional revision (which requires a two-thirds supermajority in both houses); or (2) consensus among the two major political parties, currently the LDP and the DPJ, to craft the contours of a new security identity, which may or may not necessitate constitutional revision.[19]

At present, even barring any new dramatic domestic or international developments, both of these factors appear to be converging to some extent. After a brief period of internal disarray, resulting in the loss of its ruling majority, in the past decade the LDP has revived to once again dominate Japanese politics (although in coalition first with the Democratic Socialist Party, and currently with the KMT). Under the charismatic and popular prime minister Junichiro Koizumi, the LDP enjoyed support levels not seen since the 1960s, and after the September 2005 elections it enjoys a substantial majority in the Lower House of the Diet, including the two-thirds majority needed to initiate constitutional revision in this house when the seats of its coalition partner, Komeitō (KMT), are included. Although Prime Minister Yasuo Fukuda does not enjoy the same high level of support, neither do opposition leaders. Moreover, the major opposition party, the DPJ, is moving to the right in its foreign policy orientation, largely agreeing with many key LDP positions in the security arena related to Japan's overarching security identity—on such questions as the foreign deployment of the SDF; the pursuit of missile defense, surveillance satellites, more liberal arms exports, and greater offensive capability of the SDF; and even constitutional revision. Thus, both possible scenarios for an identity shift at the political level appear to be converging.

Appearances can be deceiving, however. Apparent agreement on broad questions of security policy is not the same as actual agreement on specific security practices. Moreover, when electoral politics enters in, even general agreement among major political actors in principle can lead to public disagreement when one side perceives electoral advantage. DPJ leader Ichiro Ozawa's position on the extension of "special measures" to allow continued MSDF deployment in the Indian Ocean is a case in point. Ozawa's determination to scuttle this deployment likely had more to do with perceived electoral advantage than outright policy disagreement. Still, the DPJ and the LDP *do* disagree about the degree to which Japan should play a more active military role in the region and globally, as do coalition partners LDP and KMT. The potential for the formation of a new consensus across parties that would result in substantial policy shift is therefore greatly constrained. On the one hand, the DPJ landslide in the July 2007 Upper House election—which resulted in a sort of "divided government" never before seen in Japan—puts forth an opportunity to forge a cross-party consensus on security issues. On the other hand, the new procedural powers of the opposition that have resulted from the DPJ victory seem at the outset to have emboldened the party to suggest a different, more moderate path rather than to join the LDP in setting a new course.

Moreover, apart from party politics, public opinion—as discussed above—does not yet appear to support a dramatic new security program, even if it is more willing than in previous decades to consider incremental change somewhat beyond previous constraints. As developed in Chapter 1, both ideational and material factors can lead to changes in security practice (as summarized in Table 2). However, the nature of this change, and therefore our ability to predict change, is affected by which factor is causing the shift. So far in Japan today, the preponderance of shift in security practice is due to changes in material factors. If pressure generated by such material change leads to a shift in security identity (as realist theory predicts), we should expect far greater change in Japanese security practice than we have seen to date. Thus, in addition to examining changes in material forces, we must consider factors likely to lead to a shift in the postwar security identity of domestic antimilitarism.

This chapter concludes with three scenarios. While none of these scenarios are as likely as the continuation of incremental change bounded by the continued though stretched resilience of Japan's long-standing security identity, they are nonetheless scenarios that should be examined carefully: (1) a substantial change to Japan's international strategic environment, or sudden reinterpretation of this environment; (2) a rupture in the U.S.-Japan alliance; or (3) a domestically driven attempt to gain political advantage within inter- or intraparty competition, including possibly through a broader party realignment, or by one party capitalizing on populism linked to nationalism and a new security program or security identity. These three scenarios are not necessarily mutually exclusive but will be considered individually at the outset.

A Substantial Change in Japan's International Strategic Environment. A substantial change in Japan's international strategic environment could quickly result in Japanese elite and public reassessment of the proper role of Japan's military within the state, and Japan's proper role in the international system in general, much like the September 11 attacks on the United States led to a substantial reassessment of military strategy in that country. Unlike the European case, where scholars have noted a growing "security community" of like-minded nations devoted to the rule of law and institutionalized norms (e.g., Kagan 2002), Japan faces an uncertain and at times hostile regional environment, where a sudden shift is easily imaginable: a substantial hot war between Taiwan and China, into which the United States and Japan would likely be drawn; a surprise missile attack by North Korea on Japan, or on American forces in Japan or South Korea, or even on South Korea; an unexpected outbreak of shooting between Japanese and Chinese forces over disputed territory, likely through miscalculation and nationalist agitation on both sides; or more broadly, a radical Islamist terrorist attack on Tokyo, against American forces elsewhere in Japan, or even elsewhere abroad along the lines of the surprise attacks on the United States on September 11, 2001. Judging by Japan's multiple policy responses enacted after the relatively minor Taepodong missile overflight of August 1998,[20] and further policy responses to the terrorist attacks on the United States on September 11, 2001, it is reasonable to expect a substantial policy—and even identity—shift as a result of a substantial change in Japan's international environment.

A Rupture in the U.S.-Japan Alliance. A rupture in the U.S.-Japan alliance could also serve as a catalyst for identity shift. While this appears unlikely given the marked deepening of the alliance in the past decade, the close political, economic, and cultural relationship between the United States and Japan, and Japan's few viable other security options, such a potential rupture should not be dismissed out of hand. Anti-American riots over the rape of a school-age girl by U.S. marines in Okinawa in 1995 spread throughout Japan and exerted considerable political pressure on the United States for a major force realignment—one arguably averted more as a result of a worsening international environment (first with North Korea, then with the September 11 attacks, and with a rising China in the background) than due to resolution of Japanese complaints regarding U.S. forces in Japan. Three years later, Japan's first non-LDP prime minister in nearly forty years published an article in the influential English-language journal *Foreign Affairs* calling for "an alliance without bases"—that is, a continued U.S.-Japan alliance, but one without permanent American forces stationed in Japan (Hosokawa 1998). While not overtly calling for such a policy, the current opposition DPJ also flirts with such rhetoric, leaving open the possibility that it would pursue such a line if it were to come into power.

Although seemingly well under control, nationalism in Japan is rising, according to many observers in Japan and especially outside of Japan. This is a force that could potentially latch on to the presence of U.S. bases in Japan and a deepening interoperability of U.S. and Japanese military forces as unacceptable affronts to Japanese national pride or sovereignty. That concerns about the apparent permanence of U.S. forces in Japan, about U.S. pressure on Japan to further increase military activities and capabilities, and about the increased threat that the presence of U.S. forces on Japanese soil may cause Japan are heard not only from those on the far right (those traditionally associated with nationalism) but also among many on the left and even among government officials themselves also suggests that this scenario must be considered seriously.

Domestic Political Realignment Driven by Rising Political Populism. Finally, and perhaps relatedly, a domestically driven attempt to gain political advantage within inter- or intraparty competition, including possibly through a broader party realignment, or by one party capitalizing on populism linked to nationalism and a new security program or security identity, should be considered. Within the current context of two major political parties in Japan vying for supremacy—the LDP and the DPJ—such a drive for political advantage using security policy as a tool would most likely take one of three forms: (1) as part of a factional battle within the dominant party, the LDP—such as in the context of a leadership race; (2) as part of a drive by the opposition party, the DPJ, to remake itself to be more politically appealing; or (3) as part of a drive by a new group of politicians to form a new party that would be viable nationally.

Such party competition might result simply from a recrafting of how Japan's existing international environment is perceived and presented—for example, a vilifying of North Korea, China, or even the United States despite no new policy developments. Certainly at least for the former two states, ample recent actions by nationals of those states could lay the groundwork for a more negative policy to be crafted toward those states,[21] and a new security identity being formed around the idea that Japan must be better prepared to defend itself against such regimes. Some analysts have argued that Koizumi's landslide victory in the September 2005 Lower House election was fueled in part by the strident attitude he expressed toward Japan's Asian neighbors by such actions as visiting the controversial Yasukuni Shrine and statements related to Japan's history textbook controversies (Clemons and Oros 2005). It is imaginable that other politicians will similarly seek to employ such a strategy in future elections to gain political advantage. The current unusual political situation of the DPJ controlling a majority of the seats in the Upper House while the LDP controls a majority in the Lower House puts further pressure for political realignment to restore a functional majority in both houses.

Thus, all three of these subscenarios for gaining political advantage could, in principle, take place without any substantial international development sparking them, but given current Japanese public opinion related to the perceived utility of international cooperation and the pursuit of friendly relations abroad, it does not currently seem likely that such a strategy would appeal to a majority of voters.[22] More likely, such a shift in domestic party rhetoric would be in response to an outside factor such as those outlined in the preceding two scenarios. Absent such a development, a substantial departure from Japan's long-standing security identity of domestic antimilitarism seems unlikely for at least the next decade. Moreover, further incremental steps toward a larger global military role appear to be greatly limited by the pervasive institutionalization of domestic antimilitarism—beginning, of course, with Article Nine of the constitution, which despite much discussion of revision politically looks unlikely to be substantially modified any time soon. This question of institutionalization—and, relatedly, reproduction—of Japan's security identity over time is critical to an argument positing a sustained role for Japan's long-standing security practices. It is on this topic, therefore, that this volume will conclude.

(Re)Producing a Twenty-first-Century Security Identity

The examples of the evolution of Japan's security practices presented in this volume illustrate three ways that security identity affects security practice: (1) through its influence on policy rhetoric, (2) its structuring of public opinion and the coalition-building opportunities this enables, and (3) its institutionalization into the policy-making process. The central tenets of the security identity of domestic antimilitarism are reproduced through all of these means: through adoption into common language and discourse, through attitudes and opinions adopted and reflected in public and elite opinion polls, and perhaps most importantly, through the institutionalization of the central tenets into laws, rules, and procedures of government and other political actors. Thus, although these principles were crafted in the early postwar period, as early as fifty years ago, the security identity is not a static phenomenon, but rather must be produced and reproduced through human agency.

This final section of this volume will consider how—or whether—these principles that have grounded Japan's postwar security practice can be reproduced in the new domestic and international environment that is contemporary Japan. First, the final arguments for the central thesis will be offered—that the near-term political agenda in Japan will continue to reify the security identity of domestic antimilitarism in a new century, most fundamentally by *not* changing the constitution in a way that would negate the central tenets of this identity. Next, the alternative is considered—how a new security identity could be produced to set new principles to guide Japan in a new century. The volume will conclude with a discussion of some of the areas that might be productively explored by a new round of research in the important topic areas of Japan's security future and the broader theoretical question of how ideational factors influence the development and evolution of security practice.

Reproducing Domestic Antimilitarism in a New Environment

It is notable that in this period of great change, relatively speaking, in Japanese security practice, the long-standing principles of the existing security identity are simultaneously so extensively reinforced and reified for a new generation through public debate, media interpretation of opinion polling, and new legislation designed to adapt long-standing principles to a new domestic political landscape, new demands from abroad, new military technologies, and a new international environment. Even a piece of legislation widely reported as a departure from past practice, such as the decision to deploy the SDF to Iraq in 2004, serves to reify the long-standing security identity through new legislative text that sets clear limits on SDF action largely along the lines of limits long understood. The case chapters which considered restrictions on the export of weapons, on the military use of outer space, and on missile defense cooperation with the United States all underscored how even departures from past practice buttressed—and further reified—the continuity of limits of the past.

The postwar "peace constitution" serves as the most visible and noted symbol of Japan's long-standing security identity and moreover serves an important functional role in maintaining and reproducing the security identity over time. With constitutional revision at the top of political discussion in Japan recently, it is appropriate to address in a final discussion of the reproduction—or new production—of security identity some analysis of the likely future of this important symbol and de facto constraint on Japanese security practice.

Vocal calls for constitutional revision have long been cited as a harbinger for change in Japanese security policy, dating back to the years immediately following the U.S. Occupation of Japan in the mid-1950s, the first time Japanese might have changed their constitution. At that time, conservative rightists fought hard to modify Article Nine of the constitution and other clauses such as those related to the status of the emperor, state religion, or citizen obligations to the state. That they were unsuccessful is widely viewed as a Japanese endorsement of text that is understood to have originally been imposed on an occupied people. Throughout the postwar period, increased levels of support for constitutional revision have been interpreted—probably accurately—as an indication of the level of support for change to the basic principles underlying the security identity of domestic antimilitarism. Thus, the post–Cold War rise in support for constitutional revision—now regularly exceeding 50 percent in public opinion polls, and exceeding the necessary two-thirds majority in polls of Diet members (Kliman 2006, p. 46)—is noted with foreboding by those concerned about rising Japanese "militarism" and with approval by those seeking a more "normal" Japan. This recent interpretation is mistaken, however.

As Lisa Wedeen (2002) writes in her work on cultural symbols and their political significance: "The contexts within which an action occurs help determine the range of significations that are possible and pertinent" (p. 721). For example, an avowed declaration of commitment to the peaceful use of outer space at the time of a deepening military alliance with the United States may signify an acknowledgment by political actors that they are aware of possible future entanglements within a deepening alliance. The same action in a different context, for example, at a scientific meeting of experts abroad, may signify a sense of shared community among scientists or an effort to convey a central tenet of Japan's security identity to an external audience. Practice must be contextualized to be interpreted. Moreover, it must be acknowledged that the meanings individuals attach to certain actions may be multiple, unstable, and even unknowable.

In the political arena, however, individually perceived meaning may be less important than how practices are interpreted by groups of outside actors. For example, multiple Japanese prime ministers' visits to the Yasukuni Shrine are ascribed different meaning by different sets of observers: what is perceived as a form of respect by a Japanese veterans group may be perceived as a troubling sign of militarism to Chinese nationalists. Absent participant data (such as through an interview or a personal diary), one cannot determine the individual meaning the participant ascribed to the action; and even *with* such access, a participant might not be forthcoming with the true motivation or meaning. Overall, as Wedeen (2002) notes, "Practices make sense because they are reproduced historically and conceptualized through language.... Resistance and obedience are intelligible insofar as they make reference to this shared set of oppositions, without which political activities or speech acts would hardly make sense" (p. 722).

The issue of support for constitutional revision is one such area exactly where "the contexts within which an action occurs help determine the range of significations that are possible and pertinent," for support for constitutional revision no longer signifies, necessarily, support for a change to Article Nine of the constitution, nor even support for *any* increased military role by the SDF. Increasingly today the opposite is the case—opponents of an expanded military role for the SDF and for Japan more broadly have turned to the constitution again as a way to codify the security practices dictated by the security identity of domestic antimilitarism into guiding policy documents. There is concern among many that the continual reinterpretation of the original wording of the constitution, particularly by a ruling party or its appointed Cabinet Legislation Bureau, is the clearest path to a routing of the original intent of the document.[23]

By contrast, amending the document to admit the long-standing existence of the Self-Defense Forces but also to establish in the constitution some of the key constraints on acceptable SDF action, roles, missions, and capabilities would be among the strongest methods of institutionalization of the security identity of domestic antimilitarism for the next generation. For this reason, conservative Diet members have become much less enthusiastic about constitutional revision, and despite agreement on several areas of possible change having resulted from the Diet constitutional research commissions, currently it is unclear under what time frame (if at all) legislative action to initiate constitutional revision will take place. Pushing ahead with constitutional revision in the current political environment would require the LDP to compromise with its coalition partner, the KMT, as well as with the majority-holder in the Upper House, the DPJ. Given that the constitution has not yet ever been revised—and enabling legislation to do so dictates that the required referendum not be held until 2010 at the earliest—the LDP is concerned not to initiate the process unless it is reasonably clear that it can achieve the revision points it desires.

In sum, even the holy grail of conservatives—constitutional revision—may not be what it appears in Japan today. The significance of possible constitutional revision has been greatly altered in the past decade and no longer serves as the ultimate symbol of change in Japan. Even if revision were to take place, it is not clear a priori that this would signify a change to a more "normal" Japan—except in the sense that "normal" democracies tend to change their constitution every once in a while. Constitutional revision could serve to reproduce the existing security identity as well as to signify a shift. Similarly, as the latest political phenomenon confronting Japan—divided government between the Upper and Lower Houses of the Diet—unfolds, continuing legislative battles over a range of security practices are virtually certain. Compromise over future security decisions will reproduce elements of the security identity of domestic antimilitarism well into the twenty-first century, barring clear identity shift.

Producing a New Security Identity for a New Century?

The political process of security policy formulation in postwar Japan has entailed the formation of coalitions among actors who represent both interests vying for power as well as different ideas about Japan's role in the world and the proper use of military capability to play this role. Over time, more actors in the system were socialized into the hegemonic security identity of domestic antimilitarism, but this socialization process never succeeded in homogenizing political views of defense policy in Japan. Instead, as observed by Heclo (1974) and Robert Lieberman (2002) in the European and American contexts, respectively, the very process of policy making over time perpetuated a system of clashing ideological and institutional orders and thus carries forward the possibility of dynamic political change in the future—such as under the three scenarios outlined in the previous section.

Although recent developments in Japanese security policy certainly can be interpreted as dramatic political change, they are also consistent in most ways with previous Japanese policy constraints and outcomes. At the same time, very recent policy innovations—those since 1998—begin to call into question the commitment to continuity apparent in security policy change of the 1990s. As Huntington (1981) observes, "when the gap between ideals and institutions grows large enough periods of 'creedal passion' occur in which institutional practices are reformed to align more closely with the ideals" (quoted in Wedeen 2002, p. 702). This possibility in Japan's near future—a wholesale reform of institutional practices to reflect new ideals—must not be dismissed. The scenarios for change outlined above, as well as thresholds for measuring identity shift set out in Table 1 of the introduction, can help with interpreting future policy developments. The vocal presence—and debate—of a wide range of thought about appropriate security policies for contemporary Japan further underscores the need to watch for signs of identity shift.

Conclusion

This volume has sought to contribute to the worlds of both policy and scholarship in three ways. First, in building on and refining previous "constructivist" scholarship on how security identity restricts security practices, it has demonstrated the political foundation of Japan's postwar security identity, underscoring how identity shift may occur if this underlying political basis were to substantially change and if alternative visions were convincingly presented by contending political actors. Second, by illustrating the interplay of material and ideational factors in a number of different security practices, this volume offers an explanation for shifts in security practice despite a stable security identity. Finally, by examining the principal mechanisms of identity shift based on two previous time periods as well as the current time period, this volume offers an answer to those concerned about the future of Japanese security policy. This answer is that the future will look much like the recent past, absent a substantial shock to the system. Even with such a shock—as seen in the case of the immediate post–Cold War period—the shock would have to underscore a failure in Japan's past practice rather than simply pose new challenges for identity shift to result.

Attention to security identity alone provides only a partial explanation. As Legro (2005) writes, "A full explanation of foreign policy change ... cannot ignore strategic incentives and parochial domestic interests, but must show how enterprising agents, environmental feedback, and collective ideas come together to maintain societies on their prior foreign policy tracks or switch them to new ones" (p. 162). General theory that conceptualizes state responses to strategic incentives, or how domestic actors often pursue parochial interests, is therefore important. In looking to Japan's security future, however, scholars and practitioners must redouble their efforts to investigate important sources for sustaining and altering Japan's security identity, including renewed attention to how "enterprising agents" (or as others term them, "political entrepreneurs") seek to craft ideas and boost their power. In Japan today, numerous agents are attempting to reshape Japan's security debate by drawing on the powerful forces of nationalism and historical memory. The role of political actors outside the domestic system—such as the United States through alliance mechanisms, or Chinese and South Korean actors involved in economic and social interactions—should also be investigated more systematically. The research agenda for investigating Japan's future international roles is pregnant with possibilities.

Despite numerous areas of further investigation, however, the reasons why Japan will not once again become a great, rival military power in East Asia in the foreseeable future are many. Numerous scholars and analysts have already contributed to our ability to explain this likely outcome. It is essential, however, to base one's view of Japan's future on its enduring security identity, and ultimately, on Japanese citizens themselves—a people who have come to see their way of providing for security as sufficiently "normal" to last well into this new century.

Appendixes

Appendix 1

Postwar Japanese Prime Ministers

Name	Party	Dates of office
Naruhiko Higashikuni		Aug. 17, 1945–Oct. 9, 1945
Kijuro Shidehara		Oct. 9, 1945–May 22, 1946
Shigeru Yoshida		May 22, 1946–May 24, 1947
Tetsu Katayama	JSP	May 24, 1947–Mar. 10, 1948
Hitoshi Ashida		Mar. 10, 1948–Oct. 15, 1948
Shigeru Yoshida	Liberal	Oct. 15, 1948–Dec. 10, 1954
Ichiro Hatoyama	Liberal/LDP	Dec. 10, 1954–Dec. 23, 1956
Tanzan Ishibashi	LDP	Dec. 23, 1956–Feb. 25, 1957
Nobusuke Kishi	LDP	Feb. 25, 1957–July 19, 1960
Hayato Ikeda	LDP	July 19, 1960–Nov. 9, 1964
Eisaku Sato	LDP	Nov. 9, 1964–July 7,1972
Kakuei Tanaka	LDP	July 7, 1972–Dec. 9, 1974
Takeo Miki	LDP	Dec. 9, 1974–Dec. 24, 1976
Takeo Fukuda	LDP	Dec. 24, 1976–Dec. 7, 1978
Masayoshi Ohira	LDP	Dec. 7, 1978–July 17, 1980
Zenko Suzuki	LDP	July 17, 1980–Nov. 27, 1982
Yasuhiro Nakasone	LDP	Nov. 27, 1982–Nov. 6, 1987
Noboru Takeshita	LDP	Nov. 6, 1987–June 3, 1989
Sokuke Uno	LDP	June 3, 1989–Aug. 10, 1989
Toshiki Kaifu	LDP	Aug. 10, 1989–Nov. 5, 1991
Kiichi Miyazawa	LDP	Nov. 5, 1991–Aug. 9, 1993
Morihiro Hosokawa	NFP	Aug. 9, 1993–Apr. 28, 1994
Tsutomu Hata	LDP	Apr. 28, 1994–June 30, 1994
Tomiichi Murayama	JSP	June 30, 1994–Jan. 11, 1996
Ryutaro Hashimoto	LDP	Jan. 11, 1996–July 30, 1998
Keizo Obuchi	LDP	July 30, 1998–Apr. 5, 2000
Yoshiro Mori	LDP	Apr. 5, 2000–Apr. 26, 2001
Junichiro Koizumi	LDP	Apr. 26, 2001–Sept. 26, 2006
Shinzo Abe	LDP	Sept. 26, 2006–Sept. 26, 2007
Yasuo Fukuda	LDP	Sept. 26, 2007–

Appendix 2

Postwar Japanese Election Dates for Both Houses (1946–2007)

House of Representatives (Lower House)	House of Councilors (Upper House)	House of Representatives (Lower House)	House of Councilors (Upper House)
Apr. 10, 1946		Dec. 5, 1976	
	Apr. 20, 1947		July 10, 1977
Apr. 25, 1947		Oct. 7, 1979	
Jan. 23, 1949		June 22, 1980 (Both)	
	June 4, 1950		June 26, 1983
Oct. 1, 1952		Dec. 18, 1983	
Apr. 19, 1953		July 6, 1986 (Both)	
	Apr. 24, 1953		July 23, 1989
Feb. 27, 1955		Feb. 18, 1990	
	July 8, 1956		July 26, 1992
May 22, 1958		July 18, 1993	
	June 2, 1959		July 23, 1995
Nov. 20, 1960		Oct. 20, 1996	
	July 1, 1962	July 12, 1998	
Nov. 21, 1963		June 25, 2000	
	July 4, 1965		July 29, 2001
Jan. 29, 1967		Nov. 9, 2003	
	July 7, 1968		July 11, 2004
Dec. 27, 1969		Sept. 11, 2005	
	June 27, 1971		July 29, 2007
Dec. 10, 1972			
	July 7, 1974		

Early data from Foreign Press Center (1995)

Appendix 3

Postwar Japanese Election Returns for the House of Representatives

1945–1955: The Immediate Postwar Period

	LIB		DEM		JSP (%/no.)		JCP		Other (no.)
	%	No.	%	No.	L	R	%	No.	
Apr. 10, 1946	24.4	141	18.7	94[a]	17.9/93		3.9	5	133
Apr. 25, 1947	26.7	131	10.8	126	26.2/143		3.7	4	62
Jan. 23, 1949	43.9	264	15.7	69	13.5/48		9.8	35	50
Oct. 1, 1952	47.9	240	18.2	85[b]	9.9/54	11.4/57	2.5	0	30
Apr. 19, 1953	47.7	234[c]	17.9	76[b]	13.1/72	13.5/66	1.9	1	17
Feb. 27, 1955	26.6	112	36.6	185	15.4/89	13.9/67	2.0	2	12
end of 1955		299			154		2		

Data from Curtis (1988), pp. 253–54
[a] Progressive Party
[b] Reform Party
[c] Combination of Hatoyama and Yoshida Liberals
% = Percentage of popular vote; No. = number of seats obtained
LIB = Liberal Party (Democratic Liberals in 1949)
DEM = Democratic Party
JSP = Japan Socialist Party (L = left wing; R = right wing)
JCP = Japan Communist Party
Other = minor parties and independents

Appendix 4

Postwar Japanese Election Returns for the House of Representatives

1955–1993: The 1955 System Years

	LDP		JSP		DSP		KMT		NLC		JCP	
	%	No.	%	No.	%	No.	%	No.	%	No.	%	No.
End of 1955	—	299	—	154	—	—	—	—	—			2
May 22, 1958	57.8	287	32.9	166	—	—	—	—	—		2.6	1
Nov. 20, 1960	57.6	296	27.6	145	8.8	17	—	—	—		2.9	3
Nov. 21, 1963	54.7	283	29.0	144	7.3	23	—	—	—		4.0	5
Jan. 29, 1967	48.8	277	27.9	140	7.4	30	5.4	25	—		4.8	5
Dec. 27, 1969	47.6	288	21.4	90	7.7	31	10.9	47	—		6.8	14
Dec. 10, 1972	46.9	271	21.9	118	7.0	19	8.5	29	—		10.5	38
Dec. 5, 1976	41.8	249	20.7	123	6.3	29	10.9	55	4.1	17	10.4	17
Oct. 7, 1979	44.6	248	19.7	107	6.8	35	9.8	57	3.0	4	10.4	39
June 22, 1980	47.9	284	19.3	107	6.6	32	9.0	33	3.0	12	9.8	29
Dec. 18, 1983	45.8	250	19.5	112	7.3	38	10.1	58	2.4	8	9.3	26
July 6, 1986	49.4	300	17.2	85	6.4	26	9.4	56	1.8	6	8.8	26
Feb. 18, 1990	46.1	275	24.4	136	4.8	14	8.0	45	—		8.0	16
July 18, 1993	36.6	223	15.4	70	3.5	15	8.1	51	—		8.1	15

Data from Foreign Press Center (1995; 1997)
% = Percentage of popular vote; No. = number of seats obtained
LDP = Liberal Democratic Party   DSP = Democratic Socialist Party   NLC = New Liberal Club
JSP = Japan Socialist Party   KMT = Komeitô   JCP = Japan Communist Party

Appendix 5

Major Japanese Government Policy Statements Regarding Arms Exports

The export of arms requires a license from the Minister of International Trade and Industry pursuant to the Foreign Exchange and Control Law (1949 law No. 228) and the Export Trade Control Law (1949 Cabinet order No. 378).

1. The Three Principles on Arms Export

On April 21, 1967, then Prime Minister Eisaku Satō declared the Three Principles during a House of Representatives' Audit Committee meeting.

(summary)

The Principles provide that arms export to the following countries shall not be permitted:

(1) Communist bloc countries

(2) Countries to which the export of arms is prohibited under United Nations resolutions

(3) Countries which are actually involved or likely to become involved in international conflicts

2. The Unified Government View of Arms Export (i.e., The New Three Principles)

On February 27, 1976, then Prime Minister Takeo Miki announced the government's view during a House of Representatives' Budget Committee meeting.
(full text)

1) Government Policy

With regard to the export of "arms," the government, from the standpoint of Japan as a pacifist country, has always been dealing with the problem of arms export in a cautious manner in order to prevent that from furthering international conflict. The government will continue to deal with the matter pursuant to the following policy and will not promote arms export.

(1) The export of "arms" to areas subject to the three principles on arms export shall be prohibited.

(2) The export of "arms" to other areas which are not subject to the three principles shall be restrained in line with the spirit of the Constitution and Foreign Exchange and Foreign Trade Control Law.

(3) Equipment related to arms production (Export Trade Control Order, Separate Table 1, Section No. 109, etc.) shall be treated in the same category as "arms."

2) Definition of Arms

The term "arms" is used in laws and ordinances or in terms of application, and its definition should be interpreted in accordance with the effect of law.

(1) "Arms" in the Three Principles on Arms Export are what military forces directly use for combating and specifically mean "arms" that match definitions stated in sections from No. 197 to No. 205 in the Separate Table 1 for the Export Trade Control Order.

(2) "Arms" under the Self-Defense Forces Law are interpreted as "firearms, explosives, swords and other machines, equipment and devices aimed at killing and injuring people or destroying things as means of armed struggle." Such things as destroyers, fighters and tanks that move, intrinsically carrying firearms etc. for the purposes of directly killing and injuring people or destroying things as means of armed struggle, are considered "arms."

(*Note:* Due to partial revision of the Export Trade Control Law, "the paragraph 109" in (3) of 1) and "the paragraphs from 197 to 205" in (1) of 2) have been changed to "the paragraph 1.")

3. The Resolution as to the Problem of Arms Exports and Others

Adopted at a House of Representatives plenary session on March 20, 1981, and also at a House of Councilors plenary session on March 30, 1981.

(full text)

Parliament has resolved that: Our country, from the standpoint of the Japanese constitutional idea for a pacifist nation, has been dealing with the export of arms in a cautious manner on the basis of the Three Principles on Arms Export and the unified government view of 1976.

It is regrettable, however, that there lately appeared instances which contravened the stated government policy. The government, therefore, should take effective measures, including institutional improvement, while dealing with the export of arms in strict fairness and with prudence.

4. Statement of Chief Cabinet Secretary on Transfer of Military Technologies to the United States

(January 14, 1983)

Since June 1981, the Japanese Government has received requests from the U.S. Government for exchange of defense-related technologies. After careful studies on the transfer to the U.S. of "military technologies" as a part of such exchange, the Japanese Government has reached the following conclusion, which was approved by the Cabinet meeting today:

1. Under the Japan-U.S. security arrangement, the U.S. and Japan, in cooperation with each other, are to maintain and develop their respective capacities to resist armed attack. In improving its defense capabilities, Japan has been benefiting from various kinds of coopera-

tion extended by the U.S., including transfer of U.S. technologies to Japan. In view of the new situation which has been brought about by, among other things, the recent advance of technology in Japan, it has become extremely important for Japan to reciprocate in the exchange of defense-related technologies in order to ensure the effective operation of the Japan-U.S. Security Treaty and its related arrangements, which provide for and envisage mutual cooperation between Japan and the U.S. in the field of defense, and contribute to peace and security of Japan and in the Far East.

2. The Japanese Government has so far dealt with the question of arms export (including transfer of "military technologies") in accordance with the Three Principles on Arms Export and the Government Policy Guideline on Arms Export. In view of the foregoing, however, the Japanese Government has decided to respond positively to the U.S. request for exchange of defense-related technologies and to open a way for the transfer to the U.S. of "military technologies" (including arms which are necessary to make such transfer effective) as a part of the technology exchange with the U.S. mentioned above; such transfer of "military technologies" will not be subject to the Three Principles on Arms Export. The implementation of such transfer will be made within the framework of the relevant provisions of the MDA Agreement. In this manner, the fundamental objective of refraining from aggravating international disputes, which Japan upholds as a nation committed to peace and on which the Three Principles are based, will be secured.

3. The Japanese Government will continue to maintain, basically, the Three Principles on Arms Export and to respect the spirit of the Diet Resolution on arms export adopted in March 1981.

5. Statement of Chief Cabinet Secretary on the New National Defense Program Guidelines [excerpt]

(December 10, 2004)

[1–5 omitted]

6. We will continue to firmly maintain its policy of dealing with arms exports control carefully, in light of Japan's basic philosophy as a peace-loving nation on which the Three Principles on Arms Exports and their related policy guidelines are based.

If Japan decides that it will engage in joint development and production of ballistic missile defense systems with the United States, however, the Three Principles will not be applied, under the condition that strict control is maintained, because such systems and related activities will contribute to the effective operation of the Japan-U.S. security arrangements and are conducive to the security of Japan.

In addition, through the process by which the NDPG were developed, questions were raised regarding now to handle cases of joint development and production with the United States (other than those related to the ballistic missile defense system) as well as those related to support of counterterrorism and counterpiracy. Decisions will be made on the basis of individual examination of each case, in light of Japan's basic philosophy as a peace-loving nation that aims at avoiding the escalation of international conflicts.

[7–10 omitted]

Appendix 6

Major Japanese Government Policy Statements Regarding the Peaceful Use of Outer Space

1. Resolution Concerning the Fundamentals of Space
Development and Exploitation by Japan
(adopted at the Plenary Session of the House of Representatives on May 9, 1969)

The development and exploitation by Japan of objects to be projected into space above the earth's atmosphere, and of the rockets by which they are launched, shall be confined to peaceful purposes only and shall be carried out to contribute to the progress of science, the improvement of the nation's living standards, and the welfare of human society, along with the development of industrial technology and voluntary collaboration and cooperation.
Source: JDA, *Defense of Japan* (1987), (trans. The Japan Times), appendix reference no. 22.

2. The Utilization of Satellites for "Peaceful Purposes" by Self-Defense
Forces, as Defined by Diet Resolution
(Government views clarified at the Budget Committee of the House of Representatives on Feb. 6, 1985)

In May 1969 in the House of Representatives a resolution was adopted in regard to the development and exploitation of space. This approved space development and exploitation by Japan exclusively for peaceful purposes.

With regard to the wording "for peaceful purposes only," discussions have been conducted in the Diet resulting in a range of interpretations, including "nonmilitary."

A study was recently conducted within the government to define the significance of the Diet resolution in question, in relation to the appropriation of funds in the government-sponsored FY 1985 budget bill, to finance the development of a system designed to receive information via Fleesat satellite during the dispatch of Maritime Defense Force Personnel to the U.S. for training.

It goes without saying that the legal interpretation of the aforementioned Diet resolution is a matter for the Diet, but the government, for its part, construes the meaning of the resolution as follows, and it is hoped that the parties concerned will understand the government's interpretation.

1. Clearly, the wording "for peaceful purposes only," used in the resolution, signified disapproval of direct use by the Self-Defense Forces of any satellite as a lethal or destructive weapon. The government interprets the Diet resolution as prohibiting the Self-Defense Forces from exploiting any satellite unless it is commonly used.

Accordingly, the government considered that the Self-Defense Forces may be permitted to use any satellite which is in common use and any other satellite which is capable of similar functions.

2. The Fleesat satellite, which was discussed in the Diet, is a telecommunications satellite used by the United States for military purposes, but this satellite is capable of the same functions as other satellites which are now commonly used, such as Intelsat (international telecommunications satellite), Inmalsat (international maritime telecommunications satellite), and CS-2 (Sakura No. 2). Therefore, the government does not hold that the use of the Fleesat satellite by the Self-Defense Forces runs counter to the meaning of the Diet resolution in its approval of space development and exploitation for "peaceful purposes only."

Source: JDA, *Defense of Japan* (1987), (trans. The Japan Times), appendix reference no. 23.

Appendix 7

Major Japanese Government Policy Statements Regarding
Ballistic Missile Defense Cooperation with the United States

1. Statement of the Chief Cabinet Secretary Regarding Cooperative Technical Research with the United States on Ballistic Missile Defense (BMD)

(December 25, 1998)

1. Today, with the approval of the Security Council of Japan, the Government of Japan has decided to proceed with cooperative technical research with the United States from 1999 on the Navy's Theater-Wide Defense System (NTWD).

2. Based on the proliferation of weapons of mass destruction and ballistic missiles which began at the end of the Cold War, the Government recognizes the importance to the national defense of Ballistic Missile Defense (BMD) as an exclusively defense-oriented measure and the necessity that Japan make efforts to tackle the issue independently, and has given the issue due consideration.

3. The Government considers that Japan's efforts from now would be most efficiently and successfully served by undertaking cooperative technical research with the United States on NTWD. Furthermore, it is considered that such U.S.-Japan cooperation will be valuable in improving trust in the framework of the U.S.-Japan Security Arrangements.

4. Regarding Diet resolutions on space development and its applications, this has always been a topic about which the Diet has had to provide parliamentary interpretations; however, given the circumstances of recent years that have seen the proliferation of ballistic missiles, and based on the fact that this is a purely defensive measure for the protection of the lives and property of the citizens of Japan, and that there are no alternatives to the BMD system, the Government believes that it will gain the understanding of its citizens that the independent undertaking of a BMD system is in accordance with the aims of Diet resolutions on this issue, and also with the fundamental precepts on which a peaceful nation is founded.

In relation to this, in September 1998, the House of Representatives resolved that with regard to the test-firing of a North Korean missile, "The Government will take all measures to ensure the security of the people of Japan."

As for the transfer of military technologies, U.S.-Japan cooperative technical research regarding BMD will be implemented under a framework arrangement for the transfer of military technologies to the United States.

5. This statement refers to technology research and the transition to the development and implementation stages, which will be judged separately. Judgments on the latter two stages will be made after sufficient examination of the possibility of realizing BMD and the ideal way for the defense of Japan to develop in future.

Source: JDA (1999), *Defense of Japan* (trans. Urban Connections), p. 83.

2. Statement of the Chief Cabinet Secretary on the Cabinet Decision, "On Introduction of Ballistic Missile Defense (BMD) System and Other Measures"
(December 19, 2003)

1. The Government of Japan decided "On Introduction of Ballistic Missile Defense System and Other Measures" at the Security Council and the Cabinet Council today. This decision shows the thinking behind the introduction of BMD system, and at the same time, indicates the direction of Japan's defense force review taking into account the introduction of BMD system and the new security environment. Based on this decision, the Government of Japan will formulate a new National Defense Program Outline and a new Mid-Term Defense Program by the end of the year 2004.

[2–3 omitted]

4. BMD system is the only and purely defensive measure, without alternatives, to protect life and property of the citizens of Japan against ballistic missile attacks, and meets the principle of exclusively defense-oriented national defense policy. Therefore, it is considered that this presents no threat to neighboring countries and does not affect the regional stability.

5. As for the issue of the right of collective self-defense, the BMD system that the Government of Japan is introducing aims at defending Japan. It will be operated based on Japan's independent judgment, and will not be used for the purpose of defending third countries. Therefore, it does not raise any problems with regard to the issue of the right of collective self-defense. The BMD system requires interception of missiles by Japan's own independent judgment based on the information on the target acquired by Japan's own sensors.

[6–8 omitted]

Notes

Introduction

1. The domestic market for defense-related spending is second in the world only to that of the United States. In 2004 Japan spent $42.4 billion on defense, according to the *SIPRI Yearbook*, ranking it as the fourth-largest spender in the world. Japan's defense spending roughly equals that of France ($46.2 billion) and the United Kingdom ($47.4 billion), though it spends a higher proportion of its budget on military equipment, making its domestic defense market second only to that of the United States.

2. Oros and Tatsumi (2007) develop this point further, describing the current state of Japan's defense establishment. This paragraph is adapted from that broader work.

3. The count of fourteen, as of May 2005, consists of two "special measures deployments" (to the Indian Ocean and to Iraq), eight instances of International Peace Cooperation Activities (Cambodia, Mozambique, Rwanda, Golan Heights, twice to East Timor, Afghanistan, and Iraq), and six instances of International Disaster Relief Activities (Honduras, Turkey, India, Iran, Thailand, and Indonesia). East Timor and Iraq are counted only once each, and the Indian Ocean as a single region, to reach a total of fourteen. The JDA itself lists a higher count of SDF deployments due to multiple "missions" within many of the above-mentioned cases—for example, ASDF activities based in Kuwait, GSDF activities based in Samawah, and MSDF activities in the Persian Gulf are counted as three instances (and areas) of overseas deployment despite all being coordinated as assistance to the U.S.-led coalition in Iraq. Further information about these deployments is provided in Chapters 3 and 7 of this volume and in JDA (2005).

4. JDA (2005), p. 535. Apart from limited numbers, the SDF is prohibited from directly engaging in combat, and even indirect "rear area support" is quite limited and still quite controversial at home.

5. Japanese defense producers did export weapons earlier in the postwar period, and they continue to export products and components of a dual-use nature, however—as discussed in Chapter 4 of this volume.

6. See, for example, Soeya (2005) on Japan as a middle power. Ironically, the book that coined the phrase "normal nation" (*futsu no kuni*)—Ozawa (1993)—proposes an international role for Japan much more in line with the civilian power school than the great military power school with which the term presently is associated.

7. See Oros (2007c) for analysis of this driver of change in Japanese security policy—"*gaiatsu*" (foreign pressure) from the United States.

8. Methodologically and empirically, it is therefore justified to revisit seminal works by Berger (1998) and Katzenstein (1996b), both of which argue also that identity-related concepts (antimilitarist culture and norms, respectively) shaped postwar security practice, to reexamine how their arguments withstand a decade of substantial domestic and international political change.

9. Japan's exact position in this ranking varies by year, exchange rates, or whether purchasing-power parity (PPP) is used to compute the spending. Moreover, in the case of China, it depends on whether one uses official Chinese statistics or outside estimates.

10. Samuels (2007) usefully traces the lineage of several major lines of thought apparent throughout the twentieth century; Pyle (2007) examines, in particular, these multiple schools in the early and mid-twentieth century.

11. How much total legislative time the Diet spent on security issues is an area of contention today. Fukumoto (2000) argues that such time was not as much as previous studies have assumed. It is not contested, however, that popular political discourse was deeply engaged in security questions and that this shaped political party platforms and their levels of voter support.

12. Moreover, Japan seeks to become a permanent member of the United Nations Security Council, not to change the character of the other permanent members, but rather to join this exclusive club, a club of militarily active states.

13. Two seminal works in this area are Berger (1998) and Katzenstein (1996b), which together provide an important foundation for this volume. These works themselves, moreover, draw on substantial existing scholarship, as discussed in Chapter 2 of this volume.

14. This formulation benefited greatly from that which Lieberman (2002) uses in the context of American affirmative action policy. It also complements the methodological position of Katzenstein and Okawara (2001/02), who argue that "Japan's and the Asia-Pacific's security policies are not shaped solely by power, interests, or identity but by their combination. Adequate understanding requires analytical eclecticism, not parsimony" (p. 167).

15. Pye (1997) notes the fluidity of "public opinion" on policy issues as well as their indeterminate explanation of political outcomes. What he writes regarding American politics is equally applicable to postwar Japan: "We have literally thousands of surveys of public opinion in America, but it remains a mystery as to which ones can really inform us about where American politics is going" (p. 243). Security identity offers a useful tool to decoding the mystery he refers to, making public opinion continuity and shifts more understandable.

16. Legro (2005), chapter 1, usefully explains the critical distinction between individually held and collectively held beliefs.

17. Abdelal et al. (2005) identify these two dimensions of a collective identity that apply both to the conceptualization of a security identity offered in this volume and to the framework employed in subsequent case chapters.

18. Milly (1999) employs similar theoretical tools to explain the origins of Japan's

social welfare policies in the 1960s in showing how a conflict-ridden political system debated and chose among available definitions of poverty, and then how the chosen defini-tion was institutionalized to effect future policy development.

19. Samuels (1994) also uses *ideology* in this way when he writes, "ideologies may not be consciously held," and that in the Japanese case, they constitute "a set of beliefs operative across centuries" (pp. 17, x).

20. As Bukovansky (1997) argues persuasively, "if leaders adopt a principle that con-stitutes a specific international role for the state and commands domestic legitimacy, then diverse interests will converge on that principle, generating foreign policy continuity" (abstract). It should be noted, however, that Bukovansky's use of the term *identity* differs from its use in this study.

21. Benfell (1997) ascribes a similar role to identity in his work on Japan, writing that the identity "positions the political and ideological boundaries within which the 'nation-state' acts. While it does not determine outcomes, it demarcates what is politically and ideologically possible (and impossible) within a given 'nation'" (p. 11). Thus, he argues: "Discerning the processes of national identity formulation and change, and understanding how national identity is institutionalized and de-institutionalized, therefore, are important theory-building tasks" (p. 11).

22. Only one aspect of Berger's view of Japan's "antimilitarist culture" can be ascribed directly to the security identity of domestic antimilitarism: the security identity conditions actors' ability to mobilize their resources—as opposed to the *national* resources Berger dis-cusses—for military purposes. He writes of Japan's "political-military culture" of antimili-tarism, which he argues has a fourfold impact on security policy: "(1) it supplies the funda-mental goals and norms of political actors; (2) it determines how political actors perceive the existing domestic political environment; (3) it influences the actors' assessment of the international situation; and (4) it strongly conditions their ability to mobilize the national resources for military purposes" (p. 16).

23. In this sense, this study epitomizes a classic "case study," which has been defined by Gerring (2004) as that which undertakes "an intensive study of a single unit for the pur-pose of undertaking a larger class of (similar) units" (p. 342).

24. Feagin, Orum, and Sjoberg (1991) and George and Bennett (2005), among others, advance the argument that maximizing observable phenomena in what appears to be a single case, and linking such observations to general theory, allows case-based approaches to contribute usefully to broader theory formulation and testing.

25. Notable exceptions to the lack of scholarly attention are Hummel (1988), Söder-berg (1986), and Drifte (1986), apart from the brief mention of these policies noted by a majority of scholarly work on postwar Japanese security policy, such as Berger (1998), Green (2001), and Katzenstein (1996b).

26. On the issue of defense production, important works include Drifte (1986), Rubin-stein (1987; 1999; 2001), Samuels (1994), and Green (1995). On the issue of Japan's partici-pation in United Nations Peacekeeping Operations, see Dobson (2003), Ishizuka (2005), Kim (1994), Marten Zisk (2001), and Mulgan (1993; 1995).

27. The periods of "crisis" Calder builds his argument around (1949–54, 1958–63, and 1971–76) do not correspond well to periods of policy innovation in the security realm, however. Moreover, while complementary in many ways to the argument presented here, Calder's work emphasizes the structural aspects of Japan's unusual electoral system to explain a weak defense lobby and limited defense spending in postwar Japan—due to

strong pressure in times of crisis for increased spending in public works and social welfare programs—an argument that is no longer applicable since this electoral system was abandoned in 1994.

28. The JDA became the Ministry of Defense (MOD) in January 2007, but the institution studied in the time frame of this volume is the JDA.

29. The National Diet Library in Tokyo was a particularly useful source in this area due to the "clippings collections" that were maintained (before computer databases replaced this task) on issues related to the case chapters of this volume. Extant scholarship on the earlier postwar period—discussed in Chapter 2—also greatly aided in this endeavor.

30. Officials from the following institutions were interviewed during the course of research of this volume. Many agreed to frank discussions only off the record. Thus, references to individual names are made only in selected instances in subsequent notes. Government institutions include the Ministry of Foreign Affairs (including the North American, National Security, and Policy Planning divisions); the Ministry of the Economy, Trade, and Industry (including the Export Control Division); the Japan Defense Agency; the Cabinet Intelligence Research Office; the National Institute for Defense Studies; the Japan Aeronautical Exploration Agency; the Japan Science and Technology Agency; and the three branches of the Self-Defense Forces. Private institutions include *Akahata*, *Asahi Shimbun*, the Democratic Party of Japan, Keidanren, the Liberal Democratic Party, Mitsubishi Corporation, Mitsubishi Electric Corporation, Mitsubishi Heavy Industries, *Seikyo Shimbun*, *Yomiuri Shimbun*, and a number of major research universities in Japan and the United States.

31. Legislation passed in the Diet in May 2007 sets out, for the first time, the legislative framework to hold the required national referendum to enact constitutional revision once or if both houses of the Diet approve a proposed revision by a two-thirds majority. A clause in the legislation prohibited the holding of such a referendum until 2010 at the earliest, however.

32. This area is a matter of conjecture to some degree because the powers and inclinations of the two major institutions which would ultimately determine the acceptable scope of constitutional interpretation—the Supreme Court and the Cabinet Legislation Bureau (CLB)—are not well defined, nor have they been deeply studied. Samuels (2004) has addressed this issue recently.

33. The "public acceptance" of such statements is key here—not merely in the general "public opinion" sense, but also as measured by institutionalized or ritualized responses to such statements. For example, political leader Ichiro Ozawa, shortly before becoming the president of the opposition DPJ, was widely reported to have privately expressed to Chinese political leaders that Japan had the capability to manufacture thousands of nuclear weapons at short notice, which could be interpreted as an implicit threat of the use of force. However, putting aside its explicitness, he was forced to clarify and downplay this statement once it became widely reported.

34. I credit William Vosse of International Christian University for making this initial observation. Personal communication, September 2005.

Chapter 1

1. Campbell (1992), chap. 2, provides a useful overview of important public policy and Japan-based literature. His ideas, together with those of Calder (1988a) and Legro (2005), greatly informed this chapter.

2. See Chapter 7 in particular for discussion of recent Japanese public attitudes about security.

3. Legro (2005) sets out such an argument for the cases of postwar America and China today, among other cases.

4. Scholars working in this research area are informed by earlier approaches to incorporating domestic and individual-level variables in foreign policy analysis such as those that consider actor images, roles, and perceptions at the individual and state level. For example, Jervis (1970) addresses the issue by focusing on the "images" states seek to project internationally, rather than domestically as in this volume. Holsti (1970) discusses the issue at the mass level by way of his "national role conceptions," which is more congruent with this study in its concern with the function—or "role"—a state plays in the international system. However, like Snyder (1991), Holsti conceives of such roles as generalizable categories across states, rather than tailored in their nature to specific states, as argued in this volume in the case of Japan, and by others regarding other cases (e.g., Friedberg [2000], Kier [1997], Johnston [1995a]).

5. Although this aspect of state identity broadly conceived is not a central element of this study, more theorizing clearly is necessary over how states choose among different identities *in different policy areas*—for example, among normative prescriptions suggested by Japan as Asian nation, Japan as alliance partner, Japan as technonationalist state, and Japan as domestic antimilitarist state. Social psychology and political science constructivist literature begins to address this question, but more work is necessary. Katzenstein (2005) addresses this question directly in his work on regional identities.

6. Jackson (2006) makes a similar argument regarding the political bargain that led to the United States' development of the Marshall Plan for European reconstruction—focusing both on the material and ideational aspects of creating political support for such an ambitious policy.

7. Important examples include Waltz (1979), Keohane (1984), and Katzenstein (1996a). Classical realists allow some consideration of the role of domestic politics in shaping state interests, though Morgenthau's admonition that government "be willing to compromise with public opinion on nonessentials," but fight "for what it regards to be the irreducible minimum of good foreign policy" suggests the existence of a baseline of "objective" determinations of state interests prominent in rationalist accounts (Morgenthau [1973], quoted in Katz [2000], p. 1).

8. In my view, however, they underestimate the individual ideational component that motivates many protestors in Okinawa, though their focus on the material incentives of some protesters exposes a useful theoretical distinction of individual motivations for protest among different political actors.

9. See Desch (1998) and a special issue of *International Organization* (Fall 2005) for useful critical reviews of a number of these studies.

10. Postdeployment, however, a majority of Japanese supported the decision to deploy the SDF to Iraq on a limited basis. Such a shift underscores the malleability of public opinion over some security practices, in addition to the unusual popular support enjoyed by Prime Minister Koizumi in general, and likely relief on the part of Japanese citizens that the SDF suffered no combat-related casualties during its deployment to Iraq.

11. Wendt (1992), one of the school's most respected proponents, writes that constructivists "share a cognitive, inter-subjective conception of process in which identities and

interests are endogenous to interaction, rather than a rationalist-behavioral one in which they are exogenous" (p. 394).

12. Goldstein and Keohane (1993) address this question succinctly (pp. 5–7). Important defining literature in the postpositivist tradition includes Biersteker (1989), Lapid (1989), and Wendt (1987).

13. This argument parallels that of Calder (1988a) in *Crisis and Compensation*; however, the argument here is that Japanese actors purposefully reach to advance policy objectives, rather than simply reacting to "crisis." In essence, they create their own crises.

14. See Hughes (2004b) on Japan's comprehensive security policy.

15. Midford (2006) offers a useful compilation on much such data.

16. As the dominant paradigm in the academic study of international relations, the literature in this area is vast. Two useful articles for an overview of this school of thought are Brooks (1997) and Finel (2001/02). As they note, classic realist statements would include Morgenthau (1973), Waltz (1979), Gilpin (1981), Aron (1966), and Krasner (1985). Seminal post–Cold War restatements would include Layne (1993), Schweller (1994), Taliaferro (2000/01), and Mearsheimer (1990). In the East Asian context, see Betts (1993/94) and Christensen (1999).

17. Although this tenet is at the core of realist theory, it has been problemized in academic debate, particularly in the area of "offense-defense theory," which calls into question the fungibility of state power and introduces perception to objective factors in determining state power. See, for example, Deudney (2000) and van Evera (1999). This debate can lead to arguments quite similar to those of nonrealist institutionalists, whose core claim is exactly that lack of fungibility of power calls into question the entire realist paradigm. See, for example, Art (1999) and Baldwin (1999). As discussed later in this section, the issues this debate raises call into question for many the trajectory of the realist research program—whether it is a progressive or "degenerative" endeavor, as asked by Vasquez (1997) and Legro and Moravcsik (1999).

18. Liberal institutionalist theory is a second major strand of international-level theory, though—as discussed above—many of its central claims are now also incorporated by new schools of realist thought. Legro and Moravcsik (1999) provide a good statement of the liberal institutionalist school, building on the work of Keohane and Nye (2000), Keohane (1984), and Baldwin (1993); also see Ikenberry (2001).

19. This position was restated by Waltz (1996) in response to a growing realist literature attempting to do exactly this: use realism to explain foreign policy outcomes.

20. See Elman (1996) for a review of numerous examples and their contributions to the study of foreign policy outcomes.

21. Mearsheimer (1995) makes the general point: "States temporarily led astray by the false promise of institutionalist rhetoric eventually come to their senses and start worrying about the balance of power" (p. 93). Related questions for this study would include (1) how long is "eventually," and (2) how can we explain how states are "led astray"? The argument of this volume is that a focus on a state's security identity offers an answer to both questions.

22. Among Japan-centered literature, Green (2001), Kliman (2006), Lind (2004), Midford (2002; 2004), and several others would be included in such a school of thought based on realist theory, informed by general literature that would include van Evera (1999), Schweller (1998), Christensen (1996), and Rose (1998).

23. Calder (1988b) is one such example of a two-level game model applied to foreign

economic policy. His larger work (Calder 1988a) is an exception to the above characterization, however, in that he applies a domestic politics–based argument to the formulation of defense policy as well as other cases of domestic policy change. Overviews of the bureaucratic-politician competing literature are provided in Oros (1998) and Johnson (1995).

24. The renewed interest in such approaches has been called an "identity boom," which itself has become the subject of scholarship in political science. See the introductions to Jacquin-Berdal, Oros, and Verweij (1998) and Lapid and Kratochwil (1996) for discussion of this shift in the discipline. For a perspective from the broader political science tradition, including the area of political psychology, see Pye (1997). Two good reviews of much of this new literature in the area of international relations, pointing out both contributions and shortcomings, are Hopf (1998) and Desch (1998).

25. This study owes a great debt to Berger's careful and thought-provoking research and attempts to operationalize several concepts he sets out in his study.

26. This, I believe, is a danger of loose "eclecticism" of theory as employed by Katzenstein (1996b) in his study of Japanese security policy and as advocated by Katzenstein and Okawara (2001/02) more broadly.

27. Pye's discussion of new uses of "culture" in political analysis corrects some of the flaws of previous constructivist literature on policy making by stressing the *power* dimension of policy outcomes, in addition to the *value* component upon which proponents of cultural approaches often concentrate exclusively (see Pye [1997], p. 246). Critical theory approaches to international outcomes also put power at the center of their analysis but differ from the approach adopted here due to their general rejection of causal pathways.

28. The fifteen years of national political, economic, and social rebuilding of Japan after defeat in the Second World War is the subject of literally thousands of scholarly and popular books and articles in Japanese and English. Even today substantial empirical research continues to be conducted on this period, seen in the Pulitzer prize–winning books by John Dower (1999) and Herbert Bix (2000). The great volume of work on this period is evidence of a broad consensus on the importance of the immediate postwar period to the future development of Japanese politics, Japan's economy, and broader change in Japanese society.

29. Berger (1998) is the notable exception, though he does not examine any one policy in depth, instead only briefly sketching out plausible arguments for a number of different security policies in order to make space in his study for a cross-national comparison with postwar Germany.

30. Green (2001) is representative of many who locate Japan's security identity in the "Yoshida doctrine," which Green asserts "was the only policy paradigm that would accommodate these broad views [among competing foreign policy visions]" (p. 11). In a few introductory pages he traces a linear progression of codification of this identity throughout the Cold War period. Like many post–Cold War authors, he then rediscovers debates over security policy in the post–Cold War period.

Chapter 2

1. The term *redevelopment* is important given the large arms industry that existed in Japan until its defeat in the Second World War.

2. Countless authors have categorized political actors in this period in a great variety of different ways. Berger (1998) elegantly employs the common threefold division among Right, Center, and Left political actors, building on earlier work in Japanese by Otake (1988),

which employs a threefold conservative, liberal, and socialist framework. Curtis (1988) neatly discusses this issue along party lines, as do Otake (1983) and Chuma (1985) in Japanese.

3. One example is Prime Minister Shinzo Abe, the grandson of the depurged postwar prime minister, Nobusuke Kishi.

4. Further discussion of this option is provided in Mabon (1988) and Press (1998).

5. ASEAN+3 (the ten members of the Association of Southeast Asian Nations plus Japan, China, and South Korea) and the ASEAN Regional Forum (ARF) are the two primary nascent security institutions in East Asia today. Asia-Pacific Economic Cooperation (APEC) and the Asian Free Trade Area (AFTA) are their counterparts in the economic realm.

6. Prime Minister Shigeru Yoshida especially is credited with this policy. See Dower (1979) for a full discussion.

7. Hook (1996) devotes considerable attention to this group, in particular the Peace Issues Discussion Group [*Heiwa Mondai Danwakai*]. Also see Tabata (1972; 1993), Mori (1946), and Berger (1998).

8. Dower (1999) discusses the negative feelings among the Japanese public toward the Soviet Union generated by Soviet treatment of Japan in the immediate postwar period.

9. See Samuels (2005) for a recent reconsideration of Yoshida's unusual skills as a political leader.

10. Concerns over the rise of a "military-industrial complex" were not unique to Japan. In the United States, President Eisenhower voiced similar concerns over the threat of the military-industrial complex. Friedberg (2000) skillfully traces how these concerns, fueled by American "anti-statism," shaped American postwar political development in a manner similar to how domestic antimilitarism shaped postwar Japan.

11. See Samuels (1994), Green (1995), and Keddell (1993). Two notable doctoral dissertations pay particular attention to this point: Smith (1996) and Heinrich (1997).

12. Part of Article Nine states explicitly: "the Japanese people forever renounce war as a sovereign right of the nation and the threat or use of force as a means of settling international disputes."

13. For example, Chuma (1985), Dower (1979; 1999), Katzenstein (1996b), Mori (1946), Otake (1983), and Tabata (1972; 1993).

14. Earlier post–Cold War "exceptions" involving MSDF minesweepers dispatched to the Persian Gulf after fighting ended (they began minesweeping as part of an "environmental operation" in May 1991) and SDF participation in United Nations Peacekeeping Operations (UNPKO) beginning in 1992 should not be viewed as exceptions to the third tenet of domestic antimilitarism because the SDF was allowed to be dispatched abroad only when international conflict had formally ended and a cease-fire was in place. Thus, the SDF technically was not involved in the use of force to settle international disputes—the proscription of the third tenet of domestic antimilitarism.

15. The vernacular literature and popular press of the time were full of expositions on this subject, despite the perilous economic situation. Iokibe (1985; 1989; 1990), Kanda (1983), Kojima (1987), and Takemae (1980) incorporate many such sources. In English, Katzenstein (1996b) pays particular attention to this issue in his chapter 3, providing a fascinating and illuminating discussion of how "social and legal norms"—an alternative identity variable in the political science literature—structure political interaction. In a less theoretical but utterly enjoyable format, Dower (1999) personalizes this period through his exhaus-

tive Pulitzer prize–winning social history of the time, a best seller in Japanese despite its historical subject matter and two-volume size.

16. Cited in Dower (1999), p. 45, n. 16.

17. In principle, the Far Eastern Commission—established in Washington, D.C., in 1946—determined the general course of policy for the occupation, representing the will of all of the victor states in the Second World War, and the Allied Council in Tokyo implemented the commission's directives. In practice, however, the United States had a virtual free hand in determining Occupation policy, with General Douglas MacArthur playing the central role as Supreme Commander for the Allied Powers (SCAP).

18. Occupation policy has been studied extensively by Japanese and American scholars, given the pivotal role the Occupation played in postwar Japanese political and economic development. Memoirs of central figures in the Occupation—both Japanese and American, and the odd Allied representative—have been analyzed in depth, as have reams of policy documents (many recently declassified) from both governments. Seminal work on this area—from which the brief treatment of the subject presented here draws—includes, in Japanese, Eto (1989), Iokibe (1985; 1989; 1990), Kanda (1983), Kojima (1987), and Takemae (1980); and, in English, Borton (1967), Cohen (1987), Dower (1993a; 1999), Kawai (1979), LaFeber (1997), Schaller (1985; 1997), and Ward and Sakamoto (1987).

19. Some of the most dramatic examples of the liberal reform of the early Occupation period were the release of over a million political prisoners; the "purging" of over two hundred thousand officials from government, business, and academia; and the legalization of the Japanese Communist Party (JCP) in the first months of the occupation, the first time the JCP enjoyed legal status since its formation in the early 1920s. Other important extensions of political rights included the legalization of independent labor unions with the right to organize, bargain collectively, and strike (an often-used tactic in the immediate postwar period); the decentralization of police power (with a resultant lessening of the then-common intimidation by the police) and education policy (as an effort to inhibit central government control of the minds of Japan's youth); and the extension of wide-ranging political rights to women (including the right to vote, own property, pursue higher education, and serve in the government). On the latter point, thirty-eight women were elected to the Diet in the first postwar election of 1946.

20. In December 1945, an SCAP directive ordered the dissolution of 336 corporations, followed two years later by a broader prohibition of "excessive concentrations of economic power" (Pempel [1998], p. 87). An antimonopoly law was passed by the Diet in April 1947.

21. It was a leading Diet member, Hitoshi Ashida (who soon would become prime minister), who is said to have written the actual text of Article Nine (LaFeber [1997], p. 268), though other important political actors such as Yoshida and also probably the emperor himself also played a central role in its exact wording.

22. See Samuels (2005) for a focused discussion on the role of domestic leaders, particularly prime ministers Yoshida and Kishi, in crafting Japan's postwar future.

23. Quoted in Samuels (1994), p. 131.

24. See Prime Minister Yoshida's memoirs (1962) for a Japanese perspective on U.S. pressure.

25. By 1949, almost 50 percent of the Japanese workforce had become unionized, a figure exceeding the level of unionization of workers in the United States, the United Kingdom, and even Sweden (Pempel [1998], p. 88).

26. Pempel (1998) specifically discussed the effect of U.S. Occupation policy on the creation of a new economic regime for postwar Japan, especially pp. 82–98.

27. "Special" procurement refers to procurement outside of the normal procedures for U.S. military purchases—in this case allowing the U.S. military to purchase Korean War–related material much closer to the source (from Japan) rather than from U.S.-based manufacturers.

28. See Schaller (1997) on the latter point of covert U.S. aid, though most U.S. government documents relevant to this issue remain classified, more than fifty years after the events in question.

29. Appendix 3 of this volume provides a table with the results of each election during the period 1945–1960.

30. In the post–Cold War period, as discussed in the following chapter, the JSP joined a coalition with their archrivals, the LDP, and once again provided the prime minister, Tomiichi Murayama, from their party, but in this case they were the minority coalition member and thus did not form the government.

31. See, for example, Inoki (1986), Iokibe (1985), Dower (1979), Finn (1992), and Samuels (2005).

32. Although this chapter stresses the controversial issue of rearmament, the security alliance with the United States—and in particular the issue of U.S. military bases on Japanese soil—was equally controversial. Schoppa (2002) has developed a two-dimensional matrix of party positions on these issues which illustrates that security issues such as rearmament and U.S. bases do not fall neatly on a single-dimension continuum of left to right. Unlike the issue of rearmament, however, where a domestic compromise was reached that was codified into the central tenets of the postwar state identity, no consensus was achieved on the issue of alignment.

33. The literature on Japanese politics of the period reflects a clear consensus on this point; for example, Benfell (1997), Chuma (1985), Curtis (1988), Dower (1979), Otake (1983), Samuels (2005), Yanada (1981).

34. Calder (1988a) argues that such limits on LDP power characterized a vast array of policy areas, including defense.

35. For an analysis of the impact of Japan's rearmament on postwar Japanese politics, see Ōtake (1988).

36. For an example of the kinds of issues that provoked confrontation in the Diet between conservative and progressive parties, see Matsukawa and Ienaga (1970).

37. Smith (1996), pp. 167–78, Otake (1983; 1988), Chuma (1985).

38. Submitted on December 22, 1954; the English translation is taken from *Asian Security* (1981), p. 154.

39. The development of the SDF is discussed in greater detail in Chuma (1985), Hata (1976), and Nakamura (1996); and in English, Heinrich (1997), chapter 2, Smith (1996), chapter 2, and Berger (1998), chapter 2.

40. Mendel (1961), p. 185 (based on surveys conducted by the author); N = 2,422.

41. Benfell (1997) and Green (1998), among others, advocate this position.

42. Etō and Yamamoto (1991) summarize polling data on the question, "Should Japan side with the communist nations, side with the Free World, or remain neutral?" roughly every three years from 1950 to 1980. Berger (1998), pp. 67 and 112, presents this data in tabular form.

43. Asagumo Shimbunsha (1987), *Boei Handobukku [Defense Handbook]*, cited in Berger (1998), p. 114. It should be noted that this survey shows the attitudes of the general public. Legal opinion on the SDF from the time of its foundation to the present day continues to express the view that the SDF is unconstitutional by wide margins.

44. *Boei Handobukku [Defense Handbook]* (1983), pp. 349–50.

45. *Boei Handobukku [Defense Handbook]* (1983), pp. 337–39.

46. The Guidelines for U.S.-Japan Defense Cooperation were carefully crafted to reflect the dissonance in purpose laid out in Articles 5 and 6 of the security treaty: Article 5 provides for U.S. assistance to Japan in case of external aggression, and Article 6 provides for cooperation in providing for peace and stability in the Far East. For English text of the guidelines, see JDA, *Defense of Japan* (1987).

47. Green (1998) writes: "For the hawks, the alliance provided a source of military technology, defense assistance, and political pressure for rearmament in the context of the Cold War. For the doves, the alliance provided a cap on that rearmament. . . . Alliance with the United States provided technology transfers, economic assistance, and markets for those conservatives who were focused primarily on economic recovery" (p. 10).

48. See Appendix 4 of this volume for a table of election returns for each election between 1955 and 1993, the 1955 System years.

49. Quoted in Nishihara (1981), p. 27.

50. Umemoto (1985), p. 81, citing *Mainichi Shimbun* polls conducted June 1968 and November 1983 and published on July 1, 1968, and January 4, 1984.

51. Asagumo Shimbunsha (1987), *Boei Handobukku*, cited in Berger (1998), p. 114.

52. Umemoto (1985), p. 86. As discussed in Chapters 3 and 7, however, in the post–Cold War period a different trend is evident. In this period, steadily rising numbers support constitutional revision, growing to a majority of the population in the late 1990s.

53. A selection of views on this debate include Muramatsu (1987), Hook (1988), Inoguchi (1986), and Langdon (1985).

54. Tabata (1972), Shimada et al. (1991), Ishida (1989); in English, Hook (1996).

55. See Field (1991) and Takagi (1989).

56. Some studies which focus on "norms" as an explanation for policy outcomes, such as Katzenstein (1996a), would not see this disjuncture as a "paradox" because some exceptions would be expected—but such arguments do not constitute the majority of scholarship on Japan.

Chapter 3

1. Literature on the rise and fall of the so-called bubble economy is voluminous. Good introductory sources, each containing extensive citations, include Katz (1998), McCormack (2002), and Pempel (1998).

2. See Field (1991) for an interesting discussion of the social dimension of the collapse of the bubble economy and the death of the emperor. Tamamoto (1994) also reflects on a similar theme, discussing Japan's "ideology of nothingness."

3. Green (1998) reviews a large volume of the English and Japanese language discourse on Japan's potential new international role in the post–Cold War period. Important overview pieces of this period include Chuma (1991), Funabashi (1991; 1991/92; 1993), Higuchi (1993), Sakai (1993), and Samuels (1991). Successive ruling parties/coalitions similarly undertook official studies of this question, including in 1992 the then-ruling LDP's report

Japan's Role in the International Society (published in 1993), which highlighted a consensus in the party that Japan should expand its participation in U.N. peacekeeping operations and demonstrate more assertive leadership on regional security issues, and in 1994, a report of a special advisory committee on defense issues convened by Prime Minister Morihiro Hosokawa, which called for a future defense policy based on three guiding principles: (1) multilateral security forums; (2) indigenous defense capacity; and (3) the U.S.-Japan alliance.

4. *Heisei*, appropriately meaning "the achievement of peace," is the name of the new Japanese emperor-based calendar era that was announced to succeed the sixty-three years of the Showa (or, somewhat ironically, Enlightened Peace) reign of Emperor Hirohito.

5. The Bank of Japan governors probably began to appreciate the absurdity of valuations in Tokyo when the price of land on which the Imperial household sits became valued greater than all of either California, or better yet, the entire nation of Canada.

6. A list of postwar prime ministers is provided in Appendix 1.

7. See Hughes (1996) for a full discussion of these incidents.

8. For example, Betts (1993/94), Friedberg (1993/94), Menon (1997). Funabashi (1998) also discusses the security implications of what he calls Japan's "depression diplomacy."

9. The burgeoning new literature on post–Cold War Japanese security policy can be grouped into several substantive topics, including the Persian Gulf War, foreign deployment of the SDF, the future of the U.S.-Japan alliance and U.S. bases in Japan, and multilateral security options for Japan. See Green (1998) for a more detailed review of literature related to the latter two topics—the U.S.-Japan alliance and multilateral security options. Literature on the former topics is considered below.

10. On Japan's new "Asian" identity, see Katzenstein and Okawara (2001/02), and Oros (2001).

11. On the issue of international hegemony and the broader theories of the rise and fall of great powers, see Gilpin (1981) and Kennedy (1987). On China's rise, see Christensen (1999), Friedberg (1993/94), and Ross (1999).

12. See, for example, Medeiros (2001), p. 14. These issues are discussed further in subsequent chapters of this volume.

13. Medeiros (2001) provides a useful overview of these individual issues.

14. This is the central thesis of Pyle (1996).

15. Some consider the September 1985 Plaza Accord to be the first shock foretelling the impending end of the Cold War because the costs of maintaining the competitive superstructure in the United States—and the Soviet Union for that matter—were becoming politically and economically more difficult to sustain (Clemons [2001b], Johnson [2000]). By 1985, the U.S. balance of payments had slipped so badly that Japan surged ahead to become the world's leading creditor nation, and the United States the leading debtor.

16. In 1990–91, the Bank of Japan began to raise interest rates to bolster the value of the yen, which had begun to fall, and to try to spark financial flows back into Japan. This set into motion a cascading collapse of investments which had been based on nearly cost-free financing. As the economy slowed and the yen lost value, Japan's stock indexes declined and the price of real estate plummeted. All of the equity and land assets that had fed the borrowing binge financing Japan's economic expansion imploded in value, starting what has now come to be called the debacle of Japan's nonperforming loan (NPL) problem.

17. Green and Samuels (1994a) make an argument similar to the one presented here—that both international and domestic changes in Japan in the early 1990s led to great

pressure for foreign policy shift. Pempel (1998) examines the economic basis of LDP power during the Cold War, arguing that changing global production patterns—leading to changes in Japan's domestic economic structure—fundamentally undermined the basis of LDP rule by the early 1990s, leading to a coming "regime shift" in Japan's party politics. Curtis (1999) considers the changes in Japan's party politics since the end of the Cold War and major electoral reform in 1994, informing the analysis presented here.

18. Green (1998) and Mochizuki (1995) provide good overviews of the diversity of opinion evident in political debates of the time. One form of media particularly popular at this time was the political manifesto of leading politicians vying for power, ranging from the Takemura (1994) vision of Japan as a "small but shining state" to the Ozawa (1994) desire for Japan to become a "normal nation"—meaning one with military power to match its economic might (though, it should be noted, this economic might was dwindling rapidly). Naoto Kan (1996), Yukio Hatoyama (1996), and Yasuhiro Nakasone (1995; 1997) each injected their views on Japan's future international role into the public debate as well.

19. These three principles were (1) no "separate peace" treaties to conclude Second World War hostilities—effectively, no peace with the United States without peace with the Soviet Union; (2) no bilateral security pacts—effectively, no U.S.-Japan security treaty; and (3) neutrality in the Cold War (Dower [1993b], p. 9).

20. Yasushi Akashi, an ambitious and internationally committed diplomat, became a senior peacekeeping operation manager in the United Nations. Sadako Ogata took on the responsibility of serving as the U.N. high commissioner for refugees. Moreover, Japan sought a permanent seat on the U.N. Security Council and greater voice, commensurate with its contributions, in such institutions as the World Bank and the International Monetary Fund.

21. Ozawa (1993) in Japanese and Ozawa (1994) in English.

22. Even before the end of the Cold War, President Jimmy Carter unambiguously stated that he wanted to substantially shrink the size of the U.S. presence in South Korea and Japan and initiated this process to pull back a significant part of U.S. deployments in the region. Despite a deepening of the U.S.-Japan security alliance during the following "Ron-Yasu" years of the early 1980s—the perceived closeness of the personal relationship between President Reagan and Prime Minister Yasuhiro Nakasone was often referred to in the press this way—and vehement Pentagon opposition to such repositioning of U.S. forces, the process continued on a lesser scale throughout the 1980s.

23. Official government views on this question were set out in United States Department of Defense (1995), the so-called Nye initiative. Quasi-official views are evident in the Council on Foreign Relations (1998) edited volume on the subject, Green and Cronin (1999), and the Pacific Forum CSIS edited volume (2001). Funabashi (1996) and Tsuru (1996) present opposing views of how the alliance should move forward in the post–Cold War world. The period of uncertainty over the alliance appears to be over, however, with the conclusion of new guidelines for deeper defense cooperation between the two states in 1997, reinforced by the recent September 11 terrorist attacks on the United States in 2001, both discussed below.

24. See Tatsumi (2007) for an overview of such changes, in this period and also in the early twenty-first century.

25. Further elaboration on these issues is available, respectively, in Oros (2002), Green (1998), and Chapter 5 of this volume.

26. Unlike the JDA, the CIRO did undergo a name change in conjunction with central government reorganization in January 2001, changing its English-language moniker from Cabinet *Information* Research Office to Cabinet *Intelligence* Research Office.

27. U.S. Arms Control and Disarmament Agency (1999). Exchange rate fluctuations at times cause Japan to drop to third in defense spending, as it did in 2001—which was also due to a one-year boost in Russian defense spending, making Russia the second-highest defense spender in that year.

28. The Japanese government has interpreted Article Nine of the Constitution to mean that Japan possesses the right of both individual and collective self-defense. In 1983 the Cabinet Legislative Affairs Bureau (*Hoseikyoku*) declared its interpretation that the SDF may aid a U.S. ship that is defending Japan from attack but not if the ship is engaged in offensive military operations not directly related to the defense of Japan. This interpretation set clear boundaries on the extent of defense cooperation and integration possible in the U.S.-Japan security alliance.

29. See Green (1998), pp. 19–20, for further details on this point. Important framing literature on this issue includes Asai (1993), Nakasone (1995; 1997), Sato (1996), Shiina and Okazaki (1996), and Sugawa (2000).

30. The text of these new guidelines is reprinted in JDA, *Defense of Japan* (2001).

31. This situation provides a good example of Legro's (2005) argument that lack of "socially salient" alternative identities will hinder identity shift and broader policy change.

32. Roughly $13 billion was provided to the United States to offset the estimated $85 billion cost of the Persian Gulf War. Japan was the only advanced industrial democracy to raise taxes explicitly to fund this massive contribution. The funds were explicitly limited to support costs and were not to be used to purchase weapons, ammunition, or other goods that were prohibited by the three principles on arms export, discussed in Chapter 4.

33. More detailed discussion of Japan's debate regarding the decision to participate in UNPKO can be found in Chuma (1993), Dobson (2003), George (1993), Heinrich (1997), Ishizuka (2005), Kim (1994), Leitenberg (1996), Marten Zisk (2001), and Mulgan (1993; 1995)—all of which have informed the brief treatment presented in this volume.

34. An additional ten deployments were authorized from September 1998 to 2005, as discussed in Chapter 7. JDA, *Defense of Japan* (2001), provides a complete list of SDF participation in UNPKO activities in the 1989–98 period.

Chapter 4

1. The domestic market for defense-related spending is second in the world only to that of the United States. In 2004 Japan spent $42.4 billion on defense, according to the *SIPRI Yearbook*, ranking it as the fourth-largest spender in the world. Japan's defense spending roughly equals that of France ($46.2b) and the United Kingdom ($47.4b), though it spends a higher proportion of its budget on military equipment, making its domestic defense market second only to that of the United States. Moreover, the vast majority of manufactures used by Japan's Self-Defense Forces are produced in Japan by Japanese firms. In addition, Japanese-produced arms used by the United States armed forces stationed in Japan are officially exempted from the export controls, despite that such sales—like other industries such as tourism—would usually be considered exports under standard economic accounting practices (Tomiyama [1981], p. 3).

2. Mitsubishi Heavy Industries ranked thirteenth in the world in 1998, fourteenth in 1999, and sixteenth in 2003. Kawasaki Heavy Industries ranked between thirtieth and

fortieth in the world in those years, and Mitsubishi Electric between fortieth and fiftieth. Other major Japanese defense manufacturers such as Ishikawajima-Harima, Toshiba, NEC, and Komatsu did not even rank in the top fifty arms producers in the world (SIPRI [2000; 2005]).

3. The extent to which Japanese firms export under this provision is unknown, but anecdotal evidence shows a wide range of areas in which this has taken place. The most comprehensive source for data on arms exports, the Stockholm International Peace Research Institute (SIPRI), similarly defines arms sales in this manner, and thus also does not track such dual-use sales. A recent SIPRI study declares: "Arms sales are defined by SIPRI as sales of military goods and services to military customers, including both sales for domestic procurement and sales for export. Military goods and services are those which are designed specifically for military purposes and the technologies related to such goods and services. They exclude sales of general-purpose goods (e.g., oil, electricity, office computers, cleaning services, uniforms and boots)" (SIPRI [2005], p. 404).

4. The most exhaustive studies to date of Japan's postwar arms export restrictions are Söderberg (1986) and Hummel (1988).

5. Katzenstein's (1996a) treatment is illustrative of this type of "laundry list" coverage, although his overall argument is based around norms as the central concept. He writes: "To date, normative constraints have made it impossible to revise Article 9 of the Constitution; to build or to possess nuclear weapons; to dispatch Japanese troops abroad as combatants, even as part of international peacekeeping forces; to sell weapons abroad; and to raise the JDA to ministerial status" (p. 120), though he later notes that in fact change did take place in arms export policy and that political and competing identity factors were the likely cause of such change (pp. 138–39). Berger (1998) also notes the ban uncritically (pp. 57, 181).

6. Green (1995), for example, writes simply: "Some small arms were eventually sold, but exports never became significant, and when demand did grow for weapons in the region in the 1960s, the domestic political controversy associated with weapons sales led to Japan's arms export ban in 1967" (p. 41).

7. Samuels's (1994) explanatory framework is based on ascribing to Japanese elite policy makers an underlying motivating ideology of "technonationalism" to explain policy outcomes. In the case of defense production, he argues that a consensus was eventually able to be framed domestically restarting arms production by focusing on the technological benefits (i.e., spin-off to nonmilitary sections) of defense production.

8. The priming of the Japanese economy at a critical moment of the Korean War is widely credited as laying the foundation for a wider economic recovery. For example, in 1952 fully 63 percent of all Japanese exports were accounted for by the Korean War (Havens [1987], p. 93). A similar phenomenon is evident at the time of the Vietnam War. Havens (1987) writes in his thorough coverage of this subject: "America's great pacifist ally earned billions of dollars through direct and indirect procurement and advanced into the markets of Southeast Asia because of the war" (p. 84). Both of these instances of arms and arms-related exports took place before the Three Principles on Arms Exports had been adopted as official government policy in 1967, while contending political forces were still battling over the fundamental contours of the security identity of domestic antimilitarism.

9. Specifically, Directive 82 ordered "the immediate cessation and future prohibition of production of all goods designed for the equipment, maintenance, or use of any military force or establishment; the imposition of a ban upon the facilities for the production or

repair of implements of war ... the elimination in Japan of those industries or branches of production which would provide Japan with the capacity to rearm for war; and the prohibition of specialized research and instruction contributing directly to the development of war making power" (quoted in Samuels [1994], p. 131).

10. COCOM was founded formally as a nontreaty organization in Paris in 1953, and it included representatives from sixteen countries: the NATO countries (except Iceland), Australia, and (later) Japan.

11. "Special" procurement refers to procurement outside of the normal procedures for U.S. military purchases—in this case allowing the U.S. military to purchase Korean War–related material much closer to the source (from Japan) than from U.S.-based manufacturers.

12. This obligation was not without cost or domestic political controversy in Japan—particularly with regard to trade with China, historically one of Japan's major trading partners (see Yasuhara [1986] and Yamamoto [2000]).

13. See Gill, Ebata, and Stephenson (1996) for further elaboration of this point.

14. Gill, Ebata, and Stephenson (1996) provide further detail on specific articles of the law, including mechanisms of enforcement and penalties for noncompliance; see page 33 in particular.

15. The National Diet Library in Tokyo maintained a clippings file on the specific issue of "arms exports" (*heiki yushutsu*) from 1953 to 1983, illustrating the regularity of press articles on this topic. This file contains over 460 articles on the topic and does not even begin to cover a full range of media publications. The clippings are centered around two daily national newspapers, the *Asahi Shimbun* and the *Nihon Keizai Shimbun*, though at times clippings come from other newspapers as well as weeklies. Approximately fifty articles date from the period covered in this section.

16. This item was added on October 1, 1996, to support international export control regimes developed after the end of the Cold War as replacements for the Coordinating Committee for Export Control (COCOM) regime, which was disbanded on March 31, 1994.

17. In addition, there was the so-called know criterion, whereby an exporter was not to export even a dual-use product if it "knew" that it would be used in a weapon, but this policy has not been applied rigorously.

18. *SIPRI Yearbook*, compiled by Hummel (1988), pp. 26–27. Also see Söderberg (1986), p. 98, "Table 1: Japan's Arms Export"—though this includes materials sold to U.S. forces stationed in Japan, production the Japanese government does not count as exports.

19. It is necessary to distinguish here between the entire Keidanren organization, which was very guarded on the issue of defense production and exports, and its own Defense Production Committee (DPC), which relentlessly advocated in favor of defense production and exports on behalf of its members.

20. The political alliance among these three groups is also acknowledged by Berger (1998), though he maintains that it is Japan's postwar "antimilitarist culture" which explains the policy outcome.

21. Berger (1998) also stresses that many on the left perceived a link between remilitarization and a threat to Japan's fledgling democratic institutions. This observation serves to underscore the point made in this study that the postwar security identity enjoyed broad and diverse bases of support, and support not necessarily rooted in common ideas or based on common beliefs.

22. The arms exports clippings file of the National Diet Library includes over 150 articles from the period covered in this section; the articles cover a wide range of perspectives—and political disagreement—over arms export policy in this period.

23. In retrospect, however, it is not clear that Sony's actions would have been targeted by arms export prohibitions that would emerge in 1967 and later in the 1970s. This incident brings to the fore MITI's dual-use doctrine, which would not proscribe Sony from selling cameras to the U.S. military if the technology—as it was—was also widely used in the civilian marketplace, and if Sony did not "know" of its ultimate use as a weapon.

24. The full text of this policy statement is regularly included in either the Japanese or the English-language version of Japan's annual defense white paper (or both), including JDA (1999), *Defense of Japan*, pp. 434–35.

25. Hummel (1988) provides a useful table, "Export of Ordnance from Japan, 1965–87," on page 29.

26. While the LDP technically lost its majority in the election, in practical terms the ruling party managed to hold on to sufficient seats to exercise a majority after a number of conservative independents were brought into the party after the election.

27. The full text is provided in JDA (1998), *The Defense of Japan*, p. 397, and in Appendix 5 of this volume.

28. Kyodo News Service (February 6, 1981) offers an overview of these efforts.

29. See, for example, Jiji Press (1981), "Foreign Office Reiterates View That Arms Exports to U.S. Are 'Possible'" (November 12).

30. Over 250 articles were clipped into the National Diet Library's arms export file between 1980 and 1983 before the category was collapsed into the larger designation of "equipment/arms" (*sōbi/heiki*). From 1984 to 1993, over 700 articles were clipped on this broader topic, roughly a third of which deal with the arms export issue. In addition, over 600 articles are provided under the category of "defense production" (*bōei sangyō*), many of which discuss the issue of exports at least in passing. The argument of this section is collectively informed by analysis of these texts.

31. Samuels (1994) writes of the emergence of the significant numbers of "spin-on" technologies that had emerged by the 1980s; that is, "the transfer of products and process technologies 'off-the-shelf' from civilian to military applications" (p. 26). He provides a number of examples of this phenomenon, including that three-quarters of the computing power of a state-of-the-art Aegis cruiser depends on commercial equipment, and that fourteen out of twenty-two "critical" items on the U.S. DOD/Department of Energy "critical technology" list issued in April 1989, the end of the period examined in this section, were classified as dual use. Samuels (1994), p. 27, citing *Defense News* (6 March 1989) and Fox (1988), p. 10. Also see U.S. Congress (1989) on the issue of maintaining a "U.S. technology base."

32. See CISTEC (2000) and Gill, Ebata, and Stephenson (1996) for details of this system, some of which are included in the following text.

33. Jiji Press (1981), "Inayama Sounds Negative on Japan's Arms Exports" (January 14).

34. An important point to note here—because it is commonly misstated in the literature—is that this exemption for the United States was only for *technology* transfer, not for the export of arms or related goods (including production equipment) to the United States. As noted earlier, this was effectively a *second* exemption for the United States in that U.S. armed forces in Japan had always been allowed to purchase Japanese defense-related products despite this technically being an "export."

35. As of January 2006, thirteen projects including missile defense have been selected by the Joint Military Technology Commission (JMTC) as technology transfer projects to the United States.

36. Hummel (1988) provides a partial list of such joint work based on a compilation of a number of Japanese and foreign media reports (p. 18).

37. The U.S. DOD's annual publication, *Soviet Military Power 1988*, explains as follows: "Continued erosion of the West's lead in technology underscores the importance of preventing additional illegal Soviet technology acquisitions. By illegally acquiring technology, the Soviets are able to forgo the substantial investment costs in the basic and applied research and development. They are also able to keep up with those technologies that might alter the character of conflict and thereby represent a greater threat to them. For example, the illegal Soviet acquisition of sophisticated machinery for producing quiet-running propellers illustrates the impact that technology acquisition and espionage can have on the West's collective security. The Soviets spent less than $25 million to acquire this technology, a small price to pay for a capability to make their submarines much harder to detect" (quoted in Gill, Ebata, and Stephenson [1996], p. 35).

38. In addition to the Toshiba Machine case, several other less-publicized incidents vexed U.S. policy makers. As early as the early 1970s, this issue had been simmering. At that time Ishikawajima-Harima Heavy Industries (IHI) was criticized by the United States for exporting to the Soviet Union a giant floating dock which could be—and was—used for the warships of the Soviet Pacific Fleet (see Gill, Ebata, and Stephenson [1996], p. 34). Similarly, after the Toshiba incident, the Japan Aviation Electronics Industry Corporation (JAE) angered U.S. policy makers (and Japanese courts) by exporting spare parts and repair technology for U.S. military equipment sold to Iran by the United States before the Iranian revolution cut off access to such supplies. JAE was fined in both Japanese and American courts and was barred from continuing its participation in the joint FSX project (see Gill, Ebata, and Stephenson [1996], p. 35).

39. Several excellent book-length studies of the FSX case examine these issues. Of particular note in English are Lorell (1996), Shear (1994), and Snow and Brown (1994). For a Japanese perspective, see Kohno (1989) and Otsuki and Honda (1991).

Chapter 5

1. Samuels (1994) and Green (1995) both discuss this pursuit in the context of defense production. Japanese space policy provides an excellent example of their arguments applied to another case.

2. The Resolution Concerning the Fundamentals of Space Development and Exploitation by Japan was adopted at a plenary session of the House of Representatives on May 9, 1969, and is reprinted in Appendix 6.

3. See McDougall (1985) and Oberg (1981) for further discussion on the military origins of outer space development.

4. Schwoch (2002) documents concern of the U.S. National Security Council (NSC) with public opinion regarding outer space activities, tracing the central role of the U.S. Information Agency (USIA), created in 1953, in shaping world opinion on U.S. technological prowess.

5. This resolution is reprinted in Appendix 6.

6. It should be noted that, while it never became a discrete political issue, the JDA and SDF continuously made use of U.S. satellite imagery for military purposes throughout this period, which would appear to have contravened the spirit if not the letter of the ban.

7. It should be noted, however, that outside of the heated political discussion of this issue in Japan during the Vietnam War era, academic specialists in the area of foreign intelligence argue that significant intelligence capability is a hallmark of a defensive military posture (e.g., Herman [1996]).

8. The postwar Japanese space program is commonly dated to 1955, when students in the engineering department at the University of Tokyo successfully designed and launched the first Japanese rocket, the so-called pencil rocket (appropriately named for its small size). Good histories of the development of Japanese government space agencies include Science and Technology Agency (1978), Chiku (1992), and Yatō (1983).

9. Two good overviews of outer space development worldwide are found in Burrows (1990) and Levine (1994).

10. The SAC was located in the Prime Minister's Office and consisted of five members: the director general of the Science and Technology Agency (who served as chair), two permanent members, and two rotating members. Its mandate was to plan long-term space policy for the nation and advise the prime minister of budget and policy issues (Yatō [1983]). The SAC itself greatly limited the scope of Japan's activities in outer space to three areas, put forth in its establishing legislation: (1) the development of satellites, (2) the development of launch vehicles (i.e., rockets), and (3) the development of infrastructure necessary for the preceding two activities (Space Activities Establishment Act 1968, Article 3).

11. This final "principle," while publicly maintained even today, was not strictly honored vis-à-vis U.S. forces. Although most relevant documentation of this period remains classified by both the U.S. and Japanese governments, some recently declassified documents point to an "understanding" between Prime Minister Satō and U.S. president Lyndon Johnson on this point; officials formerly involved in the relationship have also publicly indicated that such an understanding existed.

12. The National Diet Library clippings collection on this period includes dozens of articles expressing this theme in the late 1960s.

13. SAPC literature of the time does not advocate an alternative position to the one pursued; interviews with current SAPC members confirm this impression, as do interviews with current METI officials (March 2000; January–February 2006, Tokyo).

14. Chiku (1992) includes a list of all Japanese satellites with their percentage of domestic content in his Appendix C (p. 282).

15. Further details of the deliberations of this panel are available in Yatō (1983) and Chiku (1992).

16. The Fundamental Policy consists of fifteen chapters. They are summarized by Chiku (1992) as follows: "The first four chapters were devoted to the general: Trend of Space Activities (Chapter 1); Significance and Characteristics of Space Activities (Chapter 2); Perspectives of Space Activities (Chapter 3); and Issues of Concern Regarding Japanese Space Activities (Chapter 4). The next seven chapters, which were divided into four sections, dealt with the particular: Application of Space Flying Objects on the Activities of the Earth (Section 1), Utilization of Space Environment on the Orbit (Section 2); Challenge for the Moon and the Planets (Section 3), and Perspectives for the Means for Space Activities (Section 4)" (p. 77, ff. 31).

17. Fundamental Policy, Chapter 1, Section 1, Segment 2.

18. The Fundamental Policy was revised twice in the Cold War period, once in 1984, and again in 1989. Each revision placed an increased emphasis on the commercialization of space activities, including efforts to promote industry-oriented space activities (Chiku

[1992], p. 24). Pursuant with international developments driven by the growing availability of satellite data, the revised policy also features a new commitment to environmental activities through space technology, in particular through the use of observation satellites (e.g., Revised Fundamental Policy [1989], Chapter 2, Section 1, Paragraph 2).

19. A letter from the Japanese Embassy to the U.S. Department of State, dated December 3, 1980, states that Japan should "establish or use communication satellites launched with the ETV-II and H-I launch vehicles only in a manner compatible with the obligations, objectives and purposes of INTELSAT" and that "the equipment and/or technology transferred to Japan for the development of the ETV-II and H-I launch vehicles or components manufactured by the use of such equipment or technology will not be transferred to any third countries and will not be used to launch projects for any third countries" (reproduced in Chiku [1992], p. 41).

20. Nancy Dunne (1990), *Financial Times* (March 16), p. 8.

21. Robert Thomson (1990), *World Trade News* (March 27), p. 4.

22. A huge literature to substantiate such claims arose in the mid- to late 1980s, only to be replaced with new studies of what was *wrong* with the Japanese model, after the collapse of what now is referred to as the "bubble economy" in 1990–91. Holstein (1990) and Prestowitz (1988) are good examples of both the scale of claims made regarding unfair trading practices on the part of Japan and the increasing American paranoia about such practices.

23. However, spending only once exceeded this threshold, despite the lifting of the ceiling, and even then it was by less than 0.01 percent.

24. SDI is the precursor to ballistic missile defense (BMD), which is discussed in Chapter 6.

25. See Chapter 4 for discussion of this point.

26. Once again in this context it is important to note that, while it never became a discrete political issue, the JDA and the SDF continuously made use of U.S. satellite imagery for military purposes throughout this period, which would appear to have contravened the spirit if not the letter of the ban. According to Drifte (1986, p. 70), the first acknowledged example of purchase of such imagery was via the U.S. military satellite Landsat in March 1985.

27. Recently this was taken a step further: to allow for a Japanese firm (Mitsubishi Electric, or MELCO) to produce and operate a satellite for *foreign* military communications purposes, discussed later in this chapter.

28. Chiku (1992) quotes numerous officials from space industry firms who argue that one method of recruiting engineers to their firms was to promise the opportunity to work on space projects. He also notes the enormous popularity of the animated film *Uchūsenkan Yamato* (The Space Battleship Yamato) in the early 1970s, which is widely credited with initiating the general popularity of the cartoon (*anime*) in Japan and the development of that industry in general (if not the space industry itself at the time).

29. See Oros (2007a) for a more detailed discussion of this important policy decision. This section draws on some of the empirical detail presented in that article.

30. A similar argument is made by Johnson-Freese and Gatling (2004), the only English-language study of the satellite case published to date. They write in their conclusion: "The IGS decision seems to be a variation on a traditional decision-making theme rather than a harbinger of a shift in the policy-making paradigm of Japan" (p. 551), using "policy-making paradigm" in a similar way to security identity in this study. Sunohara (2005) provides a more detailed account (in Japanese) of the nature of the surveillance satellite program and the politics behind it.

31. Such rhetoric did not obfuscate the issue completely among the general public, however. As the weekly *Shukan Posuto* expresses forthrightly: "This sort of satellite normally would be called a spy satellite. But because the Diet resolution adopted thirty years ago declares 'peaceful use of space,' the name 'information-gathering' satellites has been chosen" (February 5, 1999).

32. See Oros (2002) for further discussion of development of intelligence capability overall. Even the dramatic boosts in intelligence personnel to support the new surveillance satellites will still leave a significant gap between the number of Japanese intelligence personnel and that of other similarly positioned states.

33. Following the Taepodong Incident, Japan also announced a variety of sanctions on North Korea, including suspension of food aid and Tokyo's participation in the Korean Peninsula Energy Development Organization (KEDO) project. It also froze talks on normalizing diplomatic ties and canceled permission for all charter flights to and from North Korea.

34. On December 11, the Diet approved a third supplementary budget for fiscal 1998 that included satellite research outlays totaling ¥3.6 billion (Taoka, January 11, 1999). Looking forward, on December 22, the Obuchi cabinet approved a draft budget for fiscal 1999 which allocated ¥6.8 billion to the Science and Technology Agency (STA) and ¥1.4 billion to the cabinet secretariat to begin implementing the plan (Deutsche Presse-Agentur, December 22, 1998).

35. Handberg and Johnson-Freese, February 12, 2001.

36. Japan has relied on U.S. intelligence derived from aerial reconnaissance since the beginnings of the alliance at the end of the Second World War—progressing from photographs taken from standard planes in the 1940s, to U-2 spy planes launched from Japan in the 1950s and 1960s, and to satellite imagery in the 1970s, 1980s, and 1990s. Since the 1980s, the JDA supplemented U.S. intelligence with commercial satellite images purchased from American and French companies. Because commercially available images possess poorer resolution than those available (properly desanitized) from the U.S. government, however, the JDA continued to rely on imagery (and analysis) from U.S. intelligence organizations as well.

37. Quoted in Taoka, January 11, 1999.

38. Quoted in *Shukan Posuto*, February 5, 1999.

39. Quoted in Taoka, January 11, 1999.

40. One report estimates that space-related business revenues generated by services, manufacturing, and support of space activities reached nearly $100 billion in 1998. In this year, 64 percent of revenue was derived from commercial activities and 36 percent from government activities. It is expected that the percentage of revenue generated by commercial sources will increase to 75 percent in 2002. Moreover, the amount of investment in space-related ventures is expected to double from under $20 billion in the 1990s to over $40 billion in the first decade of the twenty-first century (International Space Business Council [1999]).

41. Keidanren Space Activities Promotion Council (1999), author translation from the Japanese.

42. Keidanren Industrial Affairs Bureau (1999), author translation from the Japanese.

43. *Asahi Shimbun*, December 18, 1998, p. 12.

44. *Nikkan Kogyo Shimbun*, October 23, 1998, p. 15.

45. A *Nihon Keizai Shimbun* editorial on the decision reflects the lack of information provided about an information satellite: "The government has described the purpose of the

project broadly as being related to security and crisis management in cases such as natural disasters, giving little information about the extent of possible military applications" (*Nikkei Weekly*, November 16, 1998, p. 4).

46. Deutsche Presse-Agentur, "Japan to build, launch four surveillance satellites," November 5, 1998.

47. Now the Cabinet *Intelligence* Research Office in English.

48. *Nihon Keizai Shimbun*, December 10, 1998, p. 2.

49. *Nikkei Weekly*, November 16, 1998, p. 4.

50. Within the government, a different issue had taken center stage—how the satellites would be developed and where they would be manufactured. The divisive political issue of whether the satellites would be produced domestically or imported wholly or partially from the United States temporarily slowed the final decision to deploy the system but is incidental to the constraints imposed by domestic antimilitarism and so has been omitted from this chapter.

51. However, the JDA was already scheduled to begin receiving newly available improved commercial images at one-meter resolution beginning in fiscal 1999. This, in fact, is one reason some in the JDA objected to the high cost of developing a satellite system independently.

52. Resolution is likely to improve in future satellites, but this will reflect more improvements in civilian dual-use technology than an erosion of the security identity of domestic antimilitarism. For example, in March 2002 the commercial firm DigitalGlobe began offering 60cm resolution imagery from its Quickbird satellite (Johnson-Freese and Gatling [2004], p. 546).

Chapter 6

1. The decision to embark on joint research with the United States on missile defense was announced by the chief cabinet secretary on December 25, 1998—full text provided in Appendix 7. The Memorandum of Understanding between Japan and the United States was signed the following August. The decision to deploy an initial missile defense system was announced on December 19, 2003—partial text provided in Appendix 7.

2. The focus of this chapter is not on the strategic advantages and disadvantages of developing a missile defense system for Northeast Asia—whether by the United States alone, jointly with Japan, or even by Japan independently. This question is the topic of heated debate, with theoretically strong arguments for multiple positions. See, for example, Christensen (2000), Lanteigne (2000), O'Hanlon (1999), Okazaki Institute (2001), and Stimson Center (2000). For the JDA rationale for the introduction of missile defense in 2004, see JDA (2005), especially pp. 186–98.

3. On Japan specifically, see Cronin and Nakano (2001), Okazaki Institute (2001), and Swaine, Swanger, and Kawakami (2001). Also see Green and Dalton (2000), Medeiros (2001), and Stimson Center (2000) for a broader discussion of missile defense in Asia, with sections devoted to Japan.

4. Even the United States is somewhat reticent to discuss these scenarios, but numerous articles and studies on these possible scenarios have appeared within U.S. defense circles, among them Cambone (1997), Christensen (2000), Shuey, Kan, and Christofferson (1999), and Stimson Center (2000).

5. Further background on early stages of the U.S. ballistic missile defense program is provided in Lanteigne (2000) and Fitzgerald (2000).

6. Due in part to Japan's security identity and the nomenclature it requires, Japanese policy makers tend to avoid the use of "theater" missile defense due to the connotations in Japanese of a "theater" as a "military battle area" (*sentou chiiki*).

7. Mitsubishi Heavy Industries is producing the missiles under license (*Aviation Week and Space Technology*, December 2, 2004, p. 30). Overall, the three types of missile defense systems are (1) national missile defense (NMD) systems for the defense of U.S. territory; (2) theater or regional defense systems including Theater High Altitude Area Defense (THAAD) and Naval Theater-Wide (NTW) working in the upper tier, or upper atmosphere; and (3) local or area defense systems (Patriot Advanced Capability PAC-3 and Navy Area Defense) working in the lower tier, or inside the atmosphere. Land-based systems include an upper-tier Army Theater High-Altitude Air Defense (THAAD) and the lower-tier upgraded Army Patriot PAC-3. Sea-based systems are made up of the lower-tier AEGIS-based Navy Block IV A (Navy Area Defense, NAD) fleet defense system and the upper-tier NTW system. Japanese interest in missile defense revolves around moves to develop an upper-tier missile defense system, currently pursued through the sea-based Navy Theater Wide project, and plans to deploy upgraded PAC-3 Patriot missiles and to upgrade its four current AEGIS ships to NAD capability.

8. The United States unilaterally withdrew from the Anti-Ballistic Missile (ABM) Restriction Treaty in June 2002 and declared a policy to deploy a multilayered missile defense system that integrates all existing research programs. Consequently, even though many key technologies of NMD and TMD systems remain the same, the United States no longer distinguishes between their architectures and has relabeled both under the concept of national missile defense. As explained by Hughes (2004b), p. 184, the previously named NTW system is now also known as Sea-Based Midcourse System (SBMS) and is now regarded as part of the Midcourse Defense Segment (MDS) of NMD, with THAAD and PAC-3 now part of the Terminal Defense Segment (TDS). Additionally, the United States has initiated research into a new program of Boost-Phase Intercept (BPI) using sea- and air-mounted lasers as part of the Boost Defense Segment (BDS).

9. U.S. Department of Defense (1999a).

10. *Aviation Week and Space Technology*, August 23, 1999.

11. In September 1999, the JDA offered the fiscal 1999 portion of the research to Mitsubishi Heavy Industry (MHI) as the main contractor, with Mitsubishi Electric Company (MELCO), Kawasaki Heavy Industries, Ishikawajima-Harima Heavy Industries, Nissan Motors, Fujitsu Corporation, and Toshiba Corporation as subcontractors. MHI, also the licensed manufacturer of U.S. Patriot surface-to-air missiles, received ¥962 million as the main contractor (*Aviation Week and Space Technology*, August 23, 1999).

12. *Aviation Week and Space Technology*, August 23, 1999.

13. Two PAC-3 launchers were deployed at the Iruma ASDF base in Saitama, just north of Tokyo, with further plans to deploy about thirty mobile PAC-3 launchers at ten SDF bases across the country by 2010 (Mary Yamaguchi, "Japan Deploys Its First Advanced Patriot Missile Defense System in Tokyo Area," *Associated Press Worldstream*, March 30, 2007).

14. Chisaki Watanabe, "Australia to Join Japan, US Study on MD," *Associated Press Worldstream*, May 22, 2007.

15. See statement by the chief cabinet secretary in Appendix 7.

16. More broadly, "realist theory" is not uniform in its view of alliances. In particular, there is disagreement about whether states in Japan's position would likely develop independent offensive capability or join an alliance, and if an alliance, whether with the stron-

ger power (the United States), a practice known as "bandwagoning," or with another, lesser power (China) in order to "balance" against the stronger power. In any case, Japanese policy did not follow a prescription offered by *any* of these three possible (and divergent) realist predictions.

17. A possible exception here would be the argument that Japan is "hedging" in its alliance with the United States in order to avoid "entrapment" by its alliance partner. At a time of escalating tension between Japan and China, however (and, moreover, between Japan and North Korea), it appears more likely that it is the United States that may become entrapped in its alliance with Japan than vice versa.

18. Interviews with JDA and SDF officials, December 2005 and January 2006, Tokyo and Washington, DC.

19. Green (1994); JDA (2005), especially pp. 392–94.

20. Keidanren Defense Production Committee (1995).

21. See, for example, interview data cited in Cronin and Nakano (2001).

22. Each of these goals is elaborated upon in Swaine, Swanger, and Kawakami (2001), pp. x–xi, 19–23.

23. *Asahi Shimbun*, May 11, 2001.

24. The Japanese government's official stand on NMD has been summarized by the *Asahi Shimbun* (June 5, 2001) as follows: First, the Japanese government welcomes President George W. Bush's plan to further decrease nuclear weapons in a new strategic framework that includes the missile defense plan. Second, Tokyo shares concerns with Washington over the serious threat posed by the proliferation of ballistic missiles. Third, Tokyo understands Washington has made efforts to deal with this proliferation and is considering a missile defense plan. Fourth, Tokyo wants Japan-U.S. technological research on Ballistic Missile Defense to continue. Fifth, Japan wants the missile defense issue dealt with in a way that improves international security, including arms control and reduction. Tokyo welcomes Washington's intention to hold talks with its allies, plus Russia and China.

25. *Asahi Shimbun*, May 11, 2001.

26. Interview data; Green and Dalton (2000), Stimson Center (2000).

27. See Jervis (1978) for elaboration on the concept of a security dilemma.

28. For a discussion of the Chinese threat, including concrete data on Chinese missile capabilities, see Swaine, Swanger, and Kawakami (2001), pp. 14–17, and JDA (2005).

29. Midford (2002) argues that concern for Japan's reputation among its neighbors is a central driver of security policy making in Japan. While this chapter does not go that far, clearly reputational concerns have played into Japanese policy regarding missile defense.

30. See Okazaki Institute (2001) and Gary Klintworth, "Why NMD Is Good for Asia," *Japan Times*, June 7, 2001. U.S. studies have made similar claims, such as Stimson Center (2000) and Swaine, Swanger, and Kawakami (2001), and JDA (2005), pp. 45–65.

31. This issue is discussed in greater detail in Chapter 4.

32. Many analysts have written that fear of angering China is one of the main obstacles to Japan proceeding with missile defense in future. For example, Christensen (2000), Cronin and Nakano (2001), Urayama (2000), and sections of Green and Dalton (2000) and Swaine, Swanger, and Kawakami (2001) address this issue. This fear of angering China is generally posed simply in terms of Japan developing the system with the United States. The specific issue of transfer of the technology to Taiwan is not stressed in the existing literature but has the potential to create an even larger diplomatic standoff between Japan and China.

33. See the chief cabinet secretary statement of December 25, 1998, reprinted in Appendix 7.

34. *Nihon Keizai Shimbun* (2001), "LDP Panel Proposes Reviewing Japan's Arms Export Principles" (March 24), p. 2.

35. In principle, the United States may agree to this condition under the type of "don't ask, don't tell" agreement concluded in the case of Japan's Three Nonnuclear Principles, which in reality turned a blind eye to the United States' de facto "introduction" of nuclear weapons into Japan via the U.S. naval fleet, a violation of one of the three principles.

36. It should be noted, however, that one could make a "defensive" argument even for this type of deployment, as such a laser would still be for the purpose of intercepting hostile missiles. The U.S. government is actively researching such space-based lasers as offensive weapons targeted at foreign satellites used by hostile militaries.

37. As discussed in Chapter 5, Japan launched the first two of four "information-gathering" surveillance satellites in March 2003, a third in September 2006, and fourth in February 2007 (after a launch failure destroyed the original second pair in 2005). These satellites do not include early-warning capabilities, but the design could be modified in future versions of the satellites—which must be replaced roughly every five years.

38. Yamashita, Takai, and Wada (1994), pp. 232–51. The Outer Space Treaty states in Article 4: "The moon and other celestial bodies shall be used by all States Party to the Treaty exclusively for peaceful purposes. The establishment of military bases, installations and fortifications, the testing of any type of weapons, and the conduct of military maneuvers on celestial bodies shall be forbidden" (Treaty on Principles Governing the Activities of States in the Exploration and Use of Outer Space, Including Moon and Other Celestial Bodies).

39. Swaine, Swanger, and Kawakami (2001), p. 72.

40. Interviews with JDA and related officials, January–February 2006, Tokyo.

41. This doctrine is discussed in greater detail in Chapter 4.

42. The development of the policy prohibiting the exercise of the right of collective self-defense is discussed in further detail in Chapters 2 and 3.

43. JDA (1998), *Defense of Japan*, appendix.

44. This concern of the implications of a joint system was surely on the mind of JDA director-general Nakatani when he declared in June 2001 that any future BMD system Japan might codevelop should be operated by Japan "independently" (*shutaiteki ni*)—despite technological and budgetary obstacles already foreseen by many (quoted in *Yomiuru Shimbun*, evening edition, June 23, 2001).

45. These two scenarios are discussed in Okazaki Institute (2001), p. 49.

46. Quoted in *Yomiuri Shimbun* (January 25, 2003), "Ishiba: Japan to 'Counter-attack' if N. Korea Prepares for Attack."

Chapter 7

1. A chronology of such important security decisions is provided in Table 11, along with further discussion of these pivotal events later in this chapter.

2. The defense budget declined from the previous year in fiscal years 2003, 2004, 2005, and 2006. Moreover, the 1 percent decline in fiscal 2004 was the record high decline to that point, matched by another 1 percent decline the following year as well (Kliman [2006], p. 23). This is in contrast to Chinese defense budget increases in the double-digits for over a decade, as discussed below. It is notable that the primary mission of the SDF was expanded to include international peace cooperation activities in the December 2006 legislation that elevated the JDA to the MOD. However, there are no significant plans currently under way (and, importantly, no new budget) to reorganize the branches of the SDF to operationalize this new primary mission, which remains in practice focused on the defense of Japan.

3. The Diet passed legislation in May 2007 setting out a process by which a required public referendum could take place to enact constitutional revision, but this legislation included a clause that precludes such a referendum until 2010.

4. *An International Study of Attitudes and Global Engagement (SAGE): A Comparative Study of the American and Japanese Citizenry.* Washington State University and International Christian University, 2005, http://subsite.icu.ac.jp/coe/sage/.

5. See Chapter 3 for a brief discussion of the impact of these events, or Oros (2002) for a longer discussion.

6. Note that the terminology for this plan has changed from "Outline" to "Guideline," though the basic function of the planning remains the same. Moreover, this should not be confused with the U.S.-Japan Defense Guidelines, first passed in 1978 and later revised in 1997 (as discussed in Chapter 3).

7. Kliman (2006) provides insightful analysis of polling data showing increasingly unfavorable attitudes toward China, noting in particular a marked increase in such views among Japan's elderly (pp. 59–61).

8. Tatsumi (2007), based on data provided at http://www.houko.com/00/FS_ON.htm.

9. A full account of the Maritime Safety Agency and SDF's engagement with the suspicious ships—including purported lessons learned from the encounter—is provided in JDA (1999), pp. 208–215.

10. This section draws on scholarship presented in Kliman (2006), Midford (2003), Shinoda (2001), and numerous media accounts and other sources.

11. Japan is Pakistan's largest aid donor, though new yen loans and grants were stopped in 1998 to protest Pakistan's nuclear weapons testing. Japan also provides significant non-military aid to a number of other countries in the region, including Iran. In addition to significant new aid to Pakistan in the wake of September 11 (totaling ¥4.7 billion), Japan also offered neighboring Tajikistan an additional ¥240 million in aid. See Keiko Yoshioka, *Asahi Shimbun*, October 25, 2001.

12. These bills passed in the Lower House on October 18 and the Upper House on October 29, 2001.

13. *Asahi Shimbun* (October 4, 2001), "46% Oppose Plan for SDF," cited in Midford (2003), p. 340.

14. Kliman (2006) includes as one of his four variables to explain Japan's security policy shift post-9/11 the issue of such "executive leadership."

15. Perhaps itself an indication of a degree of shifting attitudes related to security policy, the Japanese Maritime Safety Agency was renamed the Japan Coast Guard in April 2000.

16. A number of more specific differences between the two cases are also apparent, such as the time frame in which the incident took place, the larger number of ships involved in the 1999 case, and that it was the Japanese Coast Guard (formerly called the Maritime Safety Agency), not the MSDF, which engaged the suspicious ship in 2001.

17. Berkofsky, *Asia Times*, January 16, 2002.

18. Berkofsky, *Asia Times*, January 16, 2002.

19. This analysis ignores a third possibility—identity shift through nondemocratic means, such as a military coup—given the utter implausibility of this scenario in Japan today, despite the fears expressed by some.

20. Empirically speaking, however, it is important to note that a number of other issues related to North Korea and also the broader international environment were also unfold-

ing at this same time, and therefore it is unlikely that the post–Taepodong policy responses were motivated solely by this single missile overflight. Indeed, there had already been a North Korean missile incursion earlier in the decade, and concerns over North Korean nuclear weapons development and the subsequent revelation of North Korean abductions of Japanese citizens contributed greatly to concerns over the North Korean threat in particular.

21. Such actions as widespread anti-Japanese riots and violence in China, Japan-China citizen and military clashes over disputed islands, and North Korean nuclear weapons and Japanese citizen abduction policies are just a few possible examples that could be exploited.

22. As a possible electoral strategy for a new minority party, however, this might have more traction.

23. Boyd and Samuels (2005) offer a much more detailed account of the role of the CLB in reinterpreting core security legislation and constitutional interpretation, though they argue that constitutional revision is much more likely than the argument developed here.

Bibliography

Theory and Methodology

Abdelal, Rawi, Yoshiko M. Herrera, Alastair Iain Johnston, and Rose McDermott. 2005. Identity as a Variable. Unpublished manuscript.

Adamson, Fiona. 2000. Rethinking the "Identity Debate" in International Relations Theory: Factoring in the Role of International Migration and Transnational Identities. Paper presented at the annual meeting of the American Political Science Association, Washington, DC (September).

Adler, Emanuel. 1987. *The Power of Ideology: The Quest for Technological Autonomy in Argentina and Brazil.* Berkeley: University of California Press.

——. 1997. Seizing the Middle Ground: Constructivism in World Politics. *European Journal of International Relations* 3: 3: 319–63.

Almond, Gabriel, and Sidney Verba. 1963. *The Civic Culture: Political Attitudes and Democracy in Five Nations.* Newbury Park, CA: Sage Publications.

Aron, Raymond. 1966. *Peace and War.* New York: Doubleday.

Art, Robert. 1999. Force and Fungibility Reconsidered. *Security Studies* 8: 4 (Summer): 184–90.

Baldwin, David. 1999. Force, Fungibility, and Foreign Policy. *Security Studies* 8: 4 (Summer): 174–84.

—— (ed.). 1993. *Neorealism and Neoliberalism: The Contemporary Debate.* New York: Columbia University Press.

Biersteker, Thomas. 1989. Critical Reflections on Post-Positivism in International Relations. *International Studies Quarterly 33* (September): 263–67.

Blyth, Mark. 1997. "Any More Bright Ideas?" The Ideational Turn of Comparative Political Economy. *Comparative Politics* (January): 229–50.

Brady, Henry E., and David Collier. 2004. *Rethinking Social Inquiry: Diverse Tools, Shared Standards.* Boulder, CO: Rowman and Littlefield.

Brooks, Stephen G. 1997. Dueling Realisms. *International Organization 51*: 3 (Summer): 445–77.

Brooks, Stephen G., and William C. Wohlforth. 2002. From Old Thinking to New Thinking in Qualitative Research. *International Security 26*: 4 (Spring): 93–111.

Brown, Michael, Sean Lynn-Jones, and Steven Miller (eds.). 1996. *Debating the Democratic
Peace: An International Security Reader.* Cambridge, MA: MIT Press.

Bukovansky, Mlada. 1997. American Identity and Neutral Rights from Independence to
the War of 1812. *International Organization 51*: 2 (Spring): 209–43.

Campbell, John Creighton. 1992. *How Policies Change: The Japanese Government and the Aging
Society.* Princeton, NJ: Princeton University Press.

Checkel, Jeffrey. 1998. The Constructivist Turn in International Relations Theory. *World
Politics 20*: 2.

Deaver, Michael. 1999. Toward a Constructive Method: State Identity and Government
Tactics. Paper presented at the annual meeting of the American Political Science Association, Atlanta, GA (September).

Desch, Michael C. 1998. Culture Clash: Assessing the Importance of Ideas in Security
Studies. *International Security 23*: 1 (Summer): 141–70.

Deudney, David. 2000. Regrounding Realism: Anarchy, Security, and Changing Material
Contexts. *Security Studies 10*: 1 (autumn): 1–42.

Dittmer, Lowell. 1977. Political Culture and Political Symbolism: Toward a Theoretical
Synthesis. *World Politics 29* (July): 552–83.

Eckstein, Harry. 1975. Case Study and Theory in Political Science. In Fred Greenstein and
Nelson Polsby (eds.), *Handbook of Political Science,* vol. 7. Reading, MA: Addison-Wesley.

———. 1988. A Culturalist Theory of Political Change. *American Political Science Review 82*:
(June): 789–804.

Elman, Colin. 1996. Horses for Courses: Why Not Neorealist Theories of Foreign Policy?
Security Studies 6: 1 (Fall): 7–53.

Elster, Jon. 1989a. *Nuts and Bolts for the Social Sciences.* New York: Press Syndicate of the
University of Cambridge.

———. 1989b. *Possible Worlds.* Chicago: University of Chicago Press.

Epstein, Rachel. 2000. International Sources of Domestic Policy: Persuasion and Coercion
in Post-Communist Poland. Paper presented at joint Columbia-Princeton Workshop
on National Identity and Public Policy. Princeton, NJ (October).

Frankel, Benjamin (ed.). 1996. *Realism: Restatements and Renewal.* London: Frank Cass.

Feagin, Joe R., Anthony M. Orum, and Gideon Sjoberg. 1991. *A Case for the Case Study.*
Chapel Hill: University of North Carolina Press.

Fearon, James. 1991. Counterfactuals and Hypothesis Testing. *World Politics 43* (January):
169–95.

Finel, Bernard I. 2001/02. Black Box or Pandora's Box: State Level Variables and Progressiv-
ity in Realist Research Programs. *Security Studies 11*: 2 (Winter): 187–227.

Finnemore, Martha. 1996. Constructing Norms of Humanitarian Intervention. In Peter
Katzenstein (ed.), *The Culture of National Security: Norms and Identity in World Politics* (pp.
153–85). New York: Columbia University Press.

Friedberg, Aaron. 1993/94. Ripe for Rivalry: Prospects for Peace in a Multipolar Asia. *International Security 18*: 3 (Winter): 5–33.

———. 2000. *In the Shadow of the Garrison State: America's Anti-Statism and Its Cold War
Grand Strategy.* Princeton, NJ: Princeton University Press.

Garrett, Geoffrey, and Barry Weingast. 1993. Ideas, Interests and Institutions: Constructing
the European Communities' Internal Market. In Goldstein and Keohane (eds.), *Ideas
and Foreign Policy,* pp. 173–206. Ithaca, NY: Cornell University Press.

George, Alexander L., and Andrew Bennett. 2005. *Case Studies and Theory Development in the Social Sciences*. Boston: MIT Press.

Gerring, John. 2004. What Is a Case Study and What Is It Good for? *American Political Science Review 98*: 2 (May): 341–54.

Gilpin, Robert. 1981. *War and Change in World Politics*. Cambridge: Cambridge University Press.

———. 1989. Where Does Japan Fit In? *Millennium 18*: 3 (Winter): 329–42.

Goldstein, Judith, and Robert O. Keohane (eds.). 1993. *Ideas and Foreign Policy: Beliefs, Institutions, and Political Change*. Ithaca, NY: Cornell University Press.

Hall, Peter A. 1986. *Governing the Economy: The Politics of State Intervention in Britain and France*. Oxford: Oxford University Press.

———. 1993. Policy Paradigms, Social Learning, and the State. *Comparative Politics 25* (April): 275–96.

——— (ed.). 1989. *The Political Power of Economic Ideas: Keynesianism across Nations*. Princeton, NJ: Princeton University Press.

Heclo, Hugh. 1974. *Modern Social Politics in Britain and Sweden*. New Haven, CT: Yale University Press.

Herman, Michael. 1996. *Intelligence Power in War and Peace*. Cambridge: Cambridge University Press.

Holsti, Kal. 1970. National Role Conceptions in the Study of Foreign Policy. *International Studies Quarterly 14*: 233–309.

Hopf, Ted. 1998. The Promise of Constructivism in International Relations Theory. *International Security 23*: 1 (Summer): 171–200.

Huntington, Samuel P 1981. *American Politics: The Promise of Disharmony*. Cambridge, MA: Harvard University Press.

———. 1993. Why International Primacy Matters. *International Security 14*: 4 (Spring): 68–83.

Ikenberry, G. John. 2001. *After Victory: Institutions, Strategic Restraint, and the Rebuilding of Order after Major Wars*. Princeton, NJ: Princeton University Press.

Ikenberry, G. John, and Michael Mastanduno (eds.). 2003. *International Relations Theory and the Asia-Pacific*. New York: Columbia University Press.

Inglehart, Ronald. 1990. *Culture Shift in Advanced Industrial Society*. Princeton, NJ: Princeton University Press.

Jackson, Patrick. 1999. Discursive Spaces: Identity, Legitimacy, and the Politics of Agency. Draft dissertation chapter (unpublished), Columbia University (November).

Jackson, Patrick Thaddeus. 2006. *Civilizing the Enemy: German Reconstruction and the Invention of the West*. Ann Arbor, MI: University of Michigan Press.

Jacobsen, Kurt. 1995. Much Ado About Ideas: The Cognitive Factor in Economic Policy. *World Politics 47* (January): 283–310.

Jacquin-Berdal, Dominique, Andrew Oros, and Marco Verweij (eds.). 1998. *Culture in World Politics*. New York: St. Martin's Press.

Jervis, Robert. 1970. *The Logic of Images in International Relations*. Princeton, NJ: Princeton University Press.

———. 1976. *Perception and Misperception in International Politics*. Princeton, NJ: Princeton University Press.

———. 1978. Cooperation Under the Security Dilemma. *World Politics 30*: 167–214.

Johnson, Chalmers. 2000. *Blowback: The Costs and Consequences of American Empire*. New York: Metropolitan Books.

Johnston, Alastair Iain. 1995a. *Cultural Realism: Strategic Culture and Grand Strategy in Chinese History*. Princeton, NJ: Princeton University Press.

———. 1995b. Thinking about Strategic Culture. *International Security 18*: 4 (Spring): 32–64.

Kagan, Robert. 2002. Power and Weakness: Why the United States and Europe See the World Differently. *Policy Review*, no. 113 (June/July).

Katz, Andrew. 2000. A Constructivist Understanding of the Legacy of Vietnam. Paper presented at the annual meeting of the American Political Science Association, Washington, DC (September).

Katzenstein, Peter (ed.). 1996a. *The Culture of National Security: Norms and Identity in World Politics*. New York: Columbia University Press.

———. 2005. *A World of Regions: Asia and Europe in the American Imperium*. Ithaca, NY: Cornell University Press.

Katzenstein, Peter, and Nobuo Okawara. 2001/02. Japan, Asian-Pacific Security, and the Case for Analytical Eclecticism. *International Security 26*: 3 (Winter): 153–85.

Kennedy, Paul. 1987. *The Rise and Fall of Great Powers: Economic Change and Military Conflict from 1500–2000*. New York: Random House.

Keohane, Robert. 1984. *After Hegemony: Cooperation and Discord in the World Political Economy*. Princeton, NJ: Princeton University Press.

———. 1986. Theory of World Politics: Structural Realism and Beyond. In R. O. Keohane (ed.), *Neorealism and Its Critics*. New York: Columbia University Press.

Keohane, Robert, and Joseph Nye. 2000. *Power and Interdependence*, 3rd ed. New York: Longman.

Kier, Elizabeth. 1996. Culture and French Military Doctrine before World War II. In Peter Katzenstein (ed.), *The Culture of National Security: Norms and Identity in World Politics* (pp. 186–215). New York: Columbia University Press.

———. 1997. *Imagining War: French Military Doctrine between the Wars*. Princeton, NJ: Princeton University Press.

King, Gary, Robert Keohane, and Sidney Verba. 1994. *Designing Social Inquiry: Scientific Inference in Qualitative Research*. Princeton, NJ: Princeton University Press.

Kowert, Paul, and Jeffrey Legro. 1996. Norm, Identity, and Their Limits: A Theoretical Reprise. In P. J. Katzenstein (ed.), *The Culture of National Security: Norms and Identity in World Politics* (pp. 451–97). New York: Columbia University Press.

Krasner, Stephen D. 1985. *Structural Conflict: The Third World Against Liberalism*. Berkeley: University of California Press.

Krotz, Ulrich Bernhard. 2000. National Role Conceptions, National Interests, and Foreign Policies: France and Germany Compared. Paper presented at the Joint Columbia-Princeton Workshop on National Identity and Public Policy. Princeton, NJ (October).

Kuhn, Thomas. 1970. *The Structure of Scientific Revolutions*. Chicago: University of Chicago Press.

Lakatos, Imre, and Harold Musgrave (eds.). 1970. *Criticism and the Growth of Knowledge*. Oxford: Oxford University Press.

Lapid, Yosef. 1989. The Third Debate: On the Prospects of International Theory in a Post-Positivist Era. *International Studies Quarterly 33* (Summer): 235–54.

Lapid, Yosef, and Friedrich V. Kratochwil (eds.). 1996. *The Return of Culture and Identity in IR Theory*. Boulder, CO: Lynne Reinner Press.

Layne, Christopher. 1993. The Unipolar Illusion: Why New Great Powers Will Rise. *International Security 17*: 4 (Spring): 5–51.

Lebow, Richard Ned. 2000. What's So Different About a Counterfactual? *World Politics* 52: 2 (July): 550–85.

Legro, Jeffrey W. 1996. Culture and Preferences in the International Cooperation Two-Step. *American Political Science Review* 90: 1 (March): 118–37.

———. 2005. *Rethinking the World: Great Power Strategies and International Order.* Ithaca, NY: Cornell University Press.

Legro, Jeffrey W., and Andrew Moravcsik. 1999. Is Anybody Still a Realist? *International Security* 24: 2 (Fall): 5–55.

Lewis, David. 1973. *Counterfactuals.* Cambridge, MA: Harvard University Press.

Lieberman, Robert C. 2002. Ideas, Institutions, and Political Order: Explaining Political Change. *American Political Science Review* 96: 4 (December): 697–712.

Lijphart, Arend. 1971. Comparative Politics and the Comparative Method. *American Political Science Review* (September): 682–93.

Lobell, Steven E. 2002/03. War Is Politics: Offensive Realism, Domestic Politics, and Security Strategies. *Security Studies* 12: 2 (Winter): 165–95.

March, James G., and Johan Olsen. 1989. *Rediscovering Institutions: The Organizational Basis of Politics.* New York: The Free Press.

Mearsheimer, John J. 1990. Back to the Future: Instability in Europe after the Cold War. *International Security* 15: 1 (Summer): 5–56.

———. 1994/95. The False Promise of International Institutions. *International Security* 19: 3 (Winter): 5–49.

———. 1995. A Realist Reply. *International Security* 20: 1 (Summer): 93.

———. 2001. *The Tragedy of Great Power Politics.* New York: Norton.

Milner, Helen V. 1997. *Interests, Institutions, and Information.* Princeton, NJ: Princeton University Press.

Moravcik, Andrew. 1999. Taking Preferences Seriously: A Liberal Theory of International Politics. *International Organization* 51: 4 (Autumn): 513–53.

Morgenthau, Hans. 1973. *Politics Among Nations,* 5th ed. New York: Knopf.

Nathan, Andrew. 1993. Is Chinese Culture Distinctive? *Journal of Asian Studies* 52 (November): 923–36.

Nau, Henry. 2002. *At Home Abroad: Identity and Power in American Foreign Policy.* Ithaca, NY: Cornell University Press.

Olson, Mancur. 1970. *The Logic of Collective Action.* Cambridge, MA: Harvard University Press.

Oros, Andrew. 1995. Asian Values or Asian Ideology? The Role of Culture in the International Relations of East Asia. *Journal of Public and International Affairs* 6: 129–47.

Polvi-Lohikoski, Johanna. 2000. The Europeanization of National Policy Objectives in Finland and Sweden: Instrumental Identity Politics. Paper presented at the Joint Columbia-Princeton Workshop on National Identity and Public Policy. Princeton, NJ (October).

Pye, Lucian. 1997. Introduction: The Elusive Concept of Culture and the Vivid Reality of Personality. *Political Psychology* 18: 2: 241–54.

Risse-Kappen, Thomas. 1991. Public Opinion, Domestic Structure, and Foreign Policy in Liberal Democracies. *World Politics* 43: 4 (July): 479–512.

Rose, Gideon. 1998. Neoclassical Realism and Theories of Foreign Policy. *World Politics* 51: 1 (October): 151.

Schweller, Randall. 1994. Bandwagoning for Profit: Bringing the Revisionist State Back In. *International Security* 19: 1 (Summer): 72–107.

————. 1998. *Deadly Imbalances: Tripolarity and Hitler's Strategy of World Conquest.* New York: Columbia University Press.

Sikkink, Kathryn. 1991. *Ideas and Institutions: Developmentalism in Argentina and Brazil.* Ithaca, NY: Cornell University Press.

Snyder, Jack. 1991. *Myths of Empire: Domestic Politics and International Ambition.* Ithaca, NY: Cornell University Press.

Steimo, Sven, Kathleen Thelen, and Frank Longstreth (eds.). *Structuring Politics: Historical Institutionalism in Comparative Analysis.* Cambridge: Cambridge University Press.

Taliaferro, Jeffrey W. 2000/01. Security Seeking under Anarchy: Defensive Realism Revisited. *International Security* 25: 3 (Winter): 128–61.

Trubowitz, Peter. 1998. *Defining the National Interest: Conflict and Change in American Foreign Policy.* Chicago: University of Chicago Press.

Trubowitz, Peter, Emily O. Goldman, and Edward Rhodes (eds.). 1999. *The Politics of Strategic Adjustment: Ideas, Institutions, and Interests.* New York: Cambridge University Press.

van Evera, Stephen. 1997. *Guide to Methods for Students of Political Science.* Ithaca, NY: Cornell University Press.

————. 1999. *The Causes of War.* Ithaca, NY: Cornell University Press.

Vasquez, John. 1997. The Realist Paradigm and Degenerative vs. Progressive Research Programs: An Appraisal of Neotraditional Research on Waltz's Balancing Proposition. *American Political Science Review* 91: 4 (December): 899–912.

Walker, Stephen G. 1987. *Role Theory in Foreign Policy Analysis.* Durham, NC: Duke University Press.

Walt, Steven. 1987. *The Origin of Alliances.* Ithaca, NY: Cornell University Press.

Waltz, Kenneth. 1979. *Theory of International Politics.* New York: McGraw-Hill.

————. 1981. The Spread of Nuclear Weapons May Be Better (No. 171). London: International Institute of Strategic Studies.

————. 1996. International Politics Is Not Foreign Policy. *Security Studies* 6: 1 (Autumn): 54–57.

Wedeen, Lisa. 2002. Conceptualizing Culture: Possibilities for Political Science. *American Political Science Review* 96: 4 (December): 713–28.

Weldes, Jutta, Mark Laffey, Hugh Gusterson, and Raymond Duvall (eds.). 1999. *Cultures of Insecurity: States, Communities, and the Production of Danger.* Minneapolis: University of Minnesota Press.

Wendt, Alexander. 1987. The Agent-Structure Problem in International Relations Theory. *International Organization* 41 (Summer): 335–70.

————. 1992. Anarchy Is What States Make of It: The Social Construction of Power Politics. *International Organization* 46:2 (Spring): 391–425.

Empirical Cases

Books, Articles, Documents (English)

Abe, Kazuyoshi. 1991. The Japanese Business Community: Response to the Gulf War. *Japanese Review of International Affairs* 5 (Fall/Winter): 177–200.

Aid, Matthew M., and Cees Wiebes (eds.). 2001. *Secrets of Signals Intelligence During the Cold War and Beyond.* London: Frank Cass & Co.

Akaha, Tsuneo. 2000. U.S.-Japan Relations in the Post-Cold War Era: Ambiguous Adjustment to a Changing Strategic Environment. In Inoguchi and Jain (eds.), *Japanese Foreign Policy Today* (pp. 177–93). New York: Palgrave.

Alagappa, Muthiah (ed.). 1998. *Asian Security Practice: Material and Ideational Influences*. Stanford, CA: Stanford University Press.

Amemiya, Kozy K. 1999. The Law Promotes Blind Patriotism. *JPRI Critique 6*: 9 (September). Cardiff, CA: Japan Policy Research Institute.

Arima, Tatsuya. 2003. Japanese Security Policy in the Next Ten Years. Unpublished manuscript. Washington, DC: Stimson Center.

Armacost, Michael. 1996. *Friends or Rivals: The Insider's Account of U.S.-Japan Relations*. New York: Columbia University Press.

Asai, Motofumi. 1991. Pacifism in a New International Order. *Japan Quarterly* (April-June): 130–41.

Asher, David. 1997. A U.S.-Japan Alliance for the Next Century. *Orbis 41*: 3 (Summer): 343–75.

Aspen Strategy Group. 1986. *Anti-Satellite Weapons and U.S. Military Space Policy*. Lanham, MD: University Press of America.

Benfell, Steven. 1997. Rich Nation, No Army. University of Pennsylvania, doctoral dissertation.

———. 1999. A Past Worth Forgetting: Politics and the Institutionalization of War Memories in Japan. Paper presented at the annual meeting of the American Political Science Association, Atlanta, GA (September).

Berger, Thomas U. 1991. America's Reluctant Allies: The Genesis of the Political Military Cultures of Japan and West Germany. Massachusetts Institute of Technology, doctoral dissertation.

———. 1993. From Sword to Chrysanthemum: Japan's Culture of Anti-Militarism. *International Security 17*: 4 (Spring): 119–50.

———. 1996. Norms, Identity, and National Security in Germany and Japan. In P. J. Katzenstein (ed.), *The Culture of National Security: Norms and Identity in World Politics* (pp. 317–56). New York: Columbia University Press.

———. 1998. *Cultures of Antimilitarism: National Security in Germany and Japan*. Baltimore: Johns Hopkins University Press.

Betts, Richard K. 1993/94. Wealth, Power, and Instability: East Asia and the United States after the Cold War. *International Security 18*: 3 (Winter): 34–77.

Bix, Herbert. 2000. *Hirohito and the Making of Modern Japan*. New York: Harper Collins.

Bobrow, Davis B. 1989. Japan in the World: Opinion from Defeat to Success. *Journal of Conflict Resolution 33*: 4 (December): 571–604.

Bobrow, Davis B., and Steven R. Hill. 1991. Non-Military Determinants of Military Budgets: The Japanese Case. *International Studies Quarterly 35* (March): 39–61.

Borton, Hugh. 1967. American Presurrender Planning for Postwar Japan. Occasional paper of the East Asian Institute. New York: Columbia University.

Boyd, J. Patrick, and Richard Samuels. 2005. Nine Lives? The Politics of Constitutional Reform in Japan. *Policy Studies 19*. Washington, DC: East-West Center Washington.

Brooks, Stephen G. 2005. *Producing Security: Multinational Corporations, Globalization, and the Changing Calculus of Conflict*. Princeton, N.J.: Princeton University Press.

Burrows, William E. 1986. *Deep Black: Space Espionage and National Security*. New York: Random House.

———. 1990. *Exploring Space: Voyages in the Solar System and Beyond*. New York: Random House.

CISTEC. 2000. *Export Control System in Japan*. Tokyo (February).

Calder, Kent. 1988a. *Crisis and Compensation: Public Policy and Political Stability in Japan, 1949–1986*. Princeton, NJ: Princeton University Press.

———. 1988b. Japanese Foreign Economic Policy Formation: Explaining the Reactive State. *World Politics 40*: 4: 517–41.

Cambone, Stephen. 1997. The United States and Theater Missile Defense in Northeast Asia. *Survival 39: 3* (Autumn): 66–84.

Center for Nonproliferation Studies. 1999. *Theater Missile Defense (TMD) in Northeast Asia: An Annotated Chronology, 1990–Present*. Monterey, CA. http://cns.miis.edu/research/neasia/tmdchron.htm.

Cha, Victor. 1999. *Alignment Despite Antagonism: The United States-Korea-Japan Security Triangle*. Stanford, CA: Stanford University Press.

———. 2003. Defensive Realism and Japan's Approach toward Korean Reunification. *NBR Analysis 14*: 1 (June).

Chiku, Takemi. 1992. Japanese Space Policy in the Changing World. Massachusetts Institute of Technology, master's thesis.

Chinworth, Michael. 1992. *Inside Japan's Defense: Technology, Economics, and Strategy*. New York: Brassey's.

———. 1997. Defense-Economic Linkages in U.S.-Japan Relations: An Overview of Policy Positions and Objectives. *TASC Working Paper No. 8*. Paper presented at "Power and Prosperity: Linkages between Security and Economics in U.S.-Japanese Relations." Washington, DC: National Security Archive.

Christensen, Raymond V. 1994. Electoral Reform in Japan: How It Was Enacted and Changes It May Bring. *Asian Survey* (July): 589–605.

———. 1996. The New Japanese Electoral System. *Pacific Affairs 69*: 1 (Spring): 49–70.

Christensen, Thomas J. 1999. China, the U.S.-Japan Alliance, and the Security Dilemma in East Asia. *International Security 23: 4* (Spring): 49–80.

———. 2000. Theater Missile Defense and Taiwan's Security. *Orbis* (Winter): 79–90.

Chuma, Kiyofuku. 1991. The Choice Is Clear: Diplomacy Over Force. *Japan Quarterly* (April-June): 142–48.

Clemons, Steven C. 2000. Nuclear Policy in Japan. *Foreign Policy 117* (Winter): 156.

———. 2001a. American Triumphalism and the Conditions That Led to September 11. *Le Monde Diplomatique* (October): 1.

———. 2001b. The Armitage Report. *JPRI Occasional Paper No. 20* (February). Cardiff, CA: Japan Policy Research Institute.

Clemons, Steven C. and Andrew L. Oros. 2005. Betting on a Bolder Japan. *Japan Times* (September 15).

Cohen, Theodore. 1987. *Remaking Japan: The American Occupation as New Deal*. New York: Free Press.

Constantine, G. Ted. 1995. Intelligence Support to Humanitarian-Disaster Relief Operations. *Center for the Study of Intelligence Monograph*. Langley, VA: Central Intelligence Agency.

Council on Foreign Relations. 1998. *The Tests of War and the Strains of Peace: The U.S.-Japan Security Relationship* (Bilingual Edition). Study Group Report. New York.

Council on Security and Defense Capabilities (Japan). 2004. *Japan's Vision for Future Security and Defense Capabilities [Araki Report]*. Tokyo (October).

Cronin, Richard. 1999. *Japan's Changing Security Outlook: Implications for U.S.-Japan Defense Cooperation*. CRS Report RL-20356 (July 9). Washington, DC: Congressional Research Service.

Cronin, Richard, Paul S. Giarra, and Michael Green. 1999. The Alliance Implications of Theater Missile Defense. In Green and Cronin (ed.), *The U.S.-Japan Alliance: Past, Present, and Future* (pp. 170–88). New York: Council on Foreign Relations Press.

Cronin, Richard, and Y. Jane Nakano. 2001. *Japan-U.S. Cooperation on Theater Missile Defense: Issues and Prospects*. CRS Report RL-30992. Washington, DC: Congressional Research Service.

Curtis, Gerald. 1979. Domestic Politics and Japanese Foreign Policy. In W. J. Barnds (ed.), *Japan and the United States: Challenges and Opportunities* (pp. 21–85). New York: New York University Press.

———. 1980. Japanese Security Policies and the United States. *Foreign Affairs* 59: 4 (Spring): 852–74.

———. 1988. *The Japanese Way of Politics*. New York: Columbia University Press.

———. 1999. *The Logic of Japanese Politics*. New York: Columbia University Press.

——— (ed.). 1993. *Japan's Foreign Policy After the Cold War: Coping with Change*. Armonk, NY: M. E. Sharpe.

——— (ed.). 2001. *New Perspectives on U.S.-Japan Relations*. Tokyo: Japan Center for International Exchange.

Day, Dwayne. 1996. Invitation to Struggle: The History of Civilian-Military Relations in Space. In John Logsdon (ed.), *Exploring the Unknown: Selected Documents in the History of the U.S. Civilian Space Program,* Vol. 2: *External Relationships.* Washington, DC: NASA.

Day, Dwayne, John Logsdon, and Brian Latell (eds.). 1998. *Eye in the Sky: The Story of the Corona Spy Satellites.* Washington, DC: Smithsonian Institution Press.

Dees, Bowen C. 1997. *The Allied Occupation and Japan's Economic Miracle: Building the Foundations of Japanese Science and Technology—1945–52.* Surrey, UK: Japan Library.

Ding, Arthur A. 1999. Viewpoint: China's Concerns about Missile Defense: A Critique. *The Nonproliferation Review* (Fall): 93–101. Monterey: Center for Nonproliferation Studies.

Dobson, Hugo. 2003. *Japan and United Nations Peacekeeping: New Pressures, New Responses.* London: Sheffield Centre for Japanese Studies/RoutledgeCurzon.

Doi, Ayako, and Kim Willenson. 2005. Sayonara to Japanese Pacifism? *Washington Post* (August 14), B4.

Dower, John. 1979. *Empire and Aftermath: Yoshida Shigeru and the Japanese Experience, 1878–1954.* Cambridge, MA: Harvard East Asia Monograph.

———. 1993a. *Japan in War and Peace: Selected Essays.* New York: New Press.

———. 1993b. Peace and Democracy in Two Systems: External Policy and Internal Conflict. In A. Gordon (ed.), *Postwar Japan as History.* Berkeley: University of California Press.

———. 1999. *Embracing Defeat: Japan in the Wake of World War II.* New York: W. W. Norton.

Drifte, Reinhard. 1986. *Arms Production in Japan: The Military Applications of Civilian Technology.* Boulder, CO: Westview Press.

———. 1996. *Japan's Foreign Policy in the 1990s: From Economic Superpower to What Power?* London: Macmillan.

Field, Norma. 1991. *In the Realm of a Dying Emperor: A Portrait of Japan at Century's End.* New York: Pantheon Books.

Finn, Richard B. 1992. *Winners in Peace: MacArthur, Yoshida, and Postwar Japan.* Berkeley: University of California Press.

Fitzgerald, Frances. 2000. *Way Out There in the Blue: Reagan, Star Wars, and the End of the Cold War.* New York: Simon & Schuster.

Flores, Noboru. 1999. International Armaments Cooperation Programs (IACP) in Japan. 1999. *The DISAM Journal* (Winter): 63–67.

Foley, Theresa M. 1988. Pentagon, State Department Granted Veto Over U.S. Remote Sensing Satellites. *Aviation Week and Space Technology*: 20–22.

Foreign Press Center/Japan. 1995. The Diet, Elections, and Political Parties. *"About Japan" Series No. 13, 3rd edition*, pp. 144–47. Tokyo: Foreign Press Center/Japan.

Friedman, George, and Meredith LeBard. 1991. *The Coming War with Japan*. New York: St. Martin's Press.

Frost and Sullivan. 1999. As quoted in: Bruce A. Smith, New Launchers Seek Commercial Market Share, *Aviation Week and Space Technology* (December 13, 1999): 50.

Funabashi, Yoichi. 1991/92. Japan and the New World Order. *Foreign Affairs 70*: 5 (Winter): 57–58.

———. 1998. Japan's Depression Diplomacy. *Foreign Affairs 77*: 6: 35–36.

George, Aurelia. 1993. Japan's Participation in UN Peacekeeping Operations: Radical Departure or Predictable Response? *Asian Survey 33*: 6: 573.

Gill, Bates, Kensuke Ebata, and Matthew Stephenson. 1996. Japan's Export Control Initiatives: Meeting New Nonproliferation Challenges. *The Nonproliferation Review* (Fall): 30–42.

Gordon, Andrew (ed.). 1993. *Postwar Japan as History*. Berkeley: University of California Press.

Green, Michael. 1994. The Japanese Defense Industry's Views of U.S.-Japan Defense Technology Collaboration: Findings of the MIT Japan Program Survey. *MIT-Japan Program Working Paper* (MITJP 94–01) (January). Cambridge, MA: MIT Japan Program.

———. 1995. *Arming Japan: Defense Production, Alliance Politics, and the Postwar Search for Autonomy*. New York: Columbia University Press.

———. 1998. State of the Field Report: Research on Japanese Security Policy. *AccessAsia Review 2*: 1 (September): 5–39.

———. 2000. The Forgotten Player. *The National Interest* (Summer): 42–49.

———. 2001. *Japan's Reluctant Realism: Foreign Policy Challenges in an Era of Uncertain Power*. New York: Palgrave.

Green, Michael, and Patrick Cronin (eds.). 1999. *The U.S.-Japan Alliance: Past, Present, and Future*. New York: Council on Foreign Relations Press.

Green, Michael, and Toby Dalton. 2000. Asian Reactions to U.S. Missile Defense. *NBR Analysis 11*: 3.

Green, Michael, and Richard Samuels. 1994a. Recalculating Autonomy: Japan's Choices in the New World Order. *NBR Analysis 5*: 4 (December). Seattle, WA: National Bureau of Asian Research.

———. 1994b. U.S.-Japan Defense Technology Cooperation: Ten Guidelines to Make It Work. *MIT-Japan Program Working Paper* (MITJP 94–07). (May). Cambridge, MA: MIT Japan Program.

Green, Michael, and Benjamin J. Self. 1996. Japan's Changing China Policy: From Commercial Liberalism to Reluctant Realism. *Survival 38*: 2 (Summer): 35–58.

Hall, Stephen. 1992. *Mapping the Next Millennium: The Discovery of New Geographies*. New York: Random House.

Halloran, Richard. 1991. *Chrysanthemum and Sword Revisited: Is Japanese Militarism Resurgent?*. Honolulu: East-West Center.

Hamami, Andrew K. 1993. The Emerging Military-Industrial Relationship in Japan and the U.S. Connection. *Asian Survey 33*: 592–609.

Handberg, Roger, and Joan Johnson-Freese. 2001. Japan's Move into Military Space. *Space News* (Feb. 21).

Havens, Thomas. 1987. *Fire Across the Sea: The Vietnam War and Japan 1965–1975*. Princeton, NJ: Princeton University Press.

Heinrich, L. William, Jr. 1997. Seeking an Honored Place: The Japanese Self-Defense Forces and the Use of Armed Force Abroad. Columbia University, doctoral dissertation.

Hildreth, Stephen A., and Gary J. Pagliano. 1995. Theater Missile Defense and Technology Cooperation: Implications for the U.S.-Japan Relationship. *Congressional Research Service*. Washington, DC. August 21 (95–907F).

Holstein, William J. 1990. *The Japanese Power Game: What It Means for America*. New York: Scribner's Sons.

Hook, Glenn D. 1988. The Erosion of Anti-Militaristic Principles in Contemporary Japan. *Journal of Peace Research 25*: 4 (December): 381–94.

———. 1990. *Language and Politics: The Security Discourse in Japan and the United States*. Tokyo: Kuroshio Shuppan.

———. 1996. *Militarization and Demilitarization in Contemporary Japan*. London: Routledge.

Hopper, David R. 1975. Defense Policy and the Business Community: The Keidanren Defense Production Committee. In James H. Buck (ed.), *The Modern Japanese Military System* (pp. 113–48). Beverly Hills, CA: Sage.

Hosokawa, Morihiro. 1998. Are U.S. Troops in Japan Needed? Reforming the Alliance. *Foreign Affairs 77*: 4 (July/August): 2–5.

Hughes, Christopher W. 1996. The North Korean Nuclear Crisis and Japanese Security. *Survival 38*: 2 (Summer): 79–103.

———. 2004a. *Japan's Re-emergence as a 'Normal' Military Power*. Oxford: Oxford University Press.

———. 2004b. *Japan's Security Agenda: Military, Economic, and Environmental Dimensions*. Boulder, CO: Lynne Rienner Publishers.

———. 2005. Japanese Military Modernization: In Search of a "Normal" Security Role. In Ashley J. Tellis and Michael Wills (eds.), *Strategic Asia 2005–06: Military Modernization in an Era of Uncertainty* (pp. 105–36). Seattle and Washington, DC: National Bureau of Asian Research.

Hummel, Hartwig. 1988. The Policy of Arms Export Restrictions in Japan. *Occasional Papers Series No. 4*. Tokyo: PRIME, International Peace Research Institute Meigaku.

Igarashi, Takeshi. 1985. Peace-making and Party Politics: The Formation of the Domestic Foreign Policy System in Postwar Japan. *Journal of Japanese Studies 12*: 2 (Summer): 323–56.

Ikegami-Andersson, Masako. 1998. Military Technology and U.S.-Japan Security Relations: A Study of Three Cases of Military R&D Collaboration, 1983–1998. Uppsala University, Sweden, Department of Peace and Conflict Research, doctoral dissertation.

Inbar, Efraim, and Benzion Zilberfarb (eds.). 1998. *The Politics and Economics of Defence Industries*. London: Frank Cass.

Inoguchi, Takashi. 1986. Japan's Images and Options: Not a Challenger, but a Supporter. *Journal of Japanese Studies 12*: (Winter): 95–119.

———. 1991. *Japan's International Relations*. London: Pinter Publications.

Inoguchi, Takashi, and Purnendra Jain. 2000. *Japanese Foreign Policy Today*. New York: Palgrave.

International Space Business Council [1999], as quoted in PR Newswire, Global Space Industry Exceeds $97 Billion (May 10, 1999).

Ishida, Takeshi. 1967. Japanese Public Opinion and Foreign Policy. *Peace Research in Japan*: 11–40.

Ishizuka, Isao. 1999. *Conditions for Success in the Information Gathering Satellite Project*. Working paper (September). Tokyo: Defense Research Council.

Ishizuka, Katsumi. 2005. Japan's Policy Towards U.N. Peacekeeping Operations. *International Peacekeeping 12*: 1 (Spring): 67–86.

Itoh, Mayumi. 2001. Japan's Neo-Nationalism: The Role of the Hinomaru and Kimigayo Legislation. *JPRI Working Paper No. 79* (July). Cardiff, CA: Japan Policy Research Institute.

Izumikawa, Yasuhiro. 2005. The Sources of Japanese Antimilitarism: Entrapment Fear and Japanese Pacifist Discourse. Unpublished paper delivered at the International Studies Association annual meeting, Honolulu, Hawaii.

Japan Defense Agency (JDA). Various years. *Defense of Japan*. Tokyo: The Japan Times.

Japan Ministry of Foreign Affairs. 1997. *Peacekeeping: Japan's Policy and Statements*. Tokyo.

Johnson, Chalmers. 1982. *MITI and the Japanese Miracle*. Stanford, CA: Stanford University Press.

———. 1995. *Japan: Who Governs? The Rise of the Developmental State*. New York: Norton.

———. 1993. The State and Japanese Grand Strategy. In Richard Rosecrance and Arthur A. Stein (eds.), *The Domestic Bases of Grand Strategy* (pp. 201–23). Ithaca, NY: Cornell University Press.

Johnson, Sheila K. 1999. Flags and Anthems as National Symbols. *JPRI Critique 6*: 9 (September). Cardiff, CA: Japan Policy Research Institute.

Johnson-Freese, Joan, and Lance Gatling. 2004. Security Implications of Japan's Information Gathering Satellite (IGS) System. *Intelligence and National Security 19*: 3 (Autumn): 538–52.

Kahn, Herman. 1970. *Japan: The Emerging Superstate*. Englewood Cliffs, NJ: Prentice-Hall.

Kan, Naoto. 1996. My Vision of a New Party. *Japan Echo 23*: 4 (Winter): 14–21.

Kataoka, Tetsuya. 1991. *The Prince of a Constitution: The Origins of Japan's Postwar Politics*. New York: Crane Russak.

Katz, 1998. *Japan: The System That Soured: The Rise and Fall of the Japanese Economic Miracle*. New York: M. E. Sharpe.

Katzenstein, Peter J. 1996b. *Cultural Norms and National Security: Police and Military in Postwar Japan*. Ithaca, NY: Cornell University Press.

Katzenstein, Peter J., and Nobuo Okawara. 1993. *Japan's National Security: Structures, Norms and Policy Responses in a Changing World*. Ithaca, NY: Cornell University East Asia Program.

Kawai, Kazuo. 1979. *Japan's American Interlude*. Chicago: University of Chicago Press.

Keddell, Joseph P., Jr. 1993. *The Politics of Japan's Defense*. Armonk, NY: M. E. Sharp.

Keidanren Defense Production Committee. 1991. *Defense Production in Japan*. Tokyo: Keidanren.

———. 1994. "Challenges for the Japanese Defense Industry." Speech by the delegation of the committee to the International Symposium "Challenge for the Defense Industry" in Stockholm, Sweden (November 1).

———. 1995. *A Call for a Defense Program for a New World*. Tokyo: Keidanren. May 11.

Kihara, Masao. 1977. Production of Weapons in Postwar Japan and Its Characteristics. *Kyoto University Economic Review 47*: 1–2 (April-October): 1–26.

Kim, Andrew. 1994. Japan and Peacekeeping Operations. *Military Review 74*: 4 (April): 22–34.

Kingston, Jeff. 2004. *Japan's Quiet Transformation: Social Change and Civil Society in the Twenty-first Century*. London and New York: RoutledgeCurzon.

Kinoshita, Hiroo. 1989. Mutual Security and Dual-Use Technology: A Consideration of Japanese-U.S. Cooperation. *Speaking of Japan 10*: 104: 20–24.

Klass, Philip J. 1971. *Secret Sentries in Space*. New York: Random House.

Klien, Susanne. 2002. *Rethinking Japan's Identity and International Role: An Intercultural Perspective*. New York: Routledge.

Kliman, Daniel M. 2006. *Japan's Security Strategy in the Post-9/11 World: Embracing a New Realpolitik*. Washington Papers No. 183. Westport, CT: Praeger/CSIS Press.

Kodama, Fumio. 1991. *Analyzing Japanese High Technologies: The Techno-Paradigm Shift*. London: Pinter Publishers.

Kohno, Masaru. 1989. Japanese Defense Policy Making: The FSX Selection, 1985–87. *Asian Survey 29*: 5 (May): 457–79.

KPMG. 1996. *The Satellite Remote Sensing Industry: A Global Review*. Washington, DC.

Kunihiro, Masao. 1997. The Decline and Fall of Pacifism. *Journal of the Atomic Scientist 53*: 1 (January/February): 35–39.

Kurlantzick, Joshua. 2005. Rising Sun. *The New Republic* (October 24): 12–18.

LaFeber, Walter. 1997. *The Clash: U.S-Japanese Relations Throughout History*. New York: W. W. Norton.

Langdon, Frank. 1985. The Security Debate in Japan. *Pacific Affairs 58*: 3: 397–410.

Lanteigne, Marc. 2000. Tipping the Balance: TMD and the Evolving Security Relations in Northeast Asia. Paper presented at the International Studies Association Annual Meeting (March). Los Angeles, CA.

Leitenberg, Milton. 1996. The Participation of Japanese Military Forces in United Nations Peacekeeping Operations. *Asian Perspective 20*: 1: 8–13.

Levin, Norman D. 1988. *Japan's Changing Defense Posture*. N-2739-OSD. Santa Monica, CA: RAND.

Levine, Alan J. 1994. *The Missile and the Space Race*. Westport, CT: Praeger.

Lind, Jennifer M. 2004. Pacifism or Passing the Buck? Testing Theories of Japanese Security Policy. *International Security 29*: 1 (Summer): 92–121.

Lindgren, David T. 1988. Commercial Satellites Open Skies. *Bulletin of Atomic Scientists*. (April): 30–36.

Litfin, Karen T. 2002. Public Eyes: Satellite Imagery, the Globalization of Transparency, and New Networks of Surveillance. In J. N. Rosenau and J. P Singh (eds.), *Information Technologies and Global Politics: The Changing Scope of Power* (pp. 89–126). Albany, NY: SUNY University Press.

Logsdon, John. 1992. U.S.-Japanese Space Relationships at a Crossroads. *Science 255* (January 17).

Lorell, Mark. 1996. *Troubled Partnership: A History of U.S.-Japan Collaboration on the FS-X Fighter*. New Brunswick, NJ: Transaction Publishers.

Mabon, David W. 1988. Elusive Agreements: The Pacific Pact Proposals of 1949–1951. *Pacific-Historical Review 57*:2 (May): 147–78.

Matthews, Eugene. 2003. Japan's New Nationalism. *Foreign Affairs 82*: 6 (November/December): 74–90.

Marten Zisk, Kimberley. 2001. *Asia-Pacific Review 8:* 1 (May): 21–39.

McCormack, Gavan. 2002. Breaking the Iron Triangle. *New Left Review 13* (January-February): 5–23.

McDonough, Thomas. 1987. *Space: The Next Twenty-five Years*. New York: John Wiley.

McDougall, Walter. 1985. *The Heavens and the Earth: A Political History of the Space Age*. New York: Basic Books.

McNelly, Theordore. 1975. The Constitutionality of Japan's Defense Establishment. In James H. Buck (ed.), *The Modern Japanese Military System* (pp. 99–112). Beverly Hills: Sage.

Masumi, Junnosuke. 1995. *Contemporary Politics in Japan*. (Lonny E. Carlile, trans.). Berkeley: University of California Press.

Matsuoka, Kaname. 1989. Misunderstanding about the Japanese Self Defense Forces. *Survival 5*: 4 (April): 24–27.

Matthews, Ron, and Deisuke Matsuyama (eds.). 1993. *Japan's Military Renaissance?* New York: St. Martin's Press.

Maull, Hanns W. 1990–91. Germany and Japan: The New Civilian Powers. *Foreign Affairs 69*: 5: 91–106.

Medeiros, Evan S., rapporteur. 2001. Ballistic Missile Defense and Northeast Asian Security: Views from Washington, Beijing, and Tokyo. *Joint Publication of the Stanley Foundation and the Monterey Institute Center for Nonproliferation Studies*. Washington, DC. April.

Mendel, Douglas H., Jr. 1961. *The Japanese People and Foreign Policy: A Study of Public Opinion in Post-Treaty Japan*. Berkeley: University of California Press.

———. 1969. Japanese Opinion on Key Foreign Policy Issues. *Asian Survey 9* (August): 625–39.

———. 1970. Japanese Defense in the 1970s: The Public View. *Asian Survey 10* (December): 1046–69.

———. 1971–72. Japanese Views of the American Alliance in the Seventies. *Public Opinion Quarterly 35* (Winter): 521–38.

Menon, Rajan. 1997. The Once and Future Superpower: At Some Point Japan Is Likely to Build a Military Machine That Matches Its Economic Might. *Bulletin of the Atomic Scientist 53*: 1 (January/February).

Midford, Paul. 2002. The Logic of Reassurance and Japan's Grand Strategy. *Security Studies 11*: 3 (Spring): 1–43.

———. 2003. Japan's Response to Terror: Dispatching the SDF to the Arabian Sea. *Asian Survey 43*: 2 (March/April): 329–51.

———. 2004. China Views the Revised US-Japan Defense Guidelines: Popping the Cork? *International Relations of the Asia-Pacific 4*: 113–45.

———. 2006. *Japanese Public Opinion and the War on Terrorism: Implications for Japan's Security Strategy*. Washington, DC: East-West Center Washington.

Milly, Deborah J. 1999. *Poverty, Equality, and Growth: The Politics of Economic Need in Postwar Japan*. Cambridge, MA: Harvard University Press.

Miyashita, Akitoshi. 2007. Where Do Norms Come From? Foundations of Japan's Postwar Pacifism. *International Relations of the Asia-Pacific 7*: 1: 99–120.

Mochizuki, Mike M. 1983/84. Japan's Search for Strategy. *International Security 8*: 3 (Winter): 152–79.

———. 1995. *Japan: Domestic Change and Foreign Policy*. Santa Monica, CA: RAND.

———. 2003. Strategic Thinking under Bush and Koizumi: Implications for the U.S.-Japan Alliance. *Asia-Pacific Review 10*: 1 (May): 82–98.

Morris, Charles R. 1988. *Iron Destinies, Lost Opportunities: The Postwar Arms Race*. New York: Carroll and Graf Publishers.

Morris-Suzuki, Tessa. 1994. *The Technological Transformation of Japan: From the Seventeenth to the Twenty-First Century*. Cambridge: Cambridge University Press.

Mowthorpe, Matthew. 2004. *The Militarization and Weaponization of Space*. New York: Lexington Books.

Mulgan, Aurelia George. 1993. Japan's Participation in U.N. Peacekeeping Operations. *Asian Survey 33*: 6 (June): 560–76.

———. 1995. International Peacekeeping and Japan's Role: Catalyst or Cautionary Tale? *Asian Survey 35*: 12: 1102–17.

Muramatsu, Michio. 1987. In Search of National Identity: The Politics and Policies of the Nakasone Administration. *Journal of Japanese Studies 13*: 2 (Summer): 307–42.

Muramatsu, Michio, and Ellis Krauss. 1984. Bureaucrats and Politicians in Policymaking: The Case of Japan. *American Political Science Review 78*: 1 (March): 126–46.

Murray, Charles, and Catherine Bly Cox. 1989. *Apollo: The Race to the Moon.* New York: Simon & Schuster.

Nagata, Minoru. 1987. The Impact of High Technology on Japanese Security Concepts. In *Economics and Pacific Security: The 1986 Pacific Symposium* (pp. 225–36). Washington, DC: National Defense University Press.

Nakamura, Hisashi, and Malcolm Dando. 1993. Japan's Military Research and Development: A High Technology Deterrent. *Pacific Review 6*: 177–90.

Nakasone, Yasuhiro. 1995. Yomiuri Shimbun Constitutional Studies Group: A Proposal for a Sweeping Revision of the Constitution. *Japan Echo 22*: 1.

———. 1996. *Security and Peace in the New Asia-Pacific Era.* Tokyo: Institute for International Policy Studies.

———. 1997. Rethinking the Constitution: Make It a Japanese Document. *Japan Quarterly 44*: 3 (July-September).

Nathan, John. 2004. *Japan Unbound: A Volatile Nation's Quest for Pride and Purpose.* Boston and New York: Houghton Mifflin Company.

———. 2001. Tokyo Story. *The New Yorker* (April 9): 108–12.

National Defense Panel. 1997. *Transforming Defense: National Security in the 21st Century.* Washington, DC.

National Intelligence Council. 1999. *Foreign Missile Developments and the Ballistic Missile Threat to the United States through 2015* (September). Washington, DC: Central Intelligence Agency.

Nishihara, Masashi. 1983/84. Expanding Japan's Credible Defense Role. *International Security 8*: 3: 180–205.

Nishimoto, Tetsuya. 2001a. Japan's National Emergency Legislation: Problems with the Current Status and How It Should Be in the Future. In Pacific Forum CSIS (ed.), *United States-Japan Strategic Dialogue: Beyond the Defense Guidelines* (pp. 29–40). Honolulu: Pacific Forum CSIS.

———. 2001b. Roles and Missions of the United States and Japan in the Japan-U.S. Alliance. In Pacific Forum CSIS (ed.), *United States-Japan Strategic Dialogue: Beyond the Defense Guidelines* (pp. 8–28). Honolulu.

Nye, Joseph S., Jr. 1993. The Case for Deep Engagement. *Foreign Affairs 74* (July/August): 90–102.

O'Hanlon, Michael. 1999. Star Wars Strikes Back. *Foreign Affairs 78*: 6 (November/December): 68–9.

———. 2000. Theater Missile Defense and the United States-Japan Alliance. In Mike Mochizuki (ed.), *Toward a True Alliance: Restructuring U.S.-Japan Security Relations.* Washington, DC: Brookings Institution.

———. 2001. TMD, East Asia, and the U.S.-Japan Alliance. In Pacific Forum CSIS (ed.), *United States-Japan Strategic Dialogue: Beyond the Defense Guidelines* (pp. 126–35). Honolulu.

Oberg, James E. 1981. *Red Star in Orbit*. New York: Random House.

Odawara, Atsushi. 1985. No Tampering with the Brakes on Military Expansion. *Japan Quarterly 32*: 3 (July-September): 248–54.

Okazaki, Hisahiko. 1986. *A Grand Strategy for Japanese Defense*. Lanham, MD: University Press of America.

————. 1982. Japanese Security Policy: A Time for Strategy. *International Security 7*: 2: 188–97.

Okazaki Institute. 2001. *Introduction to BMD: Does Ballistic Missile Defense Make Sense for Japan?* Tokyo: Ballistic Missile Defense Research Group.

Okimoto, Daniel. 1978. Ideas, Intellectuals, and Institutions: National Security and the Question of Nuclear Disarmament in Japan, vols. 1–2. University of Michigan, doctoral dissertation.

————. 1981. Arms Transfers: The Japanese Calculus. In John Barton and Ryukichi Imai (eds.), *Arms Control II: A New Approach to International Security* (pp. 273–317). Cambridge, MA: Oelgeschlager, Cunn, and Hain.

————. 1982. Chrysanthemum without the Sword: Japan's Nonnuclear Policy. In Martin Weinstein (ed.), *Northeast Asian Security after Vietnam* (pp. 128–56). Urbana: University of Illinois Press.

————. 1989. *Between MITI and the Market: Japanese Industrial Policy for High Technology*. Stanford, CA: Stanford University Press.

Onishi, Norimitsu. 2005. Ugly Images of Asian Rivals Become Best Sellers in Japan. *New York Times* (November 19): A1.

Oros, Andrew. 1998. Review Article: Bureaucrats and Politicians in Japan's Political Economy. *Japan Forum 10*: 2: 221–30.

————. 2001. Multilateral Governance and Japan's New Regional Grand Vision: Policies towards APEC and ARF. Annual Meeting of the Association of Asian Studies, Chicago, March 21–25.

————. 2002. Japan's Growing Intelligence Capability in the Post-Cold War Era. *International Journal of Intelligence and Counterintelligence 15*: 1 (Winter): 1–24.

————. 2007a. Explaining Japan's Tortured Course to Surveillance Satellites. *Review of Policy Research 24*: 1 (January): 29–48.

————. 2007b. Listening to the People: Japanese Democracy and the New Security Agenda. Washington, DC: Mansfield Foundation. http://www.mansfieldfdn.org/polls/commentary-07-3.htm.

————. 2007c. The United States and "Alliance" Role in Japan's New Defense Establishment. In Yuki Tatsumi and Andrew Oros (eds.), *Japan's New Defense Establishment: Institutions, Capabilities, and Implications*. Washington, DC: Henry J. Stimson Center.

Oros, Andrew, and Yuki Tatsumi. 2007. Japan's Evolving Defense Establishment. In Yuki Tatsumi and Andrew Oros (eds.), *Japan's New Defense Establishment: Institutions, Capabilities, and Implications*. Washington, DC: Henry J. Stimson Center.

Otake, Hideo. 1996. Forces for Political Reform: The Liberal Democratic Party's Young Reformers and Ozawa Ichiro. *Journal of Japanese Studies 22*: 2 (Summer): 269–94.

Ozawa, Ichiro. 1994. *Blueprint for a New Japan: The Rethinking of a Nation* (Louisa Rubinfien, trans.). Tokyo: Kodansha International.

Pacific Forum CSIS (ed.). 2001. *United States–Japan Strategic Dialogue: Beyond the Defense Guidelines*. Honolulu, HI: Pacific Forum CSIS .

Packard, George, III. 1966. *Protest in Tokyo: The Security Treaty Crisis of 1960*. Princeton, NJ: Princeton University Press.

Peebles, Curtis. 1997. *The Corona Project: America's First Spy Satellites.* Annapolis, MD: Naval Institute Press.

Pempel, T. J. 1982. *Policy and Politics in Japan: Creative Conservatism.* Philadelphia: Temple University Press.

———. 1998. *Regime Shift: Comparative Dynamics of the Japanese Political Economy.* Ithaca, NY: Cornell University Press.

Press-Barnathan, Galia. 1998. Choosing Cooperation Strategies: The United States and Regional Arrangements in Asia and Europe in the Early Post–W.W.II Years. Columbia University, doctoral dissertation.

Prestowitz, Clyde V. 1988. *Trading Places: How We Allowed Japan to Take the Lead.* New York: Basic Books.

Pyle, Kenneth B. 1987. In Pursuit of a Grand Design: Nakasone Betwixt the Past and the Future. *Journal of Japanese Studies 13*: 2 (Summer): 243–70.

———. 1996. *The Japanese Question: Power and Purpose in a New Era,* 2nd ed. Washington, DC: The AEI Press.

———. 2007. *Japan Rising: The Resurgence of Japanese Power and Purpose.* Public Affairs/Perseus Books Group.

Renwick, Neil. 1995. *Japan's Alliance Politics and Defence Production.* New York: St. Martin's Press.

Rosecrance, Richard. 1986. *The Rise of the Trading State: Commerce and Conquest in the Modern World.* New York: Basic Books.

Rosecrance, Richard, and Jennifer Taw. 1990. Japan and the Theory of International Leadership. *World Politics 42*: (January): 184–209.

Ross, Robert S. 1999. The Geography of the Peace: East Asia in the Twenty-first Century. *International Security 22*: 4 (Spring): 81–118.

Rubinstein, Gregg A. 1987. Emerging Bonds of U.S.-Japanese Defense Technology Cooperation. *Strategic Review 15*: 1 (Winter): 43–51.

———. 1999. U.S.-Japan Armaments Cooperation. In Green and Cronin (eds.), *The U.S.-Japan Alliance: Past, Present, and Future* (pp. 268–85). New York: Council on Foreign Relations.

———. 2001. Armaments Cooperation in U.S.-Japan Security Relations. In Pacific Forum CSIS (ed.), *United States-Japan Strategic Dialogue: Beyond the Defense Guidelines* (pp. 90–99). Honolulu.

Rumsfeld Commission (Commission to Assess the Ballistic Missile Threat to the United States). 1998. *Report of the Commission to Assess the Ballistic Missile Threat to the United States (Rumsfeld Report).* Washington, DC.

SIPRI. Various years. *SIPRI Yearbook.* Stockholm: Stockholm International Peace Research Institute.

Sakamoto, Kazuya. 2001. The Japan-U.S. Security Treaty and the Right to Collective Self-Defense. In Pacific Forum CSIS (ed.), *United States-Japan Strategic Dialogue: Beyond the Defense Guidelines* (pp. 50–59). Honolulu.

Samuels, Richard J. 1991. Reinventing Security: Japan Since Meiji. *Daedalus* (Fall): 47–68.

———. 1994. *"Rich Nation, Strong Army": National Security and the Technological Transformation of Japan.* Ithaca, NY: Cornell University Press.

———. 2004. Politics, Security Policy, and Japan's Cabinet Legislation Bureau: Who Elected These Guys, Anyway? *JPRI Working Paper No. 99.*

———. 2005. *Machiavelli's Children: Leaders and Their Legacies in Italy and Japan.* Ithaca, NY: Cornell University Press.

————. 2007. Securing Japan: The Current Discourse. *Journal of Japanese Studies 33*: 1: 125–52.

Samuels, Richard J., and Eric Heginbotham. 2002. Japan's Dual Hedge. *Foreign Affairs 81*: 5 (September/October): 110–21.

————. 1998. Merchantile Realism and Japanese Foreign Policy. *International Security 22*: 4 (Spring): 171–203.

Sassa, Atsuyuki. 1995. Fault Lines in Our Emergency Management System. *Japan Echo 22*: 2 (Summer): 20–27.

Sato, Isao. 1979. Debate on Constitutional Amendment: Origins and Status. *Law in Japan 12*: 1–22.

Sato, Seizaburo. 1996. Clarifying the Right of Collective Defense. *Asia-Pacific Review 3* (Fall-Winter): 91–105.

Sato, Tsuyoki. 2000. *Loopholes and Pitfalls: The Coming Collision Between Japan's Arms Export Ban and TMD.* New York: East Asia Institute, Columbia University.

Schaller, Michael. 1985. *The American Occupation of Japan: The Origins of the Cold War in Asia.* New York: Oxford University Press.

————. 1997. *Altered States: The United States and Japan since the Occupation.* New York: Oxford University Press.

Schoppa, Leonard. 1993. Two-Level Games and Bargaining Outcomes: Why Gaiatsu Succeeds in Japan in Some Cases but Not in Others. *International Organization 47*: 3 (Summer): 353–86.

————. 1997. *Bargaining with Japan: What American Pressure Can and Cannot Do.* New York: Columbia University Press.

————. 2002. International Cooperation Despite Domestic Conflict: Japanese Politics and the San Francisco Peace Treaties. Paper presented at the annual meeting of the International Studies Association. New Orleans, March 24–28.

Schwoch, James. 2002. The Cold War, the Space Race, and the Globalization of Public Opinion Polling. Paper presented at the annual meeting of the International Studies Association. New Orleans, March 24–28.

Security Consultative Committee. 2005. *U.S.-Japan Alliance: Transformation and Realignment for the Future.* Joint Statement of U.S. Secretary of State Rice, U.S. Secretary of Defense Rumsfeld, Japanese Minister of Foreign Affairs Machimura, and Japanese Minister of State for Defense Ohno (October 29).

Shear, Jeff. 1994. *The Keys to the Kingdom: The FS-X Deal and the Selling of America's Future to Japan.* New York: Doubleday.

Shibayama, Futoshi. 2001. TMD and Japan: The First Stage of Integrating TMD and NMD into Alliance Missile Defense. In Pacific Forum CSIS (ed.), *United States-Japan Strategic Dialogue: Beyond the Defense Guidelines* (pp. 100–125). Honolulu.

Shinoda, Tomohito. 2001. Japan's Response to Terrorism. Paper presented at "Japan Sets Out: Japan's Role in the Fight Against Terrorism" workshop (October 16), Woodrow Wilson Center for Scholars.

Shuey, Robert D., Shirley Kan, and Mark Christofferson. 1999. *Missile Defense Options of Japan, South Korea, and Taiwan: A Review of the Defense Department Report to Congress.* CRS Report (November 30). Washington, DC: Congressional Research Service.

Simon, Sheldon W. 1986. Is There a Japanese Regional Security Model? *Journal of Northeast Asian Studies 5*: 2 (Summer): 30–52.

Smith, Patrick. 1999. At Last, an Official Flag and Hymn for Japan. *JPRI Critique 6*: 9 (September). Cardiff, CA: Japan Policy Research Institute.

Smith, Sheila Anne. 1996. At the Intersection of the Cold War and the Postwar: The Japanese State and Security Planning. Columbia University, doctoral dissertation.

Snow, Donald, and Eugene Brown. 1994. *Puzzle Palaces and Foggy Bottom: U.S. Foreign and Defense Policy-Making in the 1990s*. New York: St. Martin's Press.

Söderberg, Marie. 1986. *Japan's Military Export Policy*. Stockholm: University of Stockholm, Institute of Oriental Languages, Department of Japanese and Korean, Japanological Studies 6.

Stimson Center, Henry L. 2000. Theater Missile Defense in the Asia-Pacific Region. *Working Group Report No. 34* (June). Washington, DC.

Sugawa, Kiyoshi. 2000. Redefining Japanese Use of Force: Three Scenarios for Constitutional Revision and Their Implications. Draft Visiting Fellow Report. Washington, DC: Brookings Institution.

Swaine, Michael, Rachel Swanger, and Takashi Kawakami. 2001. *Japan and Ballistic Missile Defense*. Santa Monica, CA: RAND.

Takagi, Masayuki. 1989. The Japanese Right Wing. *Japan Quarterly 36*: 3 (July-September): 300–305.

Takase, Shoji. 1985. What "Star Wars" Means to Japan. *Japan Quarterly* (July-September): 240–47.

Tamama, Tetsuo. 1999. Missile Defense and Its "Symbol Effects." *Annual Report of the DRC*. Tokyo: Defense Research Center.

Tamamoto, Marasu. 1990. Japan's Search for a World Role. *World Policy Journal 7*: 3 (Summer): 493–520.

———. 1991. Trial of an Ideal: Japan's Debate over the Gulf Crisis. *World Policy Journal 8*: 1 (Winter): 89–106.

———. 1994. The Ideology of Nothingness: A Meditation on Japanese National Identity. *World Policy Journal 11* (Spring): 84–99.

———. 2003. Ambiguous Japan: Japanese National Identity at Century's End. In G. John Ikenberry and Michael Mastanduno (eds.), *International Relations Theory and the Asia-Pacific* (pp. 191–212). New York: Columbia University Press.

Tanaka, Akihiko. 1994. Japan's Security Policy in the 1990s. In Y. Funabashi (ed.), *Japan's International Agenda* (pp. 28–56). New York: New York University Press.

———. 2000. Domestic Politics and Foreign Policy. In Inoguchi and Jain (eds.), *Japanese Foreign Policy Today* (pp. 3–17). New York: Palgrave.

———. 2001. The International Context of U.S.-Japan Relations in the 1990s. In Gerald Curtis (ed.), *New Perspectives on U.S.-Japan Relations* (pp. 265–94). Tokyo: Japan Center for International Exchange.

Tatsumi, Yuki. 2007. Self Defense Forces Today—Beyond an Exclusively Defense-Oriented Posture? In Yuki Tatsumi and Andrew Oros (eds.), *Japan's New Defense Establishment: Institutions, Capabilities, and Implications*. Washington, DC: Henry J. Stimson Center.

Tellis, Ashley J., and Michael Wills (eds.). 2005. *Strategic Asia 2005–06: Military Modernization in an Era of Uncertainty*. Seattle and Washington, DC: National Bureau of Asian Research.

Todd, Daniel. 1988. *Defense Industries: A Global Perspective*. London: Routledge.

Togo, Kazuhiko. 2005a. Greater Self-Assertion and Nationalism in Japan. *Copenhagen Journal of Asian Studies 21*: 8–44.

———. 2005b. *Japan Foreign Policy 1945–2003: The Quest for a Proactive Policy*. Leidan and Boston: Brill.

Tomiyama, Kazuo. 1981. Revival and Growth of Japan's Defense Industry. *Japanese Economic Studies* 9: 4 (Summer): 3–51.

Tow, William T. 1983. U.S.-Japan Military Technology Transfers: Collaboration or Conflict? *Journal of Northeast Asian Studies* 2: 4 (December): 3–23.

Tsuchiyama, Jitsuo. 2000. Ironies of Japanese Defense and Disarmament Policy. In Inoguchi and Jain (eds.), *Japanese Foreign Policy Today* (pp. 136–51). New York: Palgrave.

Umemoto, Tetsuya. 1985. Arms and Alliance in Japanese Public Opinion. Princeton University, doctoral dissertation.

———. 2003. Ballistic Missile Defense and the U.S.-Japan Alliance. In G. John Ikenberry and Takashi Inoguchi (eds.), *Reinventing the Alliance: U.S.-Japan Security Partnership in an Era of Change*. New York: Palgrave Macmillan.

United States Arms Control and Disarmament Agency. 1999. World Military Expenditures and Arms Transfers. Washington, DC.

United States Congress, Office of Technology Assessment. 1985a. *Anti-Satellite Weapons, Countermeasures, and Arms Control*. OTA-ISC-281. Washington, DC: Government Printing Office.

———. 1985b. *International Cooperation and Competition in Civilian Space Activities*. OTA-ISC-239. Washington, DC: Government Printing Office.

———. 1989. *Holding the Edge: Maintaining the Defense Technology Base*. OTA-ISC-420. Washington, DC: Government Printing Office.

———. 1990. *Arming Our Allies: Cooperation and Competition in Defense Technology*. OTA-ISC-449. Washington, DC: Government Printing Office.

———. 1995. *Other Approaches to Civil-Military Integration: The Chinese and Japanese Arms Industries*. BP-ISS-143. Washington, DC: Government Printing Office.

United States Department of Defense. 1992. *A Strategic Framework for the Asian Pacific Rim: Report to Congress*. Washington, DC: Department of Defense.

———. 1998a. Affordable Weapons Systems: A Design for the Future. Remarks by Jacques S. Gansler, Under Secretary of Defense for Acquisition and Technology, at the Precision Strike Association Annual Programs Review (May 19). Fort Belvoir, VA.

———. 1998b. News: Contracts: Air Force (June 24). No. 321–98.

———. 1999a. News: Memorandum for Correspondents (August 16). No. 134-M.

———. 1999b. *Report to Congress on Theater Missile Defense Architecture Options for the Asia-Pacific Region* (May 4). Washington, DC.

———. 1999c. U.S.-Japan Defense Industry Cooperation in an Era of Globalization. Remarks as prepared for delivery by Deputy Secretary of Defense John J. Hamre, at Keidanren Defense Production Committee (November 26). Tokyo.

———. 1999d. National Defense Industrial Association's Tech Trends 2000 Conference 'R&D in the New Millennium'. Remarks as delivered by Deputy Secretary of Defense John J. Hamre (April 6). Philadelphia.

United States Department of Defense, Office of International Security Affairs. 1995. *United States Security Strategy for the East Asia-Pacific Region*. Washington, DC: Department of Defense.

United States Department of State. 1946. *Occupation of Japan: Policy and Progress*. Washington, DC: Government Printing Office.

———. 1976. *Foreign Relations of the United States, 1950, VI, East Asia and the Pacific*. Washington, DC: Government Printing Office.

United States Information Agency (USIA). 1998. *Briefing Paper: Japanese Public Opinion on*

Economic Issues: North Korea. Office of Research and Media Reaction. November 16, Washington, DC.

Urayama, Kori. 2000. Chinese Perspectives on Theater Missile Defense: Policy Implications for Japan. *Asian Survey* (July/August).

Uriu, Robert M. 1996. *Troubled industries: Confronting Economic Change in Japan.* Ithaca, NY: Cornell University Press.

Van de Velde, James R. 1987. Article Nine of the Postwar Japanese Constitution: Codified Ambiguity. *Journal of Northeast Asian Studies* 6: 1: 26–45.

Van Staaveren, Jacob. 1994. *An American in Japan, 1945–1948: A Civilian View of the Occupation.* Seattle: University of Washington Press.

Vogt, William. 1997. Japan's Third Way: Seeking a Robust BMD. *Jane's International Defense Review Extra 2*: 10 (October): 1–7.

Vosse, Wilhelm. 2006. Are Americans from Mars and Japanese from Venus? A Comparative Look at Public Attitudes on Peace and Security in Japan and the United States. Unpublished paper delivered at the Asian Studies Conference Japan (ASCJ), Tokyo, June 24.

Ward, Robert, and Sakamoto Yoshikazu. 1987. *Democratizing Japan: The Allied Occupation.* Honolulu: University of Hawaii Press.

Watanabe, Akio. 1977. Japanese Public Opinion and Foreign Affairs: 1964–73. In Robert Scalapino (ed.), *The Foreign Policy of Modern Japan* (pp. 105–46). Berkeley: University of California Press.

Yamamoto, Takehiko. 2000. The Japanese Decision to Join COCOM in 1952: Its Lessons and Legacy. Paper presented at the annual meeting of the International Studies Association (March 15–18), Los Angeles.

Yamauchi, Toshihiro. 1992. Gunning for Japan's Peace Constitution. *Japan Quarterly* (April–June): 159–67.

Yan Xuetong. 1999. Viewpoint: Theater Missile Defense and Northeast Asian Security. *The Nonproliferation Review* (Spring/Summer): 65–74.

Yasuhara, Yoko. 1986. Japan, Communist China, and Export Controls in Asia, 1948–52. *Diplomatic History 10*: 1: 75–89.

Yasutomo, Dennis T. 1995. *The New Multilateralism in Japan's Foreign Policy.* London: Macmillan.

Yoshida, Shigeru. 1951. Japan and the Crisis in Asia. *Foreign Affairs 29*: 2 (January): 171–81.

———. 1962. *The Yoshida Memoirs.* (Trans. Kenichi Yoshida). Cambridge, MA: Riverside Press.

Yoshino, Kosaku. 1992. *Cultural Nationalism in Contemporary Japan: A Sociological Enquiry.* London and New York: Routledge.

Ziegler, J. Nicholas. 1992. Cross-National Comparisons. In John Alic et al. (eds.), *Beyond Spinoff: Military and Commercial Technologies in a Changing World* (pp. 209–47). Boston: Harvard Business School Press.

Zisk Marten, Kimberly, and Alexander Cooley. 2003. Base Bargains: The Political Economy of Okinawa's Antimilitarism. Paper presented at the annual meeting of the American Political Science Association. Philadelphia, August 30.

Books, Articles, Documents (Japanese)

Arisawa, Hiromi. 1953. Heiki Seisan to Nihon Keizai [Arms Production and the Japanese Economy]. *Chūō Kōron* (April): 14–22.

Asahi Shimbun. Various years. *Asahi Nenkan [Asahi Yearbook].* Tokyo: Asahi Shimbunsha.

————. 1987. *Heiki Sangyō [The Weapons Industry].* Tokyo: Asahi Shimbunsha.

Asai, Heigo. 1953. Bōei Seisan Keikaku o Suishin Suru Mono [What Is Propelling Defense Production Planning?]. *Chūō Kōron* (April).

Asai, Motofumi. 1993. *"Kokuren Chushinshugi" to Nihon Koku Kempo ["UN Centrism" and the Japanese Constitution].* Tokyo: Iwanami Shoten.

Ashida, Hitoshi. 1986. *Ashida Hitoshi Nikki [The Hitoshi Ashida Diaries, 7 volumes].* Tokyo: Iwanami Shoten.

Chino, Keiko. 1991a. Space Activities at the Turning Point, No. 4: X-Ray Observation with More Achievements. *Yomiuri Shimbun* (February 1).

————. 1991b. Space Activities at the Turning Point, No. 5: Satellite Development; Manufacturers Disturbed by "Black Ship." *Yomiuri Shimbun* (March 4).

————. 1991c. Space Activities at the Turning Point, No. 6: Technology Transfer; Utilize National Assets. *Yomiuri Shimbun* (March 11).

————. 1991d. Space Activities at the Turning Point, No. 10: Lack of Financial Sources; Struggles to Win Budget. *Yomiuri Shimbun* (May 20).

Chino, Keiko, and Masahiro Takemura. 1991. Space Activities at the Turning Point, No. 2: H-2 Rocket, Difficulties in Engine Development. *Yomiuri Shimbun* (January 21).

Chuma, Kiyofuku. 1985. *Saigunbi no Seijigaku [The Politics of Rearmament].* Tokyo: Shōshinsha Insatsu Kabushiki Gaisha.

————. 1993. PKO: Dainiji Ronsen e [PKO: Toward a Second Round of Debate]. *Sekai 584.*

Chuo Koron. 1996. Nani ga Nihon no Kokuei na no ka? [Symposium: What Is Japan's National Interest?] *Chuo Koron* (February).

Deifensu Risaachi Senta *[Defense Research Center].* 1997. *Anzen Hosho to Uchu Riyo no Shawadai [Issues on National Security and Use of Space].* Study Report No. 2 (May). Tokyo: Defense Research Center.

————. 1997. *Nihon ni Okeru Dando Misairu Boei no Shawadai [Issues on Ballistic Missile Defense in Japan].* 1997. Study Report No. 3 (August). Tokyo: Defense Research Center.

Eto, Jun (ed.). 1989. *Senryo shiroku [Documents on the Occupation],* 4 volumes. Tokyo: Kodansha.

Etō, Shinkichi, and Yoshinobu Yamamoto. 1991. *Sōgōampo to Mirai no Sentaku [Comprehensive Security and Future Choices].* Tokyo: Kodansha.

Fujishima, Yudai. 1992. *Gunji-ka Suru Nichibei Gijutsu Kyoryoku [The Militarizing Technology Cooperation between Japan and the United States].* Tokyo: Mirai-sha.

Fukumoto, Kentaro. 2000. *Nihon no Kokkai Seiji. [Japan's Diet Politics].* Tokyo: University of Tokyo Press.

Funabashi, Yoichi. 1991. *Reisengo [After the Cold War].* Tokyo: Iwanami Shinsho.

————. 1993. *Nihon no Taigai Koso: Reisengo no Bijon wo Kaku [A Vision for Japan's External Policy: Fashioning a Post-Cold War Vision].* Tokyo: Iwanami Shoten.

————. 1996. *Nichibei Ampo Sai Teigi no Zen Kaibo [Complete Analysis of the Redefinition of the Japan-U.S. Security Treaty].* Sekai (May): 22–53.

Gaiko Seisaku Kettei Yoin Kenkyukai (eds.). 1999. *Nihon no Gaiko Seisaku Kettei Yoin [Domestic Determinants of Japanese Foreign Policy].* Tokyo: PHP Kenkyujo.

Hara, Yoshihisa. 1997. Josetsu: Nichi-Bei Ampo Taisei Jizoku to Hen'yo [Introduction: The Japan-U.S. Security Treaty System: Continuity and Change]. *Kokusai Seiji 117* (May).

————. 1988. *Sengo Nihon to Kokusai Seiji: Ampo Kaitei no Seijirikigaku [Postwar Japan and International Politics: The Political Dynamics of Security Treaty Revision].* Tokyo: Chuo Koron-sha.

Hata, Ikuhiko. 1976. *Shiroku: Nihon no Saigunbi [Record of Japanese Rearmament].* Tokyo: Bungei Shunju.

Hatoyama, Ichiro. 1951. *Watashi no Jijoden [My Autobiography].* Tokyo: Kaizosha.

———. 1952a. *Aru Daigishi no Seikatsu to Iken [The Life and Opinions of a Diet Member].* Tokyo: Tokyo Shuppan.

———. 1952b. *Watashi no Shinjo [My Beliefs].* Tokyo: Bunko.

———. 1957. *Hatoyama Ichiro Kaikoroku [Ichiro Hatoyama Memoirs].* Tokyo: Bungei Shunju Shinsha.

Hatoyama, Yukio. 1996. Minshuto: Watakushi no Seiken Koso [The Democratic Party: My Conception of Political Power]. *Bungei Shunju* (November): 112–30.

Heiwa Mondai Danwakai. 1960. Ampo Kaitei Mondai ni tsuite no Seimei [Statement about the Security Treaty Revision Issue]. *Sekai* (February).

Higuchi, Tsuneharu. 1993. *"Ikkoku Heiwa Shugi" no Sakkaku [The Illusion of "One-Country Pacifism"].* Tokyo: PHP Kenkyujo.

Hisakawa, Yoshihisa. 1953. Heiki Seisan no Jittai [The Reality of Weapons Production]. *Chūō Kōron* (April): 116–22.

Hiwatari, Yumi. 1990. *Sengo Seiji to Nichibei Kankei [Postwar Politics and Japan-U.S. Relations].* Tokyo: Tokyo University Press.

Hori, Yukio. 1983. *Sengo no Uyoku Seiryoku [Rightist Forces in Postwar Japan].* Tokyo: Keiso-shobo.

Igarashi, Takeshi. 1986. *Tainichi Kowa to Reisen: Sengo Nichibei Kankei no Keisei [The Japanese Peace Treaty and the Cold War: The Formation of Postwar Japan-U.S. Relations].* Tokyo: Tokyo University Press.

———. 1995. *Sengo Nichibei Kankei no Keisei [The Formation of Postwar Japan-U.S. Relations].* Tokyo: Kodansha.

Inoguchi, Kuniko. 1987. *Posuto Haken Shisutermu to Nihon no Sentaku [The Post-Hegemonic System and Japan's Options].* Tokyo: Chikuma Shobo.

Inoguchi, Takeshi. 1991b. *Gendai Koksai Seiji to Nihon [Contemporary International Politics and Japan].* Tokyo: Chikuma Shobo.

Inoki, Masamichi. 1986. *Yoshida Shigeru [Shigeru Yoshida].* Tokyo: Jiji Tsushinsha.

Iokibe, Makoto. 1985. *Beikoku to Nihon Senryo Seisaku [America and Japan Occupation Policy, vols 1–2].* Tokyo: Chuo Koronsha.

———. 1989. *Nichi-Bei Senso to Sengo Nihon [U.S. Japan War and Postwar Japan].* Osaka: Osaka Shoseki.

———. 1990. Senryo Kaikaku no San-ruiken [Three Types of Occupation Reforms]. *Leviathan 6* (Spring): 97–120.

Ishibashi, Masashi. 1965. Bōei Ronsō no Kongen wo Tsufuō [Pointing Out the Source of the Defense Debate]. *Chūō Kōron* (May): 126–36.

Ishida, Takeshi. 1989. *Nihon no Seiji to Kotoba [Words and Japanese Politics, vols. 1–2].* Tokyo: Tokyo University Press.

Ishihara, Nobuo. 1995. *Kantei 2668 Nichi: Seisaku Kettei no Butaiura [2668 Days in the Prime Minister's Residence: The Backstage of Decision Making].* Tokyo: NHK Shuppan.

———. 1996. Naikaku no Shikumi to Shusho no Kengen [The Mechanisms of the Cabinet and the Power of the Prime Minister]. In Yomiuri Shimbunsha (ed.), *Naikaku Goysei Kiko: Kaikaku e no Teigen [The Yomiuri Proposal for Restructuring the Cabinet and the Government Administration].* Tokyo: Yomiuri Shimbun-sha.

Ishimaru, Kazuto. 1983. *Sengo Nihon Gaikōshi [A History of Japan's Postwar Foreign Policy].* Tokyo: Sanseido.

Ishizuka, Isao. 1999. Jōhō-shūshū-eisei Seikō no Jōken [Condition for Success in the Information Gathering Satellite Project]. *Annual Report for 1999* (September). Tokyo: Defense Research Center.

Japan Defense Agency (JDA). Various years. *Nihon no Bōei [Defense of Japan]*. Tokyo.

———. 1999a. Dandō Misairu Bōei (BMD) ni Kan Suru Kenkyū ni Tsuite [Regarding Research Concerning Ballistic Missile Defense (BMD)]. Tokyo.

———. 1999b. Oshirase: Dandō Misairu Bōei ni Kakaru Nichibei Kyōdō Gijutsu Kenkyū ni Kansuru Ryōkai Oboegaki no Gaiyō [News Briefing for Correspondents: Summary of Memorandum of Understanding in the Japan-U.S. Collaborative Research of Ballistic Missile Defense] (August 13). Tokyo.

Japan-U.S. Industry Forum for Security Cooperation (IFSEC). 1997. *Nichibei Anzenhoshō Sangyō Fōramu Kyōdō Sengen: Nichibei Bōei Sangyō-kai no Kanshin Jikō [IFSEC Joint Report: U.S.-Japan Statement of Mutual Interests]* (October 31). Tokyo.

Kabashima, Ikuo. 1988. Yukensha no Hokaku Ideorogi to Nakasone Seiji [The Conservative-Progressive Ideology Dimension in the Electorate and the Politics of Nakasone]. *Leviathan* 2: 23–52.

Kaihara, Osamu. 1977. *Nihon Bōei Taisei no Uchimaku [Inside Japan's Defense System]*. Tokyo: Jiju Tsushin-sha.

———. 1985. *Nihon no Bōei wo Kangaeru [Thinking about Japan's Defense]*. Tokyo: Jiji Tsushin-sha.

Kamata, Satoshi. 1979. *Nihon no Heiki Kojo [Japan's Arms Factories]*. Tokyo: Shio.

Kan, Naoto. 1996. *Nihon O-Tenkan [Japan's Great Conversion]*. Tokyo: Kobunsha.

Kanda, Fuhito. 1983. *Senryo to Minshushugi [Occupation and Democracy]*. Tokyo: Shogakkan.

Kawabe, Ichiro. 1994. *Kokuren to Nihon [The UN and Japan]*. Tokyo: Iwanami Shoten.

Keidanren. 2000. *Uchu Seisaku Bijon [Space Policy Vision]*. (June 20). Tokyo: Keidanren.

Keidanren Boei Seisan Iinkai [Defense Production Committee]. 1964. *Boei Seisan Iinkai Junenshi [The Ten-Year History of the Defense Production Committee]*. Tokyo: Keidanren.

———. 1982. 56 Chugyo ni Taisuru Kenkai [View on the 1981 Midterm Defense Procurement Plan] (April 9). Tokyo.

———. 1998. Bōei Sangyō ni Okeru Nichibei Kyōryoku no Suishin wo: Keidanren Kurippu No. 72 [For further promotion of Japan-U.S. Cooperation in the Military Industry: *Keidanren Clip* No. 72] (February 12). Remarks by Jacques S. Gansler, Under Secretary of Defense for Acquisition and Technology on January 20 at Keidanren Defense Production Committee. Tokyo.

Keidanren Industrial Affairs Bureau. 1999. Uchū-riyō no Kakudai ni Muke, Ima Koso Jigatame wo [It Is Time to Make Concrete the Basis of Industries in Preparation for Enlarging Space Use]. (December 9). Tokyo.

Keidanren Space Activities Promotion Council. 1999. Sōgōteki na Uchū-kaihatsu-riyō Seisaku no Kakuritsu to Uchū-sangyō no Kiban-kyōka-sangyōka no Suishin [Proposal for the Establishment of Comprehensive Policy on Space Activities, and for the Strengthening and Industrization of Space Industry] (July 6). Tokyo.

Kioi, Saburō. 1976. Naze Miki de wa Dame na no Ka? [What's Wrong with Having Miki (as Prime Minister)?] *Shokun* (September): 58–77.

Kishi, Nobusuke. *Kishi Nobusuke Kaikoroku [Nobusuke Kishi Memoirs]*. Tokyo: Kosaido Shuppan.

Kitamura, Yukitaka, and Keiko Chino. 1991. Space Activities at the Turning Point, No. 9: Japanese Shuttle; Vague Future of the HOPE. *Yomiuri Shimbun* (May 6).

Klien, Susanne. 2002. *Rethinking Japan's Identity and International Role: An Intercultural Perspective*. New York and London: Routledge.

Kobayashi, Norioki. 1986. *Sekai ga Nihon no Uchū Sangyō ni Furueru Riyū [Reasons Why the World Fears the Japanese Space Industry]*. Tokyo: Kōbunsha.

Kojima, Noboru. 1987. *Nihon Senryo [Japan's Occupation]*, 3 volumes. Tokyo: Bungei Shunju.

Kosaka, Masataka. 1975. Tsusho Kokka Nihon no Unmei [The Fate of Commercial Nation Japan]. *Chuo Koron* (November).

Koseki, Shoichi. 1985. *Shin Kempo no Tanjo [The Birth of the New Constitution]*. Tokyo: Chuo Koron-sha.

Koyama, Hirotake, and Shinzo Shimizu. 1965. *Nihon Shakaito-shi [A History of the Japan Socialist Party]*. Tokyo: Hoga Shoten.

Kuriki, Kyoichi. 1988. *Uchū Kankyō no Riyō [Utilization of the Space Environment]*. Tokyo: Maruzen.

Kuroda, Takaji. 1992. From Competition to Supplement and Cooperation. *Nikkei Business* (January 20).

Kurokawa, Shuji. 1986. Keidanren Boei Seisan Iinkai no Seiji Kodo. [The Political Behavior of Keidanren's Defense Production Committee]. In Minoru Nakano (ed.), *Nihon-gata Seisaku Kettei no Henyo [Transformation of Japanese-style Policymaking]* (pp. 210–36). Tokyo: Toyo Keizai Shimpo-sha.

Kusano, Atsushi. 1989. Taigai Seisaku Kettei no Koko to Katei [Structure and Process in Foreign Policy Making]. In Tadashi Aruga, Shigeaki Uno, Shigeru Kido, Yoshinobu Yamamoto, and Akio Watanabe (eds.), *Nihon no Gaiko: Koza Kokusai Seiji*, vol. 4 *[Japanese Diplomacy: Handbook of International Politics*, vol. 4] (pp. 53–92). Tokyo: Tokyo University Press.

Maeda, Tetsuo. 1983. *Heiki Taikoku Nihon [Japan, the Military Superpower]*. Tokyo: Tokkan Shoten.

Mainichi Shimbun (ed.). 1969. *Ampo to Boei Seisan: Nihon no Heiwa to Anzen [Security and Defense Production: Japan's Peace and Security]*. Tokyo: Mainichi Shimbun-sha.

Matsukawa, Hiroshi, and Saburo Ienaga (eds.). 1970. *Nichibei Anpo Joyaku Taisei-shi [A History of the U.S.-Japan Security Treaty System, Vols. 1–4]*. Tokyo: Sanseido.

Mikuriya, Takashi, and Akio Watanabe (eds.). 1997. *Shusho Kantei no Ketsudan: Naikaku Fukukanbochokan Ishihara Nobuo no 2600 nichi [Decisions at the Prime Minister's Residence: 2600 Days of Deputy Chief Cabinet Secretary Ishihara Nobuo]*. Tokyo: Chuo Koron-sha.

Ministry of Foreign Affairs. Various years. *Gaiko Seisho [Diplomatic Bluebook]*. Tokyo: Ministry of Finance Printing Bureau.

Miyawaki, Mineo. 1980. Nihon no Boei Seisaku Kettei Kiko to Kettei Katei [Structures and Processes in Japanese Defense Policymaking]. *Kokusai Mondai 247* (October): 34–62.

Mori, Nobutatsuo. 1946. Heiwa Kokka no Kensetsu [Construction of a Peace State]. *Kenso* (January).

Murakami, Kaoru. 1978. Sengō Bōei Mondai Ronsō Shi [A History of the Postwar Defense Debate]. *Shokun* (October): 130–43.

Muramatsu, Takeshi. 1991. Daraku no 'Shōnin Kokka' wa Sukuwareru Ka? [Can a Depraved 'Merchant State' Be Saved?]. *Seiron* (March): 94–103.

Nagasue, Eiichi. 1989. Shakaitō no Bōei Seisaku ni Gimon Ari [Doubts about the Japan Socialist Party's Defense Policy]. *Kakushin* (November): 22–26.

Nakamura, Akira. 1984. Jiyuminshuto no Yottsu no Kao: Jiminto wo meguru Seisaku Ketteri Katei no Shironteki Kosatsu [The Four Faces of the Liberal Democratic Party: A Tentative Analysis of the Policymaking Process Centering on the LDP]. In Nakamura and Yuzuru Takeshita (eds.), *Nihon no Seisaku Katei: Jiminto, Yato, Kanryo [The Policy Process in Japan: LDP, Opposition Parties, and Bureaucracy]*. Matsudo: Azusa Shuppan-sha.

————. 1996. *Sengo Seiji ni Yureta Kenpo 9-jo [The Ups and Downs of Article 9 of the Constitution in Postwar Politics]*. Tokyo: Chuo Keizai-sha.

Nakasone, Yasuhiro. 1992. *Seiji to Jinsei: Nakasone Yasuhiro Kaikoroku [Politics and Life: Yasuhiro Nakasone's Memoirs]*. Tokyo: Kodansha.

————. 1994. Ima no Mama de ha Nihon ga Abunai [As It Is, Japan Is in Danger]. *Chuo Koron* (May): 64–78.

Nakayama, Shippu. 1991. Boeicho to Gunji Sangyo [The JDA and the Arms Industry]. *Zaikai Tembo* (January): 234–39.

Nihon Seiji Gakkai (ed.). 1996. *55-nen Taisei no Hokai [Collapse of the 1955 System]*. Tokyo: Iwanami Shoten.

Nishihara, Masashi. 1990. Nichibei Kankei ni okeru Anzen Hosho Joyaku no Igi [The Significance of the Security Treaty in the Japan–U.S. Relationship]. *Kokusai Mondai 369* (December): 2–14.

Nishihara, Shigeki. 1981. Yoron Chosa ni Miru Do-Jidai-shi (5): Nichibei Ampo Taisei [Public Opinion Surveys of the Era (5): The Japan–U.S. Security Treaty System]. *Jiyu 23*: 1 (January).

Okazaki, Hisahiko. 1980. *Kokka to Jōhō: Nihon no Gaikō Senryaku wo Motomete [State and Intelligence: Looking for Japan's Diplomatic Strategy]*. Tokyo: Bungei Shunjū.

————. 1986. Ima Kōsō Jizen no Senryaku-teki Shikō Wo [Now Is the Time for Independent Strategic Thinking]. *Bungei Shunjū* (March): 110–26.

————. 1990. *Joho Senryakuron Noto, Parto II: Rekishi to Senryaku ni tsuite [Intelligence and Strategic Thinking, Part II: On History and Strategy]*. Tokyo: PHP Kenkyujo.

————. 1997. *Kokka ha Dare ga Mamoru no ka? [Who Will Defend the Nation?]*. Tokyo: Tokkan Shoten.

Okazaki, Hisahiko, Shigeki Nishimura, and Seizaburo Sato. 1991. *Nichibei Domei to Nihon no Senryaku [Japan–U.S. Alliance and Japan's Strategy]*. Tokyo: PHP Kenkyujo.

Okazaki, Hisahiko, and Yonosuki Nagai. 1984. Nani ga Senryakuteki Riarizumu ka? [What Is Strategic Realism?] *Chuo Koron* (July): 46–61.

Ōtake, Hideo. 1981. Gunsan Fukugotai Riron kara Mita Nihon no Seiji [Japanese Politics Seen from the Theory of the Military Industrial Complex]. *Hogaku 45*: 4 (Tohoku University): 465–502.

————. 1983. *Nihon no Bōei to Kokunai Seiji [Japan's Defense and Domestic Politics]*. Tokyo: Sanichi Shōbō.

————. 1984. Bōeihi Zōgaku wo Meguru Jimintō no Tōnai Rikigaku [The Dynamics of Defense Spending Increases within the LDP]. In H. Ōtake (ed.), *Nihon Seiji no Sōten [Issues in Japanese Politics]* (pp. 281–96). Tokyo: San'ichi Shobo.

————. 1986. *Adenaua to Yoshida Shigeru [Adenauer and Shigeru Yoshida]*. Tokyo: Chuo Koron.

————. 1988. *Saibunbi no Nashonarizumu: Honshu, Riberaru, Shakai Minshushugihsa no Boeikan [Rearmament and Nationalism: The Defense Views of Conservatives, Liberals, and Socialists]*. Tokyo: Chuko Shinsho.

————. 1992. *Futatsu no Sengo: Doitsu to Nihon [Two Postwars: Germany and Japan]*. Tokyo: NHK Books.

———— (ed.). 1993. *Sengo Nihon Boei Mondai Shiryoshu [Collection of Materials on Postwar Japan's Defense Question]*. Tokyo: San-ichi Shobo.

Otsuka, Ryuichi. 1991. Space Activities at the Turning Point, No. 3: Rocket Commercial Competition; Severe Competition to Gain Pie. *Yomiuri Shimbun* (February 28).

Otsuka, Takamasa. 1992. *Gaiko to Nihonkoku Kempo:Yoshida Shigeru no Kenkyu [Foreign Relations and the Japanese Constitution: Research on Yoshida Shigeru].* Tokyo: Bushindo.

Otsuki, Shinji, and Masaru Honda. 1991. *Nichibei FSX Senso: Nichibei Domei wo Yurugasu Gijutsu Masatsu [The Japan-U.S. War over the FSX: Technology Conflict that Rocks the Japan-U.S. Alliance].* Tokyo: Ronso-sha.

Ozawa, Ichiro. 1993. *Nihon Kaizo Keikaku [Plan for Restructuring Japan].* Tokyo: Kodansha.

Sakai, Akio. 1986. Nihon Gunji Sangyo no Tenkan [The Transformation of Japan's Defense Industry]. *Sekai* (February): 130–43.

Sakai, Tetsuya. 1993. Kyujo-Anpotaisei no Shuen [The End of the Article 9/Security Treaty System]. *Kokusai Mondai* (March): 32–45.

Sakamoto, Yoshikazu. 1963. Nihon ni okeru Kokusai Reisen to Kokunai Reisen [Japan's International and Domestic Cold War]. In Reisen: Seiji-teki Kosatsu [The Cold War: A Political Inquiry] (pp. 331–70). Tokyo: Iwanami Shoten.

Sakuragawa, Akiyoshi. 1995. Nihon no Buki Kinyu Seisaku: Buki Yushutsu San-gensoku no Kokkai Rongi wo Megutte. [Japan's Arms Export Prohibition Policies: The Diet Discourse Surrounding the Three Principles on Arms Exports]. *Nihon Kokusai Seiji Gakkai Ron 108* (March): 84–100.

Sassa, Atsuyuki. 1991. Shin no Anzen Hosho Taisei no Kakuritsu wo Mezashite [Aiming at the Establishment of a Real Security Regime]. In Haruo Shimada, Yukio Okamoto, Kazuo Ijiri, and Masato Kimura (eds.). *Seikinin aru Heiwa Shugi wo Kangaeru: Kokusai Shakai to Kyozon Suru tame ni [Thoughts on Responsible Pacifism: To Co-Exist with International Society]* (pp. 54–65). Tokyo: PHP Kenkyujo.

———. 2000. *Waga Jōshi: Gotoda Masaharu [My Superior: Masaharu Gotoda].* Tokyo: Bungei Shunjū.

Sato, Seizaburo. 1990. Ima Koso Anzaen Hosho Senryaku wo Tenkan Seyo [Now Is the Time for National Security Strategy]. *Chuo Koron* (October): 577–89.

Sato, Seizaburo, and Tetsuhisa Matsuzaki. 1986. *Jiminto Seiken [LDP Government].* Tokyo: Chuo Koron-sha.

Science and Technology Agency. 1978. *Wagakuni no Uchū Kaihatsu no Aymi [A History of the Space Development of Our Nation].* Tokyo: Ministry of Finance Printing Bureau.

Science and Technology Agency, Research and Development Bureau. Various Years. *Uchū Kaihatsu Handobukku [Space Activities Handbook].* Tokyo: Keidanren Space Activities Promotion Council.

———. 1989. *Uchū Kaihatsu Shinjidai [A New Age of Space Activities].* Tokyo: Nikkan Kogyō Shimbunsha.

Sekai Henshu-bu. 1987. *"Gunji Taikoku" Nihon: Doko made Gunji-ka Saretaka?* [Japan the "Military Great Power": How Far Has It Come?] Tokyo: Iwanami Shoten.

Sentaku. 1991. Harjimaru "Nichibei Gunji Gijutsu Domei" e no Taido [A Quickening of Moves toward a "Japan-U.S. Military Technology Alliance"]. April: 96–99.

Shiina, Motoo, and Hisahiko Okazaki. 1996. Shudanteki Jieiken Rongi wo Nigeru na [Don't Run Away from a Discussion of the Right to Collective Defense]. *Chuo Koron* (July): 62–69.

Shimada, Haruo, Yukio Okamoto, Kazuo Ijiri, and Masato Kimura (eds.). 1991. *Seikinin aru Heiwa Shugi wo Kangaeru: Kokusai Shakai to Kyozon Suru tame ni [Thoughts on Responsible Pacifism: To Co-Exist with International Society].* Tokyo: PHP Kenkyujo.

Shiota, Ushio. 1986. *60-nen Anpo Toso [The 1960 Security Treaty Struggle].* Tokyo: Shin Nippon Shuppansha.

————. 1987. "1% Waku" Kekkai no 500 Nichi [500 Days of the Collapse of the "1% Ceiling"]. *Chuo Koron* (March): 140–55.

Soeya, Yoshihide. 2005. *Nihon no 'Midoru Powaa' Gaiko: Sengo Nihon no Sentaku to Kousou [Japan's 'Middle Power' Diplomacy: Choice and Framework of Postwar Japan].* Tokyo: Chikuma Shobo.

Sunohara, Tsuyoshi. 2005. *Tanjo Kokusan Supai Eisei [English title: Birth of Japan's First Spy Satellite].* Tokyo: Nihonkeizai Shimbunsha.

Tabata, Shinobu. 1972. *Nihon no Heiwa Shinso: Meiji-Taisho-Showa no Heiwa Shiso Katachi [Japanese Pacifist Thought: Pacifist Thinkers in Meiji, Taisho, and Showa].* Kyoto: Mineruba Shobo.

———— (ed.). 1993. *Kingendai Nihon no Heiwa Shiso: Heiwa Kenpo no Shisoteki Genryu to Hatten [Pacifism in Early Modern and Modern Japan: The Sources and Development of the Peace Constitution].* Kyoto: Mineruba Shobo.

Takemae, Eiji. 1980. *Senryo Sengoshi [Occupation and Postwar Japanese History].* Tokyo: Futagakisha.

Takemura, Masahiro. 1991a. Space Activities at the Turning Point, No. 7: Station Program; Miniaturization Forced by Financial Difficulties. *Yomiuri Shimbun* (March 18).

————. 1991b. Space Activities at the Turning Point, No.8: Objection from the U.S.; Persistence with the Logic of Priority for Itself. *Yomiuri Shimbun* (April 15).

Takemura, Masayoshi. 1994. *Chisakutomo Kirari to Hikaru Kuni: Nihon [A Small but Shining Country: Japan].* Tokyo: Kobunsha.

Takemura, Masayoshi, and Tanaka Shusei. 1995. *Sakigake no Kokorozashi [Sakigake's Intentions].* Tokyo: Toyo Keizai Shimpo-sha.

Tamama, Tetsuo. 2000. Uchu to Misairu to Ampo: Nihon ga Towareru Mono [Space and Missiles: What Japan Is in Need Of]. *DRC: A Quarterly Review* (May): 32–33. Tokyo: Defense Research Center.

Tanaka, Aiji. 1995. "55-nen Taisei" no Hokai to Shisutemu Ripoto no Keizoku [The Collapse of the 1955 System and the Continuation of System Report]. *Leviathan 17* (Fall): 52–83.

Tanaka, Akihiko. 1997. *Anzen Hoshō: Sengo 50-nen no Mosaku* [Security: 50 Postwar Years of Groping]. Tokyo: Yomiuri Shimbunsha.

Tanaka, Hitoshi. 1996. Shin Jidai no Nichi-Bei Anpo Taisei wo Kangaeru [Thoughts on the Japan-U.S. Security System for a New Era]. *Chuo Koron* (December): 112–20.

Tsuchiyama, Jitsuo. 1997. Nichi-Bei Domei no Kokusai Seijiron: Riarizumu, Riberaru Seidoron, Konsutorakutibizumu [International Relations Theories of the U.S.-Japan Alliance: Realism, Liberal-Institutionalism, and Constructivism]. *Kokusai Seiji 115*: 161–79.

Tomiyama, Kazuo. 1979. *Nihon no Bōei Sangyō [Japan's Defense Industry].* Tokyo: Tōyō Keizai Shimpō-sha.

Tsuji, Kiyoaki. 1970. *Shiryō Sengo Nijūnenshi I: Seiji [A Documentary History of 20 Postwar Years].* Tokyo: Nihon Hyōronsha.

Tsuru, Shigeto. 1996. *Nichibei Ampo Kaisho e no Michi [Pathway to the Dissolution of the U.S.-Japan Security Alliance].* Tokyo: Iwanami Shoten.

Uchida, Kenzo, Kunimasa Takeshige, and Yasunori Sone. 1996. Nihon no Kiro wo Tou: Nagata-cho, Kokkai Giin no Anketo [Asking about Japan's Options: Survey of Diet Members]. *Bungei Shunju* (August): 94–124.

Watanabe, Akio. 1985. *Sengo Nihon no Taigai Seisaku [Postwar Japan's Foreign Policy].* Tokyo: Yuhikaku.

———— (ed.). 1995. *Sengo Nihon no Saishotachi [Postwar Japan's Prime Ministers]*. Tokyo: Chuo Koron-sha.

Watanabe, Takeshi. 1983. *Senryo Tryogun Kosho Hitsuroku: Watanabe Takeshi Nikki [The Confidential Record of Negotiations with GHQ: The Diary of Watanabe Takeshi]*. Tokyo: Tokyo Keizai Shinposha.

Watanabe, Yozo. 1991. *Nichibei Ampo Taisei to Nihon-koku Kempo [The Japan-U.S. Security Regime and the Constitution of Japan]*. Toyo: Rodo Junpo-sha.

Yamaguchi, Asao. 1991. *Nihon no Kiki Kanri [Japan's Crisis Management]*. Tokyo: Nisshin Hodo.

Yamashita, Masamitsu, Susumu Takai, and Shuichiro Wada. 1994. *TMD: Seniiki Dando Misairu Boei [TMD: Theater Ballistic Missile Defense]*. Tokyo: TBS Buritanica.

Yanada, Hiroshi. 1981. *55-nen Taisei to Nihon Shakaito [The 1955 System and the Japan Socialist Party]*. Tokyo: Ariesu Shobo.

Yatō, Tōki. 1983. Uchū Kaihatsu Seisaku Keisei no Kiseki [The Steps of the Space Development Policy Formulation]. Tokyo: International Communication and Culture Association.

Yomiuri Shimbun. 1981. Shōwa Sensō Shi: "Saigunbi" no Kiseki [Postwar Showa History: A Record of "Rearmament"]. Tokyo: Yomiuri Shimbun-sha.

Yoshida, Shigeru. 1957. *Kaiso Junen [Reminiscences of Ten Years*, vols. 1–2]. Tokyo: Shinchosha.

————. 1967. *Nihon no Kettei Shita Hyaku-nen [Japan's Decisive Century]*. Tokyo: Nihon Keizai Shimbun-sha.

Yoshihara, Koichiro. 1988. *Nihon no Heiki Sangyo [Japan's Arms Industry]*. Tokyo: Shakai Shiso-sha.

Yoshioka, Hitoshi. 1990. Nihon no Uchu Kaihatsu no Ichi Danmen [One Aspect of the History of Space Development in Japan]. *Rekishi-gaku Chiri-gaku Nempo 14* (Kyushu University): 105–45.

Index

Abdelal, Rawi, 9, 28

Abe, Shinzo, 4, 20, 175, 187, 220n3

Aegis cruisers, 141, 151, 153, 154, 229n31

Afghanistan war, 176, 180

Aircraft: fighter planes, 115–16, 156; U-2 spy planes, 125, 126, 233n36

Aircraft Manufacturing Industry Law, 96, 97

Air Self-Defense Forces (ASDF): Kuwait deployment, 20, 34, 173, 186; refugee relief in Pakistan, 181, 182. *See also* Self-Defense Forces

Alliance, *see* United States-Japan alliance

Anti-Ballistic Missile (ABM) Restriction Treaty, 235n8

Antimilitarism: in Japan, 32, 42, 50, 52, 215n22; norms, 32–33. *See also* Domestic antimilitarism

Anti-Terrorism Special Measures Law, 181–83, 185–86

Araki Report, 176

Armitage, Richard, 4

Arms: of Self-Defense Forces, 62, 99, 226n1. *See also* Missile defense; Nuclear weapons

Arms export policies: ban, 2, 91, 92–95, 112–13; categories, 97, 97 (table), 98, 98 (table), 106; challenges in 1980s, 110–16; criticism of, 97, 100; Diet resolution

(1981), 206; domestic antimilitarism and, 90–91, 92–93, 95, 100, 119–21; domestic political factors, 95–96, 99–102, 105–9, 112–13, 119; enforcement, 111, 118; evolution, 91; exceptions, 34, 91–92, 93, 94, 98, 101, 111, 113–14, 162; explanations, 91, 92–94; future, 92; institutionalization, 102–9; international control regimes, 94, 96, 107, 115, 117–18; international environment and, 117–18; issues raised by missile defense systems, 152, 154, 156–57, 162–63; as measure of normalization, 92; missile defense component transfers, 91, 154, 156–57, 162–63; MITI controls, 96–99, 102, 110, 111, 115, 229n23; of Occupation, 94–95; in post-Cold War period, 117–19; in postwar period, 95–102; public opinion on, 99–100, 103; relaxation of controls, 102; scholarship on, 13–14; spin-on technologies, 110–11, 229n31; technology transfer to United States, 91, 110–12, 113–14, 115, 116, 156–57, 206–7, 229n34; "Three Principles for Arms Exports" (1967), 97, 102–3, 104, 106–7, 205; "Three Principles for Arms Exports" (1976), 98, 102, 109, 110, 111, 115, 205–6; U.S. view of, 111–12, 114–15; violations, 96, 114–15. *See also* Dual-use exports

Outer Space Treaty, 126, 127, 164–65,
  237n38
Ozawa, Ichiro, 174–75, 189, 216n33; call for
  normalization, 79

Pacifism, distinction from domestic antimilitarism, 5
Pacifists: antimilitarism, 32, 42; concern
  over militarization of space, 127; criticism of LDP security policy, 97; opposition to U.S. military presence, 69;
  support of arms export ban, 100, 113;
  support of neutrality, 43, 78
Paine, Thomas, 132
Pakistan: foreign aid from Japan, 238n11;
  refugee relief, 181, 182
Patriot missiles, 153
Peaceful use of space policy: Diet resolution (1969), 123, 125, 128, 129, 131, 136,
  164, 208; domestic political factors, 123,
  131, 136, 147; enforcement, 165–66;
  government policy statements, 208–9;
  importance, 122–23; meaning of "peaceful," 46, 129, 164–65; missile defense and,
  164, 165; modifications, 125, 137, 164–66;
  scholarship on, 13–14. See also Outer
  space policy
Peacekeeping missions, 14, 79, 83, 87–88,
  225n20
Pempel, T. J., 77–78
People's Liberation Army (PLA), 118
Persian Gulf War, 75; challenges to domestic antimilitarism tenets, 17, 86–87;
  financial support from Japan, 82, 86,
  226n32; Japanese minesweepers, 83, 86;
  Japanese role, 81–82, 86–87; Patriot mis-
  siles, 153
Peru, takeover of Japanese ambassador's
  residence, 72, 176
PLA, see People's Liberation Army
Plaza Accord, 135, 138, 224n15
Policy change, explanations, 24–25, 25
  (table), 32. See also Security policy mak-
  ing; Security practice
Political change, 7–8
Political parties, see specific parties
Political systems, power distribution, 24–25
Politics, see Domestic politics

Post-Cold War period: arms export policies, 117–19; comparison to immediate postwar period, 71–72; domestic
  antimilitarism, 21, 71, 82–86; domestic
  environment, 34, 71, 76–79; fears of U.S.
  withdrawal from Asia, 74, 75, 80; international environment, 72, 74–76, 175–78,
  177 (table); security practice changes, 25,
  73–74; United States-Japan alliance, 65,
  75, 79–82. See also Persian Gulf War
Postwar period: arms export policies,
  95–102; foreign policy, 51; international
  environment, 51, 52–55; political groups,
  43, 56–59; security identity evolution,
  4–5, 41, 49; security policies, 24–25, 41.
  See also Cold War
Preferences, 30, 31
Prime ministers: list, 201 (table); Yasukuni
  Shrine visits, 4, 192, 195. See also individual names
Public opinion: on arms export policies, 99–100, 103; on China, 177; on
  Constitution, 68; on constitutional revision, 195; distinction from security identity, 10, 214n15; on fishing rights dispute,
  62–63; on foreign deployments of SDF,
  31, 185, 217n10; influence on foreign
  policy, 31; on missile defense policy, 166;
  on outer space policy, 166; on SDF constitutionality, 84; on SDF participation
  in war on terrorism, 183, 185, 217n10;
  security identity and, 31, 32; on security
  policy, 34, 67–68; of Self-Defense Forces,
  50, 64, 68; on U.S.-Japan alliance, 46, 63,
  64, 67

"Reach, reach, and reach" pattern, 34, 173
"Reach, reconcile, reassure" pattern, 33–35;
  changes in, 173–78; LDP actions, 68,
  78–79, 113; in outer space policy, 129,
  134; during Vietnam War, 104
"Reach, replace, and review" pattern, 34,
  173
Reagan, Ronald, 64, 117, 136–37, 225n22
Reagan administration, Strategic Defense
  Initiative, 113, 137, 152, 158
Realist theories, 23, 24, 30, 31, 33, 35,
  36–37, 154–55, 235–36n15

Studies in Asian Security

A SERIES SPONSORED BY THE EAST-WEST CENTER

Muthiah Alagappa, Chief Editor
Distinguished Senior Fellow, East-West Center